Anti-Inflammatory Cookbook for Beginners 2022

*600 Quick & Easy Recipes with 28-Day Meal Plan
to Lose Weight, Balance Hormones
and Reduce Inflammation.*

Jemma Madison

TABLE OF CONTENTS

CHAPTER 4 SANDWICHES, PIZZAS, AND WRAPS..43

CHAPTER 5 BEANS, GRAINS, AND PASTAS ..56

CHAPTER 6 VEGETABLE MAINS...................86

CHAPTER 9 FRUITS AND DESSERTS 160

CHAPTER 10 SAUCES, DIPS, AND DRESSINGS 169

CHAPTER 11 DINNER 175

INTRODUCTION

"Take food as if it were medicine, or you will take medicine as if it were food."
This concept is reminiscent of Hippocrates' phrase: "Let food be your medicine and medicine be your food". In recent years, the scientific environment is getting astounded by the incredible therapeutic properties of certain foods, which together form the so-called anti-inflammatory diet. Eventually you will understand why, if there is an elixir of long life, it is to be considered the anti-inflammatory diet! In this chapter you will discover a diet that, as a Swedish study attests, reduces mortality from all causes by 20%, from cardiovascular diseases (heart attack, stroke, hypertension, etc.) to cancer, including metabolic diseases (diabetes, hypercholesterolemia, overweight, etc.); it also makes the body slimmer, healthier, more resistant and younger, and promises to make you live fitter and longer.

Here are our 5 golden rules for an anti-inflammatory diet

1. LESS PROTEIN
The proteins included in the anti-inflammatory diet are plant-based.
Studies say that you don't get fat from too much fat in your diet, but from too much protein, and those who are overweight have a higher chance of getting sick from inflammatory diseases and less chance of getting well.
This means that to follow this diet you must avoid dairy products, which are rich in casein, eggs and meat (both red and white), and replace with vegetable drinks, legumes and seeds.

2. LOW GLYCEMY
In order to reduce inflammation, blood sugar must be kept under control.
In this diet we do not use refined sugar (present in soft drinks, sweets, etc.), refined flours and white potatoes (especially fried ones...). They are replaced with natural sweeteners (agave syrup, maple syrup, rice malt, etc.), whole grains (and here you can indulge in pasta, bulghur, barley, spelt, oats and even gluten-free grains such as rice, corn, quinoa).
Did you know that sick cells need 20 times more glucose than healthy ones? By lowering your blood sugar, you "starve" the sick cells and give your body a way to fight them better!

3. INCREASE FIBER
Fiber reduces C-reactive protein, which is measured in the blood and is characteristic, when elevated, of an inflammatory state. Abound in whole grains, legumes, seeds, nuts and fresh fruits and vegetables (raw if possible).

4. FATS YES, BUT HEALTHY ONES

Fats are essential for the proper functioning of the body: from the health of tissues to hormones, they should not be demonized but chosen with care.

The best fats are, once again, vegetable ones. These fats are cholesterol-free and rich in antioxidant molecules, omega-3 fatty acids and vitamins. Choose olive oil, avocados, nuts and oil seeds (walnuts, sesame seeds, sunflower), one serving per day.

5. KNOW (AND ABOUND WITH) ANTI-INFLAMMATORY FOODS

If the previous points have scared you, in this last point we will give you some tips on foods to choose when shopping and want to try to eat more anti-inflammatory foods.

Green light to:

- brown rice,
- blueberries and berries,
- red onions,
- turmeric,
- nuts,
- green tea,
- pineapple,
- avocado,
- asparagus,
- cabbage (Brussels sprouts, cauliflower, broccoli...),
- dried fruits (almonds, hazelnuts, walnuts, cashews),
- green and colorful leafy vegetables (eat the rainbow!),
- dark chocolate (at least 80%).

I bet you didn't expect the last food to be considered an anti-inflammatory food! Well, yes, it's full of benefits too, as long as you eat a square or two a day, without overdoing it.

Chapter 1

The 30-Day Meal Plan

	Breakfast	Lunch	Dinner	Total Calories
DAY 1	Spinach and Egg Breakfast Wraps Calories:434	Butternut Squash and Cauliflower SoupCalories: 415 Rice Pudding with Roasted Orange SoupCalories: 274	Veal Pot Roast (Spanish) Calories: 426 Parmesan Roasted Red Potatoes Calories: 200	1749
DAY 2	Ricotta Toast with Strawberries Calories: 274 Pumpkin Pie Parfait Calories: 263	Cheesy Sweet Potato Burgers Calories: 290 Blueberry and Oat Crisp Calories: 496	Mediterranean Rice and Sausage (Italian) Calories: 650	1973
DAY 3	Egg Bake Calories: 240 Blueberry Smoothie Calories: 459	Baked Rolled Oat with Pears and Pecans Calories: 479	Italian Style Ground Beef (Italian) Calories: 365 Salad Skewers (Greek) Calories: 316	1859
DAY 4	Cauliflower Breakfast Porridge Calories: 381 Tzatziki Calories: 286	Lemon Beef (Spanish) Calories: 355 Guacamole Calories: 81	Macadamia Pork Calories: 436 Lentil-Tahini Dip Calories: 100	1639
DAY 5	Tomato and Egg Scramble Calories: 260 Creamy Peach Smoothie Calories: 212	Delicious Tomato Broth (Spanish) Calories: 460 Chocolate, Almond, and Cherry Clusters Calories: 197	Slow Cooker Salmon in Foil (Italian) Calories: 446 Lemony Blackberry Granita Calories: 183	1758
DAY 6	Quinoa Breakfast Bowls Calories: 219 Cheesy Broccoli and Mushroom Egg Casserole Calories: 326	Lebanese Flavor Broken Thin Noodles Calories: 127 Parsley-Dijon Chicken and Potatoes Calories: 324	Ground Beef, Tomato, and Kidney Bean Chili Calories: 891	1887

DAY 7	Baked Eggs in Avocado Calories: 301 Baked Ricotta with Honey Pears Calories: 329	Ritzy Veggie Chili Calories: 633	Deliciously Simple Beef (Spanish) Calories: 553	1816
DAY 8	Spinach and Egg Breakfast Wraps Calories:434	Butternut Squash and Cauliflower SoupCalories: 415 Rice Pudding with Roasted Orange SoupCalories: 274	Veal Pot Roast (Spanish) Calories: 426 Parmesan Roasted Red Potatoes Calories: 200	1749
DAY 9	Egg Bake Calories: 240 Blueberry Smoothie Calories: 459	Baked Rolled Oat with Pears and Pecans Calories: 479	Italian Style Ground Beef (Italian) Calories: 365 Salad Skewers (Greek) Calories: 316	1859
DAY 10	Ricotta Toast with Strawberries Calories: 274 Pumpkin Pie Parfait Calories: 263	Cheesy Sweet Potato Burgers Calories: 290 Blueberry and Oat Crisp Calories: 496	Mediterranean Rice and Sausage (Italian) Calories: 650	1973
DAY 11	Cauliflower Breakfast Porridge Calories: 381 Tzatziki Calories: 286	Lemon Beef (Spanish) Calories: 355 Guacamole Calories: 81	Macadamia Pork Calories: 436 Lentil-Tahini Dip Calories: 100	1639
DAY 12	Tomato and Egg Scramble Calories: 260 Creamy Peach Smoothie Calories: 212	Delicious Tomato Broth (Spanish) Calories: 460 Chocolate, Almond, and Cherry Clusters Calories: 197	Slow Cooker Salmon in Foil (Italian) Calories: 446 Lemony Blackberry Granita Calories: 183	1758
DAY 13	Quinoa Breakfast Bowls Calories: 219 Cheesy Broccoli and Mushroom Egg Casserole Calories: 326	Lebanese Flavor Broken Thin Noodles Calories: 127 Parsley-Dijon Chicken and Potatoes Calories: 324	Ground Beef, Tomato, and Kidney Bean Chili Calories: 891	1887
DAY 14	Baked Eggs in Avocado Calories: 301 Baked Ricotta with Honey Pears Calories: 329	Ritzy Veggie Chili Calories: 633	Deliciously Simple Beef (Spanish) Calories: 553	1816

DAY 15	Low Carb Bagels (Italian) Calories: 275	Apricot Pork Meat (Spanish) Calories: 332	Baked Cod with Vegetables Calories: 1168	1775
DAY 16	Spinach and Egg Breakfast Wraps Calories:434	Butternut Squash and Cauliflower SoupCalories: 415 Rice Pudding with Roasted Orange SoupCalories: 274	Veal Pot Roast (Spanish) Calories: 426 Parmesan Roasted Red Potatoes Calories: 200	1749
DAY 17	Egg Bake Calories: 240 Blueberry Smoothie Calories: 459	Baked Rolled Oat with Pears and Pecans Calories: 479	Italian Style Ground Beef (Italian) Calories: 365 Salad Skewers (Greek) Calories: 316	1859
DAY 18	Cauliflower Breakfast Porridge Calories: 381 Tzatziki Calories: 286	Lemon Beef (Spanish) Calories: 355 Guacamole Calories: 81	Macadamia Pork Calories: 436 Lentil-Tahini Dip Calories: 100	1639
DAY 19	Tomato and Egg Scramble Calories: 260 Creamy Peach Smoothie Calories: 212	Delicious Tomato Broth (Spanish) Calories: 460 Chocolate, Almond, and Cherry Clusters Calories: 197	Slow Cooker Salmon in Foil (Italian) Calories: 446 Lemony Blackberry Granita Calories: 183	1758
DAY 20	Ricotta Toast with Strawberries Calories: 274 Pumpkin Pie Parfait Calories: 263	Cheesy Sweet Potato Burgers Calories: 290 Blueberry and Oat Crisp Calories: 496	Mediterranean Rice and Sausage (Italian) Calories: 650	1973
DAY 21	Quinoa Breakfast Bowls Calories: 219 Cheesy Broccoli and Mushroom Egg Casserole Calories: 326	Lebanese Flavor Broken Thin Noodles Calories: 127 Parsley-Dijon Chicken and Potatoes Calories: 324	Ground Beef, Tomato, and Kidney Bean Chili Calories: 891	1887
DAY 22	Baked Eggs in Avocado Calories: 301 Baked Ricotta with Honey Pears Calories: 329	Ritzy Veggie Chili Calories: 633	Deliciously Simple Beef (Spanish) Calories: 553	1816

DAY 23	Low Carb Bagels (Italian) Calories: 275	Apricot Pork Meat (Spanish) Calories: 332	Baked Cod with Vegetables Calories: 1168	1775
DAY 24	Quinoa Breakfast Bowls Calories: 219 Cheesy Broccoli and Mushroom Egg Casserole Calories: 326	Lebanese Flavor Broken Thin Noodles Calories: 127 Parsley-Dijon Chicken and Potatoes Calories: 324	Ground Beef, Tomato, and Kidney Bean Chili Calories: 891	1887
DAY 25	Baked Eggs in Avocado Calories: 301 Baked Ricotta with Honey Pears Calories: 329	Ritzy Veggie Chili Calories: 633	Deliciously Simple Beef (Spanish) Calories: 553	1816
DAY 26	Egg Bake Calories: 240 Blueberry Smoothie Calories: 459	Baked Rolled Oat with Pears and Pecans Calories: 479	Italian Style Ground Beef (Italian) Calories: 365 Salad Skewers (Greek) Calories: 316	1859
DAY 27	Tomato and Egg Scramble Calories: 260 Creamy Peach Smoothie Calories: 212	Delicious Tomato Broth (Spanish) Calories: 460 Chocolate, Almond, and Cherry Clusters Calories: 197	Slow Cooker Salmon in Foil (Italian) Calories: 446 Lemony Blackberry Granita Calories: 183	1758
DAY 28	Spinach and Egg Breakfast Wraps Calories:434	Butternut Squash and Cauliflower SoupCalories: 415 Rice Pudding with Roasted Orange SoupCalories: 274	Veal Pot Roast (Spanish) Calories: 426 Parmesan Roasted Red Potatoes Calories: 200	1749
DAY 29	Cauliflower Breakfast Porridge Calories: 381 Tzatziki Calories: 286	Lemon Beef (Spanish) Calories: 355 Guacamole Calories: 81	Macadamia Pork Calories: 436 Lentil-Tahini Dip Calories: 100	1639
DAY 30	Ricotta Toast with Strawberries Calories: 274 Pumpkin Pie Parfait Calories: 263	Cheesy Sweet Potato Burgers Calories: 290 Blueberry and Oat Crisp Calories: 496	Mediterranean Rice and Sausage (Italian) Calories: 650	1973

Please note: refer to the index to find the number of the page corresponding to the recipe. *We trust that this 30-day nutritional plan is to your liking!*

Chapter 2
Breakfasts

Spinach and Egg Breakfast Wraps

Prep time: 10 minutes | **Cook time:** 7 minutes | **Serves:**2

Ingredients:

1 tablespoon olive oil
¼ cup minced onion
3 to 4 tablespoons minced sun-dried tomatoes in olive oil and herbs
2 (8-inch) whole-wheat tortillas

3 large eggs, whisked
1½ cups packed baby spinach
1 ounce (28 g) crumbled feta cheese
Salt, to taste

Directions:

Heat the olive oil in a large skillet over medium-high heat.

Sauté the onion and tomatoes for about 3 minutes, stirring occasionally, until softened.

Reduce the heat to medium. Add the whisked eggs and stir-fry for 1 to 2 minutes.

Stir in the baby spinach and scatter with the crumbled feta cheese. Season as needed with salt. Remove the egg mixture from the heat to a plate. Set aside.

Working in batches, place 2 tortillas on a microwave-safe dish and microwave for about 20 seconds to make them warm.

Spoon half of the egg mixture into each tortilla. Fold them in half and roll up, then serve.

Per Serving
calories: 434 | fat: 28.1g | protein: 17.2g | carbs: 30.8g

Pumpkin Pie Parfait

Prep time: 5 minutes | **Cook time:** 0 minutes | **Serves:**4

Ingredients:

1 (15-ounce / 425-g) can pure pumpkin purée
1 teaspoon pumpkin pie spice
2 cups plain Greek yogurt

4 teaspoons honey
1 cup honey granola
¼teaspoon ground cinnamon

Directions:

Combine the pumpkin purée, honey, pumpkin pie spice, and cinnamon in a large bowl and stir to mix well.

Cover the bowl with plastic wrap and chill in the refrigerator for at least 2 hours.

Make the parfaits: Layer each parfait glass with ¼ cup pumpkin mixture in the bottom. Top with ¼ cup of yogurt and scatter each top with ¼ cup of honey granola. Repeat the layers until the glasses are full. Serve immediately.

Per Serving
calories: 263 | fat: 8.9g | protein: 15.3g | carbs: 34.6g

Ricotta Toast with Strawberries

Prep time: 10 minutes | **Cook time:** 0 minutes | **Serves:**2

Ingredients:

½ cup crumbled ricotta cheese
1 tablespoon honey, plus additional as needed
Pinch of sea salt, plus additional as needed

4 slices of whole-grain bread, toasted
1 cup sliced fresh strawberries
4 large fresh basil leaves, sliced into thin shreds

Directions:

Mix together the cheese, honey, and salt in a small bowl until well incorporated.

Taste and add additional salt and honey as needed.

Spoon 2 tablespoons of the cheese mixture onto each slice of bread and spread it all over.

Sprinkle the sliced strawberry and basil leaves on top before serving.

Per Serving calories: 274 | fat: 7.9g | protein: 15.1g | carbs: 39.8g

Egg Bake

Prep time: 10 minutes | **Cook time:** 30 minutes | **Serves:**2

Ingredients:

1 tablespoon olive oil
1 slice whole-grain bread
4 large eggs
3 tablespoons unsweetened almond milk

½ teaspoon onion powder
¼ teaspoon garlic powder
¾ cup chopped cherry tomatoes
¼ teaspoon salt
Pinch freshly ground black pepper

Directions:

Preheat the oven to 375ºF (190ºC).

Coat two ramekins with the olive oil and transfer to a baking sheet. Line the bottom of each ramekin with ½ of bread slice.

In a medium bowl, whisk together the eggs, almond milk, onion powder, garlic powder, tomatoes, salt, and pepper until well combined.

Pour the mixture evenly into two ramekins. Bake in the preheated oven for 30 minutes, or until the eggs are completely set.

Cool for 5 minutes before serving.

Per Serving
calories: 240 | fat: 17.4g | protein: 9.0g | carbs: 12.2g

Mediterranean Eggs (Shakshuka)

Prep time: 5 minutes | **Cook time:** 20 minutes | **Serves:**4

Ingredients:

2 tablespoons extra-virgin olive oil
1 cup chopped shallots
1 teaspoon garlic powder
1 cup finely diced potato
1 cup chopped red bell peppers
¼ cup chopped fresh cilantro

1 (14.5-ounce/ 411-g) can diced tomatoes, drained
¼ teaspoon ground cardamom
¼ teaspoon paprika
¼ teaspoon turmeric
4 large eggs

Directions:

Preheat the oven to 350ºF (180ºC).

Heat the olive oil in an ovenproof skillet over medium-high heat until it shimmers.

Add the shallots and sauté for about 3 minutes, stirring occasionally, until fragrant.

Fold in the garlic powder, potato, and bell peppers and stir to combine. Cover and cook for 10 minutes, stirring frequently. Add the tomatoes, cardamon, paprika, and turmeric and mix well.

When the mixture begins to bubble, remove from the heat and crack the eggs into the skillet.

Transfer the skillet to the preheated oven and bake for 5 to 10 minutes, or until the egg whites are set and the yolks are cooked to your liking.

Remove from the oven and garnish with the cilantro before serving.

Per Serving

calories: 223 | fat: 11.8g | protein: 9.1g | carbs: 19.5g

Creamy Peach Smoothie

Prep time: 15 minutes | **Cook time:** 0 minutes | **Serves:**2

Ingredients:

2 cups packed frozen peaches, partially thawed
½ ripe avocado
½ cup plain or vanilla Greek yogurt

2 tablespoons flax meal
1 tablespoon honey
1 teaspoon orange extract
1 teaspoon vanilla extract

Directions:

Place all the ingredients in a blender and blend until completely mixed and smooth.

Divide the mixture into two bowls and serve immediately.

Per Serving

calories: 212 | fat: 13.1g | protein: 6.0g | carbs: 22.5g

Blueberry Smoothie

Prep time: 5 minutes | **Cook time:** 0 minutes | **Serves:**1

Ingredients:

1 cup unsweetened almond milk, plus additional as needed
¼ cup frozen blueberries
2 tablespoons unsweetened almond butter
1 tablespoon extra-virgin olive oil

1 tablespoon ground flaxseed or chia seeds
1 to 2 teaspoons maple syrup
½ teaspoon vanilla extract
¼ teaspoon ground cinnamon

Directions:

Blend all the ingredients in a blender until smooth and creamy.

You can add additional almond milk to reach your preferred consistency as needed. Serve immediately.

Per Serving

calories: 459 | fat: 40.1g | protein: 8.9g | carbs: 20.0g

Cauliflower Breakfast Porridge

Prep time: 5 minutes | **Cook time:** 5 minutes | **Serves:**2

Ingredients:

2 cups riced cauliflower
¾ cup unsweetened almond milk
4 tablespoons extra-virgin olive oil, divided
2 teaspoons grated fresh orange peel (from ½ orange)

½ teaspoon almond extract or vanilla extract
½ teaspoon ground cinnamon
⅛ teaspoon salt
4 tablespoons chopped walnuts, divided
1 to 2 teaspoons maple syrup (optional)

Directions:

Place the riced cauliflower, almond milk, 2 tablespoons of olive oil, orange peel, almond extract, cinnamon, and salt in a medium saucepan. Stir to incorporate and bring the mixture to a boil over medium-high heat, stirring.

Remove from the heat and add 2 tablespoons of chopped walnuts and maple syrup (if desired).Stir again and divide the porridge into bowls. Sprinkle each bowl evenly with remaining 2 tablespoons of walnuts and olive oil.

Per Serving calories: 381 | fat: 37.8g | protein: 5.2g | carbs: 10.9g

Morning Overnight Oats with Raspberries

Prep time: 5 minutes | **Cook time:** 0 minutes | **Serves:** 2

Ingredients:

⅔ cup unsweetened almond milk

¼ cup raspberries

⅓ cup rolled oats

1 teaspoon honey

¼ teaspoon turmeric

⅛ teaspoon ground cinnamon

Pinch ground cloves

Directions:

Place the almond milk, raspberries, rolled oats, honey, turmeric, cinnamon, and cloves in a mason jar. Cover and shake to combine. Transfer to the refrigerator for at least 8 hours, preferably 24 hours. Serve chilled.

Per Serving calories: 81 | fat: 1.9g | protein: 2.1g | carbs: 13.8g

Tomato and Egg Scramble

Prep time: 10 minutes | **Cook time:** 20 minutes | **Serves:** 4

Ingredients:

2 tablespoons extra-virgin olive oil

¼ cup finely minced red onion

1½ cups chopped fresh tomatoes

2 garlic cloves, minced

½ teaspoon dried thyme

½ teaspoon dried oregano

8 large eggs

½ teaspoon salt

¼ teaspoon freshly ground black pepper

¾ cup crumbled feta cheese

¼ cup chopped fresh mint leaves

Directions:

Heat the olive oil in a large skillet over medium heat.

Sauté the red onion and tomatoes in the hot skillet for 10 to 12 minutes, or until the tomatoes are softened. Stir in the garlic, thyme, and oregano and sauté for 2 to 4 minutes, or until the garlic is fragrant. Meanwhile, beat the eggs with the salt and pepper in a medium bowl until frothy. Pour the beaten eggs into the skillet and reduce the heat to low. Scramble for 3 to 4 minutes, stirring constantly, or until the eggs are set. Remove from the heat and scatter with the feta cheese and mint. Serve warm.

Per Serving calories: 260 | fat: 21.9g | protein: 10.2g | carbs: 5.8g

Baked Eggs in Avocado

Prep time: 5 minutes | **Cook time:** 10 to 15 minutes | **Serves:** 2

Ingredients:

1 ripe large avocado

2 large eggs

Salt and freshly ground black pepper, to taste

4 tablespoons jarred pesto, for serving

2 tablespoons chopped tomato, for serving

2 tablespoons crumbled feta cheese, for serving (optional)

Directions:

Preheat the oven to 425°F (220°C).Slice the avocado in half, remove the pit and scoop out a generous tablespoon of flesh from each half to create a hole big enough to fit an egg.

Transfer the avocado halves (cut-side up) to a baking sheet. Crack 1 egg into each avocado half and sprinkle with salt and pepper.

Bake in the preheated oven for 10 to 15 minutes, or until the eggs are cooked to your preferred doneness.

Remove the avocado halves from the oven. Scatter each avocado half evenly with the jarred pesto, chopped tomato, and crumbled feta cheese (if desired). Serve immediately.

Per Serving

calories: 301 | fat: 25.9g | protein: 8.1g | carbs: 9.8g

Crustless Tiropita (Greek Cheese Pie)

Prep time: 10 minutes | **Cook time:** 35 to 40 minutes | **Serves:** 6

Ingredients:

4 tablespoons extra-virgin olive oil, divided

½ cup whole-milk ricotta cheese

1¼ cups crumbled feta cheese

2 tablespoons chopped fresh mint

½ teaspoon lemon zest

¼ teaspoon freshly ground black pepper

2 large eggs

½ teaspoon baking powder

1 tablespoon chopped fresh dill

Directions:

Preheat the oven to 350°F (180°C). Coat the bottom and sides of a baking dish with 2 tablespoons of olive oil. Set aside.Mix together the ricotta and feta cheese in a medium bowl and stir with a fork until well combined. Add the dill, mint, lemon zest, and black pepper and mix well.

In a separate bowl, whisk together the eggs and baking powder. Pour the whisked eggs into the bowl of cheese mixture. Blend well.

Slowly pour the mixture into the coated baking dish and drizzle with the remaining 2 tablespoons of olive oil.

Bake in the preheated oven for about 35 to 40 minutes, or until the pie is browned around the edges and cooked through.Cool for 5 minutes before slicing into wedges.

Per Serving

calories: 181 | fat: 16.6g | protein: 7.0g | carbs: 1.8g

Fluffy Almond Flour Pancakes with Strawberries

Prep time: 5 minutes | **Cook time:** 15 minutes | **Serves:**4

Ingredients:

1 cup plus 2 tablespoons unsweetened almond milk
1 cup almond flour
2 large eggs, whisked ⅓ cup honey

1 teaspoon baking soda
¼ teaspoon salt
2 tablespoons extra-virgin olive oil
1 cup sliced strawberries

Directions:

Combine the almond milk, almond flour, whisked eggs, honey, baking soda, and salt in a large bowl and whisk to incorporate.

Heat the olive oil in a large skillet over medium-high heat.

Make the pancakes: Pour ⅓ cup of batter into the hot skillet and swirl the pan so the batter covers the bottom evenly. Cook for 2 to 3 minutes until the pancake turns golden brown around the edges. Gently flip the pancake with a spatula and cook for 2 to 3 minutes until cooked through. Repeat with the remaining batter.

Serve the pancakes with the sliced strawberries on top.

Per Serving
calories: 298 | fat: 11.7g | protein: 11.8g | carbs: 34.8g

Breakfast Yogurt Sundae

Prep time: 5 minutes | **Cook time:** 0 minutes | **Serves:**1

Ingredients:

¾ cup plain Greek yogurt
¼ cup fresh mixed berries (blueberries, strawberries, blackberries)

2 tablespoons walnut pieces
1 tablespoon ground flaxseed
2 fresh mint leaves, shredded

Directions:

Pour the yogurt into a tall parfait glass and sprinkle with the mixed berries, walnut pieces, and flaxseed.

Garnish with the shredded mint leaves and serve immediately.

Per Serving
calories: 236 | fat: 10.8g | protein: 21.1g | carbs: 15.9g

Avocado Toast with Goat Cheese

Prep time: 5 minutes | **Cook time:** 2 to 3 minutes | **Serves:**2

Ingredients:

2 slices whole-wheat thin-sliced bread
½ avocado

2 tablespoons crumbled goat cheese
Salt, to taste

Directions:

Toast the bread slices in a toaster for 2 to 3 minutes on each side until browned.

Scoop out the flesh from the avocado into a medium bowl and mash it with a fork to desired consistency. Spread the mash onto each piece of toast.

Scatter the crumbled goat cheese on top and season as needed with salt.

Serve immediately.

Per Serving
calories: 136 | fat: 5.9g | protein: 5.0g | carbs: 17.5g

Banana-Blueberry Breakfast Cookies

Prep time: 10 minutes | **Cook time:** 13 minutes | **Serves:**4

Ingredients:

2 medium bananas, sliced
4 tablespoons almond butter
4 large eggs, lightly beaten
½ cup unsweetened applesauce

1 teaspoon vanilla extract
⅔ cup coconut flour
¼ teaspoon salt
1 cup fresh or frozen blueberries

Directions:

Preheat the oven to 375ºF (190ºC). Line a baking sheet with parchment paper.

Stir together the bananas and almond butter in a medium bowl until well incorporated.

Fold in the beaten eggs, applesauce, and vanilla and blend well.

Add the coconut flour and salt and mix well. Add the blueberries and stir to just incorporate.

Drop about 2 tablespoons of dough onto the parchment paper-lined baking sheet for each cookie. Using your clean hand, flatten each into a rounded biscuit shape, until it is 1 inch thick.

Bake in the preheated oven for about 13 minutes, or until the top is golden brown and a toothpick inserted in the center comes out clean.

Let the cookies cool for 5 to 10 minutes before serving.

Per Serving (3 cookies)
calories: 264 | fat: 13.9g | protein: 7.3g | carbs: 27.6g

Blackberry-Yogurt Green Smoothie

Prep time: 5 minutes | **Cook time:** 0 minutes | **Serves:** 2

Ingredients:

1 cup plain Greek yogurt
1 cup baby spinach
½ cup frozen blackberries
¼ cup chopped pecans
½ cup unsweetened almond milk
½ teaspoon peeled and grated fresh ginger

Directions:

Process the yogurt, baby spinach, blackberries, almond milk, and ginger in a food processor until smoothly blended.

Divide the mixture into two bowls and serve topped with the chopped pecans.

Per Serving

calories: 201 | fat: 14.5g | protein: 7.1g | carbs: 14.9g

Buckwheat Porridge

Prep time: 5 minutes | **Cook time:** 40 minutes | **Serves:** 4

Ingredients:

3 cups water
2 cups raw buckwheat groats
Pinch sea salt
1 cup unsweetened almond milk

Directions:

In a medium saucepan, add the water, buckwheat groats, and sea salt and bring to a boil over medium-high heat.

Once it starts to boil, reduce the heat to low. Cook for about 20 minutes, stirring occasionally, or until most of the water is absorbed.

Fold in the almond milk and whisk well. Continue cooking for about 15 minutes, or until the buckwheat groats are very softened. Ladle the porridge into bowls and serve warm.

Per Serving calories: 121 | fat: 1.0g | protein: 6.3g | carbs: 21.5g

Healthy Chia Pudding

Prep time: 5 minutes | **Cook time:** 0 minutes | **Serves:** 4

Ingredients:

4 cups unsweetened almond milk
¾ cup chia seeds
1 teaspoon ground cinnamon
Pinch sea salt

Directions:

In a medium bowl, whisk together the almond milk, chia seeds, cinnamon, and sea salt until well incorporated.

Cover and transfer to the refrigerator to thicken for about 1 hour, or until a pudding-like texture is achieved.

Serve chilled.

Per Serving calories: 236 | fat: 9.8g | protein: 13.1g | carbs: 24.8g

Creamy Vanilla Oatmeal

Prep time: 5 minutes | **Cook time:** 40 minutes | **Serves:** 4

Ingredients:

4 cups water
Pinch sea salt
1 cup steel-cut oats
¾ cup unsweetened almond milk
2 teaspoons pure vanilla extract

Directions:

Add the water and salt to a large saucepan over high heat and bring to a boil.

Once boiling, reduce the heat to low and add the oats. Mix well and cook for 30 minutes, stirring occasionally.

Fold in the almond milk and vanilla and whisk to combine. Continue cooking for about 10 minutes, or until the oats are thick and creamy.

Ladle the oatmeal into bowls and serve warm.

Per Serving calories: 117 | fat: 2.2g | protein: 4.3g | carbs: 20.0g

Cheesy Broccoli and Mushroom Egg Casserole

Prep time: 10 minutes | **Cook time:** 40 minutes | **Serves:** 4

Ingredients:

2 tablespoons extra-virgin olive oil
½ sweet onion, chopped
1 teaspoon minced garlic
1 cup sliced button mushrooms
1 cup chopped broccoli
8 large eggs
¼ cup unsweetened almond milk
1 tablespoon chopped fresh basil
1 cup shredded Cheddar cheese
Sea salt and freshly ground black pepper, to taste

Directions:

Preheat the oven to 375ºF (190ºC).

Heat the olive oil in a large ovenproof skillet over medium-high heat.

Add the onion, garlic, and mushrooms to the skillet and sauté for about 5 minutes, stirring occasionally.

Stir in the broccoli and sauté for 5 minutes until the vegetables start to soften.

Meanwhile, beat the eggs with the almond milk and basil in a small bowl until well mixed.

Remove the skillet from the heat and pour the egg mixture over the top. Scatter the Cheddar cheese all over.

Bake uncovered in the preheated oven for about 30 minutes, or until the top of the casserole is golden brown and a fork inserted in the center comes out clean.

Remove from the oven and sprinkle with the sea salt and pepper. Serve hot.

Per Serving

calories: 326 | fat: 27.2g | protein: 14.1g | carbs: 6.7g

Quinoa Breakfast Bowls

Prep time: 5 minutes | **Cook time:** 17 minutes | **Serves:** 1

Ingredients:

¼ cup quinoa, rinsed
¾ cup water, plus additional as needed
1 carrot, grated
½ small broccoli head, finely chopped
¼ teaspoon salt
1 tablespoon chopped fresh dill

Directions:

Add the quinoa and water to a small pot over high heat and bring to a boil. Once boiling, reduce the heat to low. Cover and cook for 5 minutes, stirring occasionally.

Stir in the carrot, broccoli, and salt and continue cooking for 1o to 12 minutes, or until the quinoa is cooked though and the vegetables are fork- tender. If the mixture gets too thick, you can add additional water as needed.

Add the dill and serve warm.

Per Serving calories: 219 | fat: 2.9g | protein: 10.0g | carbs: 40.8g

Warm Bulgur Breakfast Bowls with Fruits

Prep time: 5 minutes | **Cook time:** 15 minutes | **Serves:** 6

Ingredients:

2 cups unsweetened almond milk
1½ cups uncooked bulgur
1 cup water
½ teaspoon ground cinnamon
2 cups frozen (or fresh, pitted) dark sweet cherries
8 dried (or fresh) figs, chopped
½ cup chopped almonds
¼ cup loosely packed fresh mint, chopped

Directions:

Combine the milk, bulgur, water, and cinnamon in a medium saucepan, stirring, and bring just to a boil.

Cover, reduce the heat to medium-low, and allow to simmer for 10 minutes, or until the liquid is absorbed.

Turn off the heat, but keep the pan on the stove, and stir in the frozen cherries (no need to thaw), figs, and almonds. Cover and let the hot bulgur thaw the cherries and partially hydrate the figs, about 1 minute.

Fold in the mint and stir to combine, then serve.

Per Serving
calories: 207 | fat: 6.0g | protein: 8.0g | carbs: 32.0g

Spinach Cheese Pie

Prep time: 5 minutes | **Cook time:** 25 minutes | **Serves:** 8

Ingredients:

2 tablespoons extra-virgin olive oil
1 onion, chopped
1 pound (454 g) frozen spinach, thawed
¼ teaspoon ground nutmeg
¼ teaspoon garlic salt
¼ teaspoon freshly ground black pepper
4 large eggs, divided
1 cup grated Parmesan cheese, divided
2 puff pastry doughs, at room temperature
4 hard-boiled eggs, halved
Nonstick cooking spray

Directions:

Preheat the oven to 350ºF (180ºC). Spritz a baking sheet with nonstick cooking spray and set aside.

Heat a large skillet over medium-high heat. Add the olive oil and onion and sauté for about 5 minutes, stirring occasionally, or until translucent. Squeeze the excess water from the spinach, then add to the skillet and cook, uncovered, so that any excess water from the spinach can evaporate.

Season with the nutmeg, garlic salt, and black pepper. Remove from heat and set aside to cool.

Beat 3 eggs in a small bowl. Add the beaten eggs and ½ cup of Parmesan cheese to the spinach mixture, stirring well. Roll out the pastry dough on the prepared baking sheet. Layer the spinach mixture on top of the dough, leaving 2 inches around each edge.

Once the spinach is spread onto the pastry dough, evenly place the hard-boiled egg halves throughout the pie, then cover with the second pastry dough. Pinch the edges closed. Beat the remaining 1 egg in the bowl. Brush the egg wash over the pastry dough. Bake in the preheated oven for 15 to 20 minutes until golden brown. Sprinkle with the remaining ½ cup of Parmesan cheese. Cool for 5 minutes before cutting and serving.

Per Serving
calories: 417 | fat: 28.0g | protein: 17.0g | carbs: 25.0g

Avocado Smoothie

Prep time: 2 minutes | **Cook time:** 0 minutes | **Serves:** 2

Ingredients:

1 large avocado
1½ cups unsweetened coconut milk
2 tablespoons honey

Directions:

Place all ingredients in a blender and blend until smooth and creamy.

Serve immediately.

Per Serving
calories: 686 | fat: 57.6g | protein: 6.2g | carbs: 35.8g

Baked Ricotta with Honey Pears

Prep time: 5 minutes | **Cook time:** 22 to 25 minutes | Serves:4

Ingredients:

1 (1-pound / 454-g) container whole-milk ricotta cheese
2 large eggs
¼ cup whole-wheat pastry flour
1 teaspoon vanilla extract
¼ teaspoon ground nutmeg
1 pear, cored and diced
2 tablespoons water
1 tablespoon honey
Nonstick cooking spray
1 tablespoon sugar

Directions:

Preheat the oven to 400°F (205°C). Spray four ramekins with nonstick cooking spray.

Beat together the ricotta, eggs, flour, sugar, vanilla, and nutmeg in a large bowl until combined. Spoon the mixture into the ramekins.Bake in the preheated oven for 22 to 25 minutes, or until the ricotta is just set.

Meanwhile, in a small saucepan over medium heat, simmer the pear in the water for 10 minutes, or until slightly softened. Remove from the heat, and stir in the honey.

Remove the ramekins from the oven and cool slightly on a wire rack. Top the ricotta ramekins with the pear and serve.

Per Serving calories: 329 | fat: 19.0g | protein: 17.0g | carbs: 23.0g

Cinnamon Pistachio Smoothie

Prep time: 5 minutes | **Cook time:** 0 minutes | **Serves:**1

Ingredients:

½ cup unsweetened almond milk, plus more as needed
½ cup plain Greek yogurt
Zest and juice of ½ orange
1 tablespoon extra-virgin olive oil
1 tablespoon shelled pistachios, coarsely chopped
¼ to ½ teaspoon ground allspice
¼ teaspoon vanilla extract
¼ teaspoon ground cinnamon

Directions:

In a blender, combine ½ cup almond milk, yogurt, orange zest and juice, olive oil, pistachios, allspice, vanilla, and cinnamon. Blend until smooth and creamy, adding more almond milk to achieve your desired consistency.

Serve chilled.

Per Serving calories: 264 | fat: 22.0g | protein: 6.0g | carbs: 12.0g

Breakfast Pancakes with Berry Sauce

Prep time: 5 minutes | **Cook time:** 10 minutes | **Serves:**4

Ingredients:

Pancakes:
1 cup almond flour
1 teaspoon baking powder
¼ teaspoon salt
6 tablespoon extra-virgin olive oil, divided
2 large eggs, beaten
Zest and juice of 1 lemon
½ teaspoon vanilla extract
Berry Sauce:
1 cup frozen mixed berries
1 tablespoon water, plus more as needed
½ teaspoon vanilla extract

Directions:
Make the Pancakes

In a large bowl, combine the almond flour, baking powder, and salt and stir to break up any clumps.

Add 4 tablespoons olive oil, beaten eggs, lemon zest and juice, and vanilla extract and stir until well mixed.

Heat 1 tablespoon of olive oil in a large skillet. Spoon about 2 tablespoons of batter for each pancake. Cook until bubbles begin to form, 4 to 5 minutes. Flip and cook for another 2 to 3 minutes. Repeat with the remaining 1 tablespoon of olive oil and batter.

Make the Berry Sauce

Combine the frozen berries, water, and vanilla extract in a small saucepan and heat over medium-high heat for 3 to 4 minutes until bubbly, adding more water as needed. Using the back of a spoon or fork, mash the berries and whisk until smooth. Serve the pancakes with the berry sauce.

Per Serving calories: 275 | fat: 26.0g | protein: 4.0g | carbs: 8.0g

Banana Corn Fritters

Prep time: 5 minutes | **Cook time:** 10 minutes | **Serves:**2

Ingredients:

½ cup yellow cornmeal
¼ cup flour
2 small ripe bananas, peeled and mashed
2 tablespoons unsweetened almond milk
1 large egg, beaten
½ teaspoon baking powder
¼ to ½ teaspoon ground chipotle chili
¼ teaspoon ground cinnamon
¼ teaspoon sea salt
1 tablespoon olive oil

Directions:

Stir together all ingredients except for the olive oil in a large bowl until smooth.

Heat a nonstick skillet over medium-high heat. Add the olive oil and drop about 2 tablespoons of batter for each fritter. Cook for 2 to 3 minutes until the bottoms are golden brown, then flip. Continue cooking for 1 to 2 minutes more, until cooked through. Repeat with the remaining batter. Serve warm.

Per Serving calories: 396 | fat: 10.6g | protein: 7.3g | carbs: 68.0g

Marinara Poached Eggs

Prep time: 5 minutes | **Cook time:** 15 minutes | **Serves:** 6

Ingredients:

1 tablespoon extra-virgin olive oil

1 cup chopped onion

2 garlic cloves, minced

2 (14.5-ounce / 411-g) cans no-salt-added

Italian diced tomatoes, undrained

6 large eggs

½ cup chopped fresh flat-leaf parsley

Directions:

Heat the olive oil in a large skillet over medium-high heat.

Add the onion and sauté for 5 minutes, stirring occasionally. Add the garlic and cook for 1 minute more.

Pour the tomatoes with their juices over the onion mixture and cook for 2 to 3 minutes until bubbling.

Reduce the heat to medium and use a large spoon to make six indentations in the tomato mixture. Crack the eggs, one at a time, into each indentation.

Cover and simmer for 6 to 7 minutes, or until the eggs are cooked to your preference.

Serve with the parsley sprinkled on top.

Per Serving

calories: 89 | fat: 6.0g | protein: 4.0g | carbs: 4.0g

Savory Breakfast Oatmeal

Prep time: 5 minutes | **Cook time:** 15 minutes | **Serves:** 2

Ingredients:

½ cup steel-cut oats

1 cup water

1 medium cucumber, chopped

1 large tomato, chopped

1 tablespoon olive oil

Pinch freshly grated Parmesan cheese

Sea salt and freshly ground pepper, to taste

Flat-leaf parsley or mint, chopped, for garnish

Directions:

Combine the oats and water in a medium saucepan and bring to a boil over high heat, stirring continuously, or until the water is absorbed, about 15 minutes.

Divide the oatmeal between 2 bowls and scatter the tomato and cucumber on top. Drizzle with the olive oil and sprinkle with the Parmesan cheese.

Season with salt and pepper to taste. Serve garnished with the parsley.

Per Serving

calories: 197| fat: 8.9g | protein: 6.3g | carbs: 23.1g

Apple-Tahini Toast

Prep time: 5 minutes | **Cook time:** 0 minutes | **Serves:** 1

Ingredients:

2 slices whole-wheat bread, toasted

2 tablespoons tahini

1 small apple of your choice, cored and thinly sliced

1 teaspoon honey

Directions:

Spread the tahini on the toasted bread.

Place the apple slices on the bread and drizzle with the honey. Serve immediately.

Per Serving

calories: 458 | fat: 17.8g | protein: 11.0g | carbs: 63.5g

Feta and Spinach Frittata

Prep time: 10 minutes | **Cook time:** 15 minutes | **Serves:** 2

Ingredients:

4 large eggs, beaten

2 tablespoons fresh chopped herbs, such as rosemary, thyme, oregano, basil or 1 teaspoon dried herbs

¼ teaspoon salt

Freshly ground black pepper, to taste

4 tablespoons extra-virgin olive oil, divided

1 cup fresh spinach, arugula, kale, or other leafy greens

4 ounces (113 g) quartered artichoke hearts, rinsed, drained, and thoroughly dried

8 cherry tomatoes, halved

½ cup crumbled soft goat cheese

Directions:

Preheat the broiler to Low.

In a small bowl, combine the beaten eggs, herbs, salt, and pepper and whisk well with a fork. Set aside.

In an ovenproof skillet, heat 2 tablespoons of olive oil over medium heat. Add the spinach, artichoke hearts, and cherry tomatoes and sauté until just wilted, 1 to 2 minutes.

Pour in the egg mixture and let it cook undisturbed over medium heat for 3 to 4 minutes, until the eggs begin to set on the bottom.

Sprinkle the goat cheese across the top of the egg mixture and transfer the skillet to the oven.

Broil for 4 to 5 minutes, or until the frittata is firm in the center and golden brown on top.

Remove from the oven and run a rubber spatula around the edge to loosen the sides. Slice the frittata in half and serve drizzled with the remaining 2 tablespoons of olive oil.

Per Serving

calories: 529 | fat: 46.5g | protein: 21.4g | carbs: 7.1g

Feta and Olive Scrambled Eggs

Prep time: 5 minutes | **Cook time:** 5 minutes | **Serves:**2

Ingredients:

4 large eggs
1 tablespoon unsweetened almond milk
Sea salt and freshly ground pepper, to taste
1 tablespoon olive oil

¼ cup crumbled feta cheese
10 Kalamata olives, pitted and sliced
Small bunch fresh mint, chopped, for garnish

Directions:

Beat the eggs in a bowl until just combined. Add the milk and a pinch of sea salt and whisk well.

Heat a medium nonstick skillet over medium-high heat and add the olive oil.

Pour in the egg mixture and stir constantly, or until they just begin to curd and firm up, about 2 minutes. Add the feta cheese and olive slices, and stir until evenly combined. Season to taste with salt and pepper.

Divide the mixture between 2 plates and serve garnished with the fresh chopped mint.

Per Serving

calories: 244 | fat: 21.9g | protein: 8.4g | carbs:3.5g

Tomato and Egg Breakfast Pizza

Prep time: 5 minutes | **Cook time:** 15 minutes | **Serves:**2

Ingredients:

2 (6- to 8-inch-long) slices of whole-wheat naan bread
2 tablespoons prepared pesto

1 medium tomato, sliced
2 large eggs

Directions:

Heat a large nonstick skillet over medium-high heat. Place the naan bread in the skillet and let warm for about 2 minutes on each side, or until softened.

Spread 1 tablespoon of the pesto on one side of each slice and top with tomato slices.

Remove from the skillet and place each one on its own plate.

Crack the eggs into the skillet, keeping them separated, and cook until the whites are no longer translucent and the yolk is cooked to desired doneness.

Using a spatula, spoon one egg onto each bread slice. Serve warm.

Per Serving

calories: 429 | fat: 16.8g | protein: 18.1g | carbs: 12.0g

Avocado and Egg Toast

Prep time: 5 minutes | **Cook time:** 8 minutes | **Serves:**2

Ingredients:

2 tablespoons ground flaxseed
½ teaspoon baking powder
2 large eggs, beaten
1 teaspoon salt, plus additional for serving
½ teaspoon freshly ground black pepper, plus additional for serving

½ teaspoon garlic powder, sesame seed, caraway seed, or other dried herbs (optional)
3 tablespoons extra-virgin olive oil, divided
1 medium ripe avocado, peeled, pitted, and sliced
2 tablespoons chopped ripe tomato

Directions:

In a small bowl, combine the flaxseed and baking powder, breaking up any lumps in the baking powder.

Add the beaten eggs, salt, pepper, and garlic powder (if desired) and whisk well. Let sit for 2 minutes.

In a small nonstick skillet, heat 1 tablespoon of olive oil over medium heat. Pour the egg mixture into the skillet and let cook undisturbed until the egg begins to set on bottom, 2 to 3 minutes.

Using a rubber spatula, scrape down the sides to allow uncooked egg to reach the bottom. Cook for an additional 2 to 3 minutes.

Once almost set, flip like a pancake and allow the top to fully cook, another 1 to 2 minutes.

Remove from the skillet and allow to cool slightly, then slice into 2 pieces.

Top each piece with avocado slices, additional salt and pepper, chopped tomato, and drizzle with the remaining 2 tablespoons of olive oil. Serve immediately.

Per Serving

calories: 297 | fat: 26.1g | protein: 8.9g | carbs: 12.0g

Berry and Nut Parfait

Prep time: 10 minutes | **Cook time:** 0 minutes | **Serves:**2

Ingredients:

2 cups plain Greek yogurt
2 tablespoons honey
1 cup fresh raspberries

1 cup fresh blueberries
½ cup walnut pieces

Directions:

In a medium bowl, whisk the yogurt and honey. Spoon into 2 serving bowls.

Top each with ½ cup blueberries, ½ cup raspberries, and ¼ cup walnut pieces. Serve immediately.

Per Serving calories: 507 | fat: 23.0g | protein: 24.1g | carbs: 57.0g

Classic Shakshuka

Prep time: 15 minutes | **Cook time:** 30 minutes | **Serves:**2

Ingredients:

1 tablespoon olive oil
½ red pepper, diced
½ medium onion, diced
2 small garlic cloves, minced
½ teaspoon smoked paprika
½ teaspoon cumin
Pinch red pepper flakes
3 large eggs

1 (14.5-ounce / 411-g) can fire-roasted tomatoes
¼ teaspoon salt
Pinch freshly ground black pepper
1 ounce (28 g) crumbled feta cheese (about ¼ cup)
3 tablespoons minced fresh parsley

Directions:

Heat the olive oil in a skillet over medium-high heat and add the pepper, onion, and garlic. Sauté until the vegetables start to turn golden.

Add the paprika, cumin, and red pepper flakes and stir to toast the spices for about 30 seconds. Add the tomatoes with their juices.

Reduce the heat and let the sauce simmer for 10 minutes, or until it starts to thicken. Add the salt and pepper. Taste the sauce and adjust seasonings as necessary.

Scatter the feta cheese on top. Make 3 wells in the sauce and crack one egg into each well.

Cover and let the eggs cook for about 7 minutes. Remove the lid and continue cooking for 5 minutes more, or until the yolks are cooked to desired doneness.

Garnish with fresh parsley and serve.

Per Serving

calories: 289 | fat: 18.2g | protein: 15.1g | carbs: 18.5g

Kale and Apple Smoothie

Prep time: 5 minutes | **Cook time:** 0 minutes | **Serves:**2

Ingredients:

2 cups shredded kale
1 cup unsweetened almond milk
¼ cup 2 percent plain Greek yogurt

½ Granny Smith apple, unpeeled, cored and chopped
½ avocado, diced
3 ice cubes

Directions:

Put all ingredients in a blender and blend until smooth and thick.

Pour into two glasses and serve immediately.

Per Serving

calories: 177 | fat: 6.8g | protein: 8.2g | carbs: 22.0g

Parmesan Oatmeal with Greens

Prep time: 10 minutes | **Cook time:** 18 minutes | **Serves:**2

Ingredients:

1 tablespoon olive oil
¼ cup minced onion
2 cups greens (arugula, baby spinach, chopped kale, or Swiss chard)
¾ cup gluten-free old-fashioned oats

1½ cups water, or low-sodium chicken stock
2 tablespoons Parmesan cheese
Salt, to taste
Pinch freshly ground black pepper

Directions:

Heat the olive oil in a saucepan over medium-high heat. Add the minced onion and sauté for 2 minutes, or until softened.

Add the greens and stir until they begin to wilt. Transfer this mixture to a bowl and set aside.

Add the oats to the pan and let them toast for about 2 minutes. Add the water and bring the oats to a boil.

Reduce the heat to low, cover, and let the oats cook for 10 minutes, or until the liquid is absorbed and the oats are tender.

Stir the Parmesan cheese into the oats, and add the onion and greens back to the pan. Add additional water if needed, so the oats are creamy and not dry.

Stir well and season with salt and black pepper to taste. Serve warm.

Per Serving

calories: 257 | fat: 14.0g | protein: 12.2g | carbs: 30.2g

Creamy Breakfast Bulgur with Berries

Prep time: 2 minutes | **Cook time:** 10 minutes | **Serves:**2

Ingredients:

½ cup medium-grain bulgur wheat
1 cup water
Pinch sea salt
¼ cup unsweetened almond milk

1 teaspoon pure vanilla extract
¼ teaspoon ground cinnamon
1 cup fresh berries of your choice

Directions:

Put the bulgur in a medium saucepan with the water and sea salt, and bring to a boil.

Cover, remove from heat, and let stand for 10 minutes until water is absorbed.

Stir in the milk, vanilla, and cinnamon until fully incorporated. Divide between 2 bowls and top with the fresh berries to serve.

Per Serving calories: 173 | fat: 1.6g | protein: 5.7g | carbs: 34.0g

Mediterranean Omelet

Prep time: 8 minutes | **Cook time:** 15 minutes | **Serves:** 2

Ingredients:

2 teaspoons extra-virgin olive oil, divided
1 garlic clove, minced
½ yellow bell pepper, thinly sliced
½ red bell pepper, thinly sliced
¼ cup thinly sliced red onion

2 tablespoons chopped fresh parsley, plus extra for garnish
2 tablespoons chopped fresh basil
½ teaspoon salt
½ teaspoon freshly ground black pepper
4 large eggs, beaten

Directions:

In a large, heavy skillet, heat 1 teaspoon of the olive oil over medium heat. Add the garlic, peppers, and onion to the skillet and sauté, stirring frequently, for 5 minutes.

Add the parsley, basil, salt, and pepper, increase the heat to medium-high, and sauté for 2 minutes. Slide the vegetable mixture onto a plate and return the skillet to the heat.

Heat the remaining 1 teaspoon of olive oil in the skillet and pour in the beaten eggs, tilting the pan to coat evenly. Cook the eggs just until the edges are bubbly and all but the center is dry, 3 to 5 minutes.

Spoon the vegetable mixture onto one-half of the omelet and use a spatula to fold the empty side over the top. Slide the omelet onto a platter or cutting board.

To serve, cut the omelet in half and garnish with extra fresh parsley.

Per Serving
calories: 206 | fat: 14.2g | protein: 13.7g | carbs: 7.2g

Basil Scrambled Eggs

Prep time: 5 minutes | **Cook time:** 8 minutes | **Serves:** 2

Ingredients:

4 large eggs
2 tablespoons grated Gruyère cheese
2 tablespoons finely chopped fresh basil

1 tablespoon plain Greek yogurt
1 tablespoon olive oil
2 cloves garlic, minced
Sea salt and freshly ground pepper, to taste

Directions:

In a large bowl, beat together the eggs, cheese, basil, and yogurt with a whisk until just combined.

Heat the oil in a large, heavy nonstick skillet over medium-low heat. Add the garlic and cook until golden, about 1 minute.

Pour the egg mixture into the skillet over the garlic. Work the eggs continuously and cook until fluffy and soft.

Season with sea salt and freshly ground pepper to taste. Divide between 2 plates and serve immediately.

Per Serving
calories: 243 | fat: 19.7g | protein: 15.6g | carbs: 3.4g

Cinnamon Oatmeal with Dried Cranberries

Prep time: 5 minutes | **Cook time:** 8 minutes | **Serves:** 2

Ingredients:

1 cup almond milk
1 cup water
Pinch sea salt

1 cup old-fashioned oats
½ cup dried cranberries
1 teaspoon ground cinnamon

Directions:

In a medium saucepan over high heat, bring the almond milk, water, and salt to a boil.

Stir in the oats, cranberries, and cinnamon. Reduce the heat to medium and cook for 5 minutes, stirring occasionally.

Remove the oatmeal from the heat. Cover and let it stand for 3 minutes.

Stir before serving.

Per Serving
calories: 107 | fat: 2.1g | protein: 3.2g | carbs: 18.2g

Sautéed Dandelion Toast (Italian)

Preparation Time: 5 minutes **Cooking Time:** 10 minutes
Servings: 4

Ingredients:

1 red onion, sliced
Lemon juice: 2 tbsp.
Plain yogurt: 1/4 cup
1 bunch of dandelion greens
Mint leaves: 2 tbsp.
1 loaf of ciabatta, cut & toasted

Red pepper flakes: 1/8 tsp.
Black pepper: 1/4 tsp.
Olive oil: 2 tbsp.
Feta cheese: half cup
Grated lemon zest: 1 tsp.
Salt: 1/4 tsp.

Directions:

In a skillet, add oil on medium flame.

Add onion and pepper flakes cook for 4-5 minutes.

Add lemon juice and cook for 30 seconds. Turn off the heat and add dandelion greens, season with salt and pepper, toss well.

In a food processor, add crumbled feta cheese, and the rest of the except for bread, until smooth and creamy.

Spread this mixture on toasted ciabatta and serve with greens and mint leaves on top.

Per Serving
300 Cal | 14.5 g Fat | 34 g Carbs | 10 g Protein

Balsamic Berries with Honey Yogurt (Greek)

Preparation Time: 15 minutes **Cooking Time:** 0 minutes **Servings:** 4

Ingredients:

Blueberries: 1 cup

Raspberries: 1 cup

Plain Greek yogurt: 2/3 cup

Honey: 2 tsp.

Strawberries: 1 ½ cups, cut in halves

Balsamic vinegar: 1 tbsp.

Directions:

In a bowl, toss all berries in balsamic vinegar. Let them rest for ten minutes.

Add honey, yogurt to a separate bowl, and whisk.

In serving cups, add berries and top with yogurt mixture and serve.

Per Serving

151 Cal | 6.1 g Fat | 12.6 g Carbs | 2.8 g Protein

Smoked Salmon & Poached Eggs on Toast (Italian)

Prep time: 7 minutes **Cooking Time:** 7 minutes **Servings:** 1

Ingredients:

Smoked salmon: 3.5 oz.

Bread toasted: 2 slices

Half avocado, smashed

Salt & black pepper, to taste

Thinly sliced scallions: 1 tbsp.

Lemon juice: 1/4 tsp.

2 poached eggs

Directions:

In a bowl, add smashed avocado. Add salt and lemon juice mix well.

Poach the eggs if you have not already.

Spread the avocado mixture on toast and place smoked salmon on top.

Top with poached eggs and serve with black pepper on top.

Per Serving

178 Cal | 4 g Fat | 16.9 g Carbs | 7 g Protein

Mediterranean Breakfast Quinoa (Greek)

Prep time: 10 minutes **Cooking Time:** 15 mins **Servings:** 4

Ingredients:

Ground cinnamon: 1 tsp.

Honey: 2 tbsp.

Chopped toasted almonds:

Vanilla extract: 1 tsp. 2 dried dates, diced

Quinoa: 1 cup

5 dried apricots, diced

Sea salt: 1 tsp.

¼ cup Milk: 2 cups

Directions:

In a pan, add the quinoa, cinnamon on medium flame.

Add salt, milk, mix well and let it come to a boil.

Turn the heat low and cover the pan. Let it simmer for 15 minutes. Add apricots, vanilla, dates, honey, and half of the almond slices; mix well.

Serve with the rest of the almond slices on top.

Per Serving

327 Cal | 7.9 g Fat | 50 g Carbs | 11.5 g Protein

Greek Yogurt Pumpkin Parfait (Greek)

Preparation Time: 35 minutes **Cooking Time:** 0 minutes **Servings:** 6

Ingredients:

Low-fat Greek yogurt: 1 ¼ cup Mascarpone cheese: 3 to 4 tbsp.

Ground cinnamon: 1 ½ to 2 tsp.

Vanilla extract: 1 tsp. Pinch of nutmeg Pumpkin puree: 2 cups

Brown sugar: 2 ½ tbsp.

Molasses: 2 tbsp.

Directions:

In a bowl, add all except for nuts and chocolate chips, whisk with an electric mixer until smooth.

Adjust seasonings to taste and mix well.

In small mason jars, divide the mixture and keep it in the fridge for half an hour.

Serve with nuts and chocolate chips on top.

Per Serving

102 Cal | 1.5 g Fat | 15.6 g Carbs | 0.8 g Protein

Spinach Feta Breakfast Wraps (Italian)

Preparation Time: 5 minutes **Cooking Time:** 10 minutes
Servings: 4

Ingredients:

Baby spinach: 5 cups
4 ounces feta cheese,
crumbled
4 whole-wheat tortillas

1 cup cherry tomatoes,
halved
10 eggs
Salt & black pepper, to taste

Directions:

In a bowl, whisk eggs well.

Place a skillet on medium flame, spray the pan with oil.

Add eggs and stir occasionally until cooked.

Add black pepper and salt, take out on a plate.

Oil spray the pan again and sauté spinach until wilted.
Take out on a plate.

Place tortilla on a surface, add eggs, feta and spinach.
Wrap it tightly.

Serve right away.

Per Serving

521 Cal | 27 g Fat | 45 g Carbs | 28.1 g Protein

Pepperoni Eggs (Italian)

Prep time: 10 minutes **Cooking Time:** 20 minutes
Servings: 2

Ingredients:

1 cup of egg substitute
3 green onions
8 slices of pepperoni
1 pinch of salt and ground
black pepper to taste
1 teaspoon melted butter

1 egg
minced meat diced
1/2 teaspoon of garlic
powder
1/4 cup grated Romano
cheese

Directions:

Combine the egg substitute, the egg, the green onions, the
pepperoni slices, and the garlic powder in a bowl.

Heat the butter in a non-stick frying pan over low heat;
Add the egg mixture, cover the pan and cook until the
eggs are set, 10 to 15 minutes. Sprinkle Romano's eggs and
season with salt and pepper.

Per Serving

266 calories16.2 g fat 3.7 grams of carbohydrates 25

Low Carb Bagels (Italian)

Preparation Time: 10 minutes **Cooking Time:** 20 minutes
Servings: 4

Ingredients:

1 cups almond flour
3 eggs.
3 cups mozzarella cheese,
shredded.

2 tbsps. bagel seasoning
1 tbsp. powder for baking
¼ cup cream cheese.

Directions:

Heat your oven in advance at 400 ° c.

Get 2 baking sheets and line them well with paper made
from parchment.

Get a large mixing container and in it, mix the almond
flour with the powder for baking.

Mix the mozzarella cheese and the cream cheese in a bowl
that can be used in a microwave. Place the bowl in a
microwave for 2 minutes when the cheese melts and
combines.

Get the mixture of cheese from the bowl once out of the
microwave and pour it into the mixing container with the
flour from almonds and the powder for baking. Mix all the
until well mixed.

Take the dough when done and divide it into eight parts
that are equal in measure. Using your palms, take each of
the eight dough parts and roll them into balls.

Using your fingers, create a hole in each of the balls, and
gently stretch the dough to form the shape of a bagel.

Take one egg and beat it in a bowl. Brush the eggs on top
of each made bagel following this by sprinkling the bagel
seasoning at the top as well.

Place the bagel dough in the oven on its rack, which is in
the middle for 25 minutes when they are nice and golden
in color.

Remove the bagels from the oven and let them get cold
for about 10 minutes before serving them.

Per Serving

Calories: 275 g. Fat: 20 g. Carbs: 8 g. Protein: 20 g.

Cheesy Yogurt (Greek)

Preparation Time: 4 hours and 5 minutes
Cooking Time: 0 minutes | **Servings:** 4

Ingredients:

- 1 cup Greek yogurt
- ½ cup feta cheese, crumbled
- 1 tablespoon honey

Directions:

In a blender, combine the yogurt with the honey and the cheese and pulse well.

Divide into bowls and freeze for 4 hours before serving for breakfast.

Per Serving

Calories 161, fat 10, carbs 11.8, protein 6.6

Chard Breakfast Skillet (Greek)

Preparation Time: 10 minutes **Cooking Time:** 20 minutes
Servings: 4

Ingredients:

- Cherry tomatoes: 1 1/4 cups, quartered Olive oil: 3 tbsp.
- Chopped yellow onion: 2 cups
- 4 minced garlic cloves
- Red wine vinegar: 1 tbsp.
- 2 bunches of Swiss chard
- 4 eggs
- Black pepper: half tsp
- Sea salt: half tsp.

Directions:

In a bowl, toss tomatoes with vinegar.

Remove the stems off of chard leaves and chop the leaves and rinse them. Let them dry in a colander.

Slice the stems thinly.

In a skillet, add oil and sauté the stems and onion for ten minutes.

Turn the heat low and add garlic; cook for 60 seconds.

Add leaves and season with salt and pepper.

Toss on high heat until it wilts.

Make for wells in the pan and put one egg in each nest.

Cook for four minutes until yolks are set.

Add tomatoes to the skillet and serve.

Per Serving

245 Cal | 11 g Fat | 17 g Carbs | 15 g Protein.3 g of protein 124 mg of cholesterol

Citrus-Kissed Melon (Spanish)

Preparation Time: 11 minutes **Cooking Time:** 0 minute
Servings: 4

Ingredients:

- 2 cups melon, cubed
- ½ cup freshly squeezed orange juice
- 2 cups cantaloupe, cubed
- ¼ cup freshly squeezed lime juice
- 1 tbsp. orange zest

Directions:

In a large bowl, incorporate the melon cubes.

In a bowl, blend the orange juice, lime juice, and orange zest and pour over the fruit.

Cover and chill for at least 4 hours, stirring occasionally.

Serve chilled.

Per Serving

Calories: 101 Fat: 11 g. Protein: 2 g.

Poached Eggs Caprese (Italian)

Preparation Time: 5 minutes **Cooking Time:** 15 minutes
Servings: 2

Ingredients:

- Distilled white vinegar: 1 tbsp. Salt: 2 tsp.
- 2 English muffin, cut in half
- Salt, to taste
- 4 eggs
- Pesto: 4 tsp.
- 4 slices of mozzarella cheese
- 1 tomato, sliced thick

Directions:

In a saucepan, add 2-3" of water and let it boil.

Turn the heat low and add salt, vinegar and let it simmer.

On each half of the muffin, add cheese and tomato slices. Toast for five minutes in the oven.

In a small cup, break an egg and slip gently in the simmering water.

Cook for 3 minutes or until the whites set, take the eggs out on tissue paper.

Place on top of tomato slices, serve with black pepper, pesto on top.

Per Serving

428 Cal | 24.9 g Fat | 31.7 g Carbs | 33 g Protein

Baked Eggs with Avocado & Feta (Greek)

Preparation Time: 5 minutes **Cooking Time:** 30 minutes
Servings: 2

Ingredients:

Crumbled feta cheese: 2 tbsp. 4 eggs	Salt & black pepper, to taste 1 avocado, cut into 6 slices

Directions:

Let the oven preheat to 400F

Place 2 ramekins in the oven for ten minutes and later spray with oil.

Put avocado slices in each ramekin with 2 eggs.

Add crumbled feta, salt and pepper on top.

Bake for 12 to 15 minutes until the yolks are done the way you prefer.

Serve right away

Per Serving

391 Cal | 33 g Fat | 9.5 g Carbs | 16 g Protein

Sesame-Seared Salmon (Italian)

Prep time: 5 minutes | **Cooking Time:** 10 minutes
Servings: 4

Ingredients:

4 wild salmon fillets (about 1lb.)	2 tbsps. toasted sesame oil.
1 tsp. sea salt.	1 ½ tbsps. sesame seeds.
	1½ tbsps. avocado oil.

Directions:

Using a paper towel or a clean kitchen towel, pat the fillets to dry. Brush each with a tbsp. of sesame oil and season with a ½ tsp. of salt.

Place a large skillet over medium-high heat and drizzle with avocado oil. Once the oil is hot, add the salmon fillets with the flesh side down. Cook for about 3 minutes and flip. Cook the skin side for an additional 3–4 minutes, without overcooking it.

Remove the pan from the heat and brush with the remaining sesame oil. Season with the remaining salt and sprinkle with sesame seeds. Best served with a green salad.

Per Serving

Calories: 291 g. Fat: 14 g. Carbs: 3 g. Protein: 8 g.

Breakfast Egg on Avocado (Italian)

Preparation Time: 9 minutes | **Cooking Time:** 15 minutes |
Servings: 6

Ingredients:

1 tsp. garlic powder	½ tsp. sea salt
¼ cup Parmesan cheese, shredded	¼ tsp. black pepper
3 avocados, pitted, halved 6 eggs	

Directions:

Prep muffin tins and preheat the oven to 350°F/176°C.

Split the avocado. To ensure that the egg would fit inside the cavity of the avocado, lightly scrape off 1/3 of the meat.

Place avocado on a muffin tin to ensure that it faces the top-up. Evenly season each avocado with pepper, salt, and garlic powder.

Add 1 egg to each avocado cavity and garnish tops with cheese. Set in your oven to bake until the egg white is set, about 15 minutes. Serve and enjoy.

Per Serving

Calories: 252 Fat: 20 g. Protein: 14 g.

Tuna Sandwich (Spanish)

Preparation Time: 9 minutes | **Cooking Time:** 0 minutes |
Servings: 2

Ingredients:

6 oz. canned tuna, drained and flaked	1 avocado, pitted, peeled, and mashed
4 whole-wheat bread slices	Pinch salt and black pepper
1 tbsp. Feta cheese, crumbled	1 cup baby spinach

Directions:

Using a bowl, stir in the pepper, salt, tuna, and cheese to mix.

To the bread slices, apply a spread of the mashed avocado.

Equally, divide the tuna mixture and spinach onto 2 of the slices. Top with the remaining 2 slices. Serve.

Per Serving

Calories: 283 Fat: 11.2 g. Protein: 4.5 g.

Pita Chicken Salad (Greek)

Preparation Time: 18 minutes | **Cooking Time:** 4 minutes
Servings: 4

Ingredients:

1 tbsp. olive oil	1 piece of chicken breast
Dried basil to taste	3 tbsps. natural yogurt
2 pieces pita	1 tbsp. lemon juice
1 garlic clove	1 bunch (7 oz.) green salad
1 tomato	2 chives
1 cucumber Salt to taste	Ground black pepper to taste

Directions:

Rub the chicken slices with salt, pepper, and dried basil, fry in a pan until cooked.

Put the chicken, slices of tomato, cucumber, and onion in half the pits.

Mix the yogurt with lemon juice and garlic, add to the salad in Pita. Garnish with chives then serve.

Per Serving

Calories: 94 Fat: 1.8 g. Protein: 6 g.

Chorizo & Cheese Omelet (Italian)

Preparation Time: 10 minutes | **Cooking Time:** 10 minutes | **Servings:** 2

Ingredients:

4 eggs, beaten	4 oz. mozzarella, grated
8 chorizo slices, thin	Salt and black pepper to taste
1 tomato, sliced	
1 tbsp. butter	

Directions:

Whisk the eggs with salt and pepper.

In a cast-iron skillet, add the butter and cook the eggs for 30 seconds. Create a layer with the chorizo slices.

Arrange the sliced tomato and mozzarella over the chorizo and cook for about 3 minutes. Cover the skillet and continue cooking for 3 more minutes, or until the omelet is completely set.

With a spatula, run around the edges of the omelet and flip it onto a plate folded-side down. Serve.

Per Serving

Calories: 451 g. Fats: 36.5 g. Protein: 30g.

Ken's Hard-Boiled Egg (Italian)

Preparation Time: 5 minutes **Cooking Time:** 15 minutes | **Servings:** 8

Ingredients:

1 tablespoon of salt	1/4 cup distilled white vinegar
8 eggs	
6 cups of water	

Directions:

Mix the salt, vinegar, and water in a large saucepan and bring to a boil over high heat. Add the eggs one by one, and be careful not to split them. Lower the heat and cook over low heat and cook for 14 minutes.

Remove the eggs from the hot water and place them in a container filled with ice water or cold water. Cool completely, approximately 15 minutes.

Per Serving

72 calories 5 grams of fat 0.4 g carbohydrates 6.3 g protein 186 mg of cholesterol 947

Heart-Healthful Trail Mix (Spanish)

Preparation Time: 8 minutes | **Cooking Time:** 32 minutes | **Servings:** 12

Ingredients:

1 cup raw almonds	1 cup pumpkin seeds
1 cup dried apricots, cut into thin strips	2 tbsps. extra-virgin olive oil
1 cup dried cherries, roughly chopped	1 tsp. Salt
1 cup golden raisins	1 cup walnut halves

Directions:

Preheat the oven to 300°F. Line a baking sheet with aluminum foil.

In a large bowl, mix the almonds, walnuts, pumpkin seeds, apricots, cherries, and raisins. Pour the olive oil over all and toss well with clean hands. Add the salt and toss again to distribute.

Pour the nut mixture onto the baking sheet in a single layer and bake until the fruits begin to brown, for 30 minutes. Chill on the baking sheet to room temperature.

Store in a large airtight container or zipper-top plastic bag.

Per Serving

Calories: 109 Fat: 7 g. Protein: 1 g.

Café Cooler (Italian)

Preparation Time: 16 minutes **Cooking Time:** 0 minute
Servings: 4

Ingredients:

Ice cubes as needed
½ tsp. pure vanilla extract
2 cups low-fat milk

½ tsp. ground cinnamon
1 cup espresso, cooled to
room temperature
4 tsps. sugar (optional)

Directions:

Fill 4 tall glasses with ice cubes.

In a blender, combine the milk, cinnamon, and vanilla and blend until frothy.

Pour the milk over the ice cubes and top each drink with one-quarter of the espresso. If using sugar, stir it into the espresso until it has dissolved.

Serve immediately, with a chilled teaspoon for stirring.

Per Serving
Calories: 93 Fat: 7 g. Protein: 1 g.

Egg Breakfast Sandwich with Roasted Tomatoes(Greek)

Prep time: 5 minutes **Cooking Time:** 15 minutes
Servings: 1

Ingredients:

Olive oil: 1 tsp. Pesto: 1
tbsp.
Salt & black pepper, to taste
Provolone cheese: 1 to 2
slices 1 whole ciabatta roll

Egg whites: 1/4 cup
Roasted tomatoes: half cup
Chopped fresh herbs: 1 tsp.

Directions:

In a skillet, add oil on medium flame. Add egg whites and salt, pepper.

Sprinkle fresh herbs on top. Cook for 3 to 4 minutes.

Flip only once and toast the ciabatta bread. Spread pesto on both sides and place egg whites on top with cheese.

Add roasted tomatoes on top, sprinkle salt and pepper.

Serve right away.

Per Serving
458 Cal | 24 g Fat | 51 g Carbs | 21 g Protein

Greek Omelet Casserole (Greek)

Prep time: 10 minutes **Cooking Time:** 35-40 mins **Servings:** 12

Ingredients:

12 eggs
Whole milk: 2 cups
Lemon pepper: 1 tsp.
Artichoke with olives,
peppers, chopped without
liquid Tomato (sun dried)
feta cheese: ¾ cup,
crumbled Olive oil: 4 tsp.

Fresh spinach: 1 ½ cups
2 minced garlic cloves Dried
oregano: 1 tsp.
Fresh chopped dill: 1 tbsp.
Salt: 1 tsp.

Directions:

Let the oven preheat to 350 F.

In a skillet, add oil (1 tbsp.), add garlic and spinach, sauté for three minutes.

Take a baking dish (9 by 13") and oil spray it.

Spread the spinach mixture on the bottom evenly.

In a bowl, whisk eggs with the rest of the except for feta cheese.

Pour the mixture over spinach mixture, and spread feta cheese on top.

Bake for 35 to 40 minutes until set.

Per Serving
186 Cal | 13 g Fat | 5 g Carbs | 10 g Protein

Spinach & Goat Cheese Egg Muffins (Greek)

Preparation Time: 10 minutes **Cooking Time:** 35 minutes
Servings: 12

Ingredients:

Olive oil: 1 tbsp. Milk: half
cup
Fresh goat cheese: 1/4 cup,
crumbled
Baby spinach: 1 5-oz.,
chopped

1 red pepper, sliced into ¼"
pieces
2 scallions, diced
Salt & black pepper, to taste
6 eggs

Directions:

Let the oven preheat to 350 F. oil spray a 12-cup muffin tin.

2. In a skillet, add oil on medium flame. Add red pepper, spinach and season with salt and pepper cook for 6-8 minutes.

Turn off the heat and add in scallions.

In a bowl, whisk eggs with salt, pepper and milk. Add spinach mixture and mix.

Pour this mixture into the muffin cups and add goat cheese on top.

Bake for 20-25 minutes until eggs are set.

Cool for five minutes and serve right away

Per Serving
65 Cal | 4.5 g Fat | 2 g Carbs | 4 g Protein

Chapter 3
Sides, Salads, and Soups

Sumptuous Greek Vegetable Salad

Prep time: 20 minutes | **Cook time:** 0 minutes | **Serves:** 6

Ingredients:

Salad:
1 (15-ounce / 425-g) can chickpeas, drained and rinsed
1 (14-ounce / 397-g) can artichoke hearts, drained and halved
1 head Bibb lettuce, chopped (about 2½ cups)
1 cucumber, peeled deseeded, and chopped (about 1½ cups)
1½ cups grape tomatoes, halved
½ cup sliced black olives

½ cup cubed feta cheese
Dressing:
1 tablespoon freshly squeezed lemon juice (from about ½ small lemon)
¼ teaspoon freshly ground black pepper
1 tablespoon chopped fresh oregano
2 tablespoons extra-virgin olive oil
1 tablespoon red wine vinegar
1 teaspoon honey
¼ cup chopped basil leaves

Directions:

Combine the ingredients for the salad in a large salad bowl, then toss to combine well.

Combine the ingredients for the dressing in a small bowl, then stir to mix well. Dress the salad and serve immediately.

Per Serving
calories: 165 | fat: 8.1g | protein: 7.2g | carbs: 17.9g

Brussels Sprout and Apple Slaw

Prep time: 15 minutes | **Cook time:** 0 minutes | **Serves:** 4

Ingredients:

Salad:
1 pound (454 g) Brussels sprouts, stem ends removed and sliced thinly
1 apple, cored and sliced thinly
½ red onion, sliced thinly
Dressing:
1 teaspoon Dijon mustard

2 teaspoons apple cider vinegar
1 tablespoon raw honey
1 cup plain coconut yogurt
1 teaspoon sea salt
For Garnish:
½ cup pomegranate seeds
½ cup chopped toasted hazelnuts

Directions:

Combine the ingredients for the salad in a large salad bowl, then toss to combine well.

Combine the ingredients for the dressing in a small bowl, then stir to mix well. Dress the salad let sit for 10 minutes.

Serve with pomegranate seeds and toasted hazelnuts on top.

Per Serving
calories: 248 | fat: 11.2g | protein: 12.7g | carbs: 29.9g

Butternut Squash and Cauliflower Soup

Prep time: 15 minutes | **Cook time:** 4 hours | **Serves:** 4 to 6

Ingredients:

1 pound (454 g) butternut squash, peeled and cut into 1-inch cubes
1 small head cauliflower, cut into 1-inch pieces
1 onion, sliced
2 cups unsweetened coconut milk
1 tablespoon curry powder
½ cup no-added-sugar apple juice

4 cups low-sodium vegetable soup
2 tablespoons coconut oil
1 teaspoon sea salt
¼ teaspoon freshly ground white pepper
¼ cup chopped fresh cilantro, divided

Directions:

Combine all the ingredients, except for the cilantro, in the slow cooker. Stir to mix well.

Cook on high heat for 4 hours or until the vegetables are tender.

Pour the soup in a food processor, then pulse until creamy and smooth.

Pour the puréed soup in a large serving bowl and garnish with cilantro before serving.

Per Serving
calories: 415 | fat: 30.8g | protein: 10.1g | carbs: 29.9g

Cherry, Plum, Artichoke, and Cheese Board

Prep time: 15 minutes | **Cook time:** 0 minutes | **Serves:** 4

Ingredients:

2 cups rinsed cherries
2 cups rinsed and sliced plums
2 cups rinsed carrots, cut into sticks

1 cup canned low-sodium artichoke hearts, rinsed and drained
1 cup cubed feta cheese

Directions:

Arrange all the ingredients in separated portions on a clean board or a large tray, then serve with spoons, knife, and forks.

Per Serving
calories: 417 | fat: 13.8g | protein: 20.1g | carbs: 56.2g

Artichoke and Arugula Salad

Prep time: 10 minutes | **Cook time:** 0 minutes | **Serves:**6

Ingredients:

Salad:
6 canned oil-packed artichoke hearts, sliced
6 cups baby arugula leaves
6 fresh olives, pitted and chopped
1 cup cherry tomatoes, sliced in half

Dressing:
1 teaspoon Dijon mustard
2 tablespoons balsamic vinegar
1 clove garlic, minced
2 tablespoons extra-virgin olive oil

For Garnish:
4 fresh basil leaves, thinly sliced

Directions:

Combine the ingredients for the salad in a large salad bowl, then toss to combine well. Combine the ingredients for the dressing in a small bowl, then stir to mix well.

Dress the salad, then serve with basil leaves on top.

Per Serving calories: 134 | fat: 12.1g | protein: 1.6g | carbs: 6.2g

Baby Potato and Olive Salad

Prep time: 10 minutes | **Cook time:** 20 minutes | **Serves:**6

Ingredients:

2 pounds (907 g) baby potatoes, cut into 1-inch cubes
1 tablespoon low-sodium olive brine
3 tablespoons freshly squeezed lemon juice (from about 1 medium lemon)

¼ teaspoon kosher salt
3 tablespoons extra-virgin olive oil
½ cup sliced olives
2 tablespoons torn fresh mint
1 cup sliced celery (about 2 stalks)
2 tablespoons chopped fresh oregano

Directions:

Put the tomatoes in a saucepan, then pour in enough water to submerge the tomatoes about 1 inch. Bring to a boil over high heat, then reduce the heat to medium-low. Simmer for 14 minutes or until the potatoes are soft. Meanwhile, combine the olive brine, lemon juice, salt, and olive oil in a small bow. Stir to mix well.

Transfer the cooked tomatoes in a colander, then rinse with running cold water. Pat dry with paper towels. Transfer the tomatoes in a large salad bowl, then drizzle with olive brine mixture. Spread with remaining ingredients and toss to combine well. Serve immediately.

Per Serving calories: 220 | fat: 6.1g | protein: 4.3g | carbs: 39.2g

Barley, Parsley, and Pea Salad

Prep time: 10 minutes | **Cook time:** 10 minutes | **Serves:**4

Ingredients:

2 cups water
1 cup quick-cooking barley
1 small bunch flat-leaf parsley, chopped (about 1 to 1½ cups)
2 cups sugar snap pea pods

Juice of 1 lemon
½ small red onion, diced
2 tablespoons extra-virgin olive oil
Sea salt and freshly ground pepper, to taste

Directions:

Pour the water in a saucepan. Bring to a boil. Add the barley to the saucepan, then put the lid on.

Reduce the heat to low. Simmer the barley for 10 minutes or until the liquid is absorbed, then let sit for 5 minutes.

Open the lid, then transfer the barley in a colander and rinse under cold running water.

Pour the barley in a large salad bowl and add the remaining ingredients. Toss to combine well.

Serve immediately.

Per Serving calories: 152 | fat: 7.4g | protein: 3.7g | carbs: 19.3g

Cheesy Peach and Walnut Salad

Prep time: 10 minutes | **Cook time:** 0 minutes | **Serves:**1

Ingredients:

1 ripe peach, pitted and sliced
¼ cup chopped walnuts, toasted
¼ cup shredded Parmesan cheese

1 teaspoon raw honey
Zest of 1 lemon
1 tablespoon chopped fresh mint

Directions:

Combine the peach, walnut, and cheese in a medium bowl, then drizzle with honey. Spread the lemon zest and mint on top. Toss to combine everything well. Serve immediately.

Per Serving calories: 373 | fat: 26.4g | protein: 12.9g | carbs: 27.0g

Greek Chicken, Tomato, and Olive Salad

Prep time: 10 minutes | **Cook time:** 0 minutes | **Serves:** 2

Ingredients:

Salad:
2 grilled boneless, skinless chicken breasts, sliced (about 1 cup)
10 cherry tomatoes, halved
8 pitted Kalamata olives, halved
½ cup thinly sliced red onion

Dressing:
¼ cup balsamic vinegar
1 teaspoon freshly squeezed lemon juice
¼ teaspoon sea salt
¼ teaspoon freshly ground black pepper
2 teaspoons extra-virgin olive oil

For Serving:
2 cups roughly chopped romaine lettuce
½ cup crumbled feta cheese

Directions:

Combine the ingredients for the salad in a large bowl. Toss to combine well. Combine the ingredients for the dressing in a small bowl. Stir to mix well. Pour the dressing the bowl of salad, then toss to coat well. Wrap the bowl in plastic and refrigerate for at least 2 hours.

Remove the bowl from the refrigerator. Spread the lettuce on a large plate, then top with marinated salad. Scatter the salad with feta cheese and serve immediately.

Per Serving calories: 328 | fat: 16.9g | protein: 27.6g | carbs: 15.9g

Ritzy Summer Fruit Salad

Prep time: 10 minutes | **Cook time:** 0 minutes | **Serves:** 8

Ingredients:

Salad:
1 cup fresh blueberries
2 cups cubed cantaloupe
2 cups red seedless grapes
1 cup sliced fresh strawberries
2 cups cubed honeydew melon
Zest of 1 large lime
½ cup unsweetened toasted coconut flakes

Dressing:
¼ cup raw honey
Juice of 1 large lime
¼ teaspoon sea salt
½ cup extra-virgin olive oil

Directions:

Combine the ingredients for the salad in a large salad bowl, then toss to combine well. Combine the ingredients for the dressing in a small bowl, then stir to mix well.

Dress the salad and serve immediately.

Per Serving calories: 242 | fat: 15.5g | protein: 1.3g | carbs: 28.0g

Roasted Broccoli and Tomato Panzanella

Prep time: 10 minutes | **Cook time:** 20 minutes | **Serves:** 4

Ingredients:

1 pound (454 g) broccoli (about 3 medium stalks), trimmed, cut into 1- inch florets and ½-inch stem slices
2 tablespoons extra-virgin olive oil, divided
1½ cups cherry tomatoes
1½ teaspoons honey, divided
3 cups cubed whole-grain crusty bread
1 tablespoon balsamic vinegar
¼ teaspoon kosher salt
½ teaspoon freshly ground black pepper
¼ cup grated Parmesan cheese, for serving (optional)
¼ cup chopped fresh oregano leaves, for serving (optional)

Directions:

Preheat the oven to 450ºF (235ºC).

Toss the broccoli with 1 tablespoon of olive oil in a large bowl to coat well.

Arrange the broccoli on a baking sheet, then add the tomatoes to the same bowl and toss with the remaining olive oil. Add 1 teaspoon of honey and toss again to coat well. Transfer the tomatoes on the baking sheet beside the broccoli.

Place the baking sheet in the preheated oven and roast for 15 minutes, then add the bread cubes and flip the vegetables. Roast for an additional 3 minutes or until the broccoli is lightly charred and the bread cubes are golden brown.

Meanwhile, combine the remaining ingredients, except for the Parmesan and oregano, in a small bowl. Stir to mix well.

Transfer the roasted vegetables and bread cubes to the large salad bowl, then dress them and spread with Parmesan and oregano leaves. Toss and serve immediately.

Per Serving
calories: 162 | fat: 6.8g | protein: 8.2g | carbs: 18.9g

Grilled Bell Pepper and Anchovy Antipasto

Prep time: 15 minutes | **Cook time:** 8 minutes | **Serves:**4

Ingredients:

2 tablespoons extra-virgin olive oil, divided

4 medium red bell peppers, quartered, stem and seeds removed

6 ounces (170 g) anchovies in oil, chopped

2 tablespoons capers, rinsed and drained

1 cup Kalamata olives, pitted

1 small shallot, chopped

Sea salt and freshly ground pepper, to taste

Directions:

Heat the grill to medium-high heat. Grease the grill grates with 1 tablespoon of olive oil.

Arrange the red bell peppers on the preheated grill grates, then grill for 8 minutes or until charred.

Turn off the grill and allow the pepper to cool for 10 minutes.

Transfer the charred pepper in a colander. Rinse and peel the peppers under running cold water, then pat dry with paper towels.

Cut the peppers into chunks and combine with remaining ingredients in a large bowl. Toss to mix well.

Serve immediately.

Per Serving calories: 227 | fat: 14.9g | protein: 13.9g | carbs: 9.9g

Marinated Mushrooms and Olives

Prep time: 1 hour 10 minutes | **Cook time:** 0 minutes | **Serves:**8

Ingredients:

1 pound (454 g) white button mushrooms, rinsed and drained

1 pound (454 g) fresh olives

½ tablespoon crushed fennel seeds

1 tablespoon white wine vinegar

2 tablespoons fresh thyme leaves

Pinch chili flakes

Sea salt and freshly ground pepper, to taste

2 tablespoons extra-virgin olive oil

Directions:

Combine all the ingredients in a large bowl. Toss to mix well.

Wrap the bowl in plastic and refrigerate for at least 1 hour to marinate.

Remove the bowl from the refrigerate and let sit under room temperature for 10 minutes, then serve.

Per Serving

calories: 111 | fat: 9.7g | protein: 2.4g | carbs: 5.9g

Root Vegetable Roast

Prep time: 15 mins | **Cook time:** 25 minutes | **Serves:**4 to 6

Ingredients:

1 bunch beets, peeled and cut into 1-inch cubes

2 small sweet potatoes, peeled and cut into 1-inch cubes

3 parsnips, peeled and cut into 1-inch rounds

4 carrots, peeled and cut into 1-inch rounds

1 tablespoon raw honey

1 teaspoon sea salt

½ teaspoon freshly ground black pepper

1 tablespoon extra-virgin olive oil

2 tablespoons coconut oil, melted

Directions:

Preheat the oven to 400ºF (205ºC). Line a baking sheet with parchment paper.

Combine all the ingredients in a large bowl. Toss to coat the vegetables well.

Pour the mixture in the baking sheet, then place the sheet in the preheated oven.

Roast for 25 minutes or until the vegetables are lightly browned and soft. Flip the vegetables halfway through the cooking time.

Remove the vegetables from the oven and allow to cool before serving.

Per Serving

calories: 461 | fat: 18.1g | protein: 5.9g | carbs: 74.2g

Cucumber Gazpacho

Prep time: 10 minutes | **Cook time:** 0 minutes | **Serves:**4

Ingredients:

2 cucumbers, peeled, deseeded, and cut into chunks

½ cup mint, finely chopped

2 cups plain Greek yogurt

2 garlic cloves, minced

2 cups low-sodium vegetable soup

1 tablespoon no-salt-added tomato paste

3 teaspoons fresh dill

Sea salt and freshly ground pepper, to taste

Directions:

Put the cucumber, mint, yogurt, and garlic in a food processor, then pulse until creamy and smooth.

Transfer the puréed mixture in a large serving bowl, then add the vegetable soup, tomato paste, dill, salt, and ground black pepper. Stir to mix well.

Keep the soup in the refrigerator for at least 2 hours, then serve chilled.

Per Serving

calories: 133 | fat: 1.5g | protein: 14.2g | carbs: 16.5g

Sardines with Lemony Tomato Sauce

Prep time: 10 minutes | **Cook time:** 40 minutes | **Serves:** 4

Ingredients:

2 tablespoons olive oil, divided
4 Roma tomatoes, peeled and chopped, reserve the juice
1 small onion, sliced thinly
Zest of 1 orange

1 pound (454 g) fresh sardines, rinsed, spine removed, butterflied
½ cup white wine
2 tablespoons whole-wheat breadcrumbs
Sea salt and freshly ground pepper, to taste

Directions:

Preheat the oven to 425°F (220°C). Grease a baking dish with 1 tablespoon of olive oil. Heath the remaining olive oil in a nonstick skillet over medium-low heat until shimmering.

Add the tomatoes with juice, onion, orange zest, salt, and ground pepper to the skillet and simmer for 20 minutes or until it thickens.

Pour half of the mixture on the bottom of the baking dish, then top with the butterflied sardines. Pour the remaining mixture and white wine over the sardines.

Spread the breadcrumbs on top, then place the baking dish in the preheated oven. Bake for 20 minutes or until the fish is opaque.

Remove the baking sheet from the oven and serve the sardines warm.

Per Serving

calories: 363 | fat: 20.2g | protein: 29.7g | carbs: 9.7g

Mushroom and Soba Noodle Soup

Prep time: 15 minutes | **Cook time:** 10 minutes | **Serves:** 4

Ingredients:

2 tablespoons coconut oil
8 ounces (227 g) shiitake mushrooms, stemmed and sliced thin
1 tablespoon minced fresh ginger
4 scallions, sliced thin
1 garlic clove, minced

1 teaspoon sea salt
4 cups low-sodium vegetable broth
3 cups water
4 ounces (113 g) soba noodles
1 bunch spinach, blanched, rinsed and cut into strips
1 tablespoon freshly squeezed lemon juice

Directions:

Heat the coconut oil in a stockpot over medium heat until melted.

Add the mushrooms, ginger, scallions, garlic, and salt. Sauté for 5 minutes or until fragrant and the mushrooms are tender. Pour in the vegetable broth and water. Bring to a boil, then add the soba noodles and cook for 5 minutes or until al dente. Turn off the heat and add the spinach and lemon juice. Stir to mix well.

Pour the soup in a large bowl and serve immediately.

Per Serving

calories: 254 | fat: 9.2g | protein: 13.1g | carbs: 33.9g

Greens, Fennel, and Pear Soup with Cashews

Prep time: 15 mins | **Cook time:** 15 minutes | **Serves:** 4 to 6

Ingredients:

2 tablespoons olive oil
1 fennel bulb, cut into ¼-inch-thick slices
2 leeks, white part only, sliced
2 pears, peeled, cored, and cut into ½-inch cubes

1 teaspoon sea salt
¼ teaspoon freshly ground black pepper
½ cup cashews
2 cups packed blanched spinach
3 cups low-sodium vegetable soup

Directions:

Heat the olive oil in a stockpot over high heat until shimmering.

Add the fennel and leeks, then sauté for 5 minutes or until tender.

Add the pears and sprinkle with salt and pepper, then sauté for another 3 minutes or until the pears are soft.

Add the cashews, spinach, and vegetable soup. Bring to a boil. Reduce the heat to low. Cover and simmer for 5 minutes.

Pour the soup in a food processor, then pulse until creamy and smooth.

Pour the soup back to the pot and heat over low heat until heated through.

Transfer the soup to a large serving bowl and serve immediately.

Per Serving

calories: 266 | fat: 15.1g | protein: 5.2g | carbs: 32.9g

Garlic Wilted Greens

Prep time: 10 minutes | **Cook time:** 5 minutes | **Serves:** 2

Ingredients:

1 tablespoon olive oil
2 garlic cloves, minced
3 cups sliced greens (spinach, chard, beet greens, dandelion greens, or a combination)

Pinch salt
Pinch red pepper flakes (or more to taste)

Directions:

Heat the olive oil in a skillet over medium-high heat.

Add garlic and sauté for 30 seconds, or just until fragrant.

Add the greens, salt, and pepper flakes and stir to combine. Let the greens wilt, but do not overcook.

Remove from the skillet and serve on a plate.

Per Serving calories: 93 | fat: 6.8g | protein: 1.2g | carbs: 7.3g

Veggie Slaw

Prep time: 20 minutes | **Cook time:** 0 mins | **Serves:** 4 to 6

Ingredients:

Salad:
2 large broccoli stems, peeled and shredded
½ celery root bulb, peeled and shredded
¼ cup chopped fresh Italian parsley
1 large beet, peeled and shredded
2 carrots, peeled and shredded
1 small red onion, sliced thin
2 zucchinis, shredded

Dressing:
1 teaspoon Dijon mustard
½ cup apple cider vinegar
1 tablespoon raw honey
1 teaspoon sea salt
¼ teaspoon freshly ground black pepper
2 tablespoons extra-virgin olive oil

Topping:
½ cup crumbled feta cheese

Directions:

Combine the ingredients for the salad in a large salad bowl, then toss to combine well.

Combine the ingredients for the dressing in a small bowl, then stir to mix well.

Dress the salad, then serve with feta cheese on top.

Per Serving

calories: 387 | fat: 30.2g | protein: 8.1g | carbs: 25.9g

Green Beans with Tahini-Lemon Sauce

Prep time: 5 minutes | **Cook time:** 10 minutes | **Serves:** 2

Ingredients:

1 pound (454 g) green beans, washed and trimmed
2 tablespoons tahini
1 garlic clove, minced
Grated zest and juice of 1 lemon
Salt and black pepper, to taste
1 teaspoon toasted black or white sesame seeds (optional)

Directions:

Steam the beans in a medium saucepan fitted with a steamer basket (or by adding ¼ cup water to a covered saucepan) over medium-high heat. Drain, reserving the cooking water. Mix the tahini, garlic, lemon zest and juice, and salt and pepper to taste. Use the reserved cooking water to thin the sauce as desired.

Toss the green beans with the sauce and garnish with the sesame seeds, if desired. Serve immediately.

Per Serving calories: 188 | fat: 8.4g | protein: 7.2g | carbs: 22.2g

Moroccan Lentil, Tomato, and Cauliflower Soup

Prep time: 15 minutes | **Cook time:** 4 hours | **Serves:** 6

Ingredients:

1 cup chopped carrots
1 cup chopped onions
3 cloves garlic, minced
½ teaspoon ground coriander
1 teaspoon ground cumin
1 teaspoon ground turmeric
¼ teaspoon ground cinnamon
¼ teaspoon freshly ground black pepper
1 cup dry lentils
28 ounces (794 g) tomatoes, diced, reserve the juice
1½ cups chopped cauliflower
4 cups low-sodium vegetable soup
1 tablespoon no-salt-added tomato paste
1 teaspoon extra-virgin olive oil
1 cup chopped fresh spinach
¼ cup chopped fresh cilantro
1 tablespoon red wine vinegar (optional)

Directions:

Put the carrots and onions in the slow cooker, then sprinkle with minced garlic, coriander, cumin, turmeric, cinnamon, and black pepper. Stir to combine well.

Add the lentils, tomatoes, and cauliflower, then pour in the vegetable soup and tomato paste. Drizzle with olive oil. Stir to combine well.

Put the slow cooker lid on and cook on high for 4 hours or until the vegetables are tender.

In the last 30 minutes during the cooking time, open the lid and stir the soup, then fold in the spinach.

Pour the cooked soup in a large serving bowl, then spread with cilantro and drizzle with vinegar. Serve immediately.

Per Serving

calories: 131 | fat: 2.1g | protein: 5.6g | carbs: 25.0g

Pumpkin Soup with Crispy Sage Leaves

Prep time: 15 minutes | **Cook time:** 10 minutes | **Serves:**4

Ingredients:

1 tablespoon olive oil
2 garlic cloves, cut into ⅛-inch-thick slices
1 onion, chopped
2 cups freshly puréed pumpkin
4 cups low-sodium vegetable soup
2 teaspoons chipotle powder
1 teaspoon sea salt
½ teaspoon freshly ground black pepper
½ cup vegetable oil
12 sage leaves, stemmed

Directions:

Heat the olive oil in a stockpot over high heat until shimmering.

Add the garlic and onion, then sauté for 5 minutes or until the onion is translucent.

Pour in the puréed pumpkin and vegetable soup in the pot, then sprinkle with chipotle powder, salt, and ground black pepper. Stir to mix well.

Bring to a boil. Reduce the heat to low and simmer for 5 minutes.

Meanwhile, heat the vegetable oil in a nonstick skillet over high heat.

Add the sage leaf to the skillet and sauté for a minute or until crispy. Transfer the sage on paper towels to soak the excess oil.

Gently pour the soup in three serving bowls, then divide the crispy sage leaves in bowls for garnish. Serve immediately.

Per Serving
calories: 380 | fat: 20.1g | protein: 8.9g | carbs: 45.2g

Arugula and Fig Salad

Prep time: 15 minutes | **Cook time:** 0 minutes | **Serves:**2

Ingredients:

3 cups arugula
4 fresh, ripe figs (or 4 to 6 dried figs), stemmed and sliced
2 tablespoons olive oil
¼ cup lightly toasted pecan halves
2 tablespoons crumbled blue cheese
1 to 2 tablespoons balsamic glaze

Directions:

Toss the arugula and figs with the olive oil in a large bowl until evenly coated. Add the pecans and blue cheese to the bowl. Toss the salad lightly.

Drizzle with the balsamic glaze and serve immediately.

Per Serving calories: 517 | fat: 36.2g | protein: 18.9g | carbs: 30.2g

Mushroom Barley Soup

Prep time: 5 minutes | **Cook time:** 20 to 23 minutes
Serves:6

Ingredients:

2 tablespoons extra-virgin olive oil
1 cup chopped carrots
1 cup chopped onion
5½ cups chopped mushrooms
6 cups no-salt-added vegetable broth
1 cup uncooked pearled barley
¼ cup red wine
2 tablespoons tomato paste
4 sprigs fresh thyme or ½ teaspoon dried thyme
1 dried bay leaf
6 tablespoons grated Parmesan cheese

Directions:

In a large stockpot over medium heat, heat the oil. Add the onion and carrots and cook for 5 minutes, stirring frequently. Turn up the heat to medium-high and add the mushrooms. Cook for 3 minutes, stirring frequently.

Add the broth, barley, wine, tomato paste, thyme, and bay leaf. Stir, cover, and bring the soup to a boil. Once it's boiling, stir a few times, reduce the heat to medium-low, cover, and cook for another 12 to 15 minutes, until the barley is cooked through.

Remove the bay leaf and serve the soup in bowls with 1 tablespoon of cheese sprinkled on top of each.

Per Serving
calories: 195 | fat: 4.0g | protein: 7.0g | carbs: 34.0g

Parmesan Roasted Red Potatoes

Prep time: 10 minutes | **Cook time:** 55 minutes | **Serves:**2

Ingredients:

12 ounces (340 g) red potatoes (3 to 4 small potatoes), scrubbed and diced into 1-inch pieces
1 tablespoon olive oil
½ teaspoon garlic powder
¼ teaspoon salt
1 tablespoon grated Parmesan cheese
1 teaspoon minced fresh rosemary (from 1 sprig)

Directions:

Preheat the oven to 425ºF (220ºC). Line a baking sheet with parchment paper. In a mixing bowl, combine the potatoes, olive oil, garlic powder, and salt. Toss well to coat. Lay the potatoes on the parchment paper and roast for 10 minutes. Flip the potatoes over and roast for another 10 minutes. Check the potatoes to make sure they are golden brown on the top and bottom. Toss them again, turn the heat down to 350ºF (180ºC), and roast for 30 minutes more. When the potatoes are golden brown, scatter the Parmesan cheese over them and toss again. Return to the oven for 3 minutes to melt the cheese.

Remove from the oven and sprinkle with the fresh rosemary before serving.

Per Serving calories: 200 fat: 8.2g protein: 5.1g | carbs: 30.0g

Paella Soup

Prep time: 6 minutes | **Cook time:** 24 minutes | **Serves:** 6

Ingredients:

2 tablespoons extra-virgin olive oil
1 cup chopped onion
1½ cups coarsely chopped green bell pepper
1½ cups coarsely chopped red bell pepper
2 garlic cloves, chopped
1 teaspoon ground turmeric
1 teaspoon dried thyme
2 teaspoons smoked paprika

2½ cups uncooked instant brown rice
2 cups low-sodium or no-salt-added chicken broth
2½ cups water
1 cup frozen green peas, thawed
1 (28-ounce / 794-g) can low-sodium or no-salt-added crushed tomatoes
1 pound (454 g) fresh raw medium shrimp, shells and tails removed

Directions:

In a large stockpot over medium-high heat, heat the oil. Add the onion, bell peppers, and garlic. Cook for 8 minutes, stirring occasionally. Add the turmeric, thyme, and smoked paprika, and cook for 2 minutes more, stirring often. Stir in the rice, broth, and water. Bring to a boil over high heat. Cover, reduce the heat to medium-low, and cook for 10 minutes.

Stir the peas, tomatoes, and shrimp into the soup. Cook for 4 minutes, until the shrimp is cooked, turning from gray to pink and white. The soup will be very thick, almost like stew, when ready to serve.

Ladle the soup into bowls and serve hot.

Per Serving
calories: 431 | fat: 5.7g | protein: 26.0g | carbs: 69.1g

Sautéed Kale with Olives

Prep time: 10 minutes | **Cook time:** 10 minutes | **Serves:** 2

Ingredients:

1 bunch kale, leaves chopped and stems minced
½ cup celery leaves, roughly chopped, or additional parsley
½ bunch flat-leaf parsley, stems and leaves roughly chopped

4 garlic cloves, chopped
2 teaspoons olive oil
¼ cup pitted Kalamata olives, chopped
Grated zest and juice of 1 lemon
Salt and pepper, to taste

Directions:

Place the kale, celery leaves, parsley, and garlic in a steamer basket set over a medium saucepan. Steam over medium-high heat, covered, for 15 minutes. Remove from the heat and squeeze out any excess moisture. Place a large skillet over medium heat. Add the oil, then add the kale mixture to the skillet. Cook, stirring often, for 5 minutes. Remove from the heat and add the olives and lemon zest and juice. Season with salt and pepper and serve.

Per Serving calories: 86 | fat: 6.4g | protein: 1.8g | carbs: 7.5g

Balsamic Brussels Sprouts and Delicata Squash

Prep time: 10 minutes | **Cook time:** 30 minutes | **Serves:** 2

Ingredients:

½ pound (227 g) Brussels sprouts, ends trimmed and outer leaves removed
1 medium delicata squash, halved lengthwise, seeded, and cut into 1-inch pieces
1 cup fresh cranberries

2 teaspoons olive oil
Salt and freshly ground black pepper, to taste
½ cup balsamic vinegar
2 tablespoons roasted pumpkin seeds
2 tablespoons fresh pomegranate arils (seeds)

Directions:

Preheat oven to 400°F (205°C). Line a sheet pan with parchment paper. Combine the Brussels sprouts, squash, and cranberries in a large bowl. Drizzle with olive oil, and season lightly with salt and pepper. Toss well to coat and arrange in a single layer on the sheet pan.

Roast in the preheated oven for 30 minutes, turning vegetables halfway through, or until Brussels sprouts turn brown and crisp in spots. Meanwhile, make the balsamic glaze by simmering the vinegar for 10 to 12 minutes, or until mixture has reduced to about ¼ cup and turns a syrupy consistency. Remove the vegetables from the oven, drizzle with balsamic syrup, and sprinkle with pumpkin seeds and pomegranate arils before serving.

Per Serving calories: 203 | fat: 6.8g | protein: 6.2g | carbs: 22.0g

Mixed Salad With Balsamic Honey Dressing

Prep time: 15 minutes | **Cook time:** 0 minutes | **Serves:** 2

Ingredients:

Dressing:
¼ cup balsamic vinegar
¼ cup olive oil
1 tablespoon honey
1 teaspoon Dijon mustard
¼ teaspoon garlic powder
¼ teaspoon salt, or more to taste
Pinch freshly ground black pepper
Salad:

½ cup cherry or grape tomatoes, halved
½ English cucumber, sliced in quarters lengthwise and then cut into bite-size pieces
Any combination fresh, torn herbs (parsley, oregano, basil, or chives)
1 tablespoon roasted sunflower seeds
4 cups chopped red leaf lettuce

Directions:

Combine the vinegar, olive oil, honey, mustard, garlic powder, salt, and pepper in a jar with a lid. Shake well.

In a large bowl, combine the lettuce, tomatoes, cucumber, and herbs. Toss well. Pour all or as much dressing as desired over the tossed salad and toss again to coat the salad with dressing. Top with the sunflower seeds before serving.

Per Serving calories: 337 | fat: 26.1g | protein: 4.2g | carbs: 22.2g

Rich Chicken and Small Pasta Broth

Prep time: 10 minutes | **Cook time:** 4 hours | **Serves:**6

6 boneless, skinless chicken thighs
4 stalks celery, cut into ½-inch pieces
4 carrots, cut into 1-inch pieces
1 medium yellow onion, halved
2 garlic cloves, minced
2 bay leaves
Sea salt and freshly ground black pepper, to taste
6 cups low-sodium chicken stock
½ cup stelline pasta
¼ cup chopped fresh flat-leaf parsley

Directions:

Combine the chicken thighs, celery, carrots, onion, and garlic in the slow cooker. Spread with bay leaves and sprinkle with salt and pepper. Toss to mix well.

Pour in the chicken stock. Put the lid on and cook on high for 4 hours or until the internal temperature of chicken reaches at least 165°F (74°C).

In the last 20 minutes of the cooking, remove the chicken from the slow cooker and transfer to a bowl to cool until ready to reserve.

Discard the bay leaves and add the pasta to the slow cooker. Put the lid on and cook for 15 minutes or until al dente. Meanwhile, slice the chicken, then put the chicken and parsley in the slow cooker and cook for 5 minutes or until well combined. Pour the soup in a large bowl and serve immediately.

Per Serving calories: 285 | fat: 10.8g | protein: 27.4g | carbs: 18.8g

Orange-Honey Glazed Carrots

Prep time: 10 minutes | **Cook time:** 15 to 20 minutes **Serves:**2

Ingredients:

½ pound (227 g) rainbow carrots, peeled
2 tablespoons fresh orange juice
1 tablespoon honey
½ teaspoon coriander
Pinch salt

Directions:

Preheat the oven to 400°F (205°C).

Cut the carrots lengthwise into slices of even thickness and place in a large bowl. Stir together the orange juice, honey, coriander, and salt in a small bowl. Pour the orange juice mixture over the carrots and toss until well coated.

Spread the carrots in a baking dish in a single layer. Roast for 15 to 20 minutes until fork-tender.

Let cool for 5 minutes before serving.

Per Serving
calories: 85 | fat: 0g | protein: 1.0g | carbs: 21.0g

Roasted Root Vegetable Soup

Prep time: 10 minutes | **Cook time:** 35 minutes | **Serves:**6

Ingredients:

2 parsnips, peeled and sliced
2 carrots, peeled and sliced
2 sweet potatoes, peeled and sliced
1 teaspoon chopped fresh rosemary
1 teaspoon chopped fresh thyme
1 teaspoon sea salt
½ teaspoon freshly ground black pepper
2 tablespoons extra-virgin olive oil
4 cups low-sodium vegetable soup
½ cup grated Parmesan cheese, for garnish (optional)

Directions:

Preheat the oven to 400°F (205°C). Line a baking sheet with aluminum foil.

Combine the parsnips, carrots, and sweet potatoes in a large bowl, then sprinkle with rosemary, thyme, salt, and pepper, and drizzle with olive oil. Toss to coat the vegetables well.

Arrange the vegetables on the baking sheet, then roast in the preheated oven for 30 minutes or until lightly browned and soft. Flip the vegetables halfway through the roasting.

Pour the roasted vegetables with vegetable broth in a food processor, then pulse until creamy and smooth.

Pour the puréed vegetables in a saucepan, then warm over low heat until heated through. Spoon the soup in a large serving bowl, then scatter with Parmesan cheese. Serve immediately.

Per Serving calories: 192 | fat: 5.7g | protein: 4.8g | carbs: 31.5g

Lemon-Tahini Hummus

Prep time: 15 minutes | **Cook time:** 0 minutes | **Serves:**6

1 (15-ounce / 425-g) can chickpeas, drained and rinsed
4 tablespoons extra-virgin olive oil, divided
2 lemons, juiced
1 lemon, zested, divided
1 tablespoon minced garlic
Pinch salt
4 to 5 tablespoons tahini (sesame seed paste)

Directions:

In a food processor, combine the chickpeas, 2 tablespoons of olive oil, tahini, lemon juice, half of the lemon zest, and garlic and pulse for up to 1 minute, scraping down the sides of the food processor bowl as necessary.

Taste and add salt as needed. Feel free to add 1 teaspoon of water at a time to thin the hummus to a better consistency. Transfer the hummus to a serving bowl. Serve drizzled with the remaining 2 tablespoons of olive oil and remaining half of the lemon zest.

Per Serving calories: 216 | fat: 15.0g | protein: 5.0g | carbs: 17.0g

Roasted Cauliflower

Prep time: 10 minutes | **Cook time:** 20 minutes | **Serves:**2

½ large head cauliflower, stemmed and broken into florets (about 3 cups)
1 tablespoon olive oil

2 tablespoons freshly squeezed lemon juice
2 tablespoons tahini
1 teaspoon harissa paste
Pinch salt

Directions:

Preheat the oven to 400°F (205°C). Line a sheet pan with parchment paper. Toss the cauliflower florets with the olive oil in a large bowl and transfer to the sheet pan.

Roast in the preheated oven for 15 minutes, flipping the cauliflower once or twice, or until it starts to become golden. Meanwhile, in a separate bowl, combine the lemon juice, tahini, harissa, and salt and stir to mix well.

Remove the pan from the oven and toss the cauliflower with the lemon tahini sauce. Return to the oven and roast for another 5 minutes. Serve hot.

Per Serving calories: 205 | fat: 15.0g | protein: 4.0g | carbs: 15.0g

Cheesy Roasted Broccolini

Prep time: 5 minutes | **Cook time:** 10 minutes | **Serves:**2

Ingredients:

1 bunch broccolini (about 5 ounces / 142 g)
1 tablespoon olive oil
½ teaspoon garlic powder

¼ teaspoon salt
2 tablespoons grated Romano cheese

Directions:

Preheat the oven to 400°F (205°C). Line a sheet pan with parchment paper.

Slice the tough ends off the broccolini and put in a medium bowl. Add the olive oil, garlic powder, and salt and toss to coat well. Arrange the broccolini on the prepared sheet pan.

Roast in the preheated oven for 7 minutes, flipping halfway through the cooking time.

Remove the pan from the oven and sprinkle the cheese over the broccolini. Using tongs, carefully flip the broccolini over to coat all sides.

Return to the oven and cook for an additional 2 to 3 minutes, or until the cheese melts and starts to turn golden. Serve warm.

Per Serving
calories: 114 | fat: 9.0g | protein: 4.0g | carbs: 5.0g

Sautéed White Beans with Rosemary

Prep time: 10 minutes | **Cook time:** 12 minutes | **Serves:**2

Ingredients:

1 tablespoon olive oil
2 garlic cloves, minced
1 (15-ounce / 425-g) can white cannellini beans, drained and rinsed
Salt, to taste

1 teaspoon minced fresh rosemary plus
1 whole fresh rosemary sprig
¼ teaspoon dried sage
½ cup low-sodium chicken stock

Directions:

Heat the olive oil in a saucepan over medium-high heat.

Add the garlic and sauté for 30 seconds until fragrant.

Add the beans, minced and whole rosemary, sage, and chicken stock and bring the mixture to a boil.

Reduce the heat to medium and allow to simmer for 10 minutes, or until most of the liquid is evaporated. If desired, mash some of the beans with a fork to thicken them. Season with salt to taste. Remove the rosemary sprig before serving.

Per Serving calories: 155 | fat: 7.0g | protein: 6.0g | carbs: 17.0g

Moroccan Spiced Couscous

Prep time: 10 minutes | **Cook time:** 8 minutes | **Serves:**2

Ingredients:

1 tablespoon olive oil
¾ cup couscous
¼ teaspoon cinnamon
¼ teaspoon garlic powder
¼ teaspoon salt, plus more as needed

1 cup water
2 tablespoons minced dried apricots
2 tablespoons raisins
2 teaspoons minced fresh parsley

Directions:

Heat the olive oil in a saucepan over medium-high heat until it shimmers. Add the couscous, cinnamon, garlic powder, and salt. Stir for 1 minute to toast the couscous and spices. Add the water, apricots, and raisins and bring the mixture to a boil.

Cover and turn off the heat. Allow the couscous to sit for 4 to 5 minutes and then fluff it with a fork. Sprinkle with the fresh parsley. Season with more salt as needed and serve.

Per Serving
calories: 338 | fat: 8.0g | protein: 9.0g | carbs: 59.0g

Lemon and Spinach Orzo

Prep time: 5 mins | **Cook time:** 10 minutes | **Makes** 2 cups

Ingredients:

1 cup dry orzo

1 (6-ounce / 170-g) bag baby spinach

1 cup halved grape tomatoes

2 tablespoons extra-virgin olive oil

¼ teaspoon salt

Freshly ground black pepper

¾ cup crumbled feta cheese

1 lemon, juiced and zested

Directions:

Bring a medium pot of water to a boil. Stir in the orzo and cook uncovered for 8 minutes. Drain the water, then return the orzo to medium heat. Add the spinach and tomatoes and cook until the spinach is wilted. Sprinkle with the olive oil, salt, and pepper and mix well. Top with the feta cheese, lemon juice and zest, then toss one or two more times and serve.

Per Serving (1 cup) calories: 610 | fat: 27.0g | protein: 21.0g | carbs: 74.0g

Zesty Spanish Potato Salad

Prep time: 10 minutes | **Cook time:** 5 to 7 minutes | **Serves:** 6 to 8

Ingredients:

4 russet potatoes, peeled and chopped

3 large hard-boiled eggs, chopped

1 cup frozen mixed vegetables, thawed

½ cup plain, unsweetened, full-fat Greek yogurt

5 tablespoons pitted Spanish olives

½ teaspoon freshly ground black pepper

½ teaspoon dried mustard seed

½ tablespoon freshly squeezed lemon juice

½ teaspoon dried dill Salt, to taste

Directions:

Place the potatoes in a large pot of water and boil for 5 to 7 minutes, until just fork-tender, checking periodically for doneness. You don't have to overcook them. Meanwhile, in a large bowl, mix the eggs, vegetables, yogurt, olives, pepper, mustard, lemon juice, and dill. Season with salt to taste.

Once the potatoes are cooled somewhat, add them to the large bowl, then toss well and serve.

Per Serving
calories: 192 | fat: 5.0g | protein: 9.0g | carbs: 30.0g

Greek Salad with Dressing

Prep time: 10 minutes | **Cook time:** 0 mins | **Serves:** 4 to 6

Ingredients:

1 head iceberg lettuce

2 cups cherry tomatoes

1 large cucumber

1 medium onion

¼ cup lemon juice

½ cup extra-virgin olive oil

1 teaspoon salt

1 clove garlic, minced

1 cup Kalamata olives, pitted

1 (6-ounce / 170-g) package feta cheese, crumbled

Directions:

Cut the lettuce into 1-inch pieces and put them in a large salad bowl. Cut the tomatoes in half and add them to the salad bowl. Slice the cucumber into bite-sized pieces and add them to the salad bowl.

Thinly slice the onion and add it to the salad bowl. In a separate bowl, whisk together the olive oil, lemon juice, salt, and garlic. Pour the dressing over the salad and gently toss to evenly coat.

Top the salad with the Kalamata olives and feta cheese and serve.

Per Serving calories: 539 | fat: 50.0g | protein: 9.0g | carbs: 18.0g

Tricolor Summer Salad

Prep time: 10 minutes | **Cook time:** 0 mins | **Serves:** 3 to 4

Ingredients:

¼ cup while balsamic vinegar

2 tablespoons Dijon mustard

1 tablespoon sugar

½ teaspoon garlic salt

½ teaspoon freshly ground black pepper

¼ cup extra-virgin olive oil

1½ cups chopped orange, yellow, and red tomatoes

½ cucumber, peeled and diced

1 small red onion, thinly sliced

¼ cup crumbled feta (optional)

Directions:

In a small bowl, whisk the vinegar, mustard, sugar, pepper, and garlic salt. Then slowly whisk in the olive oil. In a large bowl, add the tomatoes, cucumber, and red onion. Add the dressing. Toss once or twice, and serve with the feta crumbles (if desired) sprinkled on top.

Per Serving calories: 246 | fat: 18.0g | protein: 1.0g | carbs: 19.0g

Chicken and Pastina Soup

Prep time: 5 minutes | **Cook time:** 20 minutes | **Serves:** 6

Ingredients:

1 tablespoon extra-virgin olive oil
2 garlic cloves, minced
3 cups packed chopped kale; center ribs removed
1 cup minced carrots
8 cups no-salt-added chicken or vegetable broth
¼ teaspoon kosher or sea salt

¼ teaspoon freshly ground black pepper
¾ cup uncooked acini de pepe or pastina pasta
2 cups shredded cooked chicken (about 12 ounces / 340 g)
3 tablespoons grated Parmesan cheese

Directions:

In a large stockpot over medium heat, heat the oil. Add the garlic and cook for 30 seconds, stirring frequently. Add the kale and carrots and cook for 5 minutes, stirring occasionally. Add the broth, salt, and pepper, and turn the heat to high. Bring the broth to a boil, and add the pasta. Reduce the heat to medium and cook for 10 minutes, or until the pasta is cooked through, stirring every few minutes so the pasta doesn't stick to the bottom. Add the chicken, and cook for another 2 minutes to warm through.

Ladle the soup into six bowls. Top each with ½ tablespoon of cheese and serve.

Per Serving calories: 275 | fat: 19.0g | protein: 16.0g | carbs: 11.0g

Citrus Salad with Kale and Fennel

Prep time: 15 minutes | **Cook time:** 0 minutes | **Serves:** 2

Ingredients:

Dressing:
3 tablespoons olive oil
2 tablespoons fresh orange juice
1 tablespoon blood orange vinegar, other orange vinegar, or cider vinegar
1 tablespoon honey
Salt and freshly ground black pepper, to taste

Salad:
2 cups packed baby kale
1 medium navel or blood orange, segmented
½ small fennel bulb, stems and leaves removed, sliced into matchsticks
3 tablespoons toasted pecans, chopped
2 ounces (57 g) goat cheese, crumbled

Directions:
Make the Dressing

Mix the olive oil, orange juice, vinegar, and honey in a small bowl and whisk to combine. Season with salt and pepper to taste. Set aside.

Make the Salad

Divide the baby kale, orange segments, fennel, pecans, and goat cheese evenly between two plates.

Drizzle half of the dressing over each salad and serve.

Per Serving calories: 503 | fat: 39.1g | protein: 13.2g | carbs: 31.2g

Green Bean and Halloumi Salad

Prep time: 20 minutes | **Cook time:** 5 minutes | **Serves:** 2

Ingredients:

Dressing:
¼ cup unsweetened coconut milk
1 tablespoon olive oil
2 teaspoons freshly squeezed lemon juice
¼ teaspoon garlic powder
¼ teaspoon onion powder
Pinch salt
Pinch freshly ground black pepper

Salad:
½ pound (227 g) fresh green beans, trimmed
2 ounces (57 g) Halloumi cheese, sliced into 2 (½-inch-thick) slices
½ cup halved cherry or grape tomatoes
¼ cup thinly sliced sweet onion

Directions:

Combine the coconut milk, olive oil, lemon juice, onion powder, garlic powder, salt, and pepper in a small bowl and whisk well. Set aside.

Fill a medium-size pot with about 1 inch of water and add the green beans. Cover and steam them for about 3 to 4 minutes, or just until beans are tender. Do not overcook. Drain beans, rinse them immediately with cold water, and set them aside to cool.

Heat a nonstick skillet over medium-high heat and place the slices of Halloumi in the hot pan. After about 2 minutes, check to see if the cheese is golden on the bottom. If it is, flip the slices and cook for another minute or until the second side is golden. Remove cheese from the pan and cut each piece into cubes (about 1-inch square).

Place the green beans, halloumi slices, tomatoes, and onion in a large bowl and toss to combine.

Drizzle the dressing over the salad and toss well to combine. Serve immediately.

Per Serving calories: 274 | fat: 18.1g | protein: 8.0g | carbs: 16.8g

Mediterranean Tomato Hummus Soup

Prep time: 10 minutes | **Cook time:** 10 minutes | **Serves:** 2

Ingredients:

1 (14.5-ounce / 411-g) can crushed tomatoes with basil
2 cups low-sodium chicken stock
1 cup roasted red pepper hummus

Salt, to taste
¼ cup thinly sliced fresh basil leaves, for garnish (optional)

Directions:

Combine the canned tomatoes, hummus, and chicken stock in a blender and blend until smooth. Pour the mixture into a saucepan and bring it to a boil. Season with salt to taste. Serve garnished with the fresh basil, if desired.

Per Serving
calories: 147 | fat: 6.2g | protein: 5.2g | carbs: 20.1g

Arugula, Watermelon, and Feta Salad

Prep time: 10 minutes | **Cook time:** 0 minutes | **Serves:** 2

Ingredients:

3 cups packed arugula
2½ cups watermelon, cut into bite-size cubes
2 ounces (57 g) feta cheese, crumbled
2 tablespoons balsamic glaze

Directions:

Divide the arugula between two plates.

Divide the watermelon cubes between the beds of arugula.

Scatter half of the feta cheese over each salad.

Drizzle about 1 tablespoon of the glaze (or more if desired) over each salad. Serve immediately.

Per Serving

calories: 157 | fat: 6.9g | protein: 6.1g | carbs: 22.0g

Vegetable Fagioli Soup

Prep time: 30 minutes | **Cook time:** 60 minutes | **Serves:** 2

Ingredients:

1 tablespoon olive oil
2 medium carrots, diced
2 medium celery stalks, diced
½ medium onion, diced
1 large garlic clove, minced
3 tablespoons tomato paste
4 cups low-sodium vegetable broth
1 cup packed kale, stemmed and chopped
1 (15-ounce / 425-g) can red kidney beans, drained and rinsed
1 (15-ounce / 425-g) can cannellini beans, drained and rinsed
½ cup chopped fresh basil
Salt and freshly ground black pepper, to taste

Directions:

Heat the olive oil in a stockpot over medium-high heat. Add the carrots, celery, onion, and garlic and sauté for 10 minutes, or until the vegetables start to turn golden.

Stir in the tomato paste and cook for about 30 seconds.

Add the vegetable broth and bring the soup to a boil. Cover and reduce the heat to low. Cook the soup for 45 minutes, or until the carrots are tender.

Using an immersion blender, purée the soup so that it's partly smooth, but with some chunks of vegetables.

Add the kale, beans, and basil. Season with salt and pepper to taste, then serve.

Per Serving

calories: 217 | fat: 4.2g | protein: 10.0g | carbs: 36.2g

Avgolemono (Lemon Chicken Soup)

Prep time: 15 minutes | **Cook time:** 60 minutes | **Serves:** 2

Ingredients:

½ large onion
2 medium carrots
1 celery stalk
1 garlic clove
5 cups low-sodium chicken stock
¼ cup brown rice
1½ cups (about 5 ounces / 142 g) shredded rotisserie chicken
3 tablespoons freshly squeezed lemon juice
1 egg yolk
2 tablespoons chopped fresh dill
2 tablespoons chopped fresh parsley
Salt, to taste

Directions:

Put the onion, carrots, celery, and garlic in a food processor and pulse until the vegetables are minced.

Add the vegetables and chicken stock to a stockpot and bring it to a boil over high heat.

Reduce the heat to medium-low and add the rice, shredded chicken and lemon juice. Cover and let the soup simmer for 40 minutes, or until the rice is cooked.

In a small bowl, whisk the egg yolk lightly. Slowly, while whisking with one hand, pour about ½ of a ladle of the broth into the egg yolk to warm, or temper, the yolk. Slowly add another ladle of broth and continue to whisk.

Remove the soup from the heat and pour the whisked egg yolk–broth mixture into the pot. Stir well to combine.

Add the fresh dill and parsley. Season with salt to taste and serve.

Per Serving

calories: 172 | fat: 4.2g | protein: 18.2g | carbs: 16.1g

Minty Olives and Tomatoes Salad (Italian)

Preparation Time: 10 minutes **Cooking Time:** 0 minutes
Servings: 4

Ingredients:

1 cup kalamata olives 1 cup black olives
1 red onion, chopped
1 tablespoon mint, chopped
2 tablespoons balsamic vinegar
2 teaspoons Italian herbs, dried
1 cup cherry tomatoes 4 tomatoes
2 tablespoons oregano, chopped
¼ cup olive oil

Directions:

In a salad bowl, mix the olives with the tomatoes and the rest of the , toss, and serve cold.

Per Serving

190 Calories 8.1g Fat 4.6g Protein

Mediterranean Chicken Salad (Greek)

Preparation Time: 5 minutes **Cooking Time:** 25 minutes
Servings: 4

Ingredients:

For Chicken:
1 ¾ lb. boneless, skinless chicken breast
For Mediterranean salad:
6 cups of romaine lettuce that is torn or roughly chopped
10 pitted Kalamata olives
1 small lemon juice (it should be about 2 tablespoons)

¼ teaspoon each of pepper and salt (or as desired)
1 cup of sliced cucumber
1 pint of cherry tomatoes
1/3 cup of reduced-fat feta cheese
¼ teaspoon each of pepper and salt (or lesser)
1 ½ tablespoon of butter, melted

Directions:

Preheat your oven or grill to about 350F. Season the chicken with salt, butter, and black pepper. Roast or grill chicken until it reaches an internal temperature of 1650F in about 25 minutes.

Once your chicken breasts are cooked, remove them and keep aside to rest for about 5 minutes before you slice them.

Combine all the salad you have and toss everything together very well. Serve the chicken with Mediterranean salad.

Per Serving

Calories: 340 Protein: 45g Carbohydrate: 9g Fat: 4 g

Lentil Salmon Salad (Greek)

Preparation Time: 25 minutes **Cooking Time:** 25 minutes
Servings: 4

Ingredients:

2 cups vegetable stock
1/2 cup chopped parsley
2 tablespoons chopped cilantro
1 chopped red pepper
1 rinsed green lentil

1 chopped red onion
4 ounces shredded smoked salmon
1 lemon, juiced
Salt and pepper to taste

Directions:

1. Cook vegetable stock and lentils in a saucepan for 15 to 20 minutes, on low heat. Ensure all liquid has been absorbed and then remove from heat.
2. Pour into a salad bowl and top with red pepper, parsley, cilantro, salt and pepper (to suit your taste) and mix.
3. Mix in lemon juice and shredded salmon.
4. This salad should be served fresh.

Per Serving

Calories: 260 Fat: 2 g Carbs: 17 g Protein: 11 g

Peppy Pepper Tomato Salad (Greek)

Preparation Time: 20 minutes **Cooking Time:** 20 minutes
Servings: 4

Ingredients:

1 yellow bell pepper, cored and diced
1 tablespoon balsamic vinegar
2 cored and diced red bell peppers
1 pinch chili flakes

1 red onion, chopped
4 cucumbers, diced
2 tablespoons extra-virgin olive oil
Salt and pepper to taste
4 diced tomatoes

Directions:

Merge all the above in a salad bowl, except salt and pepper.

Season with salt and pepper to suit your taste and mix well.

Eat while fresh.

Per Serving

Calories: 260 Fat: 2 g Carbs: 17 g Protein: 11 g

Chopped Israeli Mediterranean Pasta Salad(Greek)

Preparation Time: 15 minutes **Cooking Time:** 2 minutes
Servings: 8

Ingredients:

Small bow tie or other small pasta (.5 lb.)
1/3 cup yellow bell pepper
1/3 cup orange bell pepper
1/3 cup Black olives
1/3 cup Cucumber
1/3 cup Fresh thyme leaves
Dried oregano (1 tsp.)
Dressing:

1/3 cup Radish
1/3 cup Tomato
1/3 cup green olives
1/3 cup red onions
1/3 cup Pepperoncini
1/3 cup Feta cheese
0.25 cup + more, olive oil
juice of 1 lemon

Directions:

Slice the green olives into halves. Dice the feta and pepperoncini. Finely dice the remainder of the veggies.

Prepare a pot of water with the salt, and simmer the pasta until it's al dente (checking at two minutes under the listed time). Rinse and drain in cold water.

Combine a small amount of oil with the pasta. Add the salt, pepper, oregano, thyme, and veggies. Pour in the rest of the oil, lemon juice, mix and fold in the grated feta.

Pop it into the fridge within two hours, best if overnight. Taste test and adjust the seasonings to your liking; add fresh thyme.

Per Serving

65 Calories 5.6g Fats 0.8g Protein

Tomato and Cucumber Salad with Feta (Spanish)

Preparation Time: 10 minutes **Cooking Time:** 0 minutes
Servings: 4

Ingredients:

1 tomatoe
½ bunch of spring onions
200g feta
3 tbsp balsamic vinegar salt
and pepper

½ cucumber
6 tbsp olive oil

Directions:

Thoroughly clean the tomatoes and cucumber. Eight tomatoes. Cut the cucumber into thin slices. Cut the spring onion into thin rings. Chop the herbs. Dice the feta.

Put all in a salad bowl. Add oil and balsamic vinegar, season with salt and pepper and mix well. Done! Serve and enjoy.

Per Serving
Calories: 341 Carbohydrates: 8.28g Protein: 8.-6g Fat: 31.09g

Couscous Arugula Salad (Greek)

Preparation Time: 15 minutes **Cooking Time:** 20 minutes
Servings: 4

Ingredients:

1/2 cup couscous
1 bunch, peeled asparagus
1 lemon, juiced
Salt and pepper to taste

1 cup vegetable stock
1 teaspoon dried tarragon
2 cups arugula

Directions:

Heat the vegetable stock in a pot until hot. Remove from heat and add in the couscous. Cover until the couscous has absorbed all the stock.

Pour in a bowl and fluff with a fork and then set aside to cool.

Peel asparagus with a vegetable peeler, making them into ribbons and put into a bowl with couscous.

Merge the remaining and add salt and pepper to suit your taste.

Serve the salad immediately.

Per Serving
Calories: 100 Fat: 6 g Carbs: 25 g Protein: 10g

Spinach and Grilled Feta Salad (Spanish)

Preparation Time: 10 minutes **Cooking Time:** 25 minutes
Servings: 4

Ingredients:

8 ounces feta cheese, sliced
1/4 cup green olives, sliced
4 cups baby spinach
1 teaspoon capers, chopped

2 garlic cloves, minced
1/4 cup black olives, sliced
1 tablespoon red wine vinegar
2 tablespoons extra-virgin olive oil

Directions:

Grill feta cheese slices over medium to high flame until brown on both sides.

In a salad bowl, mix green olives, black olives, and spinach.

In a separate bowl, mix vinegar, capers, and oil together to make a dressing.

Top salad with the dressing and cheese, and it is ready to serve.

Per Serving
Calories: 100 Fat: 6g Carbs: 25 g Protein: 10g

Creamy Cool Salad (Greek)

Preparation Time: 10 minutes **Cooking Time:** 25 minutes
Servings: 4

Ingredients:

1/2 cup Greek yogurt
4 cucumbers, diced
1 teaspoon lemon juice

2 tablespoons dill, chopped
2 garlic cloves, minced Salt and pepper to taste

Directions:

Mix all in a salad bowl.

Season with salt and pepper to suit your taste and eat.

Per Serving
Calories: 115 Fat: 9g Carbs: 21 g Protein: 9 g

Apples and Pomegranate Salad (Greek)

Preparation Time: 10 minutes **Cooking Time:** 0 minutes
Servings: 4

Ingredients:

2 big apples, cored and cubed
1 cup walnuts, chopped
1 tablespoon olive oil
2 tablespoons apple cider vinegar

3 cups baby arugula
1 cup pomegranate seeds
1 teaspoon white sesame seeds

Directions:

Mix the apples with the arugula and the rest of the in a bowl, toss, and serve cold.

Per Serving
Calories: 160 Fat: 4.3 g Protein: 10 g

Cranberry Bulgur Mix (Greek)

Preparation Time: 10 minutes **Cooking Time:** 0 minutes
Servings: 4

Ingredients:

1 1/2 cups hot water 1 cup bulgur
4 tablespoons cilantro, chopped
1/2 cup cranberries
1/2 cup carrots, grated
Juice of 1/2 lemon
1/2 cup red bell peppers
1 1/2 teaspoons curry powder
1/4 cup green onions
1 tablespoon olive oil

Directions:

Put bulgur into a bowl, add the water, stir, cover, leave aside for 10 minutes, fluff, and transfer to a bowl. Merge the rest of the , toss, and serve cold.

Per Serving

Calories: 300 Fat: 6.4 g Protein: 13 g

Chickpeas Corn and Black Beans Salad

Preparation Time: 10 minutes **Cooking Time:** 0 minutes
Servings: 4

Ingredients:

1 1/2 cups black beans
1 1/2 cups canned chickpeas
1 cup baby spinach
2 tablespoons lemon juice
1 tablespoon olive oil
2 teaspoons chili powder
1/2 teaspoon garlic powder
1 avocado, pitted, peeled, and chopped
1 cup corn kernels, chopped
1 tablespoon apple cider vinegar
1 teaspoon chives, chopped

Directions:

Mix the black beans with the garlic powder, chili powder, and the rest of the in a bowl, toss and serve cold.

Per Serving

Calories: 300 Fat: 13.4 g Protein: 13 g

Green Beans and Peppers Mix (Greek)

Preparation Time: 10 minutes **Cooking Time:** 10 minutes
Servings: 4

Ingredients:

2 tablespoons olive oil
Salt and black pepper to the taste
1 tablespoon dill, chopped
2 red bell peppers, cut into strips
1 tablespoon lime juice
1 and ½ pounds green beans, trimmed and halved
2 tablespoons rosemary, chopped

Directions:

Heat up a pan with the oil over medium heat, add the bell peppers and the green beans, toss and cook for 5 minutes.

Add the rest of the , toss, cook for 5 minutes more, divide between plates and serve as a side dish.

Per Serving

calories 222, fat 8.6, carbs 8.6, protein 3.4

Garlic Snap Peas Mix (Greek)

Preparation Time: 10 minutes **Cooking Time:** 10 minutes
Servings: 4

Ingredients:

½ cup walnuts, chopped
1 and ½ teaspoons garlic, minced
1 pound sugar snap peas
2 teaspoons lime juice
¼ cup olive oil
½ cup veggie stock
1 tablespoon chives, chopped
Salt and black pepper to the taste

Directions:

Heat up a pan with the stock over medium heat, add the snap peas and cook for 5 minutes.

Add the rest of the except the chives, cook for 5 minutes more and divide between plates.

Sprinkle the chives on top and serve as a side dish.

Per Serving

calories 200, fat 7.6, carbs 8.5, protein 4.3

Corn and Olives (Spanish)

Preparation Time: 5 minutes **Cooking Time:** 0 minutes
Servings: 4

Ingredients:

2 cups corn
2 tablespoons extra virgin olive oil
½ teaspoon balsamic vinegar
Salt and black pepper to the taste
4 ounces green olives, pitted and halved
1 teaspoon thyme, chopped
1 tablespoon oregano, chopped

Directions:

In a bowl, combine the corn with the olives and the rest of the , toss and serve as a side dish.

Per Serving

calories 154, fat 10, carbs 17, protein 9.3

Thyme Corn and Cheese Mix (Greek)

Preparation Time: 5 minutes **Cooking Time:** 0 minutes
Servings: 4

Ingredients:

1 tablespoon olive oil
2 cups corn
1 cup scallions, sliced
2 tablespoons blue cheese, crumbled
1 teaspoon thyme, chopped
Salt and black pepper to the taste
1 tablespoon chives, chopped

Directions:

In a salad bowl, combine the corn with scallions, thyme and the rest of the , toss, divide between plates and serve.

Per Serving

calories 183, fat 5.5, carbs 14.5

Rosemary Red Quinoa (Greek)

Preparation Time: 10 minutes **Cooking Time:** 25 minutes
Servings: 6

Ingredients:

4 cups chicken stock
2 tablespoons olive oil
1 teaspoon lemon zest, grated
2 tablespoons lemon juice
1 red onion, chopped
2 cups red quinoa, rinsed
1 tablespoon garlic, minced
Salt and black pepper to the taste
2 tablespoons rosemary, chopped

Directions:

Heat up a pan with the oil over medium heat, add the onion and the garlic and sauté for 5 minutes.

Add the quinoa, the stock and the rest of the , bring to a simmer and cook for 20 minutes stirring from time to time.

Divide the mix between plates and serve.

Per Serving
calories 193, fat 7.9, carbs 5.4, protein 1.3

Olives and Carrots Sauté (Greek)

Preparation Time: 10 minutes **Cooking Time:** 20 minutes
Servings: 4

Ingredients:

1 tablespoon green olives, pitted and sliced
½ teaspoon lemon zest, grated
¼ teaspoon rosemary, dried
Salt and black pepper to the taste
2 pounds carrots, sliced
1 tablespoon parsley, chopped
2 teaspoons capers, drained and chopped
1 and ½ teaspoons balsamic vinegar
¼ cup veggie stock
2 spring onions, chopped
3 tablespoons olive oil

Directions:

Heat up a pan with the oil over medium heat, add the carrots and brown for 5 minutes.

Add green olives, capers and the rest of the except the parsley and the chives, stir and cook over medium heat for 15 minutes.

Add the chives and parsley, toss, divide the mix between plates and serve as a side dish.

Per Serving
calories 244, fat 11, carbs 5.6, protein 6.3

Lemon Endives (Greek)

Preparation Time: 10 minutes **Cooking Time:** 35 minutes
Servings: 4

Ingredients:

Juice of 1 and ½ lemons
3 tablespoons olive oil
¼ cup veggie stock
Salt and black pepper to the taste
4 endives, halved lengthwise
1 tablespoon dill, chopped

Directions:

In a roasting pan, combine the endives with the rest of the, introduce in the oven and cook at 375 degrees F for 35 minutes.

Divide the endives between plates and serve as a side dish.

Per Serving
calories 221, fat 5.4, carbs 15.4, protein 14.3

Leeks Sauté (Greek)

Preparation Time: 10 minutes **Cooking Time:** 15 minutes
Servings: 4

Ingredients:

2 pounds leeks, sliced
Salt and black pepper to the taste
2 tablespoons chicken stock
2 tablespoons tomato paste
1 tablespoon olive oil

Directions:

Heat up a pan with the oil over medium heat, add the leeks and brown for 5 minutes.

Add the rest of the toss, increase the heat to medium-high and cook for 10 minutes more. Divide everything between plates and serve as a side dish.

Per Serving
calories 200, fat 11.4, carbs 16.4, protein 3.6

Oregano Potatoes (Spanish)

Preparation Time: 10 minutes **Cooking Time:** 40 minutes
Servings: 4

Ingredients:

6 red potatoes, peeled and cut into wedges
1 teaspoon lemon zest, grated
1 teaspoon oregano, dried
2 tablespoons olive oil ½ cup chicken stock
1 tablespoon chives, chopped
Salt and black pepper to the taste

Directions:

In a roasting pan, combine the potatoes with salt, pepper, the oil and the rest of the except the chives, toss, introduce in the oven and cook at 425 degrees F for 40 minutes.

Divide the mix between plates, sprinkle the chives on top and serve as a side dish.

Per Serving
calories 245, fat 4.5, carbs 7.1, protein 6.4

Yogurt Peppers Mix (Greek)

Preparation Time: 10 minutes **Cooking Time:** 15 minutes
Servings: 4

Ingredients:

1 red bell peppers, cut into thick strips
3 garlic cloves, minced
1 tablespoon cilantro, chopped
½ cup Greek yogurt
2 shallots, chopped
2 tablespoons olive oil
Salt and black pepper to the taste

Directions:

Heat up a pan with the oil over medium heat, add the shallots and garlic, stir and cook for 5 minutes.

Add the rest of the , toss, cook for 10 minutes more, divide the mix between plates and serve as a side dish.

Per Serving

calories 274, fat 11, protein 13.3, carbs 6.5

Beans and Rice (Spanish)

Preparation Time: 10 minutes **Cooking Time:** 55 minutes
Servings: 6

Ingredients:

1 tablespoon olive oil
2 cups brown rice
1 and ½ cup canned black beans, rinsed and drained
4 cups water
1 yellow onion, chopped
2 garlic cloves, minced
Salt and black pepper to the taste
2 celery stalks, chopped

Directions:

Heat a pan with the oil over medium heat, add the celery, garlic, and onion, stir, and cook for 10 minutes.

Add the rest of the , stir, bring to a simmer, and cook over medium heat for 45 minutes. Divide between plates and serve.

Per Serving

224 Calories 8.4g Fat 3.4g Carbs 6.2g protein

Cabbage and Mushrooms Mix (Greek)

Preparation Time: 10 minutes **Cooking Time:** 15 minutes
Servings: 2

Ingredients:

1 yellow onion, sliced
½ pound white mushrooms, sliced
1 green cabbage head, shredded
1 tablespoon balsamic vinegar
4 spring onions, chopped
Salt and black pepper to the taste
2 tablespoons olive oil

Directions:

Heat a pan with the oil over medium heat, add the yellow onion and the spring onions and cook for 5 minutes.

Add the rest of the , cook everything for 10 minutes, divide between plates and serve.

Per Serving

199 Calories 4.5g Fat 2.4g Carbs 2.2g protein

Beans and Cucumber Salad (Italian)

Preparation Time: 10 minutes **Cooking Time:** 0 minutes
Servings: 4

Ingredients:

15 oz canned great northern beans
1 tablespoon parsley
2 tablespoon balsamic vinegar
½ cup baby arugula
1 cup cucumber
2 tomatoes, cubed
2 tablespoons olive oil

1. Mix the beans with the cucumber and the rest of the in a large bowl, toss and serve cold.

Per Serving

233 Calories 9g Fat 8g protein

Chapter 4
Sandwiches, Pizzas, and Wraps

Falafel Balls with Tahini Sauce

Prep time: 2 hours 20 minutes | **Cook time:** 20 minutes | Serves:4

Ingredients:

Tahini Sauce:
½ cup tahini
2 tablespoons lemon juice
¼ cup finely chopped flat-leaf parsley
2 cloves garlic, minced
½ cup cold water, as needed
Falafel:
1 cup dried chickpeas, soaked overnight, drained
¼ cup chopped flat-leaf parsley

¼ cup chopped cilantro
1 large onion, chopped
1 teaspoon cumin
½ teaspoon chili flakes
4 cloves garlic
1 teaspoon sea salt
5 tablespoons almond flour
1½ teaspoons baking soda, dissolved in 1 teaspoon water
2 cups peanut oil
1 medium bell pepper, chopped
1 medium tomato, chopped
4 whole-wheat pita breads

Directions:
Make the Tahini Sauce

Combine the ingredients for the tahini sauce in a small bowl. Stir to mix well until smooth.

Wrap the bowl in plastic and refrigerate until ready to serve.

Make the Falafel

Put the chickpeas, parsley, cilantro, onion, cumin, chili flakes, garlic, and salt in a food processor. Pulse to mix well but not puréed.

Add the flour and baking soda to the food processor, then pulse to form a smooth and tight dough.

Put the dough in a large bowl and wrap in plastic. Refrigerate for at least 2 hours to let it rise.

Divide and shape the dough into walnut-sized small balls.

Pour the peanut oil in a large pot and heat over high heat until the temperature of the oil reaches 375°F (190°C).

Drop 6 balls into the oil each time, and fry for 5 minutes or until golden brown and crispy. Turn the balls with a strainer to make them fried evenly.

Transfer the balls on paper towels with the strainer, then drain the oil from the balls.

Roast the pita breads in the oven for 5 minutes or until golden brown, if needed, then stuff the pitas with falafel balls and top with bell peppers and tomatoes. Drizzle with tahini sauce and serve immediately.

Per Serving
calories: 574 | fat: 27.1g | protein: 19.8g | carbs: 69.7g

Glazed Mushroom and Vegetable Fajitas

Prep time: 20 minutes | **Cook time:** 20 minutes | Makes 6

Ingredients:
Spicy Glazed Mushrooms:
1 teaspoon olive oil
1 (10- to 12-ounce / 284- to 340-g) package cremini mushrooms, rinsed and drained, cut into thin slices
½ to 1 teaspoon chili powder
Sea salt and freshly ground black pepper, to taste
1 teaspoon maple syrup

Fajitas:
2 teaspoons olive oil
1 onion, chopped
Sea salt, to taste
1 bell pepper, any color, deseeded and sliced into long strips
1 zucchini, cut into large matchsticks
6 whole-grain tortilla
2 carrots, grated
3 to 4 scallions, sliced
½ cup fresh cilantro, finely chopped

Directions:
Make the Spicy Glazed Mushrooms

Heat the olive oil in a nonstick skillet over medium heat until shimmering.

Add the mushrooms and sauté for 10 minutes or until tender.

Sprinkle the mushrooms with chili powder, salt, and ground black pepper. Drizzle with maple syrup. Stir to mix well and cook for 5 to 7 minutes or until the mushrooms are glazed. Set aside until ready to use.

Make the Fajitas

Heat the olive oil in the same skillet over medium heat until shimmering.

Add the onion and sauté for 5 minutes or until translucent. Sprinkle with salt.

Add the bell pepper and zucchini and sauté for 7 minutes or until tender.

Meanwhile, toast the tortilla in the oven for 5 minutes or until golden brown.

Allow the tortilla to cool for a few minutes until they can be handled, then assemble the tortilla with glazed mushrooms, sautéed vegetables and remaining vegetables to make the fajitas. Serve immediately.

Per Serving
calories: 403 | fat: 14.8g | protein: 11.2g | carbs: 7.9g

Cheesy Fig Pizzas with Garlic Oil

Prep time: 1 day 40 minutes | **Cook time:** 10 minutes
Makes 2 pizzas

Ingredients:
Dough:
1 cup almond flour
1½ cups whole-wheat flour
¾ teaspoon instant or rapid-rise yeast
2 teaspoons raw honey
1¼ cups ice water
2 tablespoons extra-virgin olive oil
1¾ teaspoons sea salt
Garlic Oil:
4 tablespoons extra-virgin olive oil, divided

½ teaspoon dried thyme
2 garlic cloves, minced
⅛ teaspoon sea salt
½ teaspoon freshly ground pepper
Topping:
1 cup fresh basil leaves
1 cup crumbled feta cheese
8 ounces (227 g) fresh figs, stemmed and quartered lengthwise
2 tablespoons raw honey

Directions:
Make the Dough

Combine the flours, yeast, and honey in a food processor, pulse to combine well. Gently add water while pulsing. Let the dough sit for 10 minutes.

Mix the olive oil and salt in the dough and knead the dough until smooth. Wrap in plastic and refrigerate for at least 1 day.

Make the Garlic Oil

Heat 2 tablespoons of olive oil in a nonstick skillet over medium-low heat until shimmering.

Add the thyme, garlic, salt, and pepper and sauté for 30 seconds or until fragrant. Set them aside until ready to use.

Make the Pizzas

Preheat the oven to 500ºF (260ºC). Grease two baking sheets with 2 tablespoons of olive oil.

Divide the dough in half and shape into two balls. Press the balls into 13- inch rounds. Sprinkle the rounds with a tough of flour if they are sticky.

Top the rounds with the garlic oil and basil leaves, then arrange the rounds on the baking sheets. Scatter with feta cheese and figs.

Put the sheets in the preheated oven and bake for 9 minutes or until lightly browned. Rotate the pizza halfway through. Remove the pizzas from the oven, then discard the bay leaves. Drizzle with honey. Let sit for 5 minutes and serve immediately.

Per Serving (1 pizza)
calories: 1350 | fat: 46.5g | protein: 27.5g | carbs: 221.9g

Mashed Grape Tomato Pizzas

Prep time: 10 minutes | **Cook time:** 20 minutes | **Serves:** 6

Ingredients:
3 cups grape tomatoes, halved
1 teaspoon chopped fresh thyme leaves
2 garlic cloves, minced
¼ teaspoon kosher salt

¼ teaspoon freshly ground black pepper
1 tablespoon extra-virgin olive oil
¾ cup shredded Parmesan cheese
6 whole-wheat pita breads

Directions:
Preheat the oven to 425ºF (220ºC).

Combine the tomatoes, thyme, garlic, salt, ground black pepper, and olive oil in a baking pan.

Roast in the preheated oven for 20 minutes. Remove the pan from the oven, mash the tomatoes with a spatula and stir to mix well halfway through the cooking time.

Meanwhile, divide and spread the cheese over each pita bread, then place the bread in a separate baking pan and roast in the oven for 5 minutes or until golden brown and the cheese melts.

Transfer the pita bread onto a large plate, then top with the roasted mashed tomatoes. Serve immediately.

Per Serving calories: 140 | fat: 5.1g | protein: 6.2g | carbs: 16.9g

Greek Vegetable Salad Pita

Prep time: 10 minutes | **Cook time:** 0 minutes | **Serves:** 4

Ingredients:
½ cup baby spinach leaves
½ small red onion, thinly sliced
½ small cucumber, deseeded and chopped
1 tomato, chopped
1 cup chopped romaine lettuce
1 tablespoon extra-virgin olive oil

½ tablespoon red wine vinegar
1 teaspoon Dijon mustard
1 tablespoon crumbled feta cheese
Sea salt and freshly ground pepper, to taste
1 whole-wheat pita

Directions:
Combine all the ingredients, except for the pita, in a large bowl. Toss to mix well. Stuff the pita with the salad, then serve immediately.

Per Serving calories: 137 | fat: 8.1g | protein: 3.1g | carbs: 14.3g

Vegetable and Cheese Lavash Pizza

Prep time: 15 minutes | **Cook time:** 11 minutes | **Serves:**4

Ingredients:

2 (12 by 9-inch) lavash breads
2 tablespoons extra-virgin olive oil
10 ounces (284 g) frozen spinach, thawed and squeezed dry
1 cup shredded fontina cheese
1 tomato, cored and cut into ½-inch pieces
½ cup pitted large green olives, chopped
¼ teaspoon red pepper flakes
3 garlic cloves, minced
¼ teaspoon sea salt
¼ teaspoon ground black pepper
½ cup grated Parmesan cheese

Directions:

Preheat oven to 475°F (246°C).

Brush the lavash breads with olive oil, then place them on two baking sheet. Heat in the preheated oven for 4 minutes or until lightly browned. Flip the breads halfway through the cooking time.

Meanwhile, combine the spinach, fontina cheese, tomato pieces, olives, red pepper flakes, garlic, salt, and black pepper in a large bowl. Stir to mix well.

Remove the lavash bread from the oven and sit them on two large plates, spread them with the spinach mixture, then scatter with the Parmesan cheese on top.

Bake in the oven for 7 minutes or until the cheese melts and well browned. Slice and serve warm.

Per Serving calories: 431 | fat: 21.5g | protein: 20.0g | carbs: 38.4g

Pizza Pockets

Prep time: 10 minutes | **Cook time:** 0 minutes | **Serves:**2

Ingredients:

½ cup tomato sauce
½ teaspoon oregano
½ teaspoon garlic powder
½ cup chopped black olives
½ cup shredded Mozzarella cheese
2 canned artichoke hearts, drained and chopped
2 ounces (57 g) pepperoni, chopped
1 whole-wheat pita, halved

Directions:

In a medium bowl, stir together the tomato sauce, oregano, and garlic powder.

Add the olives, artichoke hearts, pepperoni, and cheese. Stir to mix.

Spoon the mixture into the pita halves and serve.

Per Serving
calories: 375 | fat: 23.5g | protein: 17.1g | carbs: 27.1g

Dulse, Avocado, and Tomato Pitas

Prep time: 10 minutes | **Cook time:** 30 mins | Makes 4 pitas

Ingredients:

2 teaspoons coconut oil
½ cup dulse, picked through and separated
Ground black pepper, to taste
2 avocados, sliced
2 tablespoons lime juice
¼ cup chopped cilantro
2 scallions, white and light green parts, sliced
Sea salt, to taste
4 (8-inch) whole wheat pitas, sliced in half
4 cups chopped romaine
4 plum tomatoes, sliced

Directions:

Heat the coconut oil in a nonstick skillet over medium heat until melted. Add the dulse and sauté for 5 minutes or until crispy. Sprinkle with ground black pepper and turn off the heat. Set aside. Put the avocado, lime juice, cilantro, and scallions in a food processor and sprinkle with salt and ground black pepper. Pulse to combine well until smooth.

Toast the pitas in a baking pan in the oven for 1 minute until soft.

Transfer the pitas to a clean work surface and open. Spread the avocado mixture over the pitas, then top with dulse, romaine, and tomato slices. Serve immediately.

Per Serving (1 pita) calories: 412 | fat: 18.7g | protein: 9.1g | carbs: 56.1g

Mini Pork and Cucumber Lettuce Wraps

Prep time: 20 mins | **Cook time:** 0 mins | Makes 12 wraps

Ingredients:

8 ounces (227 g) cooked ground pork
1 cucumber, diced
1 tomato, diced
1 red onion, sliced
1 ounce (28 g) low-fat feta cheese, crumbled
Juice of 1 lemon
1 tablespoon extra-virgin olive oil
Sea salt and freshly ground pepper, to taste
12 small, intact iceberg lettuce leaves

Directions:

Combine the ground pork, cucumber, tomato, and onion in a large bowl, then scatter with feta cheese.

Drizzle with lemon juice and olive oil, and sprinkle with salt and pepper. Toss to mix well.

Unfold the small lettuce leaves on a large plate or several small plates, then divide and top with the pork mixture.

Wrap and serve immediately.

Per Serving (1 warp)
calories: 78 | fat: 5.6g | protein: 5.5g | carbs: 1.4g

Brown Rice and Black Bean Burgers

Prep time: 20 mins | **Cook time:** 40 mins | Makes 8 burgers

Ingredients:

1 cup cooked brown rice
1 (15-ounce / 425-g) can black beans, drained and rinsed
1 tablespoon olive oil
2 tablespoons taco or Harissa seasoning
½ yellow onion, finely diced
1 beet, peeled and grated
1 carrot, peeled and grated
2 tablespoons no-salt-added tomato paste

2 tablespoons apple cider vinegar
3 garlic cloves, minced
¼ teaspoon sea salt
Ground black pepper, to taste
8 whole-wheat hamburger buns

Toppings:
16 lettuce leaves, rinsed well
8 tomato slices, rinsed well
Whole-grain mustard, to taste

Directions:

Line a baking sheet with parchment paper. Put the brown rice and black beans in a food processor and pulse until mix well. Pour the mixture in a large bowl and set aside. Heat the olive oil in a nonstick skillet over medium heat until shimmering. Add the taco seasoning and stir for 1 minute or until fragrant. Add the onion, beet, and carrot and sauté for 5 minutes or until the onion is translucent and beet and carrot are tender. Pour in the tomato paste and vinegar, then add the garlic and cook for 3 minutes or until the sauce is thickened. Sprinkle with salt and ground black pepper. Transfer the vegetable mixture to the bowl of rice mixture, then stir to mix well until smooth. Divide and shape the mixture into 8 patties, then arrange the patties on the baking sheet and refrigerate for at least 1 hour. Preheat the oven to 400°F (205°C).

Remove the baking sheet from the refrigerator and allow to sit under room temperature for 10 minutes.

Bake in the preheated oven for 40 minutes or until golden brown on both sides. Flip the patties halfway through the cooking time. Remove the patties from the oven and allow to cool for 10 minutes. Assemble the buns with patties, lettuce, and tomato slices. Top the filling with mustard and serve immediately.

Per Serving (1 burger)
calories: 544 | fat: 20.0g | protein: 15.8g | carbs: 76.0g

Classic Socca

Prep time: 10 minutes | **Cook time:** 10 minutes | **Serves:**4

Ingredients:

1½ cups chickpea flour
½ teaspoon ground turmeric
½ teaspoon sea salt

½ teaspoon ground black pepper
2 tablespoons plus 2 teaspoons extra-virgin olive oil
1½ cups water

Directions:

Combine the chickpea flour, turmeric, salt, and black pepper in a bowl. Stir to mix well, then gently mix in 2 tablespoons of olive oil and water. Stir to mix until smooth.

Heat 2 teaspoons of olive oil in an 8-inch nonstick skillet over medium- high heat until shimmering. Add half cup of the mixture into the skillet and swirl the skillet so the mixture coat the bottom evenly. Cook for 5 minutes or until lightly browned and crispy. Flip the socca halfway through the cooking time. Repeat with the remaining mixture. Slice and serve warm.

Per Serving calories: 207 | fat: 10.2g | protein: 7.9g | carbs: 20.7g

Artichoke and Cucumber Hoagies

Prep time: 10 minutes | **Cook time:** 15 minutes
Servings: 1

Ingredients:

1 (12-ounce / 340-g) whole grain baguette, sliced in half horizontally
1 cup frozen and thawed artichoke hearts, roughly chopped
1 cucumber, sliced
2 tomatoes, sliced
1 red bell pepper, sliced

⅓ cup Kalamata olives, pitted and chopped
¼ small red onion, thinly sliced
Sea salt and ground black pepper, to taste
2 tablespoons pesto
Balsamic vinegar, to taste

Directions:

range the baguette halves on a clean work surface, then cut off the top third from each half. Scoop some insides of the bottom half out and reserve as breadcrumbs.

Toast the baguette in a baking pan in the oven for 1 minute to brown lightly. Put the artichokes, cucumber, tomatoes, bell pepper, olives, and onion in a large bowl. Sprinkle with salt and ground black pepper. Toss to combine well.

Spread the bottom half of the baguette with the vegetable mixture and drizzle with balsamic vinegar, then smear the cut side of the baguette top with pesto. Assemble the two baguette halves. Wrap the hoagies in parchment paper and let sit for at least an hour before serving.

Per Serving (1 hoagies) calories: 1263 | fat: 37.7g | protein: 56.3g | carbs: 180.1g

Mushroom and Caramelized Onion Musakhan

Prep time: 20 minutes | **Cook time:** 1 hour 5 minutes
Serves: 4

Ingredients:

2 tablespoons sumac, plus more for sprinkling
1 teaspoon ground allspice
½ teaspoon ground cardamom
½ teaspoon ground cumin
3 tablespoons extra-virgin olive oil, divided
2 pounds (907 g) portobello mushroom caps, gills removed, caps halved and sliced ½ inch thick
3 medium white onions, coarsely chopped
¼ cup water
Kosher salt, to taste
1 whole-wheat Turkish flatbread
¼ cup pine nuts
lemon, wedged

Directions:

Preheat the oven to 350ºF (180ºC).

Combine 2 tablespoons of sumac, allspice, cardamom, and cumin in a small bowl. Stir to mix well.

Heat 2 tablespoons of olive oil in an oven-proof skillet over medium-high heat until shimmering.

Add the mushroom to the skillet and sprinkle with half of sumac mixture. Sauté for 8 minutes or until the mushrooms are tender. You may need to work in batches to avoid overcrowding. Transfer the mushrooms to a plate and set side.

Heat 1 tablespoon of olive oil in the skillet over medium-high heat until shimmering.

Add the onion and sauté for 20 minutes or until caramelized. Sprinkle with remaining sumac mixture, then cook for 1 more minute.

Pour in the water and sprinkle with salt. Bring to a simmer.

Turn off the heat and put the mushroom back to the skillet.

Place the skillet in the preheated oven and bake for 30 minutes.

Remove the skillet from the oven and let the mushroom sit for 10 minutes until cooled down.

Heat the Turkish flatbread in a baking dish in the oven for 5 minutes or until warmed through.

Arrange the bread on a large plate and top with mushrooms, onions, and roasted pine nuts. Squeeze the lemon wedges over and sprinkle with more sumac. Serve immediately.

Per Serving

calories: 336 | fat: 18.7g | protein: 11.5g | carbs: 34.3g

Red Pepper Coques with Pine Nuts

Prep time: 1 day 40 minutes | **Cook time:** 45 minutes
Makes 4 coques

Ingredients:

Dough:
3 cups almond flour
½ teaspoon instant or rapid-rise yeast
2 teaspoons raw honey
1⅓ cups ice water
3 tablespoons extra-virgin olive oil
1½ teaspoons sea salt
Red Pepper Topping:
4 tablespoons extra-virgin olive oil, divided
2 cups jarred roasted red peppers, patted dry and sliced thinly
2 large onions, halved and sliced thin
3 garlic cloves, minced
¼ teaspoon red pepper flakes
2 bay leaves
3 tablespoons maple syrup
1½ teaspoons sea salt
3 tablespoons red whine vinegar
For Garnish:
¼ cup pine nuts (optional)
1 tablespoon minced fresh parsley

Directions:
Make the Dough

Combine the flour, yeast, and honey in a food processor, pulse to combine well. Gently add water while pulsing. Let the dough sit for 10 minutes.

Mix the olive oil and salt in the dough and knead the dough until smooth. Wrap in plastic and refrigerate for at least 1 day.

Make the Topping

Heat 1 tablespoon of olive oil in a nonstick skillet over medium heat until shimmering.

Add the red peppers, onions, garlic, red pepper flakes, bay leaves, maple syrup, and salt. Sauté for 20 minutes or until the onion is caramelized.

Turn off the heat and discard the bay leaves. Remove the onion from the skillet and baste with wine vinegar. Let them sit until ready to use.

Make the Coques

Preheat the oven to 500ºF (260ºC). Grease two baking sheets with 1 tablespoon of olive oil.

Divide the dough ball into four balls, then press and shape them into equal-sized oval. Arrange the ovals on the baking sheets and pierce each dough about 12 times.

Rub the ovals with 2 tablespoons of olive oil and bake for 7 minutes or until puffed. Flip the ovals halfway through the cooking time.

Spread the ovals with the topping and pine nuts, then bake for an additional 15 minutes or until well browned.

Remove the coques from the oven and spread with parsley. Allow to cool for 10 minutes before serving.

Per Serving (1 coque)

calories: 658 | fat: 23.1g | protein: 3.4g | carbs: 112.0g

Ritzy Garden Burgers

Prep time: 1 hour 30 minutes | **Cook time:** 30 minutes
Serves: 6

Ingredients:

1 tablespoon avocado oil
1 yellow onion, diced
½ cup shredded carrots
4 garlic cloves, halved
1 (15 ounces / 425 g) can black beans, rinsed and drained
1 cup gluten-free rolled oats
¼ cup oil-packed sun-dried tomatoes, drained and chopped
½ cup sunflower seeds, toasted
1 teaspoon chili powder
1 teaspoon paprika
½ cup fresh parsley, stems removed
¼ teaspoon ground red pepper flakes
¾ teaspoon sea salt
¼ teaspoon ground black pepper
¼ cup olive oil

For Serving:
6 whole-wheat buns, split in half and toasted
2 ripe avocados, sliced
1 cup kaiware sprouts or mung bean sprouts
1 ripe tomato, sliced
1 teaspoon ground cumin

Directions:

1. Line a baking sheet with parchment paper.

    Heat 1 tablespoon of avocado oil in a nonstick skillet over medium heat.

    Add the onion and carrots and sauté for 10 minutes or until the onion is caramelized.

    Add the garlic and sauté for 30 seconds or until fragrant.

    Transfer them into a food processor, then add the remaining ingredients, except for the olive oil. Pulse until chopped fine and the mixture holds together. Make sure not to purée the mixture.

    Divide and form the mixture into six 4-inch diameter and ½-inch thick patties.

    Arrange the patties on the baking sheet and wrap the sheet in plastic. Put the baking sheet in the refrigerator and freeze for at least an hour until firm.

    Remove the baking sheet from the refrigerator, let them sit under room temperature for 10 minutes.

    Heat the olive oil in a nonstick skillet over medium-high heat until shimmering.

    Fry the patties in the skillet for 15 minutes or until lightly browned and crispy. Flip the patties halfway through the cooking time. You may need to work in batches to avoid overcrowding.

    Assemble the buns with patties, avocados, sprouts, and tomato slices to make the burgers.

Per Serving
calories: 613 | fat: 23.1g | protein: 26.2g | carbs: 88.3g

Alfalfa Sprout and Nut Rolls

Prep time: 40 minutes | **Cook time:** 0 minutes
Makes 16 bite-size pieces

Ingredients:

1 cup alfalfa sprouts
2 tablespoons Brazil nuts
½ cup chopped fresh cilantro
2 tablespoons flaked coconut
1 garlic clove, minced
2 tablespoons ground flaxseeds
Zest and juice of 1 lemon
Pinch cayenne pepper
Sea salt and freshly ground black pepper, to taste
1 tablespoon melted coconut oil
2 tablespoons water
2 whole-grain wraps

Directions:

Combine all ingredients, except for the wraps, in a food processor, then pulse to combine well until smooth.

Unfold the wraps on a clean work surface, then spread the mixture over the wraps.

Roll the wraps up and refrigerate for 30 minutes until set.

Remove the rolls from the refrigerator and slice into 16 bite-sized pieces, if desired, and serve.

Per Serving (1 piece)
calories: 67 | fat: 7.1g | protein: 2.2g | carbs: 2.9g

Roasted Tomato Panini

Prep time: 15 minutes | **Cook time:** 3 hours 6 minutes
Serves: 2

Ingredients:

2 teaspoons olive oil
4 Roma tomatoes, halved
4 cloves garlic
1 tablespoon Italian seasoning
Sea salt and freshly ground pepper, to taste
4 slices whole-grain bread
4 basil leaves
2 slices fresh Mozzarella cheese

Directions:

Preheat the oven to 250°F (121°C). Grease a baking pan with olive oil.

Place the tomatoes and garlic in the baking pan, then sprinkle with Italian seasoning, salt, and ground pepper. Toss to coat well.

Roast in the preheated oven for 3 hours or until the tomatoes are lightly wilted.

Preheat the panini press.

Make the panini: Place two slices of bread on a clean work surface, then top them with wilted tomatoes. Sprinkle with basil and spread with Mozzarella cheese. Top them with remaining two slices of bread.

Cook the panini for 6 minutes or until lightly browned and the cheese melts. Flip the panini halfway through the cooking. Serve immediately.

Per Serving
calories: 323 | fat: 12.0g | protein: 17.4g | carbs: 37.5mg

Salmon Salad Wraps

Prep time: 10 minutes | **Cook time:** 0 minutes | **Serves:**6

Ingredients:

1 pound (454 g) salmon fillets, cooked and flaked

½ cup diced carrots

½ cup diced celery

3 tablespoons diced red onion

3 tablespoons chopped fresh dill

2 tablespoons capers

1½ tablespoons extra-virgin olive oil

1 tablespoon aged balsamic vinegar

¼ teaspoon kosher or sea salt

½ teaspoon freshly ground black pepper

4 whole-wheat flatbread wraps or soft whole-wheat tortillas

Directions:

In a large bowl, stir together all the ingredients, except for the wraps.

On a clean work surface, lay the wraps. Divide the salmon mixture evenly among the wraps. Fold up the bottom of the wraps, then roll up the wrap. Serve immediately.

Per Serving

calories: 194 | fat: 8.0g | protein: 18.0g | carbs: 13.0g

Samosas in Potatoes

Prep time: 20 minutes | **Cook time:** 30 minutes | **Makes 8**

Ingredients:

4 small potatoes

1 teaspoon coconut oil

1 small onion, finely chopped

1 small piece ginger, minced

2 garlic cloves, minced

2 to 3 teaspoons curry powder

Sea salt and freshly ground black pepper, to taste

¼ cup frozen peas, thawed

2 carrots, grated

¼ cup chopped fresh cilantro

Directions:

Preheat the oven to 350ºF (180ºC).Poke small holes into potatoes with a fork, then wrap with aluminum foil.

Bake in the preheated oven for 30 minutes until tender.

Meanwhile, heat the coconut oil in a nonstick skillet over medium-high heat until melted. Add the onion and sauté for 5 minutes or until translucent. Add the ginger and garlic to the skillet and sauté for 3 minutes or until fragrant.

Add the curry powder, salt, and ground black pepper, then stir to coat the onion. Remove them from the heat.

When the cooking of potatoes is complete, remove the potatoes from the foil and slice in half.

Hollow to potato halves with a spoon, then combine the potato fresh with sautéed onion, peas, carrots, and cilantro in a large bowl. Stir to mix well.

Spoon the mixture back to the tomato skins and serve immediately.

Per Serving (1 samosa)

calories: 131 | fat: 13.9g | protein: 3.2g | carbs: 8.8g

Eggplant, Spinach, and Feta Sandwiches

Prep time: 10 minutes | **Cook time:** 6 to 8 minutes | **Serves:**2

Ingredients:

1 medium eggplant, sliced into ½-inch-thick slices

2 tablespoons olive oil

Sea salt and freshly ground pepper, to taste

5 to 6 tablespoons hummus

4 slices whole-wheat bread, toasted

1 cup baby spinach leaves

2 ounces (57 g) feta cheese, softened

Directions:

Preheat the grill to medium-high heat.

Salt both sides of the sliced eggplant, and let sit for 20 minutes to draw out the bitter juices.

Rinse the eggplant and pat dry with a paper towel.

Brush the eggplant slices with olive oil and season with sea salt and freshly ground pepper to taste.

Grill the eggplant until lightly charred on both sides but still slightly firm in the middle, about 3 to 4 minutes per side.

Spread the hummus on the bread slices and top with the spinach leaves, feta cheese, and grilled eggplant. Top with the other slice of bread and serve immediately.

Per Serving

calories: 493 | fat: 25.3g | protein: 17.1g | carbs: 50.9g

Zucchini Hummus Wraps

Prep time: 15 minutes | **Cook time:** 6 minutes | **Serves:**2

Ingredients:

1 zucchini, ends removed, thinly sliced lengthwise

¼ teaspoon freshly ground black pepper

¼ cup hummus

2 Roma tomatoes, cut lengthwise into slices

2 tablespoons chopped red onion

½ teaspoon dried oregano

¼ teaspoon garlic powder

2 whole wheat tortillas

1 cup chopped kale

½ teaspoon ground cumin

Directions:

In a skillet over medium heat, add the zucchini slices and cook for 3 minutes per side. Sprinkle with the oregano, pepper, and garlic powder and remove from the heat.

Spread 2 tablespoons of hummus on each tortilla. Lay half the zucchini in the center of each tortilla. Top with tomato slices, kale, red onion, and ¼ teaspoon of cumin. Wrap tightly and serve.

Per Serving

calories: 248 | fat: 8.1g | protein: 9.1g | carbs: 37.1g

Spicy Tofu Tacos with Cherry Tomato Salsa

Prep time: 20 mins | **Cook time:** 11 mins | Makes 4 tacos

Ingredients:

Cherry Tomato Salsa:
¼ cup sliced cherry tomatoes
½ jalapeño, deseeded and sliced
Juice of 1 lime
1 garlic clove, minced
Sea salt and freshly ground black pepper, to taste
2 teaspoons extra-virgin olive oil

Spicy Tofu Taco Filling:
4 tablespoons water, divided
½ cup canned black beans, rinsed and drained
2 teaspoons fresh chopped chives, divided
¾ teaspoon ground cumin, divided
¾ teaspoon smoked paprika, divided
Dash cayenne pepper (optional)
¼ teaspoon sea salt
¼ teaspoon freshly ground black pepper
1 teaspoon extra-virgin olive oil
6 ounces (170 g) firm tofu, drained, rinsed, and pressed
4 corn tortillas
¼ avocado, sliced
¼ cup fresh cilantro

Directions:
Make the Cherry Tomato Salsa

Combine the ingredients for the salsa in a small bowl. Stir to mix well. Set aside until ready to use.

Make the Spicy Tofu Taco Filling

Add 2 tablespoons of water into a saucepan, then add the black beans and sprinkle with 1 teaspoon of chives, ½ teaspoon of cumin, ¼ teaspoon of smoked paprika, and cayenne. Stir to mix well.

Cook for 5 minutes over medium heat until heated through, then mash the black beans with the back of a spoon. Turn off the heat and set aside.

Add remaining water into a bowl, then add the remaining chives, cumin, and paprika. Sprinkle with cayenne, salt, and black pepper. Stir to mix well. Set aside.

Heat the olive oil in a nonstick skillet over medium heat until shimmering.

Add the tofu and drizzle with taco sauce, then sauté for 5 minutes or until the seasoning is absorbed. Remove the tofu from the skillet and set aside.

Warm the tortillas in the skillet for 1 minutes or until heated through.

Transfer the tortillas onto a large plate and top with tofu, mashed black beans, avocado, cilantro, then drizzle the tomato salsa over. Serve immediately.

Per Serving (1 taco)
calories: 240 | fat: 9.0g | protein: 11.6g | carbs: 31.6g

Super Cheeses and Mushroom Tart

Prep time: 30 minutes | **Cook time:** 1 hour 30 minutes
Serves: 4 to 6

Ingredients:

Crust:
1¾ cups almond flour
1 tablespoon raw honey
¾ teaspoon sea salt
¼ cup extra-virgin olive oil
⅓ cup water

Filling:
2 tablespoons extra-virgin olive oil, divided
4 ounces (113 g) part-skim ricotta cheese
1 pound (454 g) white mushrooms, trimmed and sliced thinly
Sea salt, to taste
1 garlic clove, minced
2 teaspoons minced fresh thyme
¼ cup shredded Mozzarella cheese
½ cup grated Parmesan cheese
Ground black pepper, to taste
2 tablespoons ground basil

Directions:
Make the Crust

Preheat the oven to 350ºF (180ºC).

Combine the flour, honey, salt and olive oil in a large bowl. Stir to mix well. Gently mix in the water until a smooth dough forms.

Drop walnut-size clumps from the dough in the single layer on a tart pan. Press the clumps to coat the bottom of the pan.

Bake the crust in the preheated oven for 50 minutes or until firm and browned. Rotate the pan halfway through.

Make the Filling

While baking the crust, heat 1 tablespoon of olive oil in a nonstick skillet over medium-high heat until shimmering.

Add the mushrooms and sprinkle with ½ teaspoon of salt. Sauté for 15 minutes or until tender.

Add the garlic and thyme and sauté for 30 seconds or until fragrant.

Make the Tart

Meanwhile, combine the cheeses, salt, ground black pepper, and 1 tablespoon of olive oil in a bowl. Stir to mix well.

Spread the cheese mixture over the crust, then top with the mushroom mixture.

Bake in the oven for 20 minutes or until the cheeses are frothy and the tart is heated through. Rotate the pan halfway through the baking time.

Remove the tart from the oven. Allow to cool for at least 10 minutes, then sprinkle with basil. Slice to serve.

Per Serving
calories: 530 | fat: 26.6g | protein: 11.7g | carbs: 63.5g

Baked Parmesan Chicken Wraps

Prep time: 10 minutes | **Cook time:** 18 minutes | **Serves:**6

Ingredients:

1 pound (454 g) boneless, skinless chicken breasts
1 large egg
¼ cup unsweetened almond milk
⅔ cup whole-wheat bread crumbs
½ cup grated Parmesan cheese
¾ teaspoon garlic powder, divided
1 cup canned low-sodium or no-salt-added crushed tomatoes
1 teaspoon dried oregano
6 (8-inch) whole-wheat tortillas, or whole-grain spinach wraps
1 cup fresh Mozzarella cheese, sliced
1½ cups loosely packed fresh flat-leaf (Italian) parsley, chopped
Cooking spray

Directions:

1. Preheat the oven to 425ºF (220ºC). Line a large, rimmed baking sheet with aluminum foil. Place a wire rack on the aluminum foil, and spritz the rack with nonstick cooking spray. Set aside.
2. Place the chicken breasts into a large plastic bag. With a rolling pin, pound the chicken so it is evenly flattened, about ¼ inch thick. Slice the chicken into six portions.
3. In a bowl, whisk together the egg and milk. In another bowl, stir together the bread crumbs, Parmesan cheese and ½ teaspoon of the garlic powder.
4. Dredge each chicken breast portion into the egg mixture, and then into the Parmesan crumb mixture, pressing the crumbs into the chicken so they stick. Arrange the chicken on the prepared wire rack.
5. Bake in the preheated oven for 15 to 18 minutes, or until the internal temperature of the chicken reads 165ºF (74ºC) on a meat thermometer and any juices run clear.
6. Transfer the chicken to a cutting board, and cut each portion diagonally into ½-inch pieces.
7. In a small, microwave-safe bowl, stir together the tomatoes, oregano, and the remaining ¼ teaspoon of the garlic powder. Cover the bowl with a paper towel and microwave for about 1 minute on high, until very hot. Set aside.
8. Wrap the tortillas in a damp paper towel and microwave for 30 to 45 seconds on high, or until warmed through.
9. Assemble the wraps: Divide the chicken slices evenly among the six tortillas and top with the sliced Mozzarella cheese. Spread 1 tablespoon of the warm tomato sauce over the cheese on each tortilla, and top each with about ¼ cup of the parsley.
10. Wrap the tortilla: Fold up the bottom of the tortilla, then fold one side over and fold the other side over the top.
11. Serve the wraps warm with the remaining sauce for dipping.

Per Serving
calories: 358 | fat: 12.0g | protein: 21.0g | carbs: 41.0g

Grilled Caesar Salad Sandwiches

Prep time: 5 minutes | **Cook time:** 5 minutes | **Serves:**2

Ingredients:

¾ cup olive oil, divided
2 romaine lettuce hearts, left intact
3 to 4 anchovy fillets
Juice of 1 lemon
2 to 3 cloves garlic, peeled
1 teaspoon Dijon mustard
¼ teaspoon Worcestershire sauce
Sea salt and freshly ground pepper, to taste
2 slices whole-wheat bread, toasted
Freshly grated Parmesan cheese, for serving

Directions:

Preheat the grill to medium-high heat and oil the grates.

On a cutting board, drizzle the lettuce with 1 to 2 tablespoons of olive oil and place on the grates.

Grill for 5 minutes, turning until lettuce is slightly charred on all sides. Let lettuce cool enough to handle.

In a food processor, combine the remaining olive oil with the anchovies, lemon juice, garlic, mustard, and Worcestershire sauce.

Pulse the ingredients until you have a smooth emulsion. Season with sea salt and freshly ground pepper to taste. Chop the lettuce in half and place on the bread.

Drizzle with the dressing and serve, sprinkle of Parmesan cheese.

Per Serving
calories: 949 | fat: 85.6g | protein: 12.9g | carbs: 34.1g

Mediterranean Greek Salad Wraps

Prep time: 15 minutes | **Cook time:** 0 minutes | **Serves:**4

Ingredients:

1½ cups seedless cucumber, peeled and chopped
1 cup chopped tomato
½ cup finely chopped fresh mint
¼ cup diced red onion
1 (2.25-ounce / 64-g) can sliced black olives, drained
2 tablespoons extra-virgin olive oil
1 tablespoon red wine vinegar
¼ teaspoon kosher salt
¼ teaspoon freshly ground black pepper
½ cup crumbled goat cheese
4 whole-wheat flatbread wraps or soft whole-wheat tortillas

Directions:

In bowl, stir together the cucumber, tomato, mint, onion & olives.

In a small bowl, whisk together the oil, vinegar, salt, and pepper. Spread the dressing over the salad. Toss gently to combine.

On a clean work surface, lay the wraps. Divide the goat cheese evenly among the wraps. Scoop a quarter of the salad filling down the center of each wrap.

Fold up each wrap: Start by folding up the bottom, then fold one side over and fold the other side over the top. Repeat with the remaining wraps.Serve immediately.

Per Serving calories: 225 | fat: 12.0g | protein: 12.0g | carbs: 18.0g

Green Veggie Sandwiches

Prep time: 20 minutes | **Cook time:** 0 minutes | **Serves:**2

Ingredients:

Spread:
1 (15-ounce / 425-g) can cannellini beans, drained and rinsed
⅓ cup packed fresh basil leaves
⅓ cup packed fresh parsley
⅓ cup chopped fresh chives
2 garlic cloves, chopped
Zest and juice of ½ lemon
1 tablespoon apple cider vinegar

Sandwiches:
4 whole-grain bread slices, toasted
8 English cucumber slices
1 large beefsteak tomato, cut into slices
1 large avocado, halved, pitted, and cut into slices
1 small yellow bell pepper, cut into slices
2 handfuls broccoli sprouts
2 handfuls fresh spinach

Directions:

Make the Spread

In a food processor, combine the cannellini beans, basil, parsley, chives, garlic, lemon zest and juice, and vinegar. Pulse a few times, scrape down the sides, and purée until smooth. You may need to scrape down the sides again to incorporate all the basil and parsley. Refrigerate for at least 1 hour to allow the flavors to blend.

Assemble the Sandwiches

Build your sandwiches by spreading several tablespoons of spread on each slice of bread. Layer two slices of bread with the cucumber, tomato, avocado, bell pepper, broccoli sprouts, and spinach. Top with the remaining bread slices and press down lightly. Serve immediately.

Per Serving
calories: 617 | fat: 21.1g | protein: 28.1g | carbs: 86.1g

Mushroom-Pesto Baked Pizza

Prep time: 5 minutes | **Cook time:** 15 minutes | **Serves:**2

Ingredients:

1 teaspoon extra-virgin olive oil
½ cup sliced mushrooms
½ red onion, sliced
Salt and freshly ground black pepper

¼ cup store-bought pesto sauce
2 whole-wheat flatbreads
¼ cup shredded Mozzarella cheese

Directions:

Preheat the oven to 350°F (180°C). In a small skillet, heat the oil over medium heat. Add the mushrooms and onion, and season with salt and pepper. Sauté for 3 to 5 minutes until the onion and mushrooms begin to soften. Spread 2 tablespoons of pesto on each flatbread. Divide the mushroom-onion mixture between the two flatbreads. Top each with 2 tablespoons of cheese. Place the flatbreads on a baking sheet and bake for 10 to 12 minutes until the cheese is melted and bubbly. Serve warm.

Per Serving calories: 348 | fat: 23.5g | protein: 14.2g | carbs: 28.1g

Tuna and Hummus Wraps

Prep time: 10 minutes | **Cook time:** 0 minutes | **Serves:**2

Ingredients:

Hummus:
1 cup from 1 (15-ounce / 425-g) can low-sodium chickpeas, drained and rinsed
2 tablespoons tahini
1 tablespoon extra-virgin olive oil
1 garlic clove
Juice of ½ lemon

2 tablespoons water
Wraps:
4 large lettuce leaves
1 (5-ounce / 142-g) can chunk light tuna packed in water, drained
1 red bell pepper, seeded and cut into strips
1 cucumber, sliced
¼ teaspoon salt

Directions:

Make the Hummus

In a blender jar, combine the chickpeas, tahini, olive oil, garlic, lemon juice, salt, and water. Process until smooth. Taste and adjust with additional lemon juice or salt, as needed.

Make the Wraps

On each lettuce leaf, spread 1 tablespoon of hummus, and divide the tuna among the leaves. Top each with several strips of red pepper and cucumber slices.

Roll up the lettuce leaves, folding in the two shorter sides and rolling away from you, like a burrito. Serve immediately.

Per Serving calories: 192 | fat: 5.1g | protein: 26.1g | carbs: 15.1g

Chickpea Lettuce Wraps

Prep time: 15 minutes | **Cook time:** 0 minutes | **Serves:**2

Ingredients:

1 (15-ounce / 425-g) can chickpeas, drained and rinsed well
1 celery stalk, diced
½ shallot, minced
1 green apple, cored and diced
3 tablespoons tahini (sesame paste)

2 teaspoons freshly squeezed lemon juice
1 teaspoon raw honey
1 teaspoon Dijon mustard
Dash salt
Filtered water, to thin
4 romaine lettuce leaves

Directions:

In a medium bowl, stir together the chickpeas, celery, shallot, apple, tahini, lemon juice, honey, mustard, and salt. If needed, add some water to thin the mixture.

Place the romaine lettuce leaves on a plate. Fill each with the chickpea filling, using it all. Wrap the leaves around the filling. Serve immediately.

Per Serving calories: 397 | fat: 15.1g | protein: 15.1g | carbs: 53.1g

Turkish Eggplant and Tomatoes Pide with Mint

Prep time: 1 day 40 minutes | **Cook time:** 20 minutes
Makes 6 pides

Ingredients:
Dough:
3 cups almond flour
2 teaspoons raw honey
½ teaspoon instant or rapid-rise yeast
1⅓ cups ice water
1 tablespoon extra-virgin olive oil
1½ teaspoons sea salt
Eggplant and Tomato Toppings:
28 ounces (794 g) whole tomatoes, peeled and puréed

5 tablespoons extra-virgin olive oil, divided
1 pound (454 g) eggplant, cut into ½-inch pieces
½ red bell pepper, chopped
Sea salt and ground black pepper, to taste
3 garlic cloves, minced
¼ teaspoon red pepper flakes
½ teaspoon smoked paprika
6 tablespoons minced fresh mint, divided
1½ cups crumbled feta cheese

Directions:
Make the Dough

Combine the flour, yeast, and honey in a food processor, pulse to combine well. Gently add water while pulsing. Let the dough sit for 10 minutes.

Mix the olive oil and salt in the dough and knead the dough until smooth. Wrap in plastic and refrigerate for at least 1 day.

Make the Toppings

Heat 2 tablespoons of olive oil in a nonstick skillet over medium-high heat until shimmering.

Add the bell pepper, eggplant, and ½ teaspoon of salt. Sauté for 6 minutes or until the eggplant is lightly browned.

Add the red pepper flakes, paprika, and garlic. Sauté for 1 minute or until fragrant. Pour in the puréed tomatoes. Bring to a simmer, then cook for 10 minutes or until the mixture is thickened into about 3½ cups. Turn off the heat and mix in 4 tablespoons of mint, salt, and ground black pepper. Set them aside until ready to use.

Make the Turkish Pide

Preheat the oven to 500ºF (260ºC). Line three baking sheets with parchment papers.

On a clean work surface, divide and shape the dough into six 14 by 5- inch ovals. Transfer the dough to the baking sheets. Brush them with 3 tablespoons of olive oil and spread the eggplant mixture and feta cheese on top.

Bake in the preheated oven for 12 minutes or until golden brown. Rotate the pide halfway through the baking time.

Remove the pide from the oven and spread with remaining mint and serve immediately.

Per Serving (1 pide)
calories: 500 | fat: 22.1g | protein: 8.0g | carbs: 69.7g

Veg Mix and Blackeye Pea Burritos

Prep time: 15 minutes | **Cook time:** 40 minutes
Makes 6 burritos

Ingredients:
1 teaspoon olive oil
1 red onion, diced
2 garlic cloves, minced
1 zucchini, chopped
1 tomato, diced
1 bell pepper, any color, deseeded and diced

1 (14-ounce / 397-g) can blackeye peas
2 teaspoons chili powder
Sea salt, to taste
6 whole-grain tortillas

Directions:

Preheat the oven to 325ºF (160ºC).

Heat the olive oil in a nonstick skillet over medium heat or until shimmering.

Add the onion and sauté for 5 minutes or until translucent.

Add the garlic and sauté for 30 seconds or until fragrant. Add the zucchini and sauté for 5 minutes or until tender. Add the tomato and bell pepper and sauté for 2 minutes or until soft.

Fold in the black peas and sprinkle them with chili powder and salt. Stir to mix well.

Place the tortillas on a clean work surface, then top them with sautéed vegetables mix.

Fold one ends of tortillas over the vegetable mix, then tuck and roll them into burritos.

Arrange the burritos in a baking dish, seam side down, then pour the juice remains in the skillet over the burritos.

Bake in the preheated oven for 25 minutes or until golden brown. Serve immediately.

Per Serving
calories: 335 | fat: 16.2g | protein: 12.1g | carbs: 8.3g

Za'atar Pizza

Prep time: 10 minutes | **Cook time:** 1o to 12 minutes |
Serves:4 to 6

Ingredients:
1 sheet puff pastry
¼ cup extra-virgin olive oil

⅓ cup za'atar seasoning

Directions:

Preheat the oven to 350ºF (180ºC). Line a baking sheet with parchment paper.

Place the puff pastry on the prepared baking sheet. Cut the pastry into desired slices.

Brush the pastry with the olive oil. Sprinkle with the za'atar seasoning.

Put the pastry in the oven and bake for 10 to 12 minutes, or until edges are lightly browned and puffed up. Serve warm.

Per Serving
calories: 374 | fat: 30.0g | protein: 3.0g | carbs: 20.0g

Tuna and Olive Salad Sandwiches

Prep time: 10 minutes | **Cook time:** 0 minutes | **Serves:**4

Ingredients:

3 tablespoons freshly squeezed lemon juice
2 tablespoons extra-virgin olive oil
1 garlic clove, minced
½ teaspoon freshly ground black pepper

2 (5-ounce / 142-g) cans tuna, drained
1 (2.25-ounce / 64-g) can sliced olives, any green or black variety
½ cup chopped fresh fennel, including fronds
8 slices whole-grain crusty bread

Directions:

In a medium bowl, whisk together the lemon juice, oil, garlic, and pepper. Add the tuna, olives and fennel to the bowl. Using a fork, separate the tuna into chunks and stir to incorporate all the ingredients.

Divide the tuna salad equally among 4 slices of bread. Top each with the remaining bread slices.

Let the sandwiches sit for at least 5 minutes so the zesty filling can soak into the bread before serving.

Per Serving

calories: 952 | fat: 17.0g | protein: 165.0g | carbs: 37.0g

Open-Faced Margherita Sandwiches

Prep time: 10 minutes | **Cook time:** 5 minutes | **Serves:**4

Ingredients:

2 (6- to 7-inch) whole-wheat submarine or hoagie rolls, sliced open horizontally
1 tablespoon extra-virgin olive oil
1 garlic clove, halved
1 large ripe tomato, cut into 8 slices

¼ teaspoon dried oregano
1 cup fresh Mozzarella, sliced
¼ cup lightly packed fresh basil leaves, torn into small pieces
¼ teaspoon freshly ground black pepper

Directions:

Preheat the broiler to High with the rack 4 inches under the heating element. Put the sliced bread on a large, rimmed baking sheet and broil for 1 minute, or until the bread is just lightly toasted. Remove from the oven.

Brush each piece of the toasted bread with the oil, and rub a garlic half over each piece. Put the toasted bread back on the baking sheet. Evenly divide the tomato slices on each piece. Sprinkle with the oregano and top with the cheese.

Place the baking sheet under the broiler. Set the timer for 1½ minutes, but check after 1 minute. When the cheese is melted and the edges are just starting to get dark brown, remove the sandwiches from the oven. Top each sandwich with the fresh basil and pepper before serving.

Per Serving calories: 93 | fat: 2.0g | protein: 10.0g | carbs: 8.0g

Roasted Vegetable Panini

Prep time: 10 minutes | **Cook time:** 15 minutes | **Serves:**4

Ingredients:

2 tablespoons extra-virgin olive oil, divided
1½ cups diced broccoli
1 cup diced zucchini
¼ cup diced onion
¼ teaspoon dried oregano
⅛ teaspoon kosher or sea salt
⅛ teaspoon freshly ground black pepper

1 (12-ounce / 340-g) jar roasted red peppers, drained and finely chopped
2 tablespoons grated Parmesan or Asiago cheese
1 cup fresh Mozzarella (about 4 ounces / 113 g), sliced
1 (2-foot-long) whole-grain Italian loaf, cut into 4 equal lengths Cooking spray

Directions:

Place a large, rimmed baking sheet in the oven. Preheat the oven to 450ºF (235ºC) with the baking sheet inside.

In a large bowl, stir together 1 tablespoon of the oil, broccoli, zucchini, onion, oregano, salt and pepper.

Remove the baking sheet from the oven and spritz the baking sheet with cooking spray. Spread the vegetable mixture on the baking sheet and roast for 5 minutes, stirring once halfway through cooking. Remove the baking sheet from the oven. Stir in the red peppers and Parmesan cheese. In a large skillet over medium-high heat, heat the remaining 1 tablespoon of the oil.

Cut open each section of bread horizontally, but don't cut all the way through. Fill each with the vegetable mix (about ½ cup), and layer 1 ounce (28 g) of sliced Mozzarella cheese on top. Close the sandwiches, and place two of them on the skillet. Place a heavy object on top and grill for 2½ minutes. Flip the sandwiches and grill for another 2½ minutes. Repeat the grilling process with the remaining two sandwiches. Serve hot.

Per Serving calories: 116 | fat: 4.0g | protein: 12.0g | carbs: 9.0g

White Pizzas with Arugula and Spinach

Prep time: 10 minutes | **Cook time:** 20 minutes | **Serves:** 4

Ingredients:

1 pound (454 g) refrigerated fresh pizza dough
2 tablespoons extra-virgin olive oil, divided
½ cup thinly sliced onion
2 garlic cloves, minced
3 cups baby spinach
3 cups arugula
1 tablespoon water
¼ teaspoon freshly ground black pepper
1 tablespoon freshly squeezed lemon juice
½ cup shredded Parmesan cheese
½ cup crumbled goat cheese
Cooking spray

Directions:

Preheat the oven to 500°F (260°C). Spritz a large, rimmed baking sheet with cooking spray.

Take the pizza dough out of the refrigerator.

Heat 1 tablespoon of the oil in a large skillet over medium heat. Add the onion to the skillet and cook for 4 minutes, stirring constantly. Add the garlic and cook for 1 minute, stirring constantly.

Stir in the spinach, arugula, water and pepper. Cook for about 2 minutes, stirring constantly, or until all the greens are coated with oil and they start to cook down. Remove the skillet from the heat and drizzle with the lemon juice.

On a lightly floured work surface, form the pizza dough into a 12-inch circle or a 10-by-12-inch rectangle, using a rolling pin or by stretching with your hands.

Place the dough on the prepared baking sheet. Brush the dough with the remaining 1 tablespoon of the oil. Spread the cooked greens on top of the dough to within ½ inch of the edge. Top with the Parmesan cheese and goat cheese.

Bake in the preheated oven for 10 to 12 minutes, or until the crust starts to brown around the edges.

Remove from the oven and transfer the pizza to a cutting board. Cut into eight pieces before serving.

Per Serving

calories: 521 | fat: 31.0g | protein: 23.0g | carbs: 38.0g

Spicy Black Bean and Poblano Dippers

Prep time: 20 minutes | **Cook time:** 21 minutes | **Serves:** 8

Ingredients:

2 tablespoons avocado oil, plus more for brushing the dippers
1 (15 ounces / 425 g) can black beans, drained and rinsed
1 poblano, deseeded and quartered
½ cup fresh cilantro, leaves and tender stems
1 yellow onion, quartered
2 garlic cloves
1 teaspoon chili powder
1 teaspoon ground cumin
1 teaspoon sea salt
24 organic corn tortillas
1 jalapeño, halved and deseeded

Directions:

Preheat the oven to 400°F (205°C). Line a baking sheet with parchment paper and grease with avocado oil.

Combine the remaining ingredients, except for the tortillas, in a food processor, then pulse until chopped finely and the mixture holds together. Make sure not to purée the mixture.

Warm the tortillas on the baking sheet in the preheated oven for 1 minute or until softened.

Add a tablespoon of the mixture in the middle of each tortilla. Fold one side of the tortillas over the mixture and tuck to roll them up tightly to make the dippers.

Arrange the dippers on the baking sheet and brush them with avocado oil.

Bake in the oven for 20 minutes or until well browned. Flip the dippers halfway through the cooking time.

Serve immediately.

Per Serving

calories: 388 | fat: 6.5g | protein: 16.2g | carbs: 69.6g

Chapter 5
Beans, Grains, and Pastas

Baked Rolled Oat with Pears and Pecans

Prep time: 15 minutes | **Cook time:** 30 minutes | **Serves:** 6

Ingredients:

2 tablespoons coconut oil, melted, plus more for greasing the pan
3 ripe pears, cored and diced
2 cups unsweetened almond milk
1 tablespoon pure vanilla extract
¼ cup pure maple syrup

2 cups gluten-free rolled oats
½ cup raisins
¾ cup chopped pecans
¼ teaspoon ground nutmeg
1 teaspoon ground cinnamon
½ teaspoon ground ginger
¼ teaspoon sea salt

Directions:

Preheat the oven to 350°F (180°C). Grease a baking dish with melted coconut oil, then spread the pears in a single layer on the baking dish evenly.

Combine the almond milk, vanilla extract, maple syrup, and coconut oil in a bowl. Stir to mix well.

Combine the remaining ingredients in a separate large bowl. Stir to mix well. Fold the almond milk mixture in the bowl, then pour the mixture over the pears.

Place the baking dish in the preheated oven and bake for 30 minutes or until lightly browned and set. Serve immediately.

Per Serving
calories: 479 | fat: 34.9g | protein: 8.8g | carbs: 50.1g

Curry Apple Couscous with Leeks and Pecans

Prep time: 10 minutes | **Cook time:** 8 minutes | **Serves:** 4

Ingredients:

2 teaspoons extra-virgin olive oil
2 leeks, white parts only, sliced
1 apple, diced

2 cups cooked couscous
2 tablespoons curry powder
½ cup chopped pecans

Directions:

Heat the olive oil in a skillet over medium heat until shimmering.

Add the leeks and sauté for 5 minutes or until soft. Add the diced apple and cook for 3 more minutes until tender.

Add the couscous and curry powder. Stir to combine.

Transfer them in a large serving bowl, then mix in the pecans and serve.

Per Serving
calories: 254 | fat: 11.9g | protein: 5.4g | carbs: 34.3g

Brown Rice Pilaf with Pistachios and Raisins

Prep time: 5 minutes | **Cook time:** 15 minutes | **Serves:** 6

Ingredients:

1 tablespoon extra-virgin olive oil
1 cup chopped onion
½ cup shredded carrot
½ teaspoon ground cinnamon
1 teaspoon ground cumin

2 cups brown rice
1¾ cups pure orange juice
¼ cup water
½ cup shelled pistachios
1 cup golden raisins
½ cup chopped fresh chives

Directions:

Heat the olive oil in a saucepan over medium-high heat until shimmering. Add the onion, sauté for 5 minutes or until translucent.

Add the carrots, cinnamon, and cumin, then sauté for 1 minutes or until aromatic.

Pour int the brown rice, orange juice, and water. Bring to a boil. Reduce the heat to medium-low and simmer for 7 minutes or until the liquid is almost absorbed.

Transfer the rice mixture in a large serving bowl, then spread with pistachios, raisins, and chives. Serve immediately.

Per Serving
calories: 264 | fat: 7.1g | protein: 5.2g | carbs: 48.9g

Black Bean Chili with Mangoes

Prep time: 10 minutes | **Cook time:** 10 minutes | **Serves:** 4

Ingredients:

2 tablespoons coconut oil
1 onion, chopped
2 (15-ounce / 425-g) cans black beans, drained and rinsed
1 tablespoon chili powder
1 teaspoon sea salt

¼ teaspoon freshly ground black pepper
1 cup water
2 ripe mangoes, sliced thinly
¼ cup chopped fresh cilantro, divided
¼ cup sliced scallions, divided

Directions:

Heat the coconut oil in a pot over high heat until melted.

Put the onion in the pot and sauté for 5 minutes or until translucent. Add the black beans to the pot. Sprinkle with chili powder, salt, and ground black pepper. Pour in the water. Stir to mix well. Bring to a boil. Reduce the heat to low, then simmering for 5 minutes or until the beans are tender.

Turn off the heat and mix in the mangoes, then garnish with scallions and cilantro before serving.

Per Serving
calories: 430 | fat: 9.1g | protein: 20.2g | carbs: 71.9g

Cherry, Apricot, and Pecan Brown Rice Bowl

Prep time: 15 minutes | **Cook time:** 1 hour 1 minutes | Serves: 2

Ingredients:

2 tablespoons olive oil
2 green onions, sliced
½ cup brown rice
1 cup low -sodium chicken stock
2 tablespoons dried cherries

4 dried apricots, chopped
2 tablespoons pecans, toasted and chopped
Sea salt and freshly ground pepper, to taste

Directions:

Heat the olive oil in a medium saucepan over medium-high heat until shimmering.

Add the green onions and sauté for 1 minutes or until fragrant.

Add the rice. Stir to mix well, then pour in the chicken stock.

Bring to a boil. Reduce the heat to low. Cover and simmer for 50 minutes or until the brown rice is soft.

Add the cherries, apricots, and pecans, and simmer for 10 more minutes or until the fruits are tender.

Pour them in a large serving bowl. Fluff with a fork. Sprinkle with sea salt and freshly ground pepper. Serve immediately.

Per Serving

calories: 451 | fat: 25.9g | protein: 8.2g | carbs: 50.4g

Rice and Blueberry Stuffed Sweet Potatoes

Prep time: 15 minutes | **Cook time:** 20 minutes | Serves:4

Ingredients:

2 cups cooked wild rice
½ cup dried blueberries
½ cup chopped hazelnuts
½ cup shredded Swiss chard
1 teaspoon chopped fresh thyme

1 scallion, white and green parts, peeled and thinly sliced
Sea salt and freshly ground black pepper, to taste
4 sweet potatoes, baked in the skin until tender

Directions:

Preheat the oven to 400°F (205°C).

Combine all the ingredients, except for the sweet potatoes, in a large bowl. Stir to mix well.

Cut the top third of the sweet potato off length wire, then scoop most of the sweet potato flesh out.

Fill the potato with the wild rice mixture, then set the sweet potato on a greased baking sheet.

Bake in the preheated oven for 20 minutes or until the sweet potato skin is lightly charred.

Serve immediately.

Per Serving

calories: 393 | fat: 7.1g | protein: 10.2g | carbs: 76.9g

Lebanese Flavor Broken Thin Noodles

Prep time: 10 minutes | **Cook time:** 25 minutes | Serves:6

Ingredients:

1 tablespoon extra-virgin olive oil
1 (3-ounce / 85-g) cup vermicelli, broken into 1- to 1½-inch pieces
3 cups shredded cabbage
1 cup brown rice
3 cups low-sodium vegetable soup

½ cup water
2 garlic cloves, mashed
¼ teaspoon sea salt
⅛ teaspoon crushed red pepper flakes
½ cup coarsely chopped cilantro
Fresh lemon slices, for serving

Directions:

Heat the olive oil in a saucepan over medium-high heat until shimmering.

Add the vermicelli and sauté for 3 minutes or until toasted.

Add the cabbage and sauté for 4 minutes or until tender.

Pour in the brown rice, vegetable soup, and water. Add the garlic and sprinkle with salt and red pepper flakes.

Bring to a boil over high heat. Reduce the heat to medium low. Put the lid on and simmer for another 10 minutes.

Turn off the heat, then let sit for 5 minutes without opening the lid.

Pour them on a large serving platter and spread with cilantro. Squeeze the lemon slices over and serve warm.

Per Serving

calories: 127 | fat: 3.1g | protein: 4.2g | carbs: 22.9g

Italian Sautéd Cannelliqni Beans

Prep time: 10 minutes | **Cook time:** 15 minutes | Serves:6

Ingredients:

2 teaspoons extra-virgin olive oil
½ cup minced onion
¼ cup red wine vinegar
1 (12-ounce / 340-g) can no-salt-added tomato paste

2 tablespoons raw honey
½ cup water
¼ teaspoon ground cinnamon

Directions:

2 (15-ounce / 425-g) cans cannellini beans

Heat the olive oil in saucepan over medium heat until shimmering.

Add the onion and sauté for 5 minutes or until translucent.

Pour in the red wine vinegar, tomato paste, honey, and water. Sprinkle with cinnamon. Stir to mix well.

Reduce the heat to low, then pour all the beans into the saucepan. Cook for 10 more minutes. Stir constantly. Serve immediately.

Per Serving

calories: 435 | fat: 2.1g | protein: 26.2g | carbs: 80.3g

Lemony Farro and Avocado Bowl

Prep time: 5 minutes | **Cook time:** 25 minutes | **Serves:** 4

Ingredients:

1 tablespoon plus 2 teaspoons extra-virgin olive oil, divided
½ medium onion, chopped
1 carrot, shredded
2 garlic cloves, minced
1 (6-ounce / 170-g) cup pearled farro
2 cups low-sodium vegetable soup
2 avocados, peeled, pitted, and sliced
Zest and juice of 1 small lemon
¼ teaspoon sea salt

Directions:

Heat 1 tablespoon of olive oil in a saucepan over medium-high heat until shimmering.

Add the onion and sauté for 5 minutes or until translucent.

Add the carrot and garlic and sauté for 1 minute or until fragrant.

Add the farro and pour in the vegetable soup. Bring to a boil over high heat. Reduce the heat to low. Put the lid on and simmer for 20 minutes or until the farro is al dente.

Transfer the farro in a large serving bowl, then fold in the avocado slices. Sprinkle with lemon zest and salt, then drizzle with lemon juice and 2 teaspoons of olive oil.

Stir to mix well and serve immediately.

Per Serving calories: 210 | fat: 11.1g | protein: 4.2g | carbs: 27.9g

Bulgur Pilaf with Kale and Tomatoes

Prep time: 10 minutes | **Cook time:** 10 minutes | **Serves:** 2

Ingredients:

2 tablespoons olive oil,
2 cloves garlic, minced
1 bunch kale, trimmed and cut into bite-sized pieces
Juice of 1 lemon
2 cups cooked bulgur wheat
1 pint cherry tomatoes, halved
Sea salt and freshly ground pepper, to taste

Directions:

Heat the olive oil in a large skillet over medium heat. Add the garlic and sauté for 1 minute.

Add the kale leaves and stir to coat. Cook for 5 minutes until leaves are cooked through and thoroughly wilted.

Add the lemon juice, bulgur and tomatoes. Season with sea salt and freshly ground pepper to taste, then serve.

Per Serving
calories: 300 | fat: 14.0g | protein: 6.2g | carbs: 37.8g

Slow Cooked Turkey and Brown Rice

Prep time: 20 minutes | **Cook time:** 3 hours 10 minutes | **Serves:** 6

Ingredients:

1 tablespoon extra-virgin olive oil
1½ pounds (680 g) ground turkey
2 tablespoons chopped fresh sage, divided
2 tablespoons chopped fresh thyme, divided
1 teaspoon sea salt
½ teaspoon ground black pepper
2 cups brown rice
1 (14-ounce / 397-g) can stewed tomatoes, with the juice
¼ cup pitted and sliced Kalamata olives
3 medium zucchini, sliced thinly
¼ cup chopped fresh flat-leaf parsley
1 medium yellow onion, chopped
1 tablespoon plus 1 teaspoon balsamic vinegar
2 cups low-sodium chicken stock
2 garlic cloves, minced
½ cup grated Parmesan cheese, for serving

Directions:

Heat the olive oil in a nonstick skillet over medium-high heat until shimmering.

Add the ground turkey and sprinkle with 1 tablespoon of sage, 1 tablespoon of thyme, salt and ground black pepper.

Sauté for 10 minutes or until the ground turkey is lightly browned.

Pour them in the slow cooker, then pour in the remaining ingredients, except for the Parmesan. Stir to mix well.

Put the lid on and cook on high for 3 hours or until the rice and vegetables are tender.

Pour them in a large serving bowl, then spread with Parmesan cheese before serving.

Per Serving
calories: 499 | fat: 16.4g | protein: 32.4g | carbs: 56.5g

Quinoa with Baby Potatoes and Broccoli

Prep time: 5 minutes | **Cook time:** 10 minutes | **Serves:** 4

Ingredients:

2 tablespoons olive oil
1 cup baby potatoes, cut in half
1 cup broccoli florets
2 cups cooked quinoa
Zest of 1 lemon
Sea salt and freshly ground pepper, to taste

Directions:

Heat the olive oil in a large skillet over medium heat until shimmering. Add the potatoes and cook for about 6 to 7 minutes, or until softened and golden brown. Add the broccoli and cook for about 3 minutes, or until tender.

Remove from the heat and add the quinoa and lemon zest. Season with salt and pepper to taste, then serve.

Per Serving calories: 205 | fat: 8.6g | protein: 5.1g | carbs: 27.3g

Israeli Style Eggplant and Chickpea Salad

Prep time: 5 minutes | **Cook time:** 20 minutes | **Serves:**6

Ingredients:

2 tablespoons freshly squeezed lemon juice
1 teaspoon ground cumin
¼ teaspoon sea salt
2 tablespoons olive oil, divided
1 (1-pound / 454-g) medium globe eggplant, stem removed, cut into flat cubes (about ½ inch thick)
2 tablespoons balsamic vinegar
1 (15-ounce / 425-g) can chickpeas, drained and rinsed
¼ cup chopped mint leaves
1 cup sliced sweet onion
1 garlic clove, finely minced
1 tablespoon sesame seeds, toasted

Directions:

Preheat the oven to 550°F (288°C) or the highest level of your oven or broiler. Grease a baking sheet with 1 tablespoon of olive oil.

Combine the balsamic vinegar, lemon juice, cumin, salt, and 1 tablespoon of olive oil in a small bowl. Stir to mix well.

Arrange the eggplant cubes on the baking sheet, then brush with 2 tablespoons of the balsamic vinegar mixture on both sides.

Broil in the preheated oven for 8 minutes or until lightly browned. Flip the cubes halfway through the cooking time.

Meanwhile, combine the chickpeas, mint, onion, garlic, and sesame seeds in a large serving bowl. Drizzle with remaining balsamic vinegar mixture. Stir to mix well.

Remove the eggplant from the oven. Allow to cool for 5 minutes, then slice them into ½-inch strips on a clean work surface.

Add the eggplant strips in the serving bowl, then toss to combine well before serving.

Per Serving

calories: 125 | fat: 2.9g | protein: 5.2g | carbs: 20.9g

Lentil and Vegetable Curry Stew

Prep time: 20 minutes | **Cook time:** 4 hours 7 minutes | **Serves:**8

Ingredients:

1 tablespoon coconut oil
1 yellow onion, diced
¼ cup yellow Thai curry paste
2 cups unsweetened coconut milk
2 cups dry red lentils, rinsed well and drained
3 cups bite-sized cauliflower florets
2 golden potatoes, cut into chunks
2 carrots, peeled and diced
8 cups low-sodium vegetable soup, divided
1 bunch kale, stems removed and roughly chopped
Sea salt, to taste
½ cup fresh cilantro, chopped
Pinch crushed red pepper flakes

Directions:

Heat the coconut oil in a nonstick skillet over medium-high heat until melted. Add the onion and sauté for 5 minutes or until translucent. Pour in the curry paste and sauté for another 2 minutes, then fold in the coconut milk and stir to combine well. Bring to a simmer and turn off the heat.

Put the lentils, cauliflower, potatoes, and carrot in the slow cooker. Pour in 6 cups of vegetable soup and the curry mixture. Stir to combine well.

Cover and cook on high for 4 hours or until the lentils and vegetables are soft. Stir periodically.

During the last 30 minutes, fold the kale in the slow cooker and pour in the remaining vegetable soup. Sprinkle with salt. Pour the stew in a large serving bowl and spread the cilantro and red pepper flakes on top before serving hot.

Per Serving

calories: 530 | fat: 19.2g | protein: 20.3g | carbs: 75.2g

Chickpea, Vegetable, and Fruit Stew

Prep time: 20 minutes | **Cook time:** 6 hours 4 minutes | **Serves:** 6

Ingredients:

1 large bell pepper, any color, chopped

6 ounces (170 g) green beans, trimmed and cut into bite-size pieces

3 cups canned chickpeas, rinsed and drained

1 (15-ounce / 425-g) can diced tomatoes, with the juice

1 large carrot, cut into ¼-inch rounds

2 large potatoes, peeled and cubed

1 large yellow onion, chopped

1 teaspoon grated fresh ginger

2 garlic cloves, minced

1¾ cups low-sodium vegetable soup

1 teaspoon ground cumin

1 tablespoon ground coriander

¼ teaspoon ground red pepper flakes

Sea salt and ground black pepper, to taste

8 ounces (227 g) fresh baby spinach

¼ cup diced dried figs

¼ cup diced dried apricots

1 cup plain Greek yogurt

Directions:

Place the bell peppers, green beans, chicken peas, tomatoes and juice, carrot, potatoes, onion, ginger, and garlic in the slow cooker. Pour in the vegetable soup and sprinkle with cumin, coriander, red pepper flakes, salt, and ground black pepper. Stir to mix well.

Put the slow cooker lid on and cook on high for 6 hours or until the vegetables are soft. Stir periodically.

Open the lid and fold in the spinach, figs, apricots, and yogurt. Stir to mix well.

Cook for 4 minutes or until the spinach is wilted. Pour them in a large serving bowl. Allow to cool for at least 20 minutes, then serve warm.

Per Serving

calories: 611 | fat: 9.0g | protein: 30.7g | carbs: 107.4g

Quinoa and Chickpea Vegetable Bowls

Prep time: 20 minutes | **Cook time:** 15 minutes | **Serves:** 4

Ingredients:

1 cup red dry quinoa, rinsed and drained

2 cups low-sodium vegetable soup

2 cups fresh spinach

2 cups finely shredded red cabbage

1 (15-ounce / 425-g) can chickpeas, drained and rinsed

1 ripe avocado, thinly sliced

1 cup shredded carrots

1 red bell pepper, thinly sliced

½ cup fresh cilantro,

Mango Sauce:

1 mango, diced

¼ cup fresh lime juice

½ teaspoon ground turmeric

1 teaspoon finely minced fresh ginger

¼ teaspoon sea salt

Pinch of ground red pepper

1 teaspoon pure maple syrup

2 tablespoons extra-virgin olive oil

4 tablespoons Mango Sauce

Directions:

Pour the quinoa and vegetable soup in a saucepan. Bring to a boil. Reduce the heat to low. Cover and cook for 15 minutes or until tender. Fluffy with a fork.

Divide the quinoa, spinach, and cabbage into 4 serving bowls, then top with chickpeas, avocado, carrots, and bell pepper. Dress them with the mango sauce and spread with cilantro. Serve immediately.

Per Serving calories: 366 | fat: 11.1g | protein: 15.5g | carbs: 55.6g

Ritzy Veggie Chili

Prep time: 15 minutes | **Cook time:** 5 hours | **Serves:** 4

Ingredients:

1 (28-ounce / 794-g) can chopped tomatoes, with the juice

1 (15-ounce / 425-g) can black beans, drained and rinsed

1 (15-ounce / 425-g) can redly beans, drained and rinsed

1 medium green bell pepper, chopped

1 yellow onion, chopped

1 tablespoon onion powder

1 teaspoon paprika

1 teaspoon cayenne pepper

1 teaspoon garlic powder

½ teaspoon sea salt

½ teaspoon ground black pepper

1 tablespoon olive oil

1 large hass avocado, pitted, peeled, and chopped, for garnish

Directions:

Combine all the ingredients, except for the avocado, in the slow cooker. Stir to mix well.

Put the slow cooker lid on and cook on high for 5 hours or until the vegetables are tender and the mixture has a thick consistency.

Pour the chili in a large serving bowl. Allow to cool for 30 minutes, then spread with chopped avocado and serve.

Per Serving

calories: 633 | fat: 16.3g | protein: 31.7g | carbs: 97.0g

Spicy Italian Bean Balls with Marinara

Prep time: 20 minutes | **Cook time:** 30 mins | **Serves:**2 to 4

Ingredients:

Bean Balls:
1 tablespoon extra-virgin olive oil
½ yellow onion, minced
1 teaspoon fennel seeds
2 teaspoons dried oregano
½ teaspoon crushed red pepper flakes
1 teaspoon garlic powder
1 (15-ounce / 425-g) can white beans (cannellini or navy), drained and rinsed
½ cup whole-grain bread crumbs
Sea salt and ground black pepper, to taste

Marinara:
1 tablespoon extra-virgin olive oil
3 garlic cloves, minced
Handful basil leaves
1 (28-ounce / 794-g) can chopped tomatoes with juice reserved
Sea salt, to taste

Directions:

Make the Bean Balls

Preheat the oven to 350°F (180°C). Line a baking sheet with parchment paper.

Heat the olive oil in a nonstick skillet over medium heat until shimmering.

Add the onion and sauté for 5 minutes or until translucent.

Sprinkle with fennel seeds, oregano, red pepper flakes, and garlic powder, then cook for 1 minute or until aromatic.

Pour the sautéed mixture in a food processor and add the beans and bread crumbs. Sprinkle with salt and ground black pepper, then pulse to combine well and the mixture holds together.

Shape the mixture into balls with a 2-ounce (57-g) cookie scoop, then arrange the balls on the baking sheet.

Bake in the preheated oven for 30 minutes or until lightly browned. Flip the balls halfway through the cooking time.

Make the Marinara

While baking the bean balls, heat the olive oil in a saucepan over medium-high heat until shimmering.

Add the garlic and basil and sauté for 2 minutes or until fragrant. Fold in the tomatoes and juice. Bring to a boil. Reduce the heat to low. Put the lid on and simmer for 15 minutes. Sprinkle with salt. Transfer the bean balls on a large plate and baste with marinara before serving.

Per Serving

calories: 351 | fat: 16.4g | protein: 11.5g | carbs: 42.9g

Wild Rice, Celery, and Cauliflower Pilaf

Prep time: 10 minutes | **Cook time:** 45 minutes | **Serves:**4

Ingredients:

1 tablespoon olive oil, plus more for greasing the baking dish
1 cup wild rice
2 cups low-sodium chicken broth
1 sweet onion, chopped
2 stalks celery, chopped
1 teaspoon minced garlic
2 carrots, peeled, halved lengthwise, and sliced
½ cauliflower head, cut into small florets
1 teaspoon chopped fresh thyme
Sea salt, to taste

Directions:

Preheat the oven to 350°F (180°C). Line a baking sheet with parchment paper and grease with olive oil.

Put the wild rice in a saucepan, then pour in the chicken broth. Bring to a boil. Reduce the heat to low and simmer for 30 minutes or until the rice is plump.

Meanwhile, heat the remaining olive oil in an oven-proof skillet over medium-high heat until shimmering.

Add the onion, celery, and garlic to the skillet and sauté for 3 minutes or until the onion is translucent. Add the carrots and cauliflower to the skillet and sauté for 5 minutes. Turn off the heat and set aside. Pour the cooked rice in the skillet with the vegetables. Sprinkle with thyme and salt.

Set the skillet in the preheated oven and bake for 15 minutes or until the vegetables are soft. Serve immediately.

Per Serving

calories: 214 | fat: 3.9g | protein: 7.2g | carbs: 37.9g

Walnut and Ricotta Spaghetti

Prep time: 15 minutes | **Cook time:** 10 minutes | **Serves:**6

Ingredients:

1 pound (454 g) cooked whole-wheat spaghetti
2 tablespoons extra-virgin olive oil
4 cloves garlic, minced
¾ cup walnuts, toasted and finely chopped
2 tablespoons ricotta cheese
¼ cup flat-leaf parsley, chopped
½ cup grated Parmesan cheese
Sea salt and freshly ground pepper, to taste

Directions:

Reserve a cup of spaghetti water while cooking the spaghetti. Heat the olive oil in a nonstick skillet over medium-low heat or until shimmering.

Add the garlic and sauté for a minute or until fragrant. Pour the spaghetti water into the skillet and cook for 8 more minutes.

Turn off the heat and mix in the walnuts and ricotta cheese.

Put the cooked spaghetti on a large serving plate, then pour the walnut sauce over. Spread with parsley and Parmesan, then sprinkle with salt and ground pepper. Toss to serve.

Per Serving

calories: 264 | fat: 16.8g | protein: 8.6g | carbs: 22.8g

Butternut Squash, Spinach, and Cheeses Lasagna

Prep time: 30 minutes | **Cook time:** 3 hours 45 minutes | **Serves:** 4 to 6

Ingredients:

2 tablespoons extra-virgin olive oil, divided
1 butternut squash, halved lengthwise and deseeded
½ teaspoon sage
½ teaspoon sea salt
¼ teaspoon ground black pepper
¼ cup grated Parmesan cheese
2 cups ricotta cheese
½ cup unsweetened almond milk
5 layers whole-wheat lasagna noodles (about 12 ounces / 340 g in total)
4 ounces (113 g) fresh spinach leaves, divided
½ cup shredded part skim Mozzarella, for garnish

Directions:

Preheat the oven to 400°F (205°C). Line a baking sheet with parchment paper. Brush 1 tablespoon of olive oil on the cut side of the butternut squash, then place the squash on the baking sheet. Bake in the preheated oven for 45 minutes or until the squash is tender. Allow to cool until you can handle it, then scoop the flesh out and put the flesh in a food processor to purée. Combine the puréed butternut squash flesh with sage, salt, and ground black pepper in a large bowl. Stir to mix well.

Combine the cheeses and milk in a separate bowl, then sprinkle with salt and pepper, to taste.

Grease the slow cooker with 1 tablespoon of olive oil, then add a layer of lasagna noodles to coat the bottom of the slow cooker. Spread half of the squash mixture on top of the noodles, then top the squash mixture with another layer of lasagna noodles. Spread half of the spinach over the noodles, then top the spinach with half of cheese mixture. Repeat with remaining 3 layers of lasagna noodles, squash mixture, spinach, and cheese mixture. Top the cheese mixture with Mozzarella, then put the lid on and cook on low for 3 hours or until the lasagna noodles are al dente. Serve immediately.

Per Serving calories: 657 | fat: 37.1g | protein: 30.9g | carbs: 57.2g

Minestrone Chickpeas and Macaroni Casserole

Prep time: 20 minutes | **Cook time:** 7 hours 20 minutes | **Serves:** 5

Ingredients:

1 (15-ounce / 425-g) can chickpeas, drained and rinsed
1 (28-ounce / 794-g) can diced tomatoes, with the juice
1 (6-ounce / 170-g) can no-salt-added tomato paste
3 medium carrots, sliced
3 cloves garlic, minced
1 medium yellow onion, chopped
1 cup low-sodium vegetable soup
½ teaspoon dried rosemary
1 teaspoon dried oregano
2 teaspoons maple syrup
½ teaspoon sea salt
¼ teaspoon ground black pepper
½ pound (227-g) fresh green beans, trimmed and cut into bite-size pieces
1 cup macaroni pasta
2 ounces (57 g) Parmesan cheese, grated

Directions:

Except for the green beans, pasta, and Parmesan cheese, combine all the ingredients in the slow cooker and stir to mix well. Put the slow cooker lid on and cook on low for 7 hours. Fold in the pasta and green beans. Put the lid on and cook on high for 20 minutes or until the vegetable are soft and the pasta is al dente.

Pour them in a large serving bowl and spread with Parmesan cheese before serving.

Per Serving
calories: 349 | fat: 6.7g | protein: 16.5g | carbs: 59.9g

Black-Eyed Peas Salad with Walnuts

Prep time: 10 minutes | **Cook time:** 0 mins | **Serves:** 4 to 6

Ingredients:

3 tablespoons extra-virgin olive oil
3 tablespoons dukkah, divided
2 tablespoons lemon juice
2 tablespoons pomegranate molasses
¼ teaspoon salt, or more to taste
2 (15-ounce / 425-g) cans black-eyed peas, rinsed
½ cup pomegranate seeds
½ cup minced fresh parsley
½ cup walnuts, toasted and chopped
4 scallions, sliced thinly
⅛ teaspoon pepper, or more to taste

Directions:

In a large bowl, whisk together the olive oil, 2 tablespoons of the dukkah, lemon juice, pomegranate molasses, salt and pepper. Stir in the remaining ingredients. Season with salt and pepper. Sprinkle with the remaining 1 tablespoon of the dukkah before serving.

Per Serving
calories: 155 | fat: 11.5g | protein: 2.0g | carbs: 12.5g

Garlic and Parsley Chickpeas

Prep time: 10 minutes | **Cook time:** 18 to 20 minutes | **Serves:** 4 to 6

Ingredients:

¼ cup extra-virgin olive oil, divided

4 garlic cloves, sliced thinly

⅛ teaspoon red pepper flakes

1 onion, chopped finely

¼ teaspoon salt, plus more to taste

Black pepper, to taste

2 (15-ounce / 425-g) cans chickpeas, rinsed

1 cup vegetable broth

2 tablespoons minced fresh parsley

2 teaspoons lemon juice

Directions:

Add 3 tablespoons of the olive oil, garlic, and pepper flakes to a skillet over medium heat. Cook for about 3 minutes, stirring constantly, or until the garlic turns golden but not brown. Stir in the onion and ¼ teaspoon salt and cook for 5 to 7 minutes, or until softened and lightly browned.

Add the chickpeas and broth to the skillet and bring to a simmer. Reduce the heat to medium-low, cover, and cook for about 7 minutes, or until the chickpeas are cooked through and flavors meld. Uncover, increase the heat to high and continue to cook for about 3 minutes more, or until nearly all liquid has evaporated.

Turn off the heat, stir in the parsley and lemon juice. Season to taste with salt and pepper and drizzle with remaining 1 tablespoon of the olive oil. Serve warm.

Per Serving

calories: 220 | fat: 11.4g | protein: 6.5g | carbs: 24.6g

Fava and Garbanzo Bean Ful

Prep time: 10 minutes | **Cook time:** 10 minutes | **Serves:** 6

Ingredients:

1 (15-ounce / 425-g) can fava beans, rinsed and drained

1 (1-pound / 454-g) can garbanzo beans, rinsed and drained

3 cups water

½ cup lemon juice

3 cloves garlic, peeled and minced

1 teaspoon salt

3 tablespoons extra-virgin olive oil

Directions:

In a pot over medium heat, cook the beans and water for 10 minutes.

Drain the beans and transfer to a bowl. Reserve 1 cup of the liquid from the cooked beans.

Add the reserved liquid, lemon juice, minced garlic and salt to the bowl with the beans. Mix to combine well. Using a potato masher, mash up about half the beans in the bowl.

Give the mixture one more stir to make sure the beans are evenly mixed.

Drizzle with the olive oil and serve.

Per Serving calories: 199 fat: 9.0g protein: 10.0g carbs: 25.0g

Mashed Beans with Cumin

Prep time: 10 minutes | **Cook time:** 10 to 12 minutes | **Serves:** 4 to 6

Ingredients:

1 tablespoon extra-virgin olive oil, plus extra for serving

4 garlic cloves, minced

1 teaspoon ground cumin

2 (15-ounce / 425-g) cans fava beans

3 tablespoons tahini

2 tablespoons minced fresh parsley

2 tablespoons lemon juice, plus lemon wedges for serving

Salt and pepper, to taste

1 tomato, cored and cut into ½-inch pieces

1 small onion, chopped finely

2 hard-cooked large eggs, chopped

Directions:

Add the olive oil, garlic and cumin to a medium saucepan over medium heat. Cook for about 2 minutes, or until fragrant. Stir in the beans with their liquid and tahini. Bring to a simmer and cook for 8 to 10 minutes, or until the liquid thickens slightly.

Turn off the heat, mash the beans to a coarse consistency with a potato masher. Stir in the lemon juice and 1 teaspoon pepper. Season with salt and pepper.

Transfer the mashed beans to a serving dish. Top with the tomato, onion, eggs and parsley. Drizzle with the extra olive oil. Serve with the lemon wedges.

Per Serving

calories: 125 | fat: 8.6g | protein: 4.9g | carbs: 9.1g

Garlic Shrimp Fettuccine

Prep time: 10 mins | **Cook time:** 15 minutes | **Serves:** 4 to 6

Ingredients:

8 ounces (227 g) fettuccine pasta

¼ cup extra-virgin olive oil

3 tablespoons garlic, minced

1 pound (454 g) large shrimp, peeled and deveined

⅓ cup lemon juice

1 tablespoon lemon zest

½ teaspoon salt

½ teaspoon freshly ground black pepper

1. Bring a large pot of salted water to a boil. Add the fettuccine and cook for 8 minutes. Reserve ½ cup of the cooking liquid and drain the pasta.
2. In a large saucepan over medium heat, heat the olive oil. Add the garlic and sauté for 1 minute.
3. Add the shrimp to the saucepan and cook each side for 3 minutes. Remove the shrimp from the pan and set aside.
4. Add the remaining ingredients to the saucepan. Stir in the cooking liquid. Add the pasta and toss together to evenly coat the pasta.
5. Transfer the pasta to a serving dish and serve topped with the cooked shrimp.

Per Serving

calories: 615 | fat: 17.0g | protein: 33.0g | carbs: 89.0g

Turkish Canned Pinto Bean Salad

Prep time: 10 mins | **Cook time:** 3 minutes | **Serves:** 4 to 6

Ingredients:

¼ cup extra-virgin olive oil, divided
3 garlic cloves, lightly crushed and peeled
2 (15-ounce / 425-g) cans pinto beans, rinsed 2 cups plus
1 tablespoon water
Salt and pepper, to taste
¼ cup tahini
3 tablespoons lemon juice

1 tablespoon ground dried Aleppo pepper, plus extra for serving
8 ounces (227 g) cherry tomatoes, halved
¼ red onion, sliced thinly
½ cup fresh parsley leaves
2 hard-cooked large eggs, quartered
1 tablespoon toasted sesame seeds

Directions:

Add 1 tablespoon of the olive oil and garlic to a medium saucepan over medium heat. Cook for about 3 minutes, stirring constantly, or until the garlic turns golden but not brown.

Add the beans, 2 cups of the water and 1 teaspoon salt and bring to a simmer. Remove from the heat, cover and let sit for 20 minutes. Drain the beans and discard the garlic.

In a large bowl, whisk together the remaining 3 tablespoons of the oil, tahini, lemon juice, Aleppo, the remaining 1 tablespoon of the water and ¼ teaspoon salt. Stir in the beans, tomatoes, onion and parsley. Season with salt and pepper to taste.

Transfer to a serving platter and top with the eggs. Sprinkle with the sesame seeds and extra Aleppo before serving.

Per Serving calories: 402 | fat: 18.9g | protein: 16.2g | carbs: 44.4g

Triple-Green Pasta with Cheese

Prep time: 5 minutes | **Cook time:** 14 to 16 minutes | **Serves:** 4

Ingredients:

8 ounces (227 g) uncooked penne
1 tablespoon extra-virgin olive oil
2 garlic cloves, minced
¼ teaspoon crushed red pepper
2 cups chopped fresh flat-leaf parsley, including stems
5 cups loosely packed baby spinach

¼ teaspoon ground nutmeg
¼ teaspoon kosher salt
¼ teaspoon freshly ground black pepper
⅓ cup Castelvetrano olives, pitted and sliced
⅓ cup grated Parmesan cheese

Directions:

In a large stockpot of salted water, cook the pasta for about 8 to 10 minutes. Drain the pasta and reserve ¼ cup of the cooking liquid.

Meanwhile, heat the olive oil in a large skillet over medium heat. Add the garlic and red pepper and cook for 30 seconds, stirring constantly.

Add the parsley and cook for 1 minute, stirring constantly. Add the spinach, nutmeg, salt, and pepper, and cook for 3 minutes, stirring occasionally, or until the spinach is wilted.

Add the cooked pasta and the reserved ¼ cup cooking liquid to the skillet. Stir in the olives and cook for about 2 minutes, or until most of the pasta water has been absorbed.

Remove from the heat and stir in the cheese before serving.

Per Serving
calories: 262 | fat: 4.0g | protein: 15.0g | carbs: 51.0g

Mint Brown Rice

Prep time: 5 minutes | **Cook time:** 22 minutes | **Serves:** 2

Ingredients:

2 cloves garlic, minced
¼ cup chopped fresh mint, plus more for garnish
1 tablespoon chopped dried chives

1 cup short- or long-grain brown rice
1½ cups water or low-sodium vegetable broth
½ to 1 teaspoon sea salt

Directions:

Place the garlic, mint, chives, rice, and water in the Instant Pot. Stir to combine.

Secure the lid. Select the Manual mode and set the cooking time for 22 minutes at High Pressure. Once cooking is complete, do a natural pressure release for 10 minutes, then release any remaining pressure. Carefully open the lid.

Add salt to taste and serve garnished with more mint.

Per Serving
calories: 514 | fat: 6.6g | protein: 20.7g | carbs: 80.4g

Pesto Pasta

Prep time: 10 mins | **Cook time:** 8 minutes | **Serves:** 4 to 6

Ingredients:

1 pound (454 g) spaghetti
4 cups fresh basil leaves, stems removed
3 cloves garlic
1 teaspoon salt
½ teaspoon freshly ground black pepper
½ cup toasted pine nuts
¼ cup lemon juice
½ cup grated Parmesan cheese
1 cup extra-virgin olive oil

Directions:

Bring a large pot of salted water to a boil. Add the spaghetti to the pot and cook for 8 minutes.

In a food processor, place the remaining ingredients, except for the olive oil, and pulse.

While the processor is running, slowly drizzle the olive oil through the top opening. Process until all the olive oil has been added.

Reserve ½ cup of the cooking liquid. Drain the pasta and put it into a large bowl. Add the pesto and cooking liquid to the bowl of pasta and toss everything together.

Serve immediately.

Per Serving

calories: 1067 | fat: 72.0g | protein: 23.0g | carbs: 91..0g

Spaghetti with Pine Nuts and Cheese

Prep time: 10 mins | **Cook time:** 11 minutes | **Serves:** 4 to 6

Ingredients:

8 ounces (227 g) spaghetti
4 tablespoons almond butter
1 teaspoon freshly ground black pepper
½ cup pine nuts
1 cup fresh grated Parmesan cheese, divided

Directions:

Bring a large pot of salted water to a boil. Add the pasta and cook for 8 minutes.

In a large saucepan over medium heat, combine the butter, black pepper, and pine nuts. Cook for 2 to 3 minutes, or until the pine nuts are lightly toasted.

Reserve ½ cup of the pasta water. Drain the pasta and place it into the pan with the pine nuts.

Add ¾ cup of the Parmesan cheese and the reserved pasta water to the pasta and toss everything together to evenly coat the pasta.

Transfer the pasta to a serving dish and top with the remaining ¼ cup of the Parmesan cheese. Serve immediately.

Per Serving

calories: 542 | fat: 32.0g | protein: 20.0g | carbs: 46.0g

Creamy Garlic Parmesan Chicken Pasta

Prep time: 5 minutes | **Cook time:** 15 minutes | **Serves:** 4

Ingredients:

3 tablespoons extra-virgin olive oil
2 boneless, skinless chicken breasts, cut into thin strips
1 large onion, thinly sliced
3 tablespoons garlic, minced
1½ teaspoons salt
1 pound (454 g) fettuccine pasta
1 cup heavy whipping cream
¾ cup freshly grated Parmesan cheese, divided
½ teaspoon freshly ground black pepper

Directions:

In a large skillet over medium heat, heat the olive oil. Add the chicken and cook for 3 minutes.

Add the onion, garlic and salt to the skillet. Cook for 7 minutes, stirring occasionally.

Meanwhile, bring a large pot of salted water to a boil and add the pasta, then cook for 7 minutes.

While the pasta is cooking, add the heavy cream, ½ cup of the Parmesan cheese and black pepper to the chicken. Simmer for 3 minutes.

Reserve ½ cup of the pasta water. Drain the pasta and add it to the chicken cream sauce.

Add the reserved pasta water to the pasta and toss together. Simmer for 2 minutes. Top with the remaining ¼ cup of the Parmesan cheese and serve warm.

Per Serving

calories: 879 | fat: 42.0g | protein: 35.0g | carbs: 90.0g

Broccoli and Carrot Pasta Salad

Prep time: 5 minutes | **Cook time:** 10 minutes | **Serves:** 2

Ingredients:

8 ounces (227 g) whole-wheat pasta
2 cups broccoli florets
1 cup peeled and shredded carrots
¼ cup plain Greek yogurt
Juice of 1 lemon
1 teaspoon red pepper flakes
Sea salt and freshly ground pepper, to taste

Directions:

Bring a large pot of lightly salted water to a boil. Add the pasta to the boiling water and cook until al dente, about 8 to 10 minutes. Drain the pasta and let rest for a few minutes.

When cooled, combine the pasta with the veggies, yogurt, lemon juice, and red pepper flakes in a large bowl, and stir thoroughly to combine.

Taste and season to taste with salt and pepper. Serve immediately.

Per Serving

calories: 428 | fat: 2.9g | protein: 15.9g | carbs: 84.6g

Pearl Barley Risotto with Parmesan Cheese

Prep time: 5 minutes | **Cook time:** 20 minutes | **Serves:**6

Ingredients:

4 cups low-sodium or no-salt-added vegetable broth
1 tablespoon extra-virgin olive oil
1 cup chopped yellow onion
2 cups uncooked pearl barley
½ cup dry white wine
1 cup freshly grated Parmesan cheese, divided
¼ teaspoon kosher or sea salt
¼ teaspoon freshly ground black pepper
Fresh chopped chives and lemon wedges, for serving (optional)

Directions:

Pour the broth into a medium saucepan and bring to a simmer.

Heat the olive oil in a large stockpot over medium-high heat. Add the onion and cook for about 4 minutes, stirring occasionally.

Add the barley and cook for 2 minutes, stirring, or until the barley is toasted. Pour in the wine and cook for about 1 minute, or until most of the liquid evaporates. Add 1 cup of the warm broth into the pot and cook, stirring, for about 2 minutes, or until most of the liquid is absorbed.

Add the remaining broth, 1 cup at a time, cooking until each cup is absorbed (about 2 minutes each time) before adding the next. The last addition of broth will take a bit longer to absorb, about 4 minutes.

Remove the pot from the heat, and stir in ½ cup of the cheese, and the salt and pepper.

Serve with the remaining ½ cup of the cheese on the side, along with the chives and lemon wedges (if desired).

Per Serving
calories: 421 | fat: 11.0g | protein: 15.0g | carbs: 67.0g

Cranberry and Almond Quinoa

Prep time: 5 minutes | **Cook time:** 10 minutes | **Serves:**2

Ingredients:

2 cups water
1 cup quinoa, rinsed
¼ cup salted sunflower seeds
½ cup slivered almonds
1 cup dried cranberries

Directions:

Combine water and quinoa in the Instant Pot.

Secure the lid. Select the Manual mode and set the cooking time for 10 minutes at High Pressure.

Once cooking is complete, do a quick pressure release. Carefully open the lid.

Add sunflower seeds, almonds, and dried cranberries and gently mix until well combined. Serve hot.

Per Serving
calories: 445 | fat: 14.8g | protein: 15.1g | carbs: 64.1g

Israeli Couscous with Asparagus

Prep time: 5 minutes | **Cook time:** 25 minutes | **Serves:**6

Ingredients:

1½ pounds (680 g) asparagus spears, ends trimmed and stalks chopped into 1-inch pieces
1 garlic clove, minced
1 tablespoon extra-virgin olive oil
¼ teaspoon freshly ground black pepper
1¾ cups water
1 (8-ounce / 227-g) box uncooked whole-wheat or regular Israeli couscous (about 1⅓ cups)
¼ teaspoon kosher salt
1 cup garlic-and-herb goat cheese, at room temperature

Directions:

Preheat the oven to 425ºF (220ºC).

In a large bowl, stir together the asparagus, garlic, oil, and pepper. Spread the asparagus on a large, rimmed baking sheet and roast for 10 minutes, stirring a few times. Remove the pan from the oven, and spoon the asparagus into a large serving bowl. Set aside.

While the asparagus is roasting, bring the water to a boil in medium saucepan. Add couscous and season with salt, stirring well..

Reduce the heat to medium-low. Cover and cook for 12 minutes, or until the water is absorbed.

Pour the hot couscous into the bowl with the asparagus. Add the goat cheese and mix thoroughly until completely melted. Serve immediately.

Per Serving
calories: 103 | fat: 2.0g | protein: 6.0g | carbs: 18.0g

Chili Halloumi Cheese with Rice

Prep time: 10 minutes | **Cook time:** 8 minutes | **Serves:**6

Ingredients:

2 cups water
2 tablespoons brown sugar
2 tablespoons rice vinegar
1 tablespoon sweet chili sauce
1 tablespoon olive oil
1 teaspoon fresh minced garlic
20 ounces (567 g) Halloumi cheese, cubed
1 cup rice
¼ cup chopped fresh chives, for garnish

Directions:

Heat the oil on Sauté and fry the halloumi for 5 minutes until golden brown. Set aside.

To the pot, add water, garlic, olive oil, vinegar, sugar, soy sauce, and chili sauce and mix well until smooth. Stir in rice noodles. Seal the lid and cook on High Pressure for 3 minutes. Release the pressure quickly. Split the rice between bowls. Top with fried halloumi and sprinkle with fresh chives before serving.

Per Serving
calories: 534 | fat: 34.3g | protein: 24.9g | carbs: 30.1g

Caprese Pasta with Roasted Asparagus

Prep time: 5 minutes | **Cook time:** 25 minutes | **Serves:**6

Ingredients:

8 ounces (227 g) uncooked small pasta, like orecchiette (little ears) or farfalle (bow ties)

1½ pounds (680 g) fresh asparagus, ends trimmed and stalks chopped into 1-inch pieces

1½ cups grape tomatoes, halved

2 tablespoons extra-virgin olive oil

¼ teaspoon kosher salt

¼ teaspoon freshly ground black pepper

2 cups fresh Mozzarella, drained and cut into bite-size pieces (about 8 ounces / 227 g)

⅓ cup torn fresh basil leaves

2 tablespoons balsamic vinegar

Directions:

Preheat the oven to 400ºF (205ºC).

In a large stockpot of salted water, cook the pasta for about 8 to 10 minutes. Drain and reserve about ¼ cup of the cooking liquid.

Meanwhile, in a large bowl, toss together the asparagus, tomatoes, oil, salt and pepper. Spread the mixture onto a large, rimmed baking sheet and bake in the oven for 15 minutes, stirring twice during cooking.

Remove the vegetables from the oven and add the cooked pasta to the baking sheet. Mix with a few tablespoons of cooking liquid to help the sauce become smoother and the saucy vegetables stick to the pasta.

Gently mix in the Mozzarella and basil. Drizzle with the balsamic vinegar. Serve from the baking sheet or pour the pasta into a large bowl.

Per Serving

calories: 147 | fat: 3.0g | protein: 16.0g | carbs: 17.0g

Freekeh Pilaf with Dates and Pistachios

Prep time: 10 mins | **Cook time:** 10 minutes | **Serves:**4 to 6

Ingredients:

2 tablespoons extra-virgin olive oil, plus extra for drizzling

1 shallot, minced

1½ teaspoons grated fresh ginger

¼ teaspoon ground coriander

¼ teaspoon ground cumin

Salt and pepper, to taste

1¾ cups water

1½ cups cracked freekeh, rinsed

3 ounces (85 g) pitted dates, chopped

¼ cup shelled pistachios, toasted and coarsely chopped

1½ tablespoons lemon juice

¼ cup chopped fresh mint

Directions:

Set the Instant Pot to Sauté mode and heat the olive oil until shimmering. Add the shallot, ginger, coriander, cumin, salt, and pepper to the pot and cook for about 2 minutes, or until the shallot is softened. Stir in the water and freekeh.

Secure the lid. Select the Manual mode and set the cooking time for 4 minutes at High Pressure. Once cooking is complete, do a quick pressure release. Carefully open the lid. Add the dates, pistachios and lemon juice and gently fluff the freekeh with a fork to combine. Season to taste with salt and pepper.

Transfer to a serving dish and sprinkle with the mint. Serve drizzled with extra olive oil.

Per Serving

calories: 280 | fat: 8.0g | protein: 8.0g | carbs: 46.0g

Black-Eyed Pea and Vegetable Stew

Prep time: 15 minutes | **Cook time:** 40 minutes | **Serves:**2

Ingredients:

½ cup black-eyed peas, soaked in water overnight

3 cups water, plus more as needed

1 large carrot, peeled and cut into ½-inch pieces (about ¾ cup)

1 large beet, peeled and cut into ½-inch pieces (about ¾ cup)

¼ teaspoon turmeric

¼ teaspoon cayenne pepper

¼ teaspoon ground cumin seeds, toasted

¼ cup finely chopped parsley

¼ teaspoon salt (optional)

½ teaspoon fresh lime juice

Directions:

Pour the black-eyed peas and water into a large pot, then cook over medium heat for 25 minutes. Add the carrot and beet to the pot and cook for 10 minutes more, adding more water as needed.

Add the turmeric, cayenne pepper, cumin, and parsley to the pot and cook for another 6 minutes, or until the vegetables are softened. Stir the mixture periodically. Season with salt, if desired.Serve drizzled with the fresh lime juice.

Per Serving

calories: 89 | fat: 0.7g | protein: 4.1g | carbs: 16.6g

Chickpea Salad with Tomatoes and Basil

Prep time: 5 minutes | **Cook time:** 45 minutes | **Serves:**2

Ingredients:

1 cup dried chickpeas, rinsed

1 quart water, or enough to cover the chickpeas by 3 to 4 inches

1½ cups halved grape tomatoes

1 cup chopped fresh basil leaves

2 to 3 tablespoons balsamic vinegar

½ teaspoon garlic powder

½ teaspoon salt, or more to taste

Directions:

In your Instant Pot, combine the chickpeas and water.

Secure the lid. Select the Manual mode and set the cooking time for 45 minutes at High Pressure.

Once cooking is complete, do a natural pressure release for 20 minutes, then release any remaining pressure. Carefully open the lid and drain the chickpeas. Refrigerate to cool (unless you want to serve this warm, which is good, too).

While the chickpeas cool, in a large bowl, stir together the basil, tomatoes, vinegar, garlic powder, and salt. Add the beans, stir to combine, and serve.

Per Serving
calories: 395 | fat: 6.0g | protein: 19.8g | carbs: 67.1g

Mediterranean Lentils

Prep time: 7 minutes | **Cook time:** 24 minutes | **Serves:**2

Ingredients:

1 tablespoon olive oil

1 small sweet or yellow onion, diced

1 garlic clove, diced

1 teaspoon dried oregano

½ teaspoon ground cumin

½ teaspoon dried parsley

2½ cups vegetable stock

½ teaspoon salt, plus more as needed

¼ teaspoon freshly ground black pepper, plus more as needed

1 tomato, diced

1 cup brown or green lentils

1 bay leaf

Directions:

Set your Instant Pot to Sauté and heat the olive oil until it shimmers. Add the onion and cook for 3 to 4 minutes until soft. Turn off the Instant Pot and add the garlic, oregano, cumin, parsley, salt, and pepper. Cook until fragrant, about 1 minute.

Stir in the tomato, lentils, stock, and bay leaf.

Lock the lid. Select the Manual mode and set the cooking time for 18 minutes at High Pressure.

When the timer beeps, perform a natural pressure release for 10 minutes, then release any remaining pressure. Carefully open the lid. Remove and discard the bay leaf. Taste and season with more salt and pepper, as needed. If there's too much liquid remaining, select Sauté and cook until it evaporates. Serve warm.

Per Serving calories: 426 | fat: 8.1g | protein: 26.2g | carbs: 63.8g

Rich Cauliflower Alfredo

Prep time: 35 minutes | **Cook time:** 30 minutes | **Serves:**4

Ingredients:

Cauliflower Alfredo Sauce:

1 tablespoon avocado oil

½ yellow onion, diced

2 cups cauliflower florets

2 garlic cloves, minced

1½ teaspoons miso

1 teaspoon Dijon mustard

Pinch of ground nutmeg

½ cup unsweetened almond milk

1½ tablespoons fresh lemon juice

2 tablespoons nutritional yeast

Sea salt and ground black pepper, to taste

Fettuccine:

1 tablespoon avocado oil

½ yellow onion, diced

1 cup broccoli florets

1 zucchini, halved lengthwise and cut into ¼-inch-thick half-moons

Sea salt and ground black pepper, to taste

½ cup sun-dried tomatoes, drained if packed in oil

8 ounces (227 g) cooked whole-wheat fettuccine

½ cup fresh basil, cut into ribbons

Directions:
Make the Sauce

Heat the avocado oil in a nonstick skillet over medium-high heat until shimmering.

Add half of the onion to the skillet and sauté for 5 minutes or until translucent. Add the cauliflower and garlic to the skillet. Reduce the heat to low and cook for 8 minutes or until the cauliflower is tender.

Pour them in a food processor, add the remaining ingredients for the sauce and pulse to combine well. Set aside.

Make the Fettuccine

Heat the avocado oil in a nonstick skillet over medium-high heat. Add the remaining half of onion and sauté for 5 minutes or until translucent.

Add the broccoli and zucchini. Sprinkle with salt and ground black pepper, then sauté for 5 minutes or until tender.

Add the sun-dried tomatoes, reserved sauce, and fettuccine. Sauté for 3 minutes or until well-coated and heated through. Serve the fettuccine on a large plate and spread with basil before serving.

Per Serving
calories: 288 | fat: 15.9g | protein: 10.1g | carbs: 32.5g

Butternut Squash and Zucchini with Penne

Prep time: 15 minutes | **Cook time:** 30 minutes | **Serves:** 6

Ingredients:

1 large zucchini, diced
1 large butternut squash, peeled and diced
1 large yellow onion, chopped
2 tablespoons extra-virgin olive oil
1 teaspoon paprika
½ teaspoon garlic powder
½ teaspoon sea salt
½ teaspoon freshly ground black pepper
1 pound (454 g) whole-grain penne
½ cup dry white wine
2 tablespoons grated Parmesan cheese

Directions:

Preheat the oven to 400ºF (205ºC). Line a baking sheet with aluminum foil. Combine the zucchini, butternut squash, and onion in a large bowl. Drizzle with olive oil and sprinkle with paprika, garlic powder, salt, and ground black pepper. Toss to coat well.

Spread the vegetables in the single layer on the baking sheet, then roast in the preheated oven for 25 minutes or until the vegetables are tender.

Meanwhile, bring a pot of water to a boil, then add the penne and cook for 14 minutes or until al dente. Drain the penne through a colander.

Transfer ½ cup of roasted vegetables in a food processor, then pour in the dry white wine. Pulse until smooth.

Pour the puréed vegetables in a nonstick skillet and cook with penne over medium-high heat for a few minutes to heat through. Transfer the penne with the purée on a large serving plate, then spread the remaining roasted vegetables and Parmesan on top before serving.

Per Serving

calories: 340 | fat: 6.2g | protein: 8.0g | carbs: 66.8g

Super Cheesy Tagliatelle

Prep time: 10 minutes | **Cook time:** 20 minutes | **Serves:** 6

Ingredients:

¼ cup goat cheese, chevre
¼ cup grated Pecorino cheese
½ cup grated Parmesan
1 cup heavy cream
½ cup grated Gouda
2 tablespoons olive oil
1 tablespoon Italian Seasoning mix
1 cup vegetable broth
1 pound (454 g) tagliatelle

Directions:

In a bowl, mix goat cheese, pecorino, Parmesan, and heavy cream. Stir in Italian seasoning. Transfer to your instant pot. Stir in the broth and olive oil.Seal the lid and cook on High Pressure for 4 minutes. Do a quick release.

Meanwhile, drop the tagliatelle in boiling water and cook for 6 minutes. Remove the instant pot's lid and stir in the tagliatelle. Top with grated gouda and let simmer for about 10 minutes on Sauté mode.

Per Serving

calories: 511 | fat: 22.0g | protein: 14.5g | carbs: 65.7g

Mediterranean-Style Beans and Greens

Prep time: 10 minutes | **Cook time:** 15 minutes | **Serves:** 2

Ingredients:

1 (14.5-ounce / 411-g) can diced tomatoes with juice
1 (15-ounce / 425-g) can cannellini beans, drained and rinsed
2 tablespoons chopped green olives, plus 1 or 2 sliced for garnish
¼ cup vegetable broth, plus more as needed
1 teaspoon extra-virgin olive oil
2 cloves garlic, minced
4 cups arugula
¼ cup freshly squeezed lemon juice

Directions:

In a medium saucepan, bring the tomatoes, beans, and chopped olives to a low boil, adding just enough broth to make the ingredients saucy (you may need more than ¼ cup if your canned tomatoes don't have a lot of juice). Reduce heat to low and simmer for about 5 minutes.

Meanwhile, in a large skillet, heat the olive oil over medium-high heat. When the oil is hot and starts to shimmer, add garlic and sauté just until it starts to turn slightly tan, about 30 seconds. Add the arugula and lemon juice, stirring to coat leaves with the olive oil and juice. Cover, reduce the heat to low, and simmer for 3 to 5 minutes. Serve the beans over the greens and garnish with olive slices.

Per Serving

calories: 262 | fat: 5.9g | protein: 13.2g | carbs: 40.4g

Swoodles with Almond Butter Sauce

Prep time: 20 minutes | **Cook time:** 20 minutes | **Serves:** 4

Ingredients:

Sauce:
1 garlic clove
1-inch piece fresh ginger, peeled and sliced
¼ cup chopped yellow onion
¾ cup almond butter
1 tablespoon tamari
1 tablespoon raw honey
1 teaspoon paprika
1 tablespoon fresh lemon juice
⅛ teaspoon ground red pepper

¼ cup water
Swoodles:
2 large sweet potatoes, spiralized
2 tablespoons coconut oil, melted
Sea salt and ground black pepper, to taste
For Serving:
½ cup fresh parsley, chopped
½ cup thinly sliced scallions
Sea salt and ground black pepper, to taste

Directions:
Make the Sauce

Put the garlic, ginger, and onion in a food processor, then pulse to combine well.

Add the almond butter, tamari, honey, paprika, lemon juice, ground red pepper, salt, and black pepper to the food processor. Pulse to combine well.

Pour in the water during the pulsing until the mixture is thick and smooth.

Make the Swoodles

Preheat the oven to 425ºF (220ºC). Line a baking sheet with parchment paper. Put the spiralized sweet potato in a bowl, then drizzle with olive oil. Toss to coat well. Transfer them on the baking sheet. Sprinkle with salt and pepper.

Bake in the preheated oven for 20 minutes or until lightly browned and al dente.

Check the doneness during the baking and remove any well- cooked swoodles.

Transfer the swoodles on a large plate and spread with sauce, parsley, and scallions. Toss to serve.

Per Serving calories: 441 | fat: 33.6g | protein: 12.0g | carbs: 29.6g

Small Pasta and Beans Pot

Prep time: 20 minutes | **Cook time:** 15 mins | **Serves:** 2 to 4

Ingredients:

1 pound (454 g) small whole wheat pasta
1 (14.5-ounce / 411-g) can diced tomatoes, juice reserved
1 (15-ounce / 425-g) can cannellini beans, drained and rinsed
2 tablespoons no-salt-added tomato paste
1 red or yellow bell pepper, chopped
1 yellow onion, chopped

1 tablespoon Italian seasoning mix
3 garlic cloves, minced
¼ teaspoon crushed red pepper flakes, optional
1 tablespoon extra-virgin olive oil
5 cups water
1 bunch kale, stemmed and chopped
½ cup pitted Kalamata olives, chopped
1 cup sliced basil

Directions:

Except for the kale, olives, and basil, combine all the ingredients in a pot. Stir to mix well. Bring to a boil over high heat. Stir constantly. Reduce the heat to medium high and add the kale.

Cook for 10 minutes or until the pasta is al dente. Stir constantly. Transfer all of them on a large plate and serve with olives and basil on top.

Per Serving calories: 357 | fat: 7.6g | protein: 18.2g | carbs: 64.5g

Tomato Sauce and Basil Pesto Fettuccine

Prep time: 15 minutes | **Cook time:** 15 minutes | **Serves:** 4

Ingredients:

4 Roma tomatoes, diced
2 teaspoons no-salt-added tomato paste
1 tablespoon chopped fresh oregano
2 garlic cloves, minced
1 cup low-sodium vegetable soup
½ teaspoon sea salt

1 packed cup fresh basil leaves
¼ cup pine nuts
¼ cup grated Parmesan cheese
2 tablespoons extra-virgin olive oil
1 pound (454 g) cooked whole-grain fettuccine

Directions:

Put the tomatoes, tomato paste, oregano, garlic, vegetable soup, and salt in a skillet. Stir to mix well.

Cook over medium heat for 10 minutes or until lightly thickened. Put the remaining ingredients, except for the fettuccine, in a food processor and pulse to combine until smooth.

Pour the puréed basil mixture into the tomato mixture, then add the fettuccine. Cook for a few minutes or until heated through and the fettuccine is well coated.

Serve immediately.

Per Serving
calories: 389 | fat: 22.7g | protein: 9.7g | carbs: 40.2g

Bean and Veggie Pasta

Prep time: 10 minutes | **Cook time:** 15 minutes | **Serves:**2

Ingredients:

16 ounces (454 g) small whole wheat pasta, such as penne, farfalle, or macaroni
5 cups water
1 (15-ounce / 425-g) can cannellini beans, drained and rinsed
1 (14.5-ounce / 411-g) can diced (with juice) or crushed tomatoes
1 yellow onion, chopped
1 red or yellow bell pepper, chopped

2 tablespoons tomato paste
1 tablespoon olive oil
3 garlic cloves, minced
¼ teaspoon crushed red pepper (optional)
1 bunch kale, stemmed and chopped
1 cup sliced basil
½ cup pitted Kalamata olives, chopped

Directions:

Add the pasta, water, beans, tomatoes (with juice if using diced), onion, bell pepper, tomato paste, oil, garlic, and crushed red pepper (if desired), to a large stockpot. Bring to a boil over high heat, stirring often.

Reduce the heat to medium-high, add the kale, and cook, continuing to stir often, until the pasta is al dente, about 10 minutes.

Remove from the heat and let sit for 5 minutes. Garnish with the basil and olives and serve.

Per Serving

calories: 565 | fat: 17.7g | protein: 18.0g | carbs: 85.5g

Gouda Beef and Spinach Fettuccine

Prep time: 10 minutes | **Cook time:** 15 minutes | **Serves:**6

Ingredients:

10 ounces (283 g) ground beef
1 pound (454 g) fettuccine pasta
1 cup gouda cheese, shredded
1 cup fresh spinach, torn
1 medium onion, chopped

2 cups tomatoes, diced
1 tablespoon olive oil
1 teaspoon salt
½ teaspoon ground black pepper

Directions:

Heat the olive oil on Sauté mode in the Instant Pot. Stir-fry the beef and onion for 5 minutes. Add the pasta. Pour water enough to cover and season with salt and pepper. Cook on High Pressure for 5 minutes. Do a quick release. Press Sauté and stir in the tomato and spinach; cook for 5 minutes. Top with Gouda to serve.

Per Serving calories: 493 | fat: 17.7g | protein: 20.6g | carbs: 64.3g

Roasted Ratatouille Pasta

Prep time: 10 minutes | **Cook time:** 30 minutes | **Serves:**2

Ingredients:

1 small eggplant (about 8 ounces / 227 g)
1 small zucchini
1 portobello mushroom
1 Roma tomato, halved
½ medium sweet red pepper, seeded
½ teaspoon salt, plus additional for the pasta water

1 teaspoon Italian herb seasoning
1 tablespoon olive oil
2 cups farfalle pasta (about 8 ounces / 227 g)
2 tablespoons minced sun-dried tomatoes in olive oil with herbs
2 tablespoons prepared pesto

Directions:

Slice the ends off the eggplant and zucchini. Cut them lengthwise into ½- inch slices. Place the eggplant, zucchini, mushroom, tomato, and red pepper in a large bowl and sprinkle with ½ teaspoon of salt. Using your hands, toss the vegetables well so that they're covered evenly with the salt. Let them rest for about 10 minutes.

While the vegetables are resting, preheat the oven to 400°F (205°C). Line a baking sheet with parchment paper.

When the oven is hot, drain off any liquid from the vegetables and pat them dry with a paper towel. Add the Italian herb seasoning and olive oil to the vegetables and toss well to coat both sides.

Lay the vegetables out in a single layer on the baking sheet. Roast them for 15 to 20 minutes, flipping them over after about 10 minutes or once they start to brown on the underside. When the vegetables are charred in spots, remove them from the oven.

While the vegetables are roasting, fill a large saucepan with water. Add salt and cook the pasta until al dente, about 8 to 10 minutes. Drain the pasta, reserving ½ cup of the pasta water. When cool enough to handle, cut the vegetables into large chunks (about 2 inches) and add them to the hot pasta. Stir in the sun-dried tomatoes and pesto and toss everything well. Serve immediately.

Per Serving calories: 613 | fat: 16.0g | protein: 23.1g | carbs: 108.5g

Lentil and Mushroom Pasta

Prep time: 10 minutes | **Cook time:** 50 minutes | **Serves:** 2

Ingredients:

2 tablespoons olive oil
1 large yellow onion, finely diced
2 portobello mushrooms, trimmed and chopped finely
2 tablespoons tomato paste
3 garlic cloves, chopped
1 teaspoon oregano
2½ cups water
1 cup brown lentils
1 (28-ounce / 794-g) can diced tomatoes with basil (with juice if diced)
1 tablespoon balsamic vinegar
Salt and black pepper, to taste
Chopped basil, for garnish
8 ounces (227 g) pasta of choice, cooked

Directions:

Place a large stockpot over medium heat and add the olive oil. Once the oil is hot, add the onion and mushrooms. Cover and cook until both are soft, about 5 minutes. Add the tomato paste, garlic, and oregano and cook 2 minutes, stirring constantly. Stir in the water and lentils. Bring to a boil, then reduce the heat to medium-low and cook covered for 5 minutes. Add the tomatoes (and juice if using diced) and vinegar. Reduce the heat to low and cook until the lentils are tender, about 30 minutes.

Remove from the heat and season with salt and pepper to taste. Garnish with the basil and serve over the cooked pasta.

Per Serving

calories: 463 | fat: 15.9g | protein: 12.5g | carbs: 70.8g

Lentil Risotto

Prep time: 10 minutes | **Cook time:** 20 minutes | **Serves:** 2

Ingredients:

½ tablespoon olive oil
½ medium onion, chopped
½ cup dry lentils, soaked overnight
½ celery stalk, chopped
1 sprig parsley, chopped
½ cup Arborio (short-grain Italian) rice
1 garlic clove, lightly mashed
2 cups vegetable stock

Directions:

Press the Sauté button to heat your Instant Pot.

Add the oil and onion to the Instant Pot and sauté for 5 minutes.

Add the remaining ingredients to the Instant Pot, stirring well.

Secure the lid. Select the Manual mode and set the cooking time for 15 minutes at High Pressure.

Once cooking is complete, do a natural pressure release for 20 minutes, then release any remaining pressure. Carefully open the lid. Stir and serve hot.

Per Serving

calories: 261 | fat: 3.6g | protein: 10.6g | carbs: 47.1g

Tomato Basil Pasta

Prep time: 3 minutes | **Cook time:** 2 minutes | **Serves:** 2

Ingredients:

2 cups dried campanelle or similar pasta
1¾ cups vegetable stock
½ teaspoon salt, plus more as needed
2 tomatoes, cut into large dices
1 or 2 pinches red pepper flakes
½ teaspoon garlic powder
½ teaspoon dried oregano
10 to 12 fresh sweet basil leaves
Freshly ground black pepper, to taste

Directions:

In your Instant Pot, stir together the pasta, stock, and salt. Scatter the tomatoes on top (do not stir).

Secure the lid. Select the Manual mode and set the cooking time for 2 minutes at High Pressure.

Once cooking is complete, do a quick pressure release. Carefully open the lid.

Stir in the red pepper flakes, oregano, and garlic powder. If there's more than a few tablespoons of liquid in the bottom, select Sauté and cook for 2 to 3 minutes until it evaporates.

When ready to serve, chiffonade the basil and stir it in. Taste and season with more salt and pepper, as needed. Serve warm.

Per Serving

calories: 415 | fat: 2.0g | protein: 15.2g | carbs: 84.2g

Pork and Spinach Spaghetti

Prep time: 15 minutes | **Cook time:** 16 minutes | **Serves:** 4

Ingredients:

2 tablespoons olive oil
½ cup onion, chopped
1 garlic clove, minced
1 pound (454 g) ground pork
2 cups water
1 (14-ounce / 397-g) can diced tomatoes, drained
½ cup sun-dried tomatoes
1 tablespoon dried oregano
1 teaspoon Italian seasoning
1 fresh jalapeño chile, stemmed, seeded, and minced
1 teaspoon salt
8 ounces (227 g) dried spaghetti, halved
1 cup spinach

Directions:

Warm oil on Sauté. Add onion and garlic and cook for 2 minutes until softened. Stir in pork and cook for 5 minutes. Stir in jalapeño, water, sun-dried tomatoes, Italian seasoning, oregano, diced tomatoes, and salt with the chicken; mix spaghetti and press to submerge into the sauce.

Seal the lid and cook on High Pressure for 9 minutes. Release the pressure quickly. Stir in spinach, close lid again, and simmer on Keep Warm for 5 minutes until spinach is wilted.

Per Serving

calories: 621 | fat: 32.2g | protein: 29.1g | carbs: 53.9g

Rigatoni and Zucchini Minestrone

Prep time: 20 minutes | **Cook time:** 7 minutes | **Serves:** 4

Ingredients:

3 tablespoons olive oil
1 onion, diced
1 celery stalk, diced
1 large carrot, peeled and diced
14 ounces (397 g) canned chopped tomatoes
4 ounces (113 g) rigatoni
3 cups water
1 cup chopped zucchini
1 bay leaf
1 teaspoon mixed herbs
¼ teaspoon cayenne pepper
½ teaspoon salt
¼ cup shredded Pecorino Romano cheese
1 garlic clove, minced
⅓ cup olive oil-based pesto

Directions:

Heat oil on Sauté and cook onion, celery, garlic, and carrot for 3 minutes, stirring occasionally until the vegetables are softened. Stir in rigatoni, tomatoes, water, zucchini, bay leaf, herbs, cayenne, and salt. Seal the lid and cook on High for 4 minutes. Do a natural pressure release for 5 minutes. Adjust the taste of the soup with salt and black pepper, and remove the bay leaf. Ladle the soup into serving bowls and drizzle the pesto over. Serve with the garlic toasts.

Per Serving

calories: 278 | fat: 23.4g | protein: 6.7g | carbs: 12.2g

Asparagus and Broccoli Primavera Farfalle

Prep time: 15 minutes | **Cook time:** 12 minutes | **Serves:** 4

Ingredients:

1 bunch asparagus, trimmed, cut into 1-inch pieces
2 cups broccoli florets
3 tablespoons olive oil
3 teaspoons salt
10 ounces (283 g) egg noodles
3 garlic cloves, minced
2½ cups vegetable stock
½ cup heavy cream
1 cup small tomatoes, halved
¼ cup chopped basil
½ cup grated Parmesan cheese

Directions:

Pour 2 cups of water, add the noodles, 2 tablespoons of olive oil, garlic and salt. Place a trivet over the water. Combine asparagus, broccoli, remaining olive oil and salt in a bowl. Place the vegetables on the trivet. Seal the lid and cook on Steam for 12 minutes on High. Do a quick release. Remove the vegetables to a plate. Stir the heavy cream and tomatoes in the pasta. Press Sauté and simmer the cream until desired consistency.

Gently mix in the asparagus and broccoli. Garnish with basil and Parmesan, to serve.

Per Serving

calories: 544 | fat: 23.8g | protein: 18.5g | carbs: 66.1g

Chickpea Curry

Prep time: 10 minutes | **Cook time:** 24 minutes | **Serves:** 4

Ingredients:

½ cup raw chickpeas
1½ tablespoons cooking oil
½ cup chopped onions
1 bay leaf
½ tablespoon grated garlic
¼ tablespoon grated ginger
¾ cup water
Boiled white rice, for serving
1 cup fresh tomato purée
½ green chili, finely chopped
¼ teaspoon turmeric
½ teaspoon coriander powder
1 teaspoon chili powder
1 cup chopped baby spinach
Salt, to taste

Directions:

Add the oil and onions to the Instant Pot. Sauté for 5 minutes.

Stir in ginger, garlic paste, green chili and bay leaf. Cook for 1 minute, then add all the spices.

Add the chickpeas, tomato purée and the water to the pot.

Cover and secure the lid. Turn its pressure release handle to the sealing position.

Cook on the Manual function with High Pressure for 15 minutes.

After the beep, do a Natural release for 20 minutes.

Stir in spinach and cook for 3 minutes on the Sauté setting. Serve hot with boiled white rice.

Per Serving

calories: 176 | fat: 6.8g | protein: 6.7g | carbs: 24.1g

Cumin Quinoa Pilaf

Prep time: 5 minutes | **Cook time:** 5 minutes | **Serves:** 2

Ingredients:

2 tablespoons extra virgin olive oil
2 cloves garlic, minced
3 cups water
2 cups quinoa, rinsed
2 teaspoons ground cumin
2 teaspoons turmeric
Salt, to taste
1 handful parsley, chopped

Directions:

Press the Sauté button to heat your Instant Pot.

Once hot, add the oil and garlic to the pot, stir and cook for 1 minute. Add water, quinoa, cumin, turmeric, and salt, stirring well. Lock the lid. Select the Manual mode and set the cooking time for 1 minute at High Pressure.

When the timer beeps, perform a natural pressure release for 10 minutes, then release any remaining pressure. Carefully remove the lid. Fluff the quinoa with a fork. Season with more salt, if needed.

Sprinkle the chopped parsley on top and serve.

Per Serving

calories: 384 | fat: 12.3g | protein: 12.8g | carbs: 57.4g

Shrimp and Asparagus Risotto

Prep time: 15 minutes | **Cook time:** 58 minutes | **Serves:** 4

Ingredients:

1 tablespoon olive oil
1 pound (454 g) asparagus, trimmed and roughly chopped
1 cup spinach, chopped
1½ cups mushrooms, chopped
1 cup rice, rinsed and drained
1¼ cups chicken broth
¾ cup milk
1 tablespoon coconut oil
16 shrimp, cleaned and deveined
Salt and ground black pepper, to taste
¾ cup Parmesan cheese, shredded

Directions:

Warm the oil on Sauté. Add spinach, mushrooms and asparagus and Sauté for 10 minutes until cooked through. Press Cancel. Add rice, milk and chicken broth to the pot as you stir. Seal the lid, press Multigrain and cook for 40 minutes on High Pressure. Do a quick release, open the lid and put the rice on a serving plate.

Take back the empty pot to the pressure cooker, add coconut oil and press Sauté. Add shrimp and cook each side for 4 minutes until cooked through and turns pink. Set shrimp over rice, add pepper and salt for seasoning. Serve topped with shredded Parmesan cheese.

Per Serving

calories: 385 | fat: 14.3g | protein: 16.5g | carbs: 48.4g

Pancetta with Garbanzo Beans

Prep time: 10 minutes | **Cook time:** 38 minutes | **Serves:** 6

Ingredients:

3 strips pancetta
1 onion, diced
15 ounces (425 g) canned garbanzo beans
2 cups water
1 cup apple cider
2 garlic cloves, minced
½ cup ketchup
¼ cup sugar
1 teaspoon ground mustard powder
1 teaspoon salt
1 teaspoon black pepper
Fresh parsley, for garnish

Directions:

Cook pancetta for 5 minutes, until crispy, on Sauté mode. Add onion and garlic, and cook for 3 minutes until soft. Mix in garbanzo beans, ketchup, sugar, salt, apple cider, mustard powder, water, and pepper.

Seal the lid, press Bean/Chili and cook on High Pressure for 30 minutes. Release pressure naturally for 10 minutes. Serve in bowls garnished with parsley.

Per Serving

calories: 163 | fat: 5.7g | protein: 5.4g | carbs: 22.1g

Rice and Sweet Poqtato Pilaf

Prep time: 15 minutes | **Cook time:** 10 mins | **Serves:** 4 to 6

Ingredients:

2 tablespoons extra-virgin olive oil
1 onion, chopped fine
½ teaspoon table salt
2 garlic cloves, minced
1½ teaspoons ground turmeric
1 teaspoon ground coriander
⅛ teaspoon cayenne pepper
2 cups chicken broth
1½ cups long-grain white rice, rinsed
12 ounces (340 g) sweet potato, peeled, quartered lengthwise, and sliced ½ inch thick
½ preserved lemon, pulp and white pith removed, rind rinsed and minced (2 tablespoons)
½ cup shelled pistachios, toasted and chopped
¼ cup fresh cilantro leaves
¼ cup pomegranate seeds

Directions:

Using highest Sauté function, heat oil in Instant Pot until shimmering. Add onion and salt and cook until onion is softened, about 5 minutes.

Stir in garlic, turmeric, coriander, and cayenne and cook until fragrant, about 30 seconds. Stir in broth, rice, and sweet potato. Lock lid in place and close pressure release valve. Select Manual function and cook for 4 minutes. Turn off Instant Pot and quick release pressure. Carefully remove lid, allowing steam to escape away from you.

Add preserved lemon and gently fluff rice with fork to combine. Lay clean dish towel over pot, replace lid, and let sit for 5 minutes. Season with salt and pepper to taste. Transfer to serving dish and sprinkle with pistachios, cilantro, and pomegranate seeds. Serve.

Per Serving

calories: 698 | fat: 22.8g | protein: 36.8g | carbs: 85.5g

Spinach and Ricotta Stuffed Pasta Shells

Prep time: 15 minutes | **Cook time:** 35 minutes | **Serves:** 6

Ingredients:

2 cups onion, chopped
1 cup carrot, chopped
3 garlic cloves, minced
3½ tablespoons olive oil,
1 (28-ounce / 794-g)
canned tomatoes, crushed
12 ounces (340 g) conchiglie
pasta
1 tablespoon olive oil
2 cups ricotta cheese,
crumbled

1½ cups feta cheese,
crumbled
2 cups spinach, chopped
¾ cup grated Pecorino
Romano cheese
2 tablespoons chopped
fresh chives
1 tablespoon chopped fresh
dill
Salt and ground black
pepper to taste
1 cup shredded Cheddar
cheese

Directions:

Warm olive oil on Sauté. Add onion, carrot, and garlic, and cook for 5 minutes until tender. Stir in tomatoes and cook for another 10 minutes.

Remove to a bowl and set aside.

Wipe the pot with a damp cloth, add pasta and cover with enough water. Seal the lid and cook for 5 minutes on High Pressure. Do a quick release and drain the pasta. Lightly Grease olive oil to a baking sheet.

In a bowl, combine feta and ricotta cheese.

Add spinach, Pecorino Romano cheese, dill, and chives, and stir well. Adjust the seasonings. Using a spoon, fill the shells with the mixture.

Spread 4 cups tomato sauce on the baking sheet. Place the stuffed shells over with seam-sides down and sprinkle Cheddar cheese atop. Use aluminum foil to the cover the baking dish.

Pour 1 cup of water in the pot of the Pressure cooker and insert the trivet. Lower the baking dish onto the trivet. Seal the lid, and cook for 15 minutes on High Pressure.

Do a quick pressure release. Take away the foil. Place the stuffed shells to serving plates and top with tomato sauce before serving.

Per Serving

calories: 730 | fat: 41.5g | protein: 30.0g | carbs: 62.7g

Grana Padano Risotto

Prep time: 10 minutes | **Cook time:** 23 minutes | **Serves:** 6

Ingredients:

1 tablespoon olive oil
1 white onion,
chopped
2 cups Carnaroli rice,
rinsed
¼ cup dry white wine
4 cups chicken stock

1 teaspoon salt
½ teaspoon ground white pepper
2 tablespoons Grana padano
cheese, grated
¼ tablespoon Grana padano
cheese, flakes

Directions:

Warm oil on Sauté. Stir-fry onion for 3 minutes until soft and translucent. Add rice and cook for 5 minutes stirring occasionally.

Pour wine into the pot to deglaze, scrape away any browned bits of food from the pan.

Stir in stock, pepper, and salt to the pot. Seal the lid, press Rice and cook on High Pressure for 15 minutes. Release the pressure quickly.

Sprinkle with grated Parmesan cheese and stir well. Top with flaked cheese for garnish before serving.

Per Serving

calories: 307 | fat: 6.0g | protein: 8.2g | carbs: 53.2g

Brown Rice Stuffed Portobello Mushrooms

Prep time: 15 minutes | **Cook time:** 10 minutes | **Serves:** 4

Ingredients:

4 large portobello
mushrooms, stems and gills
removed
2 tablespoons olive oil
½ cup brown rice, cooked
1 tomato, seed removed and
chopped
¼ cup black olives, pitted
and chopped

1 green bell pepper, seeded
and diced
½ cup feta cheese,
crumbled
Juice of 1 lemon
½ teaspoon salt
½ teaspoon ground black
pepper
Minced fresh cilantro, for
garnish
1 cup vegetable broth

Directions:

Brush the mushrooms with olive oil.

Arrange the mushrooms in a single layer in an oiled baking pan. In a bowl, mix the rice, tomato, olives, bell pepper, feta cheese, lemon juice, salt, and black pepper.

Spoon the rice mixture into the mushrooms. Pour in the broth, seal the lid and cook on High Pressure for 10 minutes. Do a quick release. Garnish with fresh cilantro and serve immediately.

Per Serving

calories: 190 | fat: 12.5g | protein: 5.9g | carbs: 15.2g

Turkey and Bell Pepper Tortiglioni

Prep time: 20 minutes | **Cook time:** 10 minutes | **Serves:** 6

Ingredients:

2 teaspoons chili powder
1 teaspoon salt
1 teaspoon cumin
1 teaspoon onion powder
1 teaspoon garlic powder
½ teaspoon thyme
1½ pounds (680 g) turkey breast, cut into strips
1 tablespoon olive oil
1 red onion, cut into wedges
4 garlic cloves, minced
3 cups chicken broth
1 cup salsa
1 pound (454 g) tortiglioni
1 red bell pepper, chopped diagonally
1 yellow bell pepper, chopped diagonally
1 green bell pepper, chopped diagonally
1 cup shredded Gouda cheese
½ cup sour cream
½ cup chopped parsley

Directions:

In a bowl, mix chili powder, cumin, garlic powder, onion powder, salt, and oregano. Reserve 1 teaspoon of seasoning. Coat turkey with the remaining seasoning.

Warm oil on Sauté. Add turkey strips and sauté for 4 to 5 minutes until browned. Place the turkey in a bowl. Sauté the onion and garlic for 1 minute in the cooker until soft. Press Cancel. Mix in salsa, broth, and scrape the bottom of any brown bits. Into the broth mixture, stir in tortiglioni pasta and cover with bell peppers and chicken.

Seal lid, cook for 5 minutes , HighPressure.1 quick Pressure release.

Open the lid and sprinkle with shredded gouda cheese and reserved seasoning, and stir well. Divide into plates and top with sour cream. Add parsley for garnishing and serve.

Per Serving

calories: 646 | fat: 21.7g | protein: 41.1g | carbs: 72.9g

Carrot Risoni

Prep time: 5 minutes | **Cook time:** 11 minutes | **Serves:** 6

Ingredients:

1 cup orzo, rinsed
2 cups water
2 carrots, cut into sticks
1 large onion, chopped
2 tablespoons olive oil
Salt, to taste
Fresh cilantro, chopped, for garnish

Directions:

Heat oil on Sauté. Add onion and carrots and stir-fry for about 10 minutes until tender and crispy. Remove to a plate and set aside. Add water, salt and orzo in the instant pot.

Seal the lid and cook on High Pressure for 1 minute. Do a quick release. Fluff the cooked orzo with a fork. Transfer to a serving plate and top with the carrots and onion. Serve scattered with cilantro.

Per Serving

calories: 121 | fat: 4.9g | protein: 1.7g | carbs: 18.1g

Roasted Butternut Squash and Rice

Prep time: 15 minutes | **Cook time:** 15 minutes | **Serves:** 4

Ingredients:

½ cup water
2 cups vegetable broth
1 small butternut squash, peeled and sliced
2 tablespoons olive oil, divided
1 teaspoon salt
1 teaspoon freshly ground black pepper
1 cup feta cheese, cubed
1 tablespoon coconut aminos
2 teaspoons arrowroot starch
1 cup jasmine rice, cooked

Directions:

Pour the rice and broth in the pot and stir to combine. In a bowl, toss butternut squash with 1 tablespoon of olive oil and season with salt and black pepper.

In another bowl, mix the remaining olive oil, water and coconut aminos. Toss feta in the mixture, add the arrowroot starch, and toss again to combine well. Transfer to a greased baking dish.

Lay a trivet over the rice and place the baking dish on the trivet. Seal the lid and cook on High for 15 minutes. Do a quick pressure release. Fluff the rice with a fork and serve with squash and feta.

Per Serving

calories: 258 | fat: 14.9g | protein: 7.8g | carbs: 23.2g

Pesto Arborio Rice and Veggie Bowls

Prep time: 10 minutes | **Cook time:** 1 minute | **Serves:** 2

Ingredients:

1 cup arborio rice, rinsed and drained
2 cups vegetable broth
Salt and black pepper to taste
1 potato, peeled, cubed
1 head broccoli, cut into small florets
1 bunch baby carrots, peeled
¼ cabbage, chopped
2 eggs
¼ cup pesto sauce
Lemon wedges, for serving

Directions:

In the pot, mix broth, pepper, rice and salt. Set trivet to the inner pot on top of rice and add a steamer basket to the top of the trivet. Mix carrots, potato, eggs and broccoli in the steamer basket. Add pepper and salt for seasoning.

Seal the lid and cook for 1 minute on High Pressure. Quick release the pressure. Take away the trivet and steamer basket from the pot.

Set the eggs in a bowl of ice water. Then peel and halve the eggs. Use a fork to fluff rice.

Adjust the seasonings. In two bowls, equally divide rice, broccoli, eggs, carrots, sweet potatoes, and a dollop of pesto. Serve alongside a lemon wedge.

Per Serving
calories: 858 | fat: 24.4g | protein: 26.4g | carbs: 136.2g

Rice and Bean Stuffed Zucchini

Prep time: 10 minutes | **Cook time:** 15 minutes | **Serves:** 4

Ingredients:

2 small zucchinis, halved lengthwise
½ cup cooked rice
½ cup canned white beans, drained and rinsed
½ cup chopped tomatoes
½ cup chopped toasted cashew nuts
½ cup grated Parmesan cheese
1 tablespoon olive oil
½ teaspoon salt
½ teaspoon freshly ground black pepper

Directions:

Pour 1 cup of water in the instant pot and insert a trivet. Scoop out the pulp of zucchini and chop roughly.

In a bowl, mix the zucchini pulp, rice, tomatoes, cashew nuts, ¼ cup of Parmesan, olive oil, salt, and black pepper. Fill the zucchini boats with the mixture, and arrange the stuffed boats in a single layer on the trivet. Seal the lid and cook for 15 minutes on Steam on High. Do a quick release and serve.

Per Serving calories: 239 | fat: 14.7g | protein: 9.4g

Chard and Mushroom Risotto

Prep time: 15 minutes | **Cook time:** 20 minutes | **Serves:** 4

Ingredients:

3 tablespoons olive oil
1 onion, chopped
2 Swiss chard, stemmed and chopped
1 cup risotto rice
⅓ cup white wine
3 cups vegetable stock
½ teaspoon salt
½ cup mushrooms
4 tablespoons pumpkin seeds, toasted
⅓ cup grated Pecorino Romano cheese

Directions:

Heat oil on Sauté, and cook onion and mushrooms for 5 minutes, stirring, until tender. Add the rice and cook for a minute. Stir in wine and cook for 2 to 3 minutes until almost evaporated.

Pour in stock and season with salt. Seal the lid and cook on High Pressure for 10 minutes.

Do a quick release. Stir in chard until wilted, mix in cheese to melt, and serve scattered with pumpkin seeds.

Per Serving

calories: 420 | fat: 17.7g | protein: 11.8g | carbs: 54.9g

Beef and Bean Stuffed Pasta Shells

Prep time: 15 minutes | **Cook time:** 17 minutes | **Serves:** 4

Ingredients:

2 tablespoons olive oil
1 pound (454 g) ground beef
1 pound (454 g) pasta shells
2 cups water
15 ounces (425 g) tomato sauce
1 (15-ounce / 425-g) can black beans, drained and rinsed
15 ounces (425 g) canned corn, drained (or 2 cups frozen corn)
10 ounces (283 g) red enchilada sauce
4 ounces (113 g) diced green chiles
1 cup shredded Mozzarella cheese
Salt and ground black pepper to taste
Additional cheese for topping
Finely chopped parsley for garnish

Directions:

Heat oil on Sauté. Add ground beef and cook for 7 minutes until it starts to brown.

Mix in pasta, tomato sauce, enchilada sauce, black beans, water, corn, and green chiles and stir to coat well. Add more water if desired.

Seal the lid and cook on High Pressure for 10 minutes. Do a quick Pressure release. Into the pasta mixture, mix in Mozzarella cheese until melted; add black pepper and salt. Garnish with parsley to serve.

Per Serving

calories: 1006 | fat: 30.0g | protein: 53.3g | carbs: 138.9g

Caprese Fusilli

Prep time: 15 minutes | **Cook time:** 7 minutes | **Serves:** 3

Ingredients:

1 tablespoon olive oil
1 onion, thinly chopped
6 garlic cloves, minced
1 teaspoon red pepper flakes
2½ cups dried fusilli
1 (15-ounce / 425-g) can tomato sauce
1 cup tomatoes, halved
1 cup water
¼ cup basil leaves
1 teaspoon salt
1 cup Ricotta cheese, crumbled
2 tablespoons chopped fresh basil

Directions:

Warm oil on Sauté. Add red pepper flakes, garlic and onion and cook for 3 minutes until soft.

Mix in fusilli, tomatoes, half of the basil leaves, water, tomato sauce, and salt. Seal the lid, and cook on High Pressure for 4 minutes. Release the pressure quickly.

Transfer the pasta to a serving platter and top with the crumbled ricotta and remaining chopped basil.

Per Serving

calories: 589 | fat: 17.7g | protein: 19.5g | carbs: 92.8g

Chicken and Spaghetti Ragù Bolognese

Prep time: 15 minutes | **Cook time:** 42 minutes | **Serves:** 8

Ingredients:

2 tablespoons olive oil
6 ounces (170 g) bacon, cubed
1 onion, minced
1 carrot, minced
1 celery stalk, minced
2 garlic cloves, crushed
¼ cup tomato paste
¼ teaspoon crushed red pepper flakes
1½ pounds (680 g) ground chicken
½ cup white wine
1 cup milk
1 cup chicken broth
Salt, to taste
1 pound (454 g) spaghetti

Directions:

Warm oil on Sauté. Add bacon and fry for 5 minutes until crispy. Add celery, carrot, garlic and onion and cook for 5 minutes until fragrant. Mix in red pepper flakes and tomato paste, and cook for 2 minutes. Break chicken into small pieces and place in the pot.

Cook for 10 minutes, as you stir, until browned. Pour in wine and simmer for 2 minutes. Add chicken broth and milk. Seal the lid and cook for 15 minutes on High Pressure. Release the pressure quickly.

Add the spaghetti and stir. Seal the lid, and cook on High Pressure for another 5 minutes.

Release the pressure quickly. Check the pasta for doneness. Taste, adjust the seasoning and serve hot.

Per Serving calories: 477 | fat: 20.6g | protein: 28.1g | carbs: 48.5g

Cheesy Tomato Linguine

Prep time: 15 minutes | **Cook time:** 11 minutes | **Serves:** 4

Ingredients:

2 tablespoons olive oil
1 small onion, diced
2 garlic cloves, minced
1 cup cherry tomatoes, halved
1½ cups vegetable stock
¼ cup julienned basil leaves
1 teaspoon salt
½ teaspoon ground black pepper
¼ teaspoon red chili flakes
1 pound (454 g) Linguine noodles, halved
Fresh basil leaves for garnish
½ cup Parmigiano-Reggiano cheese, grated

Directions:

Warm oil on Sauté. Add onion and Sauté for 2 minutes until soft. Mix garlic and tomatoes and sauté for 4 minutes. To the pot, add vegetable stock, salt, julienned basil, red chili flakes and pepper.

Add linguine to the tomato mixture until covered. Seal the lid and cook on High Pressure for 5 minutes.

Naturally release the pressure for 5 minutes. Stir the mixture to ensure it is broken down.

Divide into plates. Top with basil and Parmigiano-Reggiano cheese and serve.

Per Serving calories: 311 fat: 11.3g protein: 10.3g carbs: 42.1g

Parmesan Squash Linguine

Prep time: 15 minutes | **Cook time:** 5 minutes | **Serves:** 4

Ingredients:

1 cup flour
2 teaspoons salt
2 eggs
4 cups water
1 cup seasoned breadcrumbs
½ cup grated Parmesan cheese, plus more for garnish
1 yellow squash, peeled and sliced
1 pound (454 g) linguine
24 ounces (680 g) canned seasoned tomato sauce
2 tablespoons olive oil
1 cup shredded Mozzarella cheese
Minced fresh basil, for garnish

Directions:

Break the linguine in half. Put it in the pot and add water and half of salt. Seal the lid and cook on High Pressure for 5 minutes. Combine the flour and 1 teaspoon of salt in a bowl. In another bowl, whisk the eggs and 2 tablespoons of water. In a third bowl, mix the breadcrumbs and Mozzarella cheese.

Coat each squash slices in the flour. Shake off excess flour, dip in the egg wash, and dredge in the bread crumbs. Set aside. Quickly release the pressure. Remove linguine to a serving bowl and mix in the tomato sauce and sprinkle with fresh basil. Heat oil on Sauté and fry breaded squash until crispy.

Serve the squash topped Mozzarella cheese with the linguine on side.

Per Serving
calories: 857 | fat: 17.0g | protein: 33.2g | carbs: 146.7g

Italian Chicken Pasta (Italian)

Preparation Time: 10 minutes **Cooking Time:** 9 minutes
Servings: 8

Ingredients:

1 lb. chicken breast, skinless, boneless, and cut into chunks
1 tsp garlic, minced
1/2 cup cream cheese
2 tomatoes, diced 2 cups of water
1 cup mozzarella cheese, shredded
1 1/2 tsp Italian seasoning
1 cup mushrooms, diced
1/2 onion, diced
16 oz whole wheat penne pasta Pepper, Salt

Directions:

Add all except cheeses into the inner pot of instant pot and stir well.

Seal pot with lid and cook on high for 9 minutes.

Once done, allow to release pressure naturally for 5 minutes then release remaining using quick release. Remove lid.

Add cheeses and stir well and serve.

Per Serving
Calories 328 Fat 8.5 g Carbohydrates 42.7 g Sugar 1.4 g Protein 23.7 g Cholesterol 55 mg

Red Bean Curry

Prep time: 10 minutes | **Cook time:** 24 minutes | **Serves:** 4

Ingredients:

½ cup raw red beans
1½ tablespoons cooking oil
½ cup chopped onions
1 bay leaf
½ tablespoon grated garlic
¼ tablespoon grated ginger
¾ cup water
1 cup fresh tomato purée
Boiled white rice or quinoa, for serve

½ green chili, finely chopped
¼ teaspoon turmeric
½ teaspoon coriander powder
1 teaspoon chili powder
1 cup chopped baby spinach
Salt, to taste

Directions:

Add the oil and onions to the Instant Pot. Sauté for 5 minutes.

Stir in ginger, garlic paste, green chili and bay leaf. Cook for 1 minute, then add all the spices.

Add the red beans, tomato purée and water to the pot.

Cover and secure the lid. Turn its pressure release handle to the sealing position.

Cook on the Manual function with High Pressure for 15 minutes. After the beep, do a Natural release for 20 minutes.

Stir in spinach and cook for 3 minutes on the Sauté setting.

Serve hot with boiled white rice or quinoa.

Per Serving

calories: 159 | fat: 5.6g | protein: 6.8g | carbs: 22.5g

Easy Simple Pesto Pasta (Italian)

Preparation Time: 10 minutes **Cooking Time:** 8 minutes
Servings: 4 to 6

Ingredients:

1-pound (454 g) spaghetti
3 cloves garlic
1 teaspoon salt
1/2 cup toasted pine nuts
1/4 cup lemon juice
1 cup extra-virgin olive oil

4 cups fresh basil leaves, stems removed
1/2 teaspoon freshly ground black pepper
1/2 cup grated Parmesan cheese

Directions:

Bring a large pot of salted water to a boil. Add the spaghetti to the pot and cook for 8 minutes. In a food processor, place the remaining , except for the olive oil, and pulse.

While the processor is running, slowly drizzle the olive oil through the top opening. Process until all the olive oil has been added. Reserve ½ cup of the cooking liquid. Drain the pasta and put it into a large bowl. Add the pesto and cooking liquid to the bowl of pasta and toss everything together. Serve immediately.

Per Serving

calories: 1067 fat: 72.0g protein: 23.0g carbs: 91.0g

Pesto Chicken Pasta (Italian)

Preparation Time: 10 minutes **Cooking Time:** 10 minutes
Servings: 6

Ingredients:

1 lb. chicken breast, skinless, boneless, and diced
3 tbsp olive oil
1/4 cup heavy cream
3 1/2 cups water Pepper
6 oz basil pesto

1/2 cup parmesan cheese, shredded
1 tsp Italian seasoning
16 oz whole wheat pasta
Salt

Directions:

Season chicken with Italian seasoning, pepper, and salt.

Add oil into the inner pot of instant pot and set the pot on sauté mode.

Add chicken to the pot and sauté until brown.

Add remaining except for parmesan cheese, heavy cream, and pesto and stir well.

Seal pot with lid and cook on high for 5 minutes.

Once done, release pressure using quick release. Remove lid.

Stir in parmesan cheese, heavy cream, and pesto and serve.

Per Serving

Calories 475 Fat 14.7 g Carbohydrates 57 g Sugar 2.8 g Protein 28.7 g Cholesterol 61 mg

Mac & Cheese (Italian)

Preparation Time: 10 minutes **Cooking Time:** 4 minutes
Servings: 8

Ingredients:

1 lb. whole grain pasta
4 cups cheddar cheese, shredded
1/4 tsp garlic powder
1/2 tsp ground mustard
2 tbsp olive oil

1/2 cup parmesan cheese, grated
1 cup milk
4 cups of water Pepper
Salt

Directions:

Add pasta, garlic powder, mustard, oil, water, pepper, and salt into the instant pot. Seal pot with lid and cook on high for 4 minutes. Once done, release pressure using quick release. Remove lid. Add remaining and stir well and serve.

Per Serving

Calories 509 Fat 25.7 g Carbohydrates 43.8 g Sugar 3.8 g Protein 27.3 g Cholesterol 66 mg

Fresh Sauce Pasta (Italian)

Preparation Time: 15 minutes **Cooking Time:** 15 minutes
Servings: 4

Ingredients:

1/8 teaspoon salt, plus more for cooking the pasta
1 garlic clove, crushed
3 tomatoes, diced
2 tablespoons chopped fresh basil
1/4 cup olive oil
1-pound penne pasta
3 cups chopped scallions, white and green parts
1/8 teaspoon freshly ground black pepper
Freshly grated Parmesan cheese, for serving

Directions:

Bring a large pot of salted water to a boil over high heat. Drop in the pasta, stir, and return the water to a boil. Boil the pasta for about 6 minutes or until al dente.

A couple minutes before the pasta is completely cooked, in a medium saucepan over medium heat, heat the olive oil.

Add the garlic and cook for 30 seconds.

Stir in the scallions and tomatoes. Cover the pan and cook for 2 to 3 minutes.

Drain the pasta and add it to the vegetables. Stir in the basil and season with the salt and pepper. Top with the Parmesan cheese.

Per Serving

Calories: 477; Total Fat: 16g; Saturated Fat: 2g; Carbohydrates: 72g; Protein: 15g

Caprese Fusilli

Prep time: 15 minutes | **Cook time:** 7 minutes | **Serves:** 3

Ingredients:

1 tablespoon olive oil
1 onion, thinly chopped
6 garlic cloves, minced
1 teaspoon red pepper flakes
2½ cups dried fusilli
1 (15-ounce / 425-g) can tomato sauce
1 cup tomatoes, halved
1 cup water
¼ cup basil leaves
1 teaspoon salt
1 cup Ricotta cheese, crumbled
2 tablespoons chopped fresh basil

Directions:

Warm oil on Sauté. Add red pepper flakes, garlic and onion and cook for 3 minutes until soft.

Mix in fusilli, tomatoes, half of the basil leaves, water, tomato sauce, and salt. Seal the lid, and cook on High Pressure for 4 minutes. Release the pressure quickly.

Transfer the pasta to a serving platter and top with the crumbled ricotta and remaining chopped basil.

Per Serving

calories: 589 | fat: 17.7g | protein: 19.5g | carbs: 92.8g

Broccoli Pesto Spaghetti (Italian)

Preparation Time: 5 minutes **Cooking Time:** 35 minutes
Servings: 4

Ingredients:

8 oz. Spaghetti
2 tablespoons olive oil
4 garlic cloves, chopped
4 basil leaves
Salt and pepper to taste
1-pound broccoli, cut into florets
2 tablespoons blanched almonds
1 lemon, juiced

Directions:

For the pesto, combine the broccoli, oil, garlic, basil, lemon juice and almonds in a blender and pulse until well mixed and smooth.

Cook the spaghetti in a large pot of salty water for 8 minutes or until al dente. Drain well.

Mix the warm spaghetti with the broccoli pesto and serve right away.

Per Serving

Calories: 284, Fat:10.2g, Protein:10.4g, Carbohydrates:40.2g

Very Vegan Patras Pasta (Italian)

Prep time: 5 minutes **Cooking Time:** 10 mins **Servings:** 6

Ingredients:

4 quarts salted water
10 oz. gluten-free and whole-grain pasta
5 cloves garlic, minced
½ cup walnuts
2 tbsp dried cranberries (optional)
1 cup hummus Salt and pepper
1/3 cup water
½ cup olives

Directions:

Bring the salted water to a boil for cooking the pasta.

In the meantime, prepare for the hummus sauce. Combine the garlic, hummus, salt, and pepper with water in a mixing bowl. Add the walnuts, olive, and dried cranberries, if desired. Set aside.

Add the pasta in the boiling water. Cook the pasta following the manufacturer's specifications until attaining an al dente texture. Drain the pasta.

Transfer the pasta to a large serving bowl and combine with the sauce.

Per Serving

Calories: 329 Protein: 12 g Fat: 13 g Carbs: 43 g

Cheesy Spaghetti with Pine Nuts (Italian)

Prep time: 10 minutes **Cooking Time:** 10 mins **Servings:** 4

Ingredients:

8 oz. spaghetti	4 tbsp. (½ stick) unsalted butter
1 tsp. freshly ground black pepper	½ cup pine nuts
1 cup fresh grated Parmesan cheese, divided	

Directions:

Bring a large pot of salted water to a boil. Add the pasta and cook for 8 minutes.

In a large saucepan over medium heat, combine the butter, black pepper, and pine nuts. Cook for 2 to 3 minutes or until the pine nuts are lightly toasted.

Reserve ½ cup of the pasta water. Drain the pasta and put it into the pan with the pine nuts.

Add ¾ cup of Parmesan cheese and the reserved pasta water to the pasta and toss everything together to coat the pasta evenly.

To serve, put the pasta in a serving dish and top with the remaining ¼ cup of Parmesan cheese.

Per Serving

Calories: 238; Protein: 12.3g; Carbs: 3.4g; Fat: 6.3g

Italian Mac & Cheese (Italian)

Prep time: 10 minutes **Cooking Time:** 6 mins **Servings:** 4

Ingredients:

1 lb. whole grain pasta	4 cups of water
2 tsp Italian seasoning	1 cup sour cream
4 oz parmesan cheese, shredded	Pepper Salt
12 oz ricotta cheese	1 1/2 tsp onion powder
	1 1/2 tsp garlic powder

Directions:

Add all except ricotta cheese into the inner pot of instant pot and stir well.

Seal pot with lid and cook on high for 6 minutes.

Once done, allow to release pressure naturally for 5 minutes then release remaining using quick release. Remove lid.

Add ricotta cheese and stir well and serve.

Per Serving

Calories 388 Fat 25.8 g Carbohydrates 18.1 g Sugar 4 g Protein 22.8 g Cholesterol 74 mg

Penne Bolognese Pasta (Italian)

Preparation Time: 15 minutes **Cooking Time:** 20 minutes **Servings:** 2

Ingredients:

Penne pasta 7 oz. Beef 5 oz.	Parmesan Cheese 1 oz..
Shallots 26 g	Carrot 1.5 oz.
Garlic 1 clove	Thyme 1 g
Tomatoes in own juice 6 oz.	Oregano 1 g
Parsley 3 g	Celery Stalk 1 oz
Butter 20 g	Dry white wine 50 ml Olive oil 40 ml

Directions:

Pour the penne into boiling salted water and cook for 9 minutes.

Roll the beef through a meat grinder.

Dice onion, celery, carrots and garlic in a small cube.

Fry the chopped vegetables in a heated frying pan in olive oil with minced meat for 4–5 minutes, salt and pepper.

Add oregano to the fried minced meat and vegetables, pour 50 ml of wine, add the tomatoes along with the juice and simmer for 10 minutes until the tomatoes are completely softened.

Add the boiled penne and butter to the sauce and simmer for 1-2 minutes, stirring continuously.

Put in a plate, sprinkle with grated Parmesan and chopped parsley, decorate with a sprig of thyme and serve.

Per Serving

Calories: 435 Protein: 18 g Fat: 14 g Carbs: 33 g

Spaghetti all 'Olio (Italian)

Preparation Time:5 minutes **Cooking Time:**30 minutes **Servings:** 4

Ingredients:

8 oz. Spaghetti	2 tablespoons olive oil
4 garlic cloves, minced	2 red peppers, sliced
1 tablespoon lemon juice	½ cup grated parmesan cheese
Salt and pepper to taste	

Directions:

Heat the oil in a skillet and add the garlic. Cook for 30 seconds then stir in the red peppers and cook for 1 more minute on low heat, making sure only to infuse them, not to burn or fry them.

Add the lemon juice and remove off heat.

Cook the spaghetti in a large pot of salty water for 8 minutes or as stated on the package, just until they become al dente.

Drain the spaghetti well and mix them with the garlic and pepper oil.

Serve right away.

Per Serving

Calories:268, Fat:11.9g, Protein:7.1g, Carbohydrates:34.1g

Pasta with Pesto (Italian)

Preparation Time: 10 minutes **Cooking Time:** 0 minutes
Servings: 4

Ingredients:

3 tablespoons extra-virgin olive oil ¼ cup (about 2 ounces) grated Parmesan cheese
8 ounces whole-wheat pasta, cooked

½ cup fresh basil leaves
3 garlic cloves, finely minced
¼ cup pine nuts according to package instructions and drained

Directions:

In a blender or food processor, combine the olive oil, garlic, basil, cheese, and pine nuts. Pulse for 10 to 20 (1-second) pulses until everything is chopped and blended.

Toss with the hot pasta and serve.

Per Serving

Calories: 405; Protein: 13g; Total Carbohydrates: 44g; Sugars:2g; Total Fat: 21g; Saturated Fat: 4g; Cholesterol: 10mg;

Vegan Olive Pasta (Italian)

Preparation Time: 10 minutes **Cooking Time:** 5 minutes
Servings: 4

Ingredients:

4 cups whole grain penne pasta
1/4 tsp red pepper flakes
3 cups of water
Pepper Salt

1 tbsp capers
1/2 cup olives, sliced
4 cups pasta sauce, homemade
1 tbsp garlic, minced

Directions:

Add all into the inner pot of instant pot and stir well.

Seal pot with lid and cook on high for 5 minutes.

Once done, release pressure using quick release. Remove lid.

Stir and serve.

Per Serving

Calories 441 Fat 10.1 g Carbohydrates 77.3 g Sugar 24.1 g Protein 11.8 g Cholesterol 5 mg

Penne In Tomato and Caper Sauce (Italian)

Preparation Time: 10 minutes **Cooking Time:** 15 minutes
Servings: 4

Ingredients:

2 tablespoons olive oil
2 cups Basic Tomato Basil Sauce, or store-bought
4 cups penne pasta
2 garlic cloves, minced

1 cup sliced cherry tomatoes
1 cup capers, drained and rinsed
Salt

Directions:

Set a large pot of salted water over high heat to boil.

In a medium saucepan over medium heat, heat the olive oil. Add the garlic and cook for 30 seconds. Add the cherry tomatoes and cook for 2 to 3 minutes.

Pour in the tomato sauce and bring the mixture to a boil. Stir in the capers and turn off the heat.

Once boiling add the pasta to the pot of water and cook for about 7 minutes until al dente.

Drain the pasta and stir it into the sauce. Toss gently and cook over medium heat for 1 minute or until warmed through.

Per Serving

Calories: 329; Total Fat: 8g; Saturated Fat: 1g; Carbohydrates: 55g; Protein: 10g;

Delicious Greek Chicken Pasta (Italian)

Preparation Time: 10 minutes **Cooking Time:** 10 minutes
Servings: 6

Ingredients:

2 chicken breasts, skinless, boneless, and cut into chunks
12 oz Greek vinaigrette dressing

2 cups vegetable stock
1/2 cup olives, sliced
1 lb. whole grain pasta
Pepper Salt

Directions:

Add all into the inner pot of instant pot and stir well.

Seal pot with lid and cook on high for 10 minutes.

Once done, release pressure using quick release. Remove lid.

Stir well and serve.

Per Serving

Calories 325 Fat 25.8 g Carbohydrates 10.5 g Sugar 4 g Protein 15.6 g Cholesterol 43 mg

Pasta with Lemon and Artichokes (Italian)

Preparation Time: 10 minutes **Cooking Time:** 15 minutes
Servings: 4

Ingredients:

16 ounces linguine or angel hair pasta
2 (15-ounce) jars water-packed artichoke hearts, drained and quartered
2 tablespoons freshly squeezed lemon juice
Freshly ground black pepper
8 garlic cloves, finely minced or pressed
1/4 cup thinly sliced fresh basil
1 teaspoon of sea salt
1/4 cup extra-virgin olive oil

Directions:

Boil a pot of water on high heat and cook the pasta.

While the pasta is cooking, heat the oil in a skillet over medium heat and cook the garlic, stirring often, for 1 to 2 minutes until it just begins to brown. Toss the garlic with the artichokes in a large bowl.

When the pasta is cooked, drain it very carefully and add it to the artichoke mixture, then add the lemon juice, basil, salt, and pepper. Gently stir and serve.

Per Serving

Calories: 423 Protein: 15 g Fat: 14 g

Spinach Beef Pasta (Italian)

Preparation Time: 30 minutes **Cooking Time:** 10 minutes
Servings: 4

Ingredients:

1 ¼ cups uncooked orzo pasta
1 ½ lb. beef tenderloin
1 cup cherry tomatoes, halved
¾ cup baby spinach
2 tbsp. olive oil
¾ cup feta cheese
¼ tsp. Salt
2 quarts water

Directions:

Rub the meat with pepper and cut into small cubes.

Over medium stove flame; heat the oil in a deep saucepan (preferably of medium size).

Add and stir-fry the meat until it is evenly brown.

Add the water and boil the mixture; stir in the orzo and salt.

Cook the mixture for 7-8 minutes. Add the spinach and cook until it wilts.

Add the tomatoes and cheese; combine and serve warm.

Per Serving

Calories 334 |Fat 13g|Carbs 36g| Protein 16g

Chickpea Pasta Salad (Italian)

Preparation Time: 10 minutes **Cooking Time:** 15 minutes
Servings: 6

Ingredients:

2 Tablespoons Olive Oil 16 Ounces Rotelle Pasta
2 Tablespoons Oregano, Fresh & Minced
Pepper to Taste
15 Ounces Canned Garbanzo Beans, Drained & Rinsed
½ Cup Cured Olives, Chopped
¼ Cup Red Wine Vinegar
1 Bunch Green Onions, Chopped
½ Cup Parmesan Cheese, Grated Sea Salt & Black
2 Tablespoons Parsley, Fresh & Chopped

Directions:

Bring a pot of water to a boil and cook your pasta al dente per package instructions. Drain it and rinse it using cold water.

Get out a skillet and heat up your olive oil over medium heat. Add in your scallions, chickpeas, parsley, oregano and olives. Lower the heat to low, and cook for twenty minutes more. Allow this mixture to cool.

Toss your chickpea mixture with your pasta, and then add in your grated cheese, salt, pepper and vinegar. Let it chill for four hours or overnight before serving.

Per Serving

Calories: 424 Protein: 16 g Fat: 10 g Carbs: 69 g

Spaghetti with Pine Nuts and Cheese (Italian)

Preparation Time: 10 minutes **Cooking Time:** 11 minutes
Servings: 4 to 6

Ingredients:

8 ounces (227 g) spaghetti
4 tablespoons almond butter
1 cup fresh grated Parmesan cheese, divided
1 teaspoon freshly ground black pepper
1/2 cup pine nuts

Directions:

Bring a large pot of salted water to a boil. Add the pasta and cook for 8 minutes.

In a large saucepan over medium heat, combine the butter, black pepper, and pine nuts. Cook for 2 to 3 minutes, or until the pine nuts are lightly toasted.

Reserve ½ cup of the pasta water. Drain the pasta and place it into the pan with the pine nuts.

Add ¾ cup of the Parmesan cheese and the reserved pasta water to the pasta and toss everything together to coat the pasta evenly.

Transfer the pasta to a serving dish and top with the remaining ¼ cup of the Parmesan cheese. Serve immediately.

Per Serving

calories: 542 fats: 32.0g protein: 20.0g carbs: 46.0g

Homemade Pasta Bolognese (Italian)

Preparation Time: 20 minutes **Cooking Time:** 10 minutes
Servings: 4

Ingredients:

Minced meat 17 oz. Pasta	Sweet red onion1 piece
12 oz.	Garlic 2 cloves
2 oz. Bacon 3 pieces	Vegetable oil 1 tbsp.
Tomato pastes 3 tbsp.	Grated Parmesan Cheese

Directions:

1. Fry finely chopped onions and garlic in a frying pan in vegetable oil until a characteristic smell.
2. Add minced meat and chopped bacon to the pan. Constantly break the lumps with a spatula and mix so that the minced meat is crumbly.
3. When the mince is ready, add tomato paste, grated Parmesan to the pan, mix, reduce heat and leave to simmer.
4. At this time, boil the pasta. I don't salt water, because for me tomato paste and sauce as a whole turn out to be quite salty.
5. When the pasta is ready, discard it in a colander, arrange it on plates, add meat sauce with tomato paste on top of each serving.

Per Serving
Calories: 1091, Fat: 54.7g, Carbs: 92.8g, Protein: 74g

Arugula Pasta Soup (Italian)

Preparation Time: 15 minutes **Cooking Time:** 5 minutes
Servings: 6

Ingredients:

7 oz. chickpeas, rinsed 4	3 cups arugula, chopped
eggs, lightly beaten 2 tbsp.	6 tbsp. parmesan cheese
lemon juice	6 cups chicken broth
1 pinch of nutmeg	1 bunch scallions, sliced
1 1/3 cups whole-wheat	(greens and whites sliced
pasta shells	separately)
2 cups water	Ground black pepper, to taste

Directions:

In a cooking pot or deep saucepan, combine the pasta, scallion whites, chickpeas, water, broth and nutmeg.

Heat the mixture; cover and bring to a boil.

Take off the lid and simmer the mixture for about 4 minutes. Add the arugula and cook until it is wilted.

Mix in the eggs and season with black pepper and salt.

Mix in the lemon juice and scallion greens. Top with the parmesan cheese; serve warm.

Per Serving
Calories 317 Fat 7g Carbs Protein 38g

Stuffed Pasta Shells (Italian)

Preparation Time: 15 minutes **Cooking Time:** 10 minutes
Servings: 4

Ingredients:

5 Cups Marinara Sauce 15	1 ½ Cups Mozzarella
Oz. Ricotta Cheese	Cheese, Grated
¾ Cup Parmesan Cheese,	¼ Cup Basil Leaves, Fresh
Grated 2 tbsp. Parsley,	& Chopped 8 Oz. Spinach,
Fresh & Chopped	Fresh & Chopped
½ tsp. Thyme	Sea Salt & Black Pepper to
1 lb. Ground Beef	Taste
1 Cup Onions, Chopped	2 tbsp. Olive Oil, Divided
4 Cloves Garlic, Diced	12 Oz. Jumbo Pasta Shells

Directions:

Start by cooking your pasta shells by following your package instructions. Once they're cooked, then set them to the side.

Press sauté and then add in half of your olive oil. Cook your garlic and onions, which should take about four minutes. Your onions should be tender, and your garlic should be fragrant.

Add your ground beef in, seasoning it with thyme, salt, and pepper, cooking for another four minutes.

Add in your basil, parsley, spinach and marinara sauce.

Cover your pot, and cook for five minutes on low pressure.

Use a quick release, and top with cheeses.

Press sauté again, making sure that it stays warm until your cheese melts.

Take a tbsp. of the mixture, stuffing it into your pasta shells.Top with your remaining sauce before serving warm.

Per Serving
Calories: 710, Protein: 45.2 g, Fat: 23.1 g, Carbs: 70 g

Mediterranean Pasta with Tomato Sauce and Vegetables (Italian)

Preparation Time: 15 minutes **Cooking Time:** 25 minutes
Servings: 8

Ingredients:

8 oz. linguine or spaghetti, cooked
1 tsp. garlic powder
1 (8 oz.) can tomato sauce
8 oz. mushrooms, sliced
8 oz. yellow squash, sliced
½ cup grated Parmesan cheese

1 (28 oz.) can whole peeled tomatoes, drained and sliced
1 tbsp. olive oil
½ tsp. Italian seasoning
8 oz. zucchini, sliced
½ tsp. sugar

Directions:

In a medium saucepan, mix tomato sauce, tomatoes, sugar, Italian seasoning, and garlic powder. Bring to boil on medium heat. Reduce heat to low. Cover and simmer for 20 minutes.

In a large skillet, heat olive oil on medium-high heat. Add squash, mushrooms, and zucchini. Cook, stirring, for 4 minutes or until tender-crisp. Stir vegetables into the tomato sauce.

Place pasta in a serving bowl. Spoon vegetable mixture over pasta and toss to coat. Top with grated Parmesan cheese.

Per Serving Calories: 154 Protein: 6 g Fat: 2 g Carbs: 28 g

Penne Pasta with Tomato Sauce and MitzithraCheese (Italian)

Preparation Time: 15 minutes **Cooking Time:** 20 minutes
Servings: 5

Ingredients:

2 tablespoons olive oil
2 green garlic stalks, minced
10 ounces penne
1/2 teaspoon dried oregano
1/4 teaspoon cayenne pepper
1/2 teaspoon dried basil
1 cup Mitzithra cheese, grated
2 overripe tomatoes, pureed

2 scallion stalks, chopped
1/3 teaspoon ground black pepper, to taste Sea salt, to taste
1/2 cup marinara sauce
2 cups vegetable broth
1/4 teaspoon dried marjoram

Directions:

Press the "Sauté" button to preheat your Instant Pot. Heat the oil until sizzling. Now, sauté the scallions and garlic until just tender and fragrant.

Secure the lid. Choose the "Manual" mode and cook for 7 minutes at High pressure. Once cooking is complete, use a natural pressure release for 5 minutes; carefully remove the lid.

Fold in the cheese and seal the lid. Let it sit in the residual heat until the cheese melts. Bon appetite

Per Serving
395 Calories; 15.6g Fat; 51.8g Carbs; 14.9g Protein; 2.5g Sugars;

Lentil and Mushroom Pasta (Italian)

Preparation Time: 10 minutes **Cooking Time:** 50 minutes
Servings: 2

Ingredients:

2 tablespoons olive oil
2 tablespoons tomato paste
2 portobello mushrooms, trimmed and chopped finely
2½ cups water
1 (28-ounce / 794-g) can diced tomatoes with basil (with juice if diced)
1 tablespoon balsamic vinegar

1 large yellow onion, finely diced
3 garlic cloves, chopped
1 teaspoon oregano
1 cup brown lentils
8 ounces (227 g) pasta of choice, cooked Salt and black pepper, to taste
Chopped basil, for garnish

Directions:

Place a large stockpot over medium heat. Add the oil. Once the oil is hot, add the onion and mushrooms. Cover and cook until both are soft, about 5 minutes. Add the tomato paste, garlic, and oregano and cook 2 minutes, stirring constantly.

Stir in the water and lentils. Bring to a boil, then reduce the heat to medium-low and cook for 5 minutes, covered.

Add the tomatoes (and juice if using diced) and vinegar. Replace the lid, reduce the heat to low and cook until the lentils are tender, about 30 minutes.

Remove the sauce from the heat and season with salt and pepper to taste. Garnish with the basil and serve over the cooked pasta.

Per Serving
calories: 463 fats: 15.9g protein: 12.5g carbs: 70.0g

Chapter 6
Vegetable Mains

Stuffed Portobello Mushrooms with Spinach

Prep time: 5 minutes | **Cook time:** 20 minutes | **Serves:**4

Ingredients:

8 large portobello mushrooms, stems removed
3 teaspoons extra-virgin olive oil, divided
1 medium red bell pepper, diced
4 cups fresh spinach
¼ cup crumbled feta cheese

Directions:

Preheat the oven to 450°F (235°C).

Using a spoon to scoop out the gills of the mushrooms and discard them. Brush the mushrooms with 2 teaspoons of olive oil.

Arrange the mushrooms (cap-side down) on a baking sheet. Roast in the preheated oven for 20 minutes.

Meantime, in a medium skillet, heat the remaining olive oil over medium heat until it shimmers.

Add the bell pepper and spinach and sauté for 8 to 10 minutes, stirring occasionally, or until the spinach is wilted.

Remove the mushrooms from the oven to a paper towel-lined plate. Using a spoon to stuff each mushroom with the bell pepper and spinach mixture. Scatter the feta cheese all over. Serve immediately.

Per Serving (2 mushrooms)

calories: 115 | fat: 5.9g | protein: 7.2g | carbs: 11.5g

Chickpea Lettuce Wraps with Celery

Prep time: 10 minutes | **Cook time:** 0 minutes | **Serves:**4

Ingredients:

1 (15-ounce / 425-g) can low-sodium chickpeas, drained and rinsed
1 celery stalk, thinly sliced
2 tablespoons finely chopped red onion
2 tablespoons unsalted tahini
3 tablespoons honey mustard
1 tablespoon capers, undrained
12 butter lettuce leaves

Directions:

In a bowl, mash the chickpeas with a potato masher or the back of a fork until mostly smooth.

Add the celery, red onion, tahini, honey mustard, and capers to the bowl and stir until well incorporated.

For each serving, place three overlapping lettuce leaves on a plate and top with ¼ of the mashed chickpea filling, then roll up. Repeat with the remaining lettuce leaves and chickpea mixture.

Per Serving

calories: 182 | fat: 7.1g | protein: 10.3g | carbs: 19.6g

Zoodles with Walnut Pesto

Prep time: 10 minutes | **Cook time:** 10 minutes | **Serves:**4

Ingredients:

4 medium zucchinis, spiralized
¼ cup extra-virgin olive oil, divided
1 teaspoon minced garlic, divided
½ teaspoon crushed red pepper
¼ teaspoon freshly ground black pepper, divided
¼ teaspoon kosher salt, divided
2 tablespoons grated Parmesan cheese, divided
1 cup packed fresh basil leaves
¾ cup walnut pieces, divided

Directions:

In a large bowl, stir together the zoodles, 1 tablespoon of the olive oil, ½ teaspoon of the minced garlic, red pepper, ⅛ teaspoon of the black pepper and ⅛ teaspoon of the salt. Set aside.

Heat ½ tablespoon of the oil in a large skillet over medium-high heat. Add half of the zoodles to the skillet and cook for 5 minutes, stirring constantly. Transfer the cooked zoodles into a bowl. Repeat with another ½ tablespoon of the oil and the remaining zoodles. When done, add the cooked zoodles to the bowl.

Make the pesto: In a food processor, combine the remaining ½ teaspoon of the minced garlic, ⅛ teaspoon of the black pepper and ⅛ teaspoon of the salt, 1 tablespoon of the Parmesan, basil leaves and ¼ cup of the walnuts. Pulse until smooth and then slowly drizzle the remaining 2 tablespoons of the oil into the pesto. Pulse again until well combined.

Add the pesto to the zoodles along with the remaining 1 tablespoon of the Parmesan and the remaining ½ cup of the walnuts. Toss to coat well.

Serve immediately.

Per Serving

calories: 166 | fat: 16.0g | protein: 4.0g | carbs: 3.0g

Eggplant and Zucchini Gratin

Prep time: 10 minutes | **Cook time:** 19 minutes | **Serves:**6

Ingredients:

2 large zucchinis, finely chopped

1 large eggplant, finely chopped

¼ teaspoon kosher salt

¼ teaspoon freshly ground black pepper

3 tablespoons extra-virgin olive oil, divided

¾ cup unsweetened almond milk

1 tablespoon all-purpose flour

⅓ cup plus 2 tablespoons grated Parmesan cheese, divided

1 cup chopped tomato

1 cup diced fresh Mozzarella

¼ cup fresh basil leaves

Directions:

Preheat the oven to 425°F (220°C).

In a large bowl, toss together the zucchini, eggplant, salt and pepper.

In a large skillet over medium-high heat, heat 1 tablespoon of the oil. Add half of the veggie mixture to the skillet. Stir a few times, then cover and cook for about 4 minutes, stirring occasionally. Pour the cooked veggies into a baking dish. Place the skillet back on the heat, add 1 tablespoon of the oil and repeat with the remaining veggies. Add the veggies to the baking dish.

Meanwhile, heat the milk in the microwave for 1 minute. Set aside.

Place a medium saucepan over medium heat. Add the remaining 1 tablespoon of the oil and flour to the saucepan. Whisk together until well blended.

Slowly pour the warm milk into the saucepan, whisking the entire time. Continue to whisk frequently until the mixture thickens a bit. Add ⅓ cup of the Parmesan cheese and whisk until melted. Pour the cheese sauce over the vegetables in the baking dish and mix well.

Fold in the tomatoes and Mozzarella cheese. Roast in the oven for 10 minutes, or until the gratin is almost set and not runny.

Top with the fresh basil leaves and the remaining 2 tablespoons of the Parmesan cheese before serving.

Per Serving

calories: 122 | fat: 5.0g | protein: 10.0g | carbs: 11.0g

Veggie-Stuffed Portabello Mushrooms

Prep time: 5 minutes | **Cook time:** 24 to 25 minutes | **Serves:**6

3 tablespoons extra-virgin olive oil, divided

1 cup diced onion

2 garlic cloves, minced

1 large zucchini, diced

3 cups chopped mushrooms

1 cup chopped tomato

1 teaspoon dried oregano

¼ teaspoon kosher salt

¼ teaspoon crushed red pepper

6 large portabello mushrooms, stems and gills removed

Cooking spray

4 ounces (113 g) fresh Mozzarella cheese, shredded

Directions:

In a large skillet over medium heat, heat 2 tablespoons of the oil. Add the onion and sauté for 4 minutes. Stir in the garlic and sauté for 1 minute.

Stir in the zucchini, mushrooms, tomato, oregano, salt and red pepper. Cook for 10 minutes, stirring constantly. Remove from the heat.

Meanwhile, heat a grill pan over medium-high heat.

Brush the remaining 1 tablespoon of the oil over the portabello mushroom caps. Place the mushrooms, bottom-side down, on the grill pan. Cover with a sheet of aluminum foil sprayed with nonstick cooking spray. Cook for 5 minutes.

Flip the mushroom caps over, and spoon about ½ cup of the cooked vegetable mixture into each cap. Top each with about 2½ tablespoons of the Mozzarella. Cover and grill for 4 to 5 minutes, or until the cheese is melted.

Using a spatula, transfer the portabello mushrooms to a plate. Let cool for about 5 minutes before serving.

Per Serving

calories: 111 | fat: 4.0g | protein: 11.0g | carbs: 11.0g

Quick Steamed Broccoli

Prep time: 5 minutes | **Cook time:** 0 minutes | **Serves:**2

Ingredients:

¼ cup water

3 cups broccoli florets

Salt and ground black pepper, to taste

Directions:

Pour the water into the Instant Pot and insert a steamer basket. Place the broccoli florets in the basket.

Secure the lid. Select the Manual mode and set the cooking time for 0 minutes at High Pressure.

Once cooking is complete, do a quick pressure release. Carefully open the lid.

Transfer the broccoli florets to a bowl with cold water to keep bright green color.

Season the broccoli with salt and pepper to taste, then serve.

Per Serving

calories: 16 | fat: 0.2g | protein: 1.9g | carbs: 1.7g

Stir-Fried Eggplant

Prep time: 25 minutes | **Cook time:** 15 minutes | **Serves:** 2

Ingredients:

1 cup water, plus more as needed
½ cup chopped red onion
1 tablespoon finely chopped garlic
1 tablespoon dried Italian herb seasoning
1 teaspoon ground cumin
1 small eggplant (about 8 ounces / 227 g), peeled and cut into ½-inch cubes
1 medium carrot, sliced
2 cups green beans, cut into 1-inch pieces
2 ribs celery, sliced
1 cup corn kernels
2 tablespoons almond butter
2 medium tomatoes, chopped

Directions:

Heat 1 tablespoon of water in a large soup pot over medium-high heat until it sputters.

Cook the onion for 2 minutes, adding a little more water as needed.

Add the garlic, Italian seasoning, cumin, and eggplant and stir-fry for 2 to 3 minutes, adding a little more water as needed.

Add the carrot, green beans, celery, corn kernels, and ½ cup of water and stir well. Reduce the heat to medium, cover, and cook for 8 to 10 minutes, stirring occasionally, or until the vegetables are tender.

Meanwhile, in a bowl, stir together the almond butter and ½ cup of water. Remove the vegetables from the heat and stir in the almond butter mixture and chopped tomatoes. Cool for a few minutes before serving.

Per Serving
calories: 176 | fat: 5.5g | protein: 5.8g | carbs: 25.4g

Garlic-Butter Asparagus with Parmesan

Prep time: 5 minutes | **Cook time:** 8 minutes | **Serves:** 2

Ingredients:

1 cup water
1 pound (454 g) asparagus, trimmed
2 cloves garlic, chopped
3 tablespoons almond butter
Salt and ground black pepper, to taste
3 tablespoons grated Parmesan cheese

Directions:

Pour the water into the Instant Pot and insert a trivet.

Put the asparagus on a tin foil add the butter and garlic. Season to taste with salt and pepper.

Fold over the foil and seal the asparagus inside so the foil doesn't come open. Arrange the asparagus on the trivet.

Secure the lid. Select the Manual mode and set the cooking time for 8 minutes at High Pressure.

Once cooking is complete, do a quick pressure release. Carefully open the lid. Unwrap the foil packet and serve sprinkled with the Parmesan cheese.

Per Serving calories: 243 fat: 15.7g protein: 12.3g carbs: 15.3g

Honey-Glazed Baby Carrots

Prep time: 5 minutes | **Cook time:** 6 minutes | **Serves:** 2

Ingredients:

⅔ cup water
1½ pounds (680 g) baby carrots
4 tablespoons almond butter
½ cup honey
1 teaspoon dried thyme
1½ teaspoons dried dill Salt, to taste

Directions:

Pour the water into the Instant Pot and add a steamer basket. Place the baby carrots in the basket.

Secure the lid. Select the Manual mode and set the cooking time for 4 minutes at High Pressure.

Once cooking is complete, do a quick pressure release. Carefully open the lid.

Transfer the carrots to a plate and set aside.

Pour the water out of the Instant Pot and dry it.

Press the Sauté button on the Instant Pot and heat the almond butter.

Stir in the honey, thyme, and dill.

Return the carrots to the Instant Pot and stir until well coated. Sauté for another 1 minute.

Taste and season with salt as needed. Serve warm.

Per Serving
calories: 575 | fat: 23.5g | protein: 2.8g | carbs: 90.6g

Ratatouille

Prep time: 10 minutes | **Cook time:** 6 minutes | **Serves:** 4

Ingredients:

2 large zucchinis, sliced
2 medium eggplants, sliced
4 medium tomatoes, sliced
2 small red onions, sliced
4 cloves garlic, chopped
2 tablespoons thyme leaves
2 teaspoons sea salt
1 teaspoon black pepper
2 tablespoons balsamic vinegar
4 tablespoons olive oil
2 cups water

Directions:

Line a springform pan with foil and place the chopped garlic in the bottom.

Now arrange the vegetable slices, alternately, in circles.

Sprinkle the thyme, pepper and salt over the vegetables. Top with oil and vinegar.

Pour a cup of water into the instant pot and place the trivet inside. Secure the lid and cook on Manual function for 6 minutes at High Pressure.

Release the pressure naturally and remove the lid.

Remove the vegetables along with the tin foil.

Serve on a platter and enjoy.

Per Serving
calories: 240 | fat: 14.3g | protein: 4.7g | carbs: 27.5g

Cheesy Sweet Potato Burgers

Prep time: 10 minutes | **Cook time:** 19 to 20 minutes | Serves:4

Ingredients:

1 large sweet potato (about 8 ounces / 227 g)
2 tablespoons extra-virgin olive oil, divided
1 cup chopped onion
1 large egg
¼ teaspoon kosher salt
1 garlic clove
1 cup old-fashioned rolled oats
1 tablespoon dried oregano
1 tablespoon balsamic vinegar
½ cup crumbled Gorgonzola cheese

Directions:

Using a fork, pierce the sweet potato all over and microwave on high for 4 to 5 minutes, until softened in the center. Cool slightly before slicing in half.

Meanwhile, in a large skillet over medium-high heat, heat 1 tablespoon of the olive oil. Add the onion and sauté for 5 minutes.

Spoon the sweet potato flesh out of the skin and put the flesh in a food processor. Add the cooked onion, egg, garlic, oats, oregano, vinegar and salt. Pulse until smooth. Add the cheese and pulse four times to barely combine.

Form the mixture into four burgers. Place the burgers on a plate, and press to flatten each to about ¾-inch thick.

Wipe out the skillet with a paper towel. Heat the remaining 1 tablespoon of the oil over medium-high heat for about 2 minutes. Add the burgers to the hot oil, then reduce the heat to medium. Cook the burgers for 5 minutes per side.

Transfer the burgers to a plate and serve.

Per Serving

calories: 290 | fat: 12.0g | protein: 12.0g | carbs: 43.0g

Radish and Cabbage Congee

Prep time: 5 minutes | **Cook time:** 20 minutes | Serves:3

Ingredients:

1 cup carrots, diced
½ cup radish, diced
6 cups vegetable broth
Salt, to taste
1½ cups short grain rice, rinsed
1 tablespoon grated fresh ginger
4 cups cabbage, shredded
Green onions for garnishing, chopped

Directions:

Add all the ingredients, except the cabbage and green onions, into the instant pot.

Select the Porridge function and cook on the default time and settings.

After the beep, Quick release the pressure and remove the lid Stir in the shredded cabbage and cover with the lid.

Serve after 10 minutes with chopped green onions on top.

Per Serving

calories: 438 | fat: 0.8g | protein: 8.7g | carbs: 98.4g

Mushroom and Potato Teriyaki

Prep time: 10 minutes | **Cook time:** 18 minutes | **Serves:**4

Ingredients:

¾ large yellow or white onion, chopped
1½ medium carrots, diced
1½ ribs celery, chopped
1 medium portabella mushroom, diced
¾ tablespoon garlic, chopped
2 cups water
1 pound (454 g) white potatoes, peeled and diced
¼ cup tomato paste
½ tablespoon sesame oil
2 teaspoons sesame seeds
½ tablespoon paprika
1 teaspoon fresh rosemary
¾ cups peas
¼ cup fresh parsley for garnishing, chopped

Directions:

Add the oil, sesame seeds, and all the vegetables in the instant pot and Sauté for 5 minutes.

Stir in the remaining ingredients and secure the lid. Cook on Manual function for 13 minutes at High Pressure.

After the beep, natural release the pressure and remove the lid. Garnish with fresh parsley and serve hot.

Per Serving

calories: 160 | fat: 3.0g | protein: 4.7g | carbs: 30.6g

Cauliflower with Sweet Potato

Prep time: 15 minutes | **Cook time:** 8 minutes | **Serves:**8

Ingredients:

1 small onion
4 tomatoes
4 garlic cloves, chopped
2-inch ginger, chopped
2 teaspoons olive oil
1 teaspoon turmeric
2 teaspoons ground cumin
Salt, to taste
1 teaspoon paprika
2 medium sweet potatoes, cubed small
2 small cauliflowers, diced
2 tablespoons fresh cilantro for topping, chopped

Directions:

Blend the tomatoes, garlic, ginger and onion in a blender.

Add the oil and cumin in the instant pot and Sauté for 1 minute.

Stir in the blended mixture and the remaining spices.

Add the sweet potatoes and cook for 5 minutes on Sauté

Add the cauliflower chunks and secure the lid.

Cook on Manual for 2 minutes at High Pressure.

Once done, Quick release the pressure and remove the lid.

Stir and serve with cilantro on top.

Per Serving

calories: 76 | fat: 1.6g | protein: 2.7g | carbs: 14.4g

Peanut and Coconut Stuffed Eggplants

Prep time: 15 minutes | **Cook time:** 9 minutes | **Serves:** 4

Ingredients:

1 tablespoon coriander seeds
½ teaspoon cumin seeds
½ teaspoon mustard seeds
2 to 3 tablespoons chickpea flour
2 tablespoons chopped peanuts
2 tablespoons coconut shreds
1-inch ginger, chopped
2 cloves garlic, chopped
1 hot green chili, chopped
A pinch of cinnamon
⅓ to ½ teaspoon cayenne
½ teaspoon turmeric
½ teaspoon raw sugar
½ to ¾ teaspoon salt
1 teaspoon lemon juice
Water as needed
4 baby eggplants
Fresh Cilantro for garnishing
½ teaspoon ground cardamom

Directions:

Add the coriander, mustard seeds and cumin in the instant pot.

Roast on Sauté function for 2 minutes.

Add the chickpea flour, nuts and coconut shred to the pot, and roast for 2 minutes.

Blend this mixture in a blender, then transfer to a medium-sized bowl. Roughly blend the ginger, garlic, raw sugar, chili, and all the spices in a blender.

Add the water and lemon juice to make a paste. Combine it with the dry flour mixture.

Cut the eggplants from one side and stuff with the spice mixture. Add 1 cup of water to the instant pot and place the stuffed eggplants inside.

Sprinkle some salt on top and secure the lid.

Cook on Manual for 5 minutes at High Pressure, then quick release the steam. Remove the lid and garnish with fresh cilantro, then serve hot.

Per Serving
calories: 207 | fat: 4.9g | protein: 7.9g | carbs: 39.6g

Mushroom, Potato, and Green Bean Mix

Prep time: 10 minutes | **Cook time:** 18 minutes | **Serves:** 3

Ingredients:

1 tablespoon olive oil
½ carrot, peeled and minced
½ celery stalk, minced
½ small onion, minced
1 garlic clove, minced
½ teaspoon dried sage, crushed
½ teaspoon dried rosemary, crushed
4 ounces (113 g) fresh Portabella mushrooms, sliced
4 ounces (113 g) fresh white mushrooms, sliced
¼ cup red wine
1 Yukon Gold potato, peeled and diced
¾ cup fresh green beans, trimmed and chopped
1 cup tomatoes, chopped
½ cup tomato paste
½ tablespoon balsamic vinegar
3 cups water
Salt and freshly ground black pepper to taste
2 ounces (57 g) frozen peas
½ lemon juice
2 tablespoons fresh cilantro for garnishing, chopped

Directions:

1. Put the oil, onion, tomatoes and celery into the instant pot and Sauté for 5 minutes. Stir in the herbs and garlic and cook for 1 minute. Add the mushrooms and sauté for 5 minutes. Stir in the wine and cook for a further 2 minutes

2. Add the diced potatoes and mix. Cover the pot with a lid and let the potatoes cook for 2-3 minutes.

3. Now add the green beans, carrots, tomato paste, peas, salt, pepper, water and vinegar.

4. Secure the lid and cook on Manual function for 8 minutes at High Pressure with the pressure valve in the sealing position. Do a Quick release and open the pot, stir the veggies and then add lemon juice and cilantro, then serve with rice or any other of your choice.

Per Serving
calories: 238 | fat: 5.4g | protein: 8.3g | carbs: 42.7g

Mushroom Tacos

Prep time: 10 minutes | **Cook time:** 13 minutes | **Serves:** 3

Ingredients:

4 large guajillo chilies
2 teaspoons oil
2 bay leaves
2 large onions, sliced
2 garlic cloves
2 chipotle chillies in adobo sauce
2 teaspoons ground cumin
1 teaspoon dried oregano
1 teaspoon smoked hot paprika

½ teaspoon ground cinnamon, Salt, to taste
¾ cup vegetable broth
1 teaspoon apple cider vinegar
3 teaspoons lime juice
¼ teaspoon sugar
8 ounces (227 g) mushrooms chopped
Whole-wheat tacos, for serving

Directions:

Put the oil, onion, garlic, salt and bay leaves into the instant pot and Sauté for 5 minutes.

Blend the half of this mixture, in a blender, with all the spices and chillies.

Add the mushrooms to the remaining onions and Sauté for 3 minutes. Pour the blended mixture into the pot and secure the lid. Cook on Manual function for 5 minutes at High Pressure. Once done, Quick release the pressure and remove the lid. Stir well and serve with tacos.

Per Serving

calories: 138 | fat: 4.1g | protein: 5.7g | carbs: 23.8g

Potato Curry

Prep time: 10 minutes | **Cook time:** 30 minutes | **Serves:** 2

Ingredients:

2 large potatoes, peeled and diced
1 small onion, peeled and diced
8 ounces (227 g) fresh tomatoes
1 tablespoon olive oil
1 cup water

2 tablespoons garlic cloves, grated
½ tablespoon rosemary
½ tablespoon cayenne pepper
1½ tablespoons thyme
Salt and pepper, to taste

Directions:

Pour a cup of water into the instant pot and place the steamer trivet inside.

Place the potatoes and half the garlic over the trivet and sprinkle some salt and pepper on top.

Secure the lid and cook on Steam function for 20 minutes.

After the beep, natural release the pressure and remove the lid.

Put the potatoes to one side and empty the pot.

Add the remaining ingredients to the cooker and Sauté for 10 minutes.

Use an immerse blender to purée the cooked mixture.

Stir in the steamed potatoes and serve hot.

Per Serving

calories: 398 | fat: 7.6g | protein: 9.6g | carbs: 76.2g

Lentils and Eggplant Curry

Prep time: 10 minutes | **Cook time:** 22 minutes | **Serves:** 4

Ingredients:

¾ cup lentils, soaked and rinsed
1 teaspoon olive oil
½ onion, chopped
4 garlic cloves, chopped
1 teaspoon ginger, chopped
1 hot green chili, chopped
¼ teaspoon turmeric
½ teaspoon ground cumin

2 tomatoes, chopped
1 cup eggplant, chopped
1 cup sweet potatoes, cubed
¾ teaspoon salt
2 cups water
1 cup baby spinach leaves
Cayenne and lemon/lime to taste
Pepper flakes (garnish)

Directions:

Add the oil, garlic, ginger, chili and salt into the instant pot and Sauté for 3 minutes.

Stir in the tomatoes and all the spices. Cook for 5 minutes.

Add all the remaining ingredients, except the spinach leaves and garnish.

Secure the lid and cook on Manual function for 12 minutes at High Pressure.

After the beep, release the pressure naturally and remove the lid.

Stir in the spinach leaves and let the pot simmer for 2 minutes on Sauté.

Garnish with the pepper flakes and serve warm.

Per Serving

calories: 88 | fat: 1.5g | protein: 3.4g | carbs: 17.4g

Sweet Potato and Tomato Curry

Prep time: 5 minutes | **Cook time:** 8 minutes | **Serves:** 8

Ingredients:

2 large brown onions, finely diced
4 tablespoons olive oil
4 teaspoons salt
4 large garlic cloves, diced
1 red chili, sliced
4 tablespoons cilantro, chopped
4 teaspoons ground cumin

2 teaspoons ground coriander
2 teaspoons paprika
2 pounds (907 g) sweet potato, diced
4 cups chopped, tinned tomatoes
2 cups water
2 cups vegetable stock
Lemon juice and cilantro (garnish)

Directions:

Put the oil and onions into the instant pot and Sauté for 5 minutes.

Stir in the remaining ingredients and secure the lid.

Cook on Manual function for 3 minutes at High Pressure.

Once done, Quick release the pressure and remove the lid.

Garnish with cilantro and lemon juice.

Serve.

Per Serving

calories: 224 | fat: 8.0g | protein: 4.6g | carbs: 35.9g

Veggie Chili

Prep time: 15 minutes | **Cook time:** 10 minutes | **Serves:**3

Ingredients:

½ tablespoon olive oil
1 small yellow onion, chopped
4 garlic cloves, minced
¾ (15-ounce / 425-g) can diced tomatoes
1 ounce (28 g) sugar-free tomato paste
½ (4-ounce / 113-g) can green chilies with liquid
1 tablespoon Worcestershire sauce

2 tablespoons red chili powder
½ cup carrots, diced
½ cup scallions, chopped
½ cup green bell pepper, chopped
¼ cup peas
1 tablespoon ground cumin
½ tablespoon dried oregano, crushed
Salt and freshly ground black pepper to taste

Directions:

Add the oil, onion, and garlic into the instant pot and Sauté for 5 minutes.

Stir in the remaining vegetables and stir-fry for 3 minutes.

Add the remaining ingredients and secure the lid.

Cook on Manual function for 2 minutes at High Pressure.

After the beep, natural release the pressure and remove the lid.

Stir well and serve warm.

Per Serving

calories: 106 | fat: 3.9g | protein: 3.4g | carbs: 18.0g

Creamy Potato Curry

Prep time: 10 minutes | **Cook time:** 18 minutes | **Serves:**4

Ingredients:

¾ large yellow or white onion, chopped
1½ ribs celery, chopped
¼ cup carrots, diced
¼ cup green onions
½ cup coconut milk
¾ tablespoon garlic, chopped
1 pound (454 g) white potatoes, peeled and diced

¼ cup heavy cream
¼ teaspoon thyme
¼ teaspoon rosemary
½ tablespoon black pepper
¾ cup peas Salt, to taste
2 tablespoons fresh cilantro for garnishing, chopped
1½ cups water

Directions:

1. Add the oil and all the vegetables in the instant pot and Sauté for 5 minutes.
2. Stir in the remaining ingredients and secure the lid.
3. Cook on Manual function for 13 minutes at High Pressure.
4. Once it beeps, natural release the pressure and remove the lid.
5. Garnish with fresh cilantro and serve hot.

Per Serving

calories: 210 | fat: 10.1g | protein: 4.1g | carbs: 27.6g

Cabbage Stuffed Acorn Squash

Prep time: 15 minutes | **Cook time:** 23 minutes | **Serves:**4

Ingredients:

½ tablespoon olive oil
2 medium Acorn squashes
¼ small yellow onion, chopped
1 jalapeño pepper, chopped
½ cup green onions, chopped
½ cup carrots, chopped
¼ cup cabbage, chopped
1 garlic clove, minced

½ (6-ounce / 170-g) can sugar-free tomato sauce
½ tablespoon chili powder
½ tablespoon ground cumin
Salt and freshly ground black pepper to taste
2 cups water
¼ cup Cheddar cheese, shredded

Directions:

Pour the water into the instant pot and place the trivet inside.

Slice the squash into 2 halves and remove the seeds.

Place over the trivet, skin side down, and sprinkle some salt and pepper over it.

Secure the lid and cook on Manual for 15 minutes at High Pressure.

Release the pressure naturally and remove the lid. Empty the pot into a bowl.

Now add the oil, onion, and garlic in the instant pot and Sauté for 5 minutes.

Stir in the remaining vegetables and stir-fry for 3 minutes.

Add the remaining ingredients and secure the lid.

Cook on Manual function for 2 minutes at High Pressure.

After the beep, natural release the pressure and remove the lid.

Stuff the squashes with the prepared mixture and serve warm.

Per Serving

calories: 163 | fat: 5.1g | protein: 4.8g | carbs: 28.4g

Mushroom and Spinach Stuffed Peppers

Prep time: 15 minutes | **Cook time:** 8 minutes | **Serves:** 7

Ingredients:

7 mini sweet peppers
1 cup button mushrooms, minced
5 ounces (142 g) organic baby spinach
½ teaspoon fresh garlic
½ teaspoon coarse sea salt
¼ teaspoon cracked mixed pepper
2 tablespoons water
1 tablespoon olive oil
Organic Mozzarella cheese, diced

Directions:

Put the sweet peppers and water in the instant pot and Sauté for 2 minutes.

Remove the peppers and put the olive oil into the pot.

Stir in the mushrooms, garlic, spices and spinach.

Cook on Sauté until the mixture is dry. Stuff each sweet pepper with the cheese and spinach mixture. Bake the stuffed peppers in an oven for 6 minutes at 400°F (205°C).

Once done, serve hot.

Per Serving

calories: 81 | fat: 2.4g | protein: 4.1g | carbs: 13.2g

Black Bean and Corn Tortilla Bowls

Prep time: 10 minutes | **Cook time:** 8 minutes | **Serves:** 4

Ingredients:

1½ cups vegetable broth
½ cup tomatoes, undrained diced
1 small onion, diced
2 garlic cloves, finely minced
1 teaspoon chili powder
1 teaspoon cumin
½ teaspoon paprika
½ teaspoon ground coriander
Salt and pepper to taste
2 small potatoes, cubed
½ cup bell pepper, chopped
½ can black beans, drained and rinsed
1 cup frozen corn kernels
½ tablespoon lime juice
2 tablespoons cilantro for topping, chopped
Whole-wheat tortilla chips
½ cup carrots, diced

Directions:

Add the oil and all the vegetables into the instant pot and Sauté for 3 minutes.

Add all the spices, corn, lime juice, and broth, along with the beans, to the pot.

Seal the lid and cook on Manual setting at High Pressure for 5 minutes.

Once done, natural release the pressure when the timer goes off. Remove the lid.

To serve, put the prepared mixture into a bowl.

Top with tortilla chips and fresh cilantro. Serve.

Per Serving

calories: 183 | fat: 0.9g | protein: 7.1g | carbs: 39.8g

Cauliflower and Broccoli Bowls

Prep time: 5 minutes | **Cook time:** 7 minutes | **Serves:** 3

Ingredients:

½ medium onion, diced
2 teaspoons olive oil
1 garlic clove, minced
½ cup tomato paste
½ pound (227 g) frozen cauliflower
½ pound (227 g) broccoli florets
½ cup vegetable broth
½ teaspoon paprika
¼ teaspoon dried thyme
2 pinches sea salt

Directions:

Add the oil, onion and garlic into the instant pot and Sauté for 2 minutes.

Add the broth, tomato paste, cauliflower, broccoli, and all the spices, to the pot.

Secure the lid. Cook on the Manual setting at with pressure for 5 minutes.

After the beep, Quick release the pressure and remove the lid.

Stir well and serve hot.

Per Serving

calories: 109 | fat: 3.8g | protein: 6.1g | carbs: 16.7g

Potato and Broccoli Medley

Prep time: 10 minutes | **Cook time:** 20 minutes | **Serves:** 3

Ingredients:

1 tablespoon olive oil
½ white onion, diced
1½ cloves garlic, finely chopped
1 pound (454 g) potatoes, cut into chunks
1 pound (454 g) broccoli florets, diced
1 pound (454 g) baby carrots, cut in half
¼ cup vegetable broth
½ teaspoon Italian seasoning
½ teaspoon Spike original seasoning
Fresh parsley for garnishing

Directions:

Put the oil and onion into the instant pot and Sauté for 5 minutes. Stir in the carrots, and garlic and stir-fry for 5 minutes. Add the remaining ingredients and secure the lid.

Cook on the Manual function for 10 minutes at High Pressure. After the beep, Quick release the pressure and remove the lid. Stir gently and garnish with fresh parsley , then serve.

Per Serving

calories: 256 | fat: 5.6g | protein: 9.1g | carbs: 46.1g

Mushroom and Potato Oat Burgers

Prep time: 20 minutes | **Cook time:** 21 minutes | **Serves:**5

Ingredients:

½ cup minced onion
1 teaspoon grated fresh ginger
½ cup minced mushrooms
½ cup red lentils, rinsed
¾ sweet potato, peeled and diced
1 cup vegetable stock
2 tablespoons hemp seeds
2 tablespoons chopped cilantro
1 tablespoon curry powder
1 cup quick oats
Brown rice flour, optional
5 tomato slices
Lettuce leaves
5 whole-wheat buns
2 tablespoons chopped parsley

Directions:

Add the oil, ginger, mushrooms and onion into the instant pot and Sauté for 5 minutes.

Stir in the lentils, stock, and the sweet potatoes.

Secure the lid and cook on the Manual function for 6 minutes at High Pressure.

After the beep, natural release the pressure and remove the lid. Meanwhile, heat the oven to 375°F (190°C) and line a baking tray with parchment paper.

Mash the prepared lentil mixture with a potato masher.

Add the oats and the remaining spices. Put in some brown rice flour if the mixture is not thick enough.

Wet your hands and prepare 5 patties, using the mixture, and place them on the baking tray.

Bake the patties for 10 minutes in the preheated oven.

Slice the buns in half and stack each with a tomato slice, a vegetable patty and lettuce leaves. Serve and enjoy.

Per Serving
calories: 266 | fat: 5.3g | protein: 14.5g | carbs: 48.7g

Saut é ed Spinach and Leeks

Prep time: 5 minutes | **Cook time:** 8 minutes | **Serves:**2

Ingredients:

3 tablespoons olive oil
2 garlic cloves, crushed
2 leeks, chopped
2 red onions, chopped
9 ounces (255 g) fresh spinach
1 teaspoon kosher salt
½ cup crumbled goat cheese

Directions:

Coat the bottom of the Instant Pot with the olive oil.

Add the garlic, leek, and onions and stir-fry for about 5 minutes, on Sauté mode.

Stir in the spinach. Sprinkle with the salt and sauté for an additional 3 minutes, stirring constantly.

Transfer to a plate and scatter with the goat cheese before serving.

Per Serving
calories: 447 | fat: 31.2g | protein: 14.6g | carbs: 28.7g

Potato, Corn, and Spinach Medley

Prep time: 10 minutes | **Cook time:** 10 minutes | **Serves:**6

Ingredients:

1 tablespoon olive oil
3 scallions, chopped
½ cup onion, chopped
2 large white potatoes, peeled and diced
1 tablespoon ginger, grated
3 cups frozen corn kernels
1 cup vegetable stock
1 tablespoon fish sauce
2 tablespoons light soy sauce
2 large cloves garlic, diced
⅓ teaspoon white pepper
1 teaspoon salt
3-4 handfuls baby spinach leaves
Juice of ½ lemon

Directions:

Put the oil, ginger, garlic and onions in the instant pot and Sauté for 5 minutes. Add all the remaining ingredients except the spinach leaves and lime juice

Secure the lid and cook on the Manual setting for 5 minutes at High Pressure. After the beep, Quick release the pressure and remove the lid.

Add the spinach and cook for 3 minutes on Sauté

Drizzle the lime juice over the dish and serve hot.

Per Serving
calories: 217 | fat: 3.4g | protein: 6.5g | carbs: 44.5g

Italian Zucchini Pomodoro

Prep time: 10 minutes | **Cook time:** 12 minutes | **Serves:**4

Ingredients:

1 tablespoon avocado oil
1 large onion, peeled and diced
3 cloves garlic, minced
1 (28-ounce / 794-g) can diced tomatoes, including juice
½ cup water
1 tablespoon Italian seasoning
1 teaspoon sea salt
½ teaspoon ground black pepper
2 medium zucchini, spiraled

Directions:

Press Sauté button on the Instant Pot. Heat avocado oil. Add onions and stir-fry for 3 to 5 minutes until translucent. Add garlic and cook for an additional minute. Add tomatoes, water, Italian seasoning, salt, and pepper. Add zucchini and toss to combine. Lock lid.

Press the Manual button and adjust time to 1 minute. When timer beeps, let pressure release naturally for 5 minutes. Quick release any additional pressure until float valve drops and then unlock lid.

Transfer zucchini to four bowls. Press Sauté button, press Adjust button to change the temperature to Less, and simmer sauce in the Instant Pot unlidded for 5 minutes. Ladle over zucchini and serve immediately.

Per Serving
calories: 92 | fat: 4.1g | protein: 2.5g | carbs: 13.1g

Mushroom Swoodles

Prep time: 5 minutes | **Cook time:** 3 minutes | **Serves:** 4

Ingredients:

2 tablespoons coconut aminos
1 tablespoon white vinegar
2 teaspoons olive oil
1 teaspoon sesame oil
1 tablespoon honey
¼ teaspoon red pepper flakes

3 cloves garlic, minced
1 large sweet potato, peeled and spiraled
1 pound (454 g) shiitake mushrooms, sliced
1 cup vegetable broth
¼ cup chopped fresh parsley

Directions:

In a large bowl, whisk together coconut aminos, vinegar, olive oil, sesame oil, honey, red pepper flakes, and garlic.

Toss sweet potato and shiitake mushrooms in sauce. Refrigerate covered for 30 minutes.

Pour vegetable broth into Instant Pot. Add trivet. Lower steamer basket onto trivet and add the sweet potato mixture to the basket. Lock lid.

Press the Manual button and adjust time to 3 minutes. When timer beeps, let pressure release naturally for 5 minutes. Quick release any additional pressure until float valve drops and then unlock lid.

Remove basket from the Instant Pot and distribute sweet potatoes and mushrooms evenly among four bowls; pour liquid from the Instant Pot over bowls and garnish with chopped parsley.

Per Serving

calories: 127 | fat: 4.0g | protein: 4.2g | carbs: 20.9g

Carrot and Turnip Purée

Prep time: 10 minutes | **Cook time:** 10 minutes | **Serves:** 6

Ingredients:

2 tablespoons olive oil, divided
3 large turnips, peeled and quartered
4 large carrots, peeled and cut into 2-inch pieces

2 cups vegetable broth
1 teaspoon salt
½ teaspoon ground nutmeg
2 tablespoons sour cream

Directions:

Press the Sauté button on Instant Pot. Heat 1 tablespoon olive oil. Toss turnips and carrots in oil for 1 minute. Add broth. Lock lid. Press the Manual button and adjust time to 8 minutes. When timer beeps, quick release pressure until float valve drops and then unlock lid.

Drain vegetables and reserve liquid; set liquid aside. Add 2 tablespoons of reserved liquid plus remaining ingredients to vegetables in the Instant Pot.

Use an immersion blender to blend until desired smoothness. If too thick, add more liquid 1 tablespoon at a time. Serve warm.

Per Serving

calories: 95 | fat: 5.2g | protein: 1.4g | carbs: 11.8g

Rice, Corn, and Bean Stuffed Peppers

Prep time: 15 minutes | **Cook time:** 15 minutes | **Serves:** 4

Ingredients:

4 large bell peppers
2 cups cooked white rice
1 medium onion, peeled and diced
3 small Roma tomatoes, diced
¼ cup marinara sauce
1 cup corn kernels (cut from the cob is preferred)
¼ cup sliced black olives

¼ cup canned cannellini beans, rinsed and drained
¼ cup canned black beans, rinsed and drained
1 teaspoon sea salt
1 teaspoon garlic powder
½ cup vegetable broth
2 tablespoons grated Parmesan cheese

Directions:

Cut off the bell pepper tops as close to the tops as possible. Hollow out and discard seeds. Poke a few small holes in the bottom of the peppers to allow drippings to drain.

In a medium bowl, combine remaining ingredients except for broth and Parmesan cheese. Stuff equal amounts of mixture into each of the bell peppers.

Place trivet into the Instant Pot and pour in the broth. Set the peppers upright on the trivet. Lock lid.

Press the Manual button and adjust time to 15 minutes. When timer beeps, let pressure release naturally until float valve drops and then unlock lid.

Serve immediately and garnish with Parmesan cheese.

Per Serving

calories: 265 | fat: 3.0g | protein: 8.1g | carbs: 53.1g

Zoodles

Prep time: 10 minutes | **Cook time:** 5 minutes | **Serves:** 2

Ingredients:

2 tablespoons avocado oil
2 medium zucchini, spiralized

¼ teaspoon salt
Freshly ground black pepper, to taste

Directions:

Heat the avocado oil in a large skillet over medium heat until it shimmers.

Add the zucchini noodles, salt, and black pepper to the skillet and toss to coat. Cook for 1 to 2 minutes, stirring constantly, until tender.

Serve warm.

Per Serving

calories: 128 | fat: 14.0g | protein: 0.3g | carbs: 0.3g

Garlicky Broccoli Rabe

Prep time: 10 minutes | **Cook time:** 5 to 6 minutes | **Serves:**4

Ingredients:

14 ounces (397 g) broccoli rabe, trimmed and cut into 1-inch pieces

2 teaspoons salt, plus more for seasoning

Black pepper, to taste

2 tablespoons extra-virgin olive oil

3 garlic cloves, minced

¼ teaspoon red pepper flakes

Directions:

Bring 3 quarts water to a boil in a large saucepan. Add the broccoli rabe and 2 teaspoons of the salt to the boiling water and cook for 2 to 3 minutes, or until wilted and tender. Drain the broccoli rabe. Transfer to ice water and let sit until chilled. Drain again and pat dry.

In a skillet over medium heat, heat the oil and add the garlic and red pepper flakes. Sauté for about 2 minutes, or until the garlic begins to sizzle. Increase the heat to medium-high. Stir in the broccoli rabe and cook for about 1 minute, or until heated through, stirring constantly. Season with salt and pepper. Serve immediately.

Per Serving

calories: 87 | fat: 7.3g | protein: 3.4g | carbs: 4.0g

Brussels Sprouts Linguine

Prep time: 5 minutes | **Cook time:** 25 minutes | **Serves:**4

Ingredients:

8 ounces (227 g) whole-wheat linguine

⅓ cup plus 2 tablespoons extra-virgin olive oil, divided

1 medium sweet onion, diced

2 to 3 garlic cloves, smashed

8 ounces (227 g) Brussels sprouts, chopped

½ cup chicken stock

⅓ cup dry white wine

½ cup shredded Parmesan cheese

1 lemon, quartered

Directions:

Bring a large pot of water to a boil and cook the pasta for about 5 minutes, or until al dente. Drain the pasta and reserve 1 cup of the pasta water. Mix the cooked pasta with 2 tablespoons of the olive oil. Set aside.

In a large skillet, heat the remaining ⅓ cup of the olive oil over medium heat. Add the onion to the skillet and sauté for about 4 minutes, or until tender. Add the smashed garlic cloves and sauté for 1 minute, or until fragrant.

Stir in the Brussels sprouts and cook covered for 10 minutes. Pour in the chicken stock to prevent burning. Once the Brussels sprouts have wilted and are fork-tender, add white wine and cook for about 5 minutes, or until reduced. Add the pasta to the skillet and add the pasta water as needed. Top with the Parmesan cheese and squeeze the lemon over the dish right before eating.

Per Serving

calories: 502 | fat: 31.0g | protein: 15.0g | carbs: 50.0g

Beet and Watercress Salad

Prep time: 15 minutes | **Cook time:** 8 minutes | **Serves:**4

Ingredients:

2 pounds (907 g) beets, scrubbed, trimmed and cut into ¾-inch pieces

½ cup water

1 teaspoon caraway seeds

½ teaspoon table salt, plus more for seasoning

1 cup plain Greek yogurt

1 small garlic clove, minced

5 ounces (142 g) watercress, torn into bite-size pieces

Coarse sea salt, to taste

1 tablespoon extra-virgin olive oil, divided, plus more for drizzling

1 tablespoon white wine vinegar, divided

Black pepper, to taste

1 teaspoon grated orange zest

2 tablespoons orange juice

¼ cup coarsely chopped fresh dill

¼ cup hazelnuts, toasted, skinned and chopped

Directions:

Combine the beets, water, caraway seeds and table salt in the Instant Pot. Set the lid in place. Select the Manual mode and set the cooking time for 8 minutes on High Pressure. When the timer goes off, do a quick pressure release.

Carefully open the lid. Using a slotted spoon, transfer the beets to a plate. Set aside to cool slightly.

In a small bowl, combine the yogurt, garlic and 3 tablespoons of the beet cooking liquid.

In a large bowl, toss the watercress with 2 teaspoons of the oil and 1 teaspoon of the vinegar. Season with table salt and pepper.

Spread the yogurt mixture over a serving dish. Arrange the watercress on top of the yogurt mixture, leaving 1-inch border of the yogurt mixture.

Add the beets to now-empty large bowl and toss with the orange zest and juice, the remaining 2 teaspoons of the vinegar and the remaining 1 teaspoon of the oil. Season with table salt and pepper.

Arrange the beets on top of the watercress mixture. Drizzle with the olive oil and sprinkle with the dill, hazelnuts and sea salt. Serve immediately.

Per Serving calories: 240 | fat: 15.0g | protein: 9.0g | carbs: 19.0g

Sautéed Cabbage with Parsley

Prep time: 10 minutes | **Cook time:** 12 to 14 minutes | **Serves:** 4 to 6

Ingredients:

1 small head green cabbage (about 1¼ pounds / 567 g), cored and sliced thin

2 tablespoons extra-virgin olive oil, divided

1½ teaspoons lemon juice

1 onion, halved and sliced thin

¾ teaspoon salt, divided

¼ teaspoon black pepper

¼ cup chopped fresh parsley

Directions:

Place the cabbage in a large bowl with cold water. Let sit for 3 minutes. Drain well. Heat 1 tablespoon of the oil in a skillet over medium-high heat until shimmering. Add the onion and ¼ teaspoon of the salt and cook for 5 to 7 minutes, or until softened and lightly browned. Transfer to a bowl. Heat the remaining 1 tablespoon of the oil in now-empty skillet over medium-high heat until shimmering. Add the cabbage and sprinkle with the remaining ½ teaspoon of the salt and black pepper. Cover and cook for about 3 minutes, without stirring, or until cabbage is wilted and lightly browned on bottom.

Stir and continue to cook for about 4 minutes, uncovered, or until the cabbage is crisp-tender and lightly browned in places, stirring once halfway through cooking. Off heat, stir in the cooked onion, parsley and lemon juice.

Transfer to a plate and serve.

Per Serving

calories: 117 | fat: 7.0g | protein: 2.7g | carbs: 13.4g

Grilled Romaine Lettuce

Prep time: 5 minutes | **Cook time:** 3 to 5 minutes | **Serves:** 4

Ingredients:

Romaine:

2 heads romaine lettuce, halved lengthwise

2 tablespoons extra-virgin olive oil

Dressing:

½ cup unsweetened almond milk

1 tablespoon extra-virgin olive oil

¼ bunch fresh chives, thinly chopped

1 garlic clove, pressed

1 pinch red pepper flakes

Directions:

Heat a grill pan over medium heat.

Brush each lettuce half with the olive oil. Place the lettuce halves, flat-side down, on the grill. Grill for 3 to 5 minutes, or until the lettuce slightly wilts and develops light grill marks. Meanwhile, whisk together all the ingredients for the dressing in a small bowl. Drizzle 2 tablespoons of the dressing over each romaine half and serve.

Per Serving

calories: 126 | fat: 11.0g | protein: 2.0g | carbs: 7.0g

Parmesan Stuffed Zucchini Boats

Prep time: 5 minutes | **Cook time:** 15 minutes | **Serves:** 4

Ingredients:

1 cup canned low-sodium chickpeas, drained and rinsed

1 cup no-sugar-added spaghetti sauce

2 zucchinis

¼ cup shredded Parmesan cheese

Directions:

Preheat the oven to 425°F (220°C).

In a medium bowl, stir together the chickpeas and spaghetti sauce.

Cut the zucchini in half lengthwise and scrape a spoon gently down the length of each half to remove the seeds.

Fill each zucchini half with the chickpea sauce and top with one-quarter of the Parmesan cheese. Place the zucchini halves on a baking sheet and roast in the oven for 15 minutes. Transfer to a plate. Let rest for 5 minutes before serving.

Per Serving

calories: 139 | fat: 4.0g | protein: 8.0g | carbs: 20.0g

Baby Kale and Cabbage Salad

Prep time: 10 minutes | **Cook time:** 0 minutes | **Serves:** 6

Ingredients:

2 bunches baby kale, thinly sliced

½ head green savoy cabbage, cored and thinly sliced

1 medium red bell pepper, thinly sliced

Dressing:

Juice of 1 lemon

¼ cup apple cider vinegar

1 teaspoon ground cumin

¼ teaspoon smoked paprika

1 garlic clove, thinly sliced

1 cup toasted peanuts

Directions:

In a large mixing bowl, toss together the kale and cabbage.

Make the dressing: Whisk together the lemon juice, vinegar, cumin and paprika in a small bowl.

Pour the dressing over the greens and gently massage with your hands. Add the pepper, garlic and peanuts to the mixing bowl. Toss to combine. Serve immediately.

Per Serving

calories: 199 | fat: 12.0g | protein: 10.0g | carbs: 17.0g

Cauliflower Steaks with Arugula

Prep time: 5 minutes | **Cook time:** 20 minutes | **Serves:**4

Ingredients:

Cauliflower:
1 head cauliflower
Cooking spray
½ teaspoon garlic powder
4 cups arugula

Dressing:
1½ tablespoons extra-virgin olive oil
1½ tablespoons honey mustard
1 teaspoon freshly squeezed lemon juice

Directions:

Preheat the oven to 425ºF (220ºC).

Remove the leaves from the cauliflower head, and cut it in half lengthwise. Cut 1½-inch-thick steaks from each half.

Spritz both sides of each steak with cooking spray and season both sides with the garlic powder.

Place the cauliflower steaks on a baking sheet, cover with foil, and roast in the oven for 10 minutes.

Remove the baking sheet from the oven and gently pull back the foil to avoid the steam. Flip the steaks, then roast uncovered for 10 minutes more.

Meanwhile, make the dressing: Whisk together the olive oil, honey mustard and lemon juice in a small bowl.

When the cauliflower steaks are done, divide into four equal portions. Top each portion with one-quarter of the arugula and dressing.

Serve immediately.

Per Serving
calories: 115 | fat: 6.0g | protein: 5.0g | carbs: 14.0g

Butternut Noodles with Mushrooms

Prep time: 10 minutes | **Cook time:** 12 minutes | **Serves:**4

Ingredients:

¼ cup extra-virgin olive oil
1 pound (454 g) cremini mushrooms, sliced
½ red onion, finely chopped
1 teaspoon dried thyme
½ teaspoon sea salt

3 garlic cloves, minced
½ cup dry white wine
Pinch of red pepper flakes
4 cups butternut noodles
4 ounces (113 g) grated Parmesan cheese

Directions:

In a large skillet over medium-high heat, heat the olive oil until shimmering. Add the mushrooms, onion, thyme, and salt to the skillet.

Cook for about 6 minutes, stirring occasionally, or until the mushrooms start to brown. Add the garlic and sauté for 30 seconds. Stir in the white wine and red pepper flakes. Fold in the noodles.

Cook for about 5 minutes, stirring occasionally, or until the noodles are tender. Serve topped with the grated Parmesan.

Per Serving calories: 244 fat: 14.0g protein: 4.0g carbs: 22.0g

Mini Crustless Spinach Quiches

Prep time: 10 minutes | **Cook time:** 20 minutes | **Serves:**6

Ingredients:

2 tablespoons extra-virgin olive oil
1 onion, finely chopped
2 cups baby spinach
2 garlic cloves, minced
8 large eggs, beaten

¼ cup unsweetened almond milk
½ teaspoon sea salt
¼ teaspoon freshly ground black pepper
1 cup shredded Swiss cheese
Cooking spray

Directions:

Preheat the oven to 375ºF (190ºC). Spritz a 6-cup muffin tin with cooking spray. Set aside.

In a large skillet over medium-high heat, heat the olive oil until shimmering. Add the onion and cook for about 4 minutes, or until soft. Add the spinach and cook for about 1 minute, stirring constantly, or until the spinach softens. Add the garlic and sauté for 30 seconds. Remove from the heat and let cool.

In a medium bowl, whisk together the eggs, milk, salt and pepper. Stir the cooled vegetables and the cheese into the egg mixture. Spoon the mixture into the prepared muffin tins. Bake for about 15 minutes, or until the eggs are set.

Let rest for 5 minutes before serving.

Per Serving calories: 218 | fat: 17.0g | protein: 14.0g | carbs: 4.0g

Celery and Mustard Greens

Prep time: 10 minutes | **Cook time:** 15 minutes | **Serves:**4

Ingredients:

½ cup low-sodium vegetable broth
1 celery stalk, roughly chopped
½ sweet onion, chopped

½ large red bell pepper, thinly sliced
2 garlic cloves, minced
1 bunch mustard greens, roughly chopped

Directions:

Pour the vegetable broth into a large cast iron pan and bring it to a simmer over medium heat.

Stir in the celery, onion, bell pepper, and garlic. Cook uncovered for about 3 to 5 minutes, or until the onion is softened.

Add the mustard greens to the pan and stir well. Cover, reduce the heat to low, and cook for an additional 10 minutes, or until the liquid is evaporated and the greens are wilted. Remove from the heat and serve warm.

Per Serving (1 cup)
calories: 39 | fat: 0g | protein: 1.6g

Braised Cauliflower with White Wine

Prep time: 10 minutes | **Cook time:** 12 to 16 minutes | **Serves:** 4 to 6

Ingredients:

3 tablespoons plus 1 teaspoon extra-virgin olive oil, divided
3 garlic cloves, minced
⅛ teaspoon red pepper flakes
1 head cauliflower (2 pounds / 907 g), cored and cut into 1½-inch florets

¼ teaspoon salt, plus more for seasoning
Black pepper, to taste
⅓ cup vegetable broth
⅓ cup dry white wine
2 tablespoons minced fresh parsley

Directions:

Combine 1 teaspoon of the oil, garlic and pepper flakes in small bowl.

Heat the remaining 3 tablespoons of the oil in a skillet over medium-high heat until shimmering. Add the cauliflower and ¼ teaspoon of the salt and cook for 7 to 9 minutes, stirring occasionally, or until florets are golden brown.

Push the cauliflower to sides of the skillet. Add the garlic mixture to the center of the skillet. Cook for about 30 seconds, or until fragrant. Stir the garlic mixture into the cauliflower.

Pour in the broth and wine and bring to simmer. Reduce the heat to medium-low. Cover and cook for 4 to 6 minutes, or until the cauliflower is crisp-tender. Off heat, stir in the parsley and season with salt and pepper. Serve immediately.

Per Serving
calories: 143 | fat: 11.7g | protein: 3.1g | carbs: 8.7g

Slow Cooked Buttery Mushrooms (Spanish)

Prep time: 10 minutes **Cooking Time:** 10 mins **Servings:** 2

Ingredients:

2 tablespoons butter
3 cloves of garlic, minced
Salt and pepper to taste
A dash of thyme

2 tablespoons olive oil
16 ounces fresh brown mushrooms, sliced
7 ounces fresh shiitake mushrooms, sliced

Directions:

Heat the butter and oil in a pot.

Sauté the garlic until fragrant, around 1 minute.

Stir in the rest of the and cook until soft, around 9 minutes.

Per Serving
Calories: 192; Carbs: 12.7g; Protein: 3.8g; Fat: 15.5g

Veggie Rice Bowls with Pesto Sauce

Prep time: 15 minutes | **Cook time:** 1 minute | **Serves:** 2

Ingredients:

2 cups water
1 cup arborio rice, rinsed
Salt and ground black pepper, to taste
2 eggs
1 cup broccoli florets
Lemon wedges, for serving

½ pound (227 g) Brussels sprouts
1 carrot, peeled and chopped
1 small beet, peeled and cubed
¼ cup pesto sauce

Directions:

Combine the water, rice, salt, and pepper in the Instant Pot. Insert a trivet over rice and place a steamer basket on top. Add the eggs, broccoli, Brussels sprouts, carrots, beet cubes, salt, and pepper to the steamer basket.

Lock the lid. Select the Manual mode and set the cooking time for 1 minute at High Pressure.

When the timer beeps, perform a natural pressure release for 10 minutes, then release any remaining pressure. Carefully open the lid. Remove the steamer basket and trivet from the pot and transfer the eggs to a bowl of ice water. Peel and halve the eggs. Use a fork to fluff the rice.

Divide the rice, broccoli, Brussels sprouts, carrot, beet cubes, and eggs into two bowls. Top with a dollop of pesto sauce and serve with the lemon wedges.

Per Serving
calories: 590 | fat: 34.1g | protein: 21.9g | carbs: 50.0g

Lentil and Tomato Collard Wraps

Prep time: 15 minutes | **Cook time:** 0 minutes | **Serves:** 4

Ingredients:

2 cups cooked lentils
5 Roma tomatoes, diced
½ cup crumbled feta cheese
10 large fresh basil leaves, thinly sliced
¼ cup extra-virgin olive oil
1 tablespoon balsamic vinegar

2 garlic cloves, minced
½ teaspoon raw honey
½ teaspoon salt
¼ teaspoon freshly ground black pepper
4 large collard leaves, stems removed

Directions:

Combine the lentils, tomatoes, cheese, basil leaves, olive oil, vinegar, garlic, honey, salt, and black pepper in a large bowl and stir until well blended.

Lay the collard leaves on a flat work surface. Spoon the equal-sized amounts of the lentil mixture onto the edges of the leaves. Roll them up and slice in half to serve.

Per Serving
calories: 318 | fat: 17.6g | protein: 13.2g | carbs: 27.5g

Potato Tortilla with Leeks and Mushrooms

Prep time: 30 minutes | **Cook time:** 50 minutes | **Serves:**2

Ingredients:

1 tablespoon olive oil
1 cup thinly sliced leeks
4 ounces (113 g) baby bella (cremini) mushrooms, stemmed and sliced
1 small potato, peeled and sliced ¼-inch thick
½ cup unsweetened almond milk
5 large eggs, beaten
1 teaspoon Dijon mustard
½ teaspoon salt
½ teaspoon dried thyme
Pinch freshly ground black pepper
3 ounces (85 g) Gruyère cheese, shredded

Directions:

Preheat the oven to 350ºF (180ºC).

In a large sauté pan over medium-high heat, heat the olive oil. Add the leeks, mushrooms, and potato and sauté for about 10 minutes, or until the potato starts to brown.

Reduce the heat to medium-low, cover, and cook for an additional 10 minutes, or until the potato begins to soften. Add 1 to 2 tablespoons of water to prevent sticking to the bottom of the pan, if needed.

Meanwhile, whisk together the milk, beaten eggs, mustard, salt, thyme, black pepper, and cheese in a medium bowl until combined. When the potatoes are fork-tender, turn off the heat. Transfer the cooked vegetables to an oiled nonstick ovenproof pan and arrange them in a nice layer along the bottom and slightly up the sides of the pan. Pour the milk mixture evenly over the vegetables.

Bake in the preheated oven for 25 to 30 minutes, or until the eggs are completely set and the top is golden and puffed. Remove from the oven and cool for 5 minutes before cutting and serving.

Per Serving
calories: 541 | fat: 33.1g | protein: 32.8g | carbs: 31.0g

Garlicky Zucchini Cubes with Mint

Prep time: 5 minutes | **Cook time:** 10 minutes | **Serves:**4

Ingredients:

3 large green zucchini, cut into ½-inch cubes
3 tablespoons extra-virgin olive oil
1 large onion, chopped
3 cloves garlic, minced
1 teaspoon salt
1 teaspoon dried mint

Directions:

Heat the olive oil in a large skillet over medium heat.

Add the onion and garlic and sauté for 3 minutes, stirring constantly, or until softened.

Stir in the zucchini cubes and salt and cook for 5 minutes, or until the zucchini is browned and tender.

Add the mint to the skillet and toss to combine, then continue cooking for 2 minutes. Serve warm.

Per Serving
calories: 146 | fat: 10.6g | protein: 4.2g | carbs: 11.8g

Mushrooms Ragu with Cheesy Polenta

Prep time: 20 minutes | **Cook time:** 30 minutes | **Serves:**2

Ingredients:

½ ounce (14 g) dried porcini mushrooms
1 pound (454 g) baby bella (cremini) mushrooms, quartered
2 tablespoons olive oil
1 garlic clove, minced
1 large shallot, minced
1 tablespoon flour
2 teaspoons tomato paste
½ cup red wine
1 cup mushroom stock (or reserved liquid from soaking the porcini mushrooms, if using)
1 fresh rosemary sprig
½ teaspoon dried thyme
1½ cups water
½ teaspoon salt, plus more as needed
⅓ cup instant polenta
2 tablespoons grated Parmesan cheese

Directions:

Soak the dried porcini mushrooms in 1 cup of hot water for about 15 minutes to soften them. When ready, scoop them out of the water, reserving the soaking liquid. Mince the porcini mushrooms. Heat the olive oil in a large sauté pan over medium-high heat. Add the mushrooms, garlic, and shallot and sauté for 10 minutes, or until the vegetables are beginning to caramelize.

Stir in the flour and tomato paste and cook for an additional 30 seconds. Add the red wine, mushroom stock, rosemary, and thyme. Bring the mixture to a boil, stirring constantly, or until it has thickened.

Reduce the heat and allow to simmer for 10 minutes.

Meanwhile, bring the water to a boil in a saucepan and sprinkle with the salt.

Add the instant polenta and stir quickly while it thickens. Scatter with the grated Parmesan cheese. Taste and season with more salt as needed. Serve warm.

Per Serving calories: 450 | fat: 16.0g | protein: 14.1g | carbs: 57.8g

Roasted Cauliflower and Carrots

Prep time: 10 minutes | **Cook time:** 30 minutes | **Serves:** 2

Ingredients:

4 cups cauliflower florets (about ½ small head)

2 medium carrots, peeled, halved, and then sliced into quarters lengthwise

2 tablespoons olive oil, divided

½ teaspoon salt, divided

½ teaspoon garlic powder, divided

2 teaspoons za'atar spice mix, divided

1 (15-ounce / 425-g) can chickpeas, drained, rinsed, and patted dry

¾ cup plain Greek yogurt

1 teaspoon harissa spice paste, plus additional as needed

Directions:

Preheat the oven to 400°F (205°C). Line a sheet pan with foil or parchment paper.

Put the cauliflower and carrots in a large bowl. Drizzle with 1 tablespoon of olive oil and sprinkle with ¼ teaspoon of salt, ¼ teaspoon of garlic powder, and 1 teaspoon of za'atar. Toss to combine well.

Spread the vegetables onto one half of the prepared sheet pan in a single layer.

Put the chickpeas in the same bowl and season with the remaining 1 tablespoon of olive oil, ¼ teaspoon of salt, ¼ teaspoon of garlic powder, and the remaining 1 teaspoon of za'atar. Toss to combine well.

Spread the chickpeas onto the other half of the sheet pan.

Roast in the preheated oven for 30 minutes, or until the vegetables are crisp-tender. Flip the vegetables halfway through and give the chickpeas a stir so they cook evenly.

Meanwhile, whisk the yogurt and harissa together in a small bowl. Taste and add additional harissa as needed.

Serve the vegetables and chickpeas with the yogurt mixture on the side.

Per Serving calories: 468 | fat: 23.0g | protein: 18.1g | carbs: 54.1g

Zoodles with Beet Pesto

Prep time: 10 minutes | **Cook time:** 50 minutes | **Serves:** 2

Ingredients:

1 medium red beet, peeled, chopped

½ cup walnut pieces

½ cup crumbled goat cheese

2 tablespoons freshly squeezed lemon juice

2 tablespoons plus 2 teaspoons extra-virgin olive oil, divided

¼ teaspoon salt

4 small zucchinis, spiralized

3 garlic cloves

Directions:

Preheat the oven to 375°F (190°C).

Wrap the chopped beet in a piece of aluminum foil and seal well.

Roast in the preheated oven for 30 to 40 minutes until tender.

Meanwhile, heat a skillet over medium-high heat until hot. Add the walnuts and toast for 5 to 7 minutes, or until fragrant and lightly browned.

Remove the cooked beets from the oven and place in a food processor. Add the toasted walnuts, goat cheese, garlic, lemon juice, 2 tablespoons of olive oil, and salt. Pulse until smoothly blended. Set aside.

Heat the remaining 2 teaspoons of olive oil in a large skillet over medium heat. Add the zucchini and toss to coat in the oil. Cook for 2 to 3 minutes, stirring gently, or until the zucchini is softened. Transfer the zucchini to a serving plate and toss with the beet pesto, then serve.

Per Serving

calories: 423 | fat: 38.8g | protein: 8.0g | carbs: 17.1g

Triumph of Cucumbers and Avocados (Spanish)

Preparation Time: 10 minutes **Cooking Time:** 15 minutes
Servings: 4

Ingredients:

12 oz cherry tomatoes, cut in half

½ tsp ground black pepper

¼ cup fresh cilantro, chopped

3 small avocados, chopped

5 small cucumbers, chopped

2 tbsp fresh lemon juice

1 tsp sea salt

2 tbsp olive oil

Directions:

Add cherry tomatoes, cucumbers, avocados, and cilantro into the large mixing bowl and mix well.

Mix olive oil, lemon juice, black pepper, and salt and pour over salad.

Toss well and serve immediately.

Per Serving

442 Calories 37g Fat 6.2g Protein

Fried Eggplant Rolls

Prep time: 20 minutes | **Cook time:** 10 mins | **Serves:** 4 to 6

Ingredients:

1 large eggplants, trimmed and cut lengthwise into ¼-inch-thick slices
1 teaspoon salt
1 cup ricotta cheese
Olive oil spray

4 ounces (113 g) goat cheese, shredded
¼ cup finely chopped fresh basil
½ teaspoon freshly ground black pepper

Directions:

Add the eggplant slices to a colander and season with salt. Set aside for 15 to 20 minutes.

Mix together the ricotta and goat cheese, basil, and black pepper in a large bowl and stir to combine. Set aside.

Dry the eggplant slices with paper towels and lightly mist them with olive oil spray.

Heat a large skillet over medium heat and lightly spray it with olive oil spray.

Arrange the eggplant slices in the skillet and fry each side for 3 minutes until golden brown.

Remove from the heat to a paper towel-lined plate and rest for 5 minutes.

Make the eggplant rolls: Lay the eggplant slices on a flat work surface and top each slice with a tablespoon of the prepared cheese mixture. Roll them up and serve immediately.

Per Serving

calories: 254 | fat: 14.9g | protein: 15.3g | carbs: 18.6g

Cauliflower Hash with Carrots

Prep time: 10 minutes | **Cook time:** 10 minutes | **Serves:** 4

Ingredients:

3 tablespoons extra-virgin olive oil
1 large onion, chopped
1 tablespoon minced garlic

2 cups diced carrots
4 cups cauliflower florets
½ teaspoon ground cumin
1 teaspoon salt

Directions:

In a large skillet, heat the olive oil over medium heat.

Add the onion and garlic and sauté for 1 minute. Stir in the carrots and stir-fry for 3 minutes.

Add the cauliflower florets, cumin, and salt and toss to combine.

Cover and cook for 3 minutes until lightly browned. Stir well and cook, uncovered, for 3 to 4 minutes, until softened.

Remove from the heat and serve warm.

Per Serving

calories: 158 | fat: 10.8g | protein: 3.1g | carbs: 14.9g

Roasted Veggies and Brown Rice Bowl

Prep time: 15 minutes | **Cook time:** 20 minutes | **Serves:** 4

Ingredients:

2 cups cauliflower florets
2 cups broccoli florets
1 (15-ounce / 425-g) can chickpeas, drained and rinsed
1 cup carrot slices (about 1 inch thick)
2 to 3 tablespoons extra-virgin olive oil, divided
Salt and freshly ground black pepper, to taste
Nonstick cooking spray

2 cups cooked brown rice
2 to 3 tablespoons sesame seeds, for garnish
Dressing:
3 to 4 tablespoons tahini
2 tablespoons honey
1 lemon, juiced
1 garlic clove, minced
Salt and freshly ground black pepper, to taste

Directions:

Preheat the oven to 400°F (205°C). Spritz two baking sheets with nonstick cooking spray.

Spread the cauliflower and broccoli on the first baking sheet and the second with the chickpeas and carrot slices.

Drizzle each sheet with half of the olive oil and sprinkle with salt and pepper. Toss to coat well.

Roast the chickpeas and carrot slices in the preheated oven for 10 minutes, leaving the carrots tender but crisp, and the cauliflower and broccoli for 20 minutes until fork-tender. Stir them once halfway through the cooking time.

Meanwhile, make the dressing: Whisk together the tahini, honey, lemon juice, garlic, salt, and pepper in a small bowl.

Divide the cooked brown rice among four bowls. Top each bowl evenly with roasted vegetables and dressing. Sprinkle the sesame seeds on top for garnish before serving.

Per Serving

calories: 453 | fat: 17.8g | protein: 12.1g | carbs: 61.8g

Wilted Dandelion Greens with Sweet Onion

Prep time: 15 minutes | **Cook time:** 15 minutes | **Serves:** 4

Ingredients:

1 tablespoon extra-virgin olive oil
2 garlic cloves, minced
1 Vidalia onion, thinly sliced
½ cup low-sodium vegetable broth

2 bunches dandelion greens, roughly chopped
Freshly ground black pepper, to taste

Directions:

Heat the olive oil in a large skillet over low heat.

Add the garlic and onion and cook for 2 to 3 minutes, stirring occasionally, or until the onion is translucent.

Fold in the vegetable broth and dandelion greens and cook for 5 to 7 minutes until wilted, stirring frequently.

Sprinkle with the black pepper and serve on a plate while warm.

Per Serving

calories: 81 | fat: 3.9g | protein: 3.2g | carbs: 10.8g

Zucchini and Artichokes Bowl with Farro

Prep time: 15 minutes | **Cook time:** 10 mins | **Serves:** 4 to 6

Ingredients:

⅓ cup extra-virgin olive oil
⅓ cup chopped red onions
½ cup chopped red bell pepper
2 garlic cloves, minced
1 cup zucchini, cut into ½-inch-thick slices
½ cup coarsely chopped artichokes
½ cup canned chickpeas, drained and rinsed
3 cups cooked farro

Salt and freshly ground black pepper, to taste
½ cup crumbled feta cheese, for serving (optional)
¼ cup sliced olives, for serving (optional)
2 tablespoons fresh basil, chiffonade, for serving (optional)
3 tablespoons balsamic vinegar, for serving (optional)

Directions:

Heat the olive oil in a large skillet over medium heat until it shimmers. Add the onions, bell pepper, and garlic and sauté for 5 minutes, stirring occasionally, until softened.

Stir in the zucchini slices, artichokes, and chickpeas and sauté for about 5 minutes until slightly tender.

Add the cooked farro and toss to combine until heated through. Sprinkle the salt and pepper to season.

Divide the mixture into bowls. Top each bowl evenly with feta cheese, olive slices, and basil and sprinkle with the balsamic vinegar, if desired.

Per Serving

calories: 366 | fat: 19.9g | protein: 9.3g | carbs: 50.7g

Vegetable and Tofu Scramble

Prep time: 5 minutes | **Cook time:** 10 minutes | **Serves:** 2

Ingredients:

2 tablespoons extra-virgin olive oil
½ red onion, finely chopped
1 cup chopped kale
8 ounces (227 g) mushrooms, sliced

2 garlic cloves, minced
Pinch red pepper flakes
½ teaspoon sea salt
⅛ teaspoon freshly ground black pepper
8 ounces (227 g) tofu, cut into pieces

Directions:

Heat the olive oil in a medium nonstick skillet over medium-high heat until shimmering.

Add the onion, kale, and mushrooms to the skillet and cook for about 5 minutes, stirring occasionally, or until the vegetables start to brown.

Add the tofu and stir-fry for 3 to 4 minutes until softened. Stir in the garlic, red pepper flakes, salt, and black pepper and cook for 30 seconds. Let the mixture cool for 5 minutes before serving.

Per Serving

calories: 233 | fat: 15.9g | protein: 13.4g | carbs: 11.9g

Zucchini Fritters

Prep time: 15 minutes | **Cook time:** 5 minutes
Makes 14 fritters

Ingredients:

4 cups grated zucchini
Salt, to taste
2 large eggs, lightly beaten
⅓ cup sliced scallions (green and white parts)

⅔ all-purpose flour
⅛ teaspoon black pepper
2 tablespoons olive oil

Directions:

Put the grated zucchini in a colander and lightly season with salt. Set aside to rest for 10 minutes. Squeeze out as much liquid from the grated zucchini as possible.

Pour the grated zucchini into a bowl. Fold in the beaten eggs, scallions, flour, salt, and pepper and stir until everything is well combined.

Heat the olive oil in a large skillet over medium heat until hot.

Drop 3 tablespoons mounds of the zucchini mixture onto the hot skillet to make each fritter, pressing them lightly into rounds and spacing them about 2 inches apart.

Cook for 2 to 3 minutes. Flip the zucchini fritters and cook for 2 minutes more, or until they are golden brown and cooked through.

Remove from the heat to a plate lined with paper towels. Repeat with the remaining zucchini mixture.Serve hot.

Per Serving (2 fritters)

calories: 113 | fat: 6.1g | protein: 4.0g | carbs: 12.2g

Vegetable and Red Lentil Stew

Prep time: 10 minutes | **Cook time:** 35 minutes | **Serves:** 6

Ingredients:

1 tablespoon extra-virgin olive oil
2 onions, peeled and finely diced
6½ cups water
2 zucchini, finely diced

4 celery stalks, finely diced
3 cups red lentils
1 teaspoon dried oregano
1 teaspoon salt, plus more as needed

Directions:

Heat the olive oil in a large pot over medium heat.

Add the onions and sauté for about 5 minutes, stirring constantly, or until the onions are softened.

Stir in the water, zucchini, celery, lentils, oregano, and salt and bring the mixture to a boil.

Reduce the heat to low and let simmer covered for 30 minutes, stirring occasionally, or until the lentils are tender.

Taste and adjust the seasoning as needed.

Per Serving

calories: 387 | fat: 4.4g | protein: 24.0g | carbs: 63.7g

Moroccan Tagine with Vegetables

Prep time: 20 minutes | **Cook time:** 40 minutes | **Serves:**2

Ingredients:

2 tablespoons olive oil
½ onion, diced
1 garlic clove, minced
2 cups cauliflower florets
1 medium carrot, cut into 1-inch pieces
1 cup diced eggplant
1 (28-ounce / 794-g) can whole tomatoes with their juices
1 (15-ounce / 425-g) can chickpeas, drained and rinsed

2 small red potatoes, cut into 1-inch pieces
1 cup water
1 teaspoon pure maple syrup
½ teaspoon cinnamon
½ teaspoon turmeric
1 teaspoon cumin
½ teaspoon salt
1 to 2 teaspoons harissa paste

Directions:

In a Dutch oven, heat the olive oil over medium-high heat. Sauté the onion for 5 minutes, stirring occasionally, or until the onion is translucent.

Stir in the garlic, cauliflower florets, carrot, eggplant, tomatoes, and potatoes. Using a wooden spoon or spatula to break up the tomatoes into smaller pieces.

Add the chickpeas, water, maple syrup, cinnamon, turmeric, cumin, and salt and stir to incorporate. Bring the mixture to a boil.

Once it starts to boil, reduce the heat to medium-low. Stir in the harissa paste, cover, allow to simmer for about 40 minutes, or until the vegetables are softened. Taste and adjust seasoning as needed.

Let the mixture cool for 5 minutes before serving.

Per Serving

calories: 293 | fat: 9.9g | protein: 11.2g | carbs: 45.5g

Steamed Zucchini-Paprika (Italian)

Prep time: 15 minutes **Cook time:** 30 minutes **Servings:** 2

Ingredients:

4 tablespoons olive oil
3 medium-sized zucchinis, sliced thinly
Λ dash of paprika

3 cloves of garlic, minced
Salt and pepper to taste
1 onion, chopped

Directions:

Place all in the Instant Pot. Give a good stir to combine all . Close the lid and make sure that the steam release valve is set to "Venting."

Press the "Slow Cook" button and adjust the cooking time to 4 hours.

Halfway through the cooking time, open the lid and give a good stir to brown the other side.

Per Serving

Calories: 93; Carbs: 3.1g; Protein: 0.6g; Fat: 10.2g

Vegan Lentil Bolognese

Prep time: 15 minutes | **Cook time:** 50 minutes | **Serves:**2

Ingredients:

1 medium celery stalk
1 large carrot
½ large onion
1 garlic clove
2 tablespoons olive oil
1 (28-ounce / 794-g) can crushed tomatoes

1 cup red wine
½ teaspoon salt, plus more as needed
½ teaspoon pure maple syrup
1 cup cooked lentils (prepared from ½ cup dry)

Directions:

Add the celery, carrot, onion, and garlic to a food processor and process until everything is finely chopped.

In a Dutch oven, heat the olive oil over medium-high heat. Add the chopped mixture and sauté for about 10 minutes, stirring occasionally, or until the vegetables are lightly browned.

Stir in the tomatoes, wine, salt, and maple syrup and bring to a boil.

Once the sauce starts to boil, cover, and reduce the heat to medium-low. Simmer for 30 minutes, stirring occasionally, or until the vegetables are softened.

Stir in the cooked lentils and cook for an additional 5 minutes until warmed through.

Taste and add additional salt, if needed. Serve warm.

Per Serving

calories: 367 | fat: 15.0g | protein: 13.7g | carbs: 44.

Grilled Vegetable Skewers

Prep time: 15 minutes | **Cook time:** 10 minutes | **Serves:**4

Ingredients:

4 medium red onions, peeled and sliced into 6 wedges
4 medium zucchinis, cut into 1-inch-thick slices
2 beefsteak tomatoes, cut into quarters
4 red bell peppers, cut into 2-inch squares

2 orange bell peppers, cut into 2-inch squares
2 yellow bell peppers, cut into 2-inch squares
2 tablespoons plus 1 teaspoon olive oil, divided
Special Equipment:
4 wooden skewers, soaked in water for at least 30 minutes

Directions:

Preheat the grill to medium-high heat.

Skewer the vegetables by alternating between red onion, zucchini, tomatoes, and the different colored bell peppers. Brush them with 2 tablespoons of olive oil.

Oil the grill grates with 1 teaspoon of olive oil and grill the vegetable skewers for 5 minutes. Flip the skewers and grill for 5 minutes more, or until they are cooked to your liking.

Let the skewers cool for 5 minutes before serving.

Per Serving

calories: 115 | fat: 3.0g | protein: 3.5g | carbs: 18.7g

Stuffed Portobello Mushroom with Tomatoes

Prep time: 10 minutes | **Cook time:** 15 minutes | **Serves:** 4

Ingredients:

4 large portobello mushroom caps
3 tablespoons extra-virgin olive oil
Salt and freshly ground black pepper, to taste

4 sun-dried tomatoes
1 cup shredded mozzarella cheese, divided
½ to ¾ cup low-sodium tomato sauce

Directions:

1. Preheat the broiler to High.
2. Arrange the mushroom caps on a baking sheet and drizzle with olive oil.
1. Sprinkle with salt and pepper.
2. Broil for 1o minutes, flipping the mushroom caps halfway through, until browned on the top.
3. Remove from the broil. Spoon 1 tomato, 2 tablespoons of cheese, and 2 to 3 tablespoons of sauce onto each mushroom cap.
4. Return the mushroom caps to the broiler and continue broiling for 2 to 3 minutes.
5. Cool for 5 minutes before serving.

Per Serving

calories: 217 | fat: 15.8g | protein: 11.2g | carbs: 11.7g

Stir-Fry Baby Bok Choy

Prep time: 12 minutes | **Cook time:** 10 to 13 minutes | **Serves:** 6

Ingredients:

2 tablespoons coconut oil
1 large onion, finely diced
2 teaspoons ground cumin
1-inch piece fresh ginger, grated
1 teaspoon ground turmeric

½ teaspoon salt
12 baby bok choy heads, ends trimmed and sliced lengthwise
Water, as needed
3 cups cooked brown rice

Directions:

Heat the coconut oil in a large pan over medium heat.

Saut é the onion for 5 minutes, stirring occasionally, or until the onion is translucent. Fold in the cumin, ginger, turmeric, and salt and stir to coat well.

Add the bok choy and cook for 5 to 8 minutes, stirring occasionally, or until the bok choy is tender but crisp. You can add 1 tablespoon of water at a time, if the skillet gets dry until you finish sautéing. Transfer the bok choy to a plate and serve over the cooked brown rice.

Per Serving calories: 443 | fat: 8.8g | protein: 30.3g | carbs: 75.7g

Sweet Pepper Stew

Prep time: 20 minutes | **Cook time:** 50 minutes | **Serves:** 2

Ingredients:

2 tablespoons olive oil
2 sweet peppers, diced (about 2 cups)
½ large onion, minced
1 garlic clove, minced
1 tablespoon gluten-free Worcestershire sauce

1 teaspoon oregano
1 cup low-sodium tomato juice
1 cup low-sodium vegetable stock
¼ cup brown rice
¼ cup brown lentils
Salt, to taste

Directions:

In a Dutch oven, heat the olive oil over medium-high heat.

Saut é the sweet peppers and onion for 10 minutes, stirring occasionally, or until the onion begins to turn golden and the peppers are wilted.

Stir in the garlic, Worcestershire sauce, and oregano and cook for 30 seconds more. Add the tomato juice, vegetable stock, rice, and lentils to the Dutch oven and stir to mix well. Bring the mixture to a boil and then reduce the heat to medium-low. Let it simmer covered for about 45 minutes, or until the rice is cooked through and the lentils are tender. Sprinkle with salt and serve warm.

Per Serving

calories: 378 | fat: 15.6g | protein: 11.4g | carbs: 52.8g

Cauliflower Rice Risotto with Mushrooms

Prep time: 5 minutes | **Cook time:** 10 minutes | **Serves:** 4

Ingredients:

1 teaspoon extra-virgin olive oil
½ cup chopped portobello mushrooms
4 cups cauliflower rice

½ cup plain Greek yogurt
¼ cup low-sodium vegetable broth
1 cup shredded Parmesan cheese

Directions:

In a medium skillet, heat the olive oil over medium-low heat until shimmering.

Add the mushrooms and stir-fry for 3 minutes.

Stir in the cauliflower rice, yogurt, and vegetable broth. Cover and bring to a boil over high heat for 5 minutes, stirring occasionally.

Add the Parmesan cheese and stir to combine. Continue cooking for an additional 3 minutes until the cheese is melted.

Divide the mixture into four bowls and serve warm.

Per Serving

calories: 167 | fat: 10.7g | protein: 12.1g | carbs: 8.1g

Roasted Vegetables

Prep time: 20 minutes | **Cook time:** 35 minutes | **Serves:**2

Ingredients:

6 teaspoons extra-virgin olive oil, divided
12 to 15 Brussels sprouts, halved
1 medium sweet potato, peeled and cut into 2-inch cubes
2 cups fresh cauliflower florets
1 medium zucchini, cut into 1-inch rounds
1 red bell pepper, cut into 1-inch slices
Salt, to taste

Directions:

Preheat the oven to 425ºF (220ºC).

Add 2 teaspoons of olive oil, Brussels sprouts, sweet potato, and salt to a large bowl and toss until they are completely coated.

Transfer them to a large roasting pan and roast for 10 minutes, or until the Brussels sprouts are lightly browned.

Meantime, combine the cauliflower florets with 2 teaspoons of olive oil and salt in a separate bowl.

Remove from the oven. Add the cauliflower florets to the roasting pan and roast for 10 minutes more.

Meanwhile, toss the zucchini and bell pepper with the remaining olive oil in a medium bowl until well coated. Season with salt.

Remove the roasting pan from the oven and stir in the zucchini and bell pepper. Continue roasting for 15 minutes, or until the vegetables are fork- tender.

Divide the roasted vegetables between two plates and serve warm.

Per Serving

calories: 333 | fat: 16.8g | protein: 12.2g | carbs: 37.6g

Ratatouille

Prep time: 10 minutes | **Cook time:** 30 minutes | **Serves:**4

Ingredients:

4 tablespoons extra-virgin olive oil, divided
1 cup diced zucchini
2 cups diced eggplant
1 cup diced onion
1 cup chopped green bell pepper
1 (15-ounce / 425-g) can no-salt-added diced tomatoes
½ teaspoon garlic powder
1 teaspoon ground thyme
Salt and freshly ground black pepper, to taste

Directions:

Heat 2 tablespoons of olive oil in a large saucepan over medium heat until it shimmers.

Add the zucchini and eggplant and sauté for 10 minutes, stirring occasionally. If necessary, add the remaining olive oil. Stir in the onion and bell pepper and sauté for 5 minutes until softened.

Add the diced tomatoes with their juice, garlic powder, and thyme and stir to combine. Continue cooking for 15 minutes until the vegetables are cooked through, stirring occasionally. Sprinkle with salt and black pepper.

Remove from the heat and serve on a plate.

Per Serving

calories: 189 | fat: 13.7g | protein: 3.1g | carbs: 14.8g

Sauté ed Green Beans with Tomatoes

Prep time: 10 minutes | **Cook time:** 20 minutes | **Serves:**4

Ingredients:

¼ cup extra-virgin olive oil
1 large onion, chopped
4 cloves garlic, finely chopped
1 pound (454 g) green beans, fresh or frozen, cut into 2-inch pieces
1½ teaspoons salt, divided
1 (15-ounce / 425-g) can diced tomatoes
½ teaspoon freshly ground black pepper

Directions:

Heat the olive oil in a large skillet over medium heat.

Add the onion and garlic and sauté for 1 minute until fragrant.

Stir in the green beans and sauté for 3 minutes. Sprinkle with ½ teaspoon of salt.

Add the tomatoes, remaining salt, and pepper and stir to mix well. Cook for an additional 12 minutes, stirring occasionally, or until the green beans are crisp and tender.

Remove from the heat and serve warm.

Per Serving

calories: 219 | fat: 13.9g | protein: 4.0g | carbs: 17.7g

Baked Tomatoes and Chickpeas

Prep time: 15 minutes | **Cook time:** 40 to 45 minutes | **Serves:**4

Ingredients:

1 tablespoon extra-virgin olive oil
½ medium onion, chopped
3 garlic cloves, chopped
¼ teaspoon ground cumin
2 teaspoons smoked paprika
1 cup crumbled feta cheese, for serving

2 (15-ounce / 425-g) cans chickpeas, drained and rinsed
4 cups halved cherry tomatoes
½ cup plain Greek yogurt, for serving

Directions:

Preheat the oven to 425°F (220°C).

Heat the olive oil in an ovenproof skillet over medium heat.

Add the onion and garlic and sauté for about 5 minutes, stirring occasionally, or until tender and fragrant.

Add the paprika and cumin and cook for 2 minutes. Stir in the chickpeas and tomatoes and allow to simmer for 5 to 10 minutes.

Transfer the skillet to the preheated oven and roast for 25 to 30 minutes, or until the mixture bubbles and thickens.

Remove from the oven and serve topped with yogurt and crumbled feta cheese.

Per Serving

calories: 411 | fat: 14.9g | protein: 20.2g | carbs: 50.7g

Creamy Cauliflower Chickpea Curry

Prep time: 5 minutes | **Cook time:** 15 minutes | **Serves:**4

Ingredients:

3 cups fresh or frozen cauliflower florets
2 cups unsweetened almond milk
1 (15-ounce / 425-g) can low-sodium chickpeas, drained and rinsed

1 tablespoon curry powder
¼ teaspoon garlic powder
¼ teaspoon ground ginger
⅛ teaspoon onion powder
¼ teaspoon salt
1 (15-ounce / 425-g) can coconut milk

Directions:

Add the cauliflower florets, almond milk, chickpeas, coconut milk, curry powder, garlic powder, ginger, and onion powder to a large stockpot and stir to combine.

Cover and cook over medium-high heat for 10 minutes, stirring occasionally.

Reduce the heat to low and continue cooking uncovered for 5 minutes, or until the cauliflower is tender.

Sprinkle with the salt and stir well. Serve warm.

Per Serving

calories: 409 | fat: 29.6g | protein: 10.0g | carbs: 29.8g

Sweet Potato Chickpea Buddha Bowl

Prep time: 10 minutes | **Cook time:** 10 to 15 minutes | **Serves:**2

Ingredients:

Sauce:
1 tablespoon tahini
2 tablespoons plain Greek yogurt
2 tablespoons hemp seeds
1 garlic clove, minced Pinch salt
Freshly ground black pepper, to taste

Bowl:
1 small sweet potato, peeled and finely diced
1 teaspoon extra-virgin olive oil
1 cup from 1 (15-ounce / 425-g) can low-sodium chickpeas, drained and rinsed
2 cups baby kale

Directions:
Make the Sauce

Whisk together the tahini and yogurt in a small bowl.

Stir in the hemp seeds and minced garlic. Season with salt pepper. Add 2 to 3 tablespoons water to create a creamy yet pourable consistency and set aside.

Make the Bowl

Preheat the oven to 425°F (220°C). Line a baking sheet with parchment paper.

Place the sweet potato on the prepared baking sheet and drizzle with the olive oil. Toss well

Roast in the preheated oven for 10 to 15 minutes, stirring once during cooking, or until fork-tender and browned.

In each of 2 bowls, place ½ cup of chickpeas, 1 cup of baby kale, and half of the cooked sweet potato. Serve drizzled with half of the prepared sauce.

Per Serving

calories: 323 | fat: 14.1g | protein: 17.0g | carbs: 36.0 g

Instant Pot Millet Pilaf (Italian)

Prep time: 20 minutes **Cooking Time:** 11 mins **Servings:** 4-5

Ingredients:

1 cup millet
1 lemon juice and zest
tbsp olive oil

Cup apricot and shelled pistachios (roughly chopped)
Cup parsley (fresh)

Directions:

Pour one and three-quarter cup of water in your instant pot. Place the millet and lid the instant pot.

Adjust time for 10 minutes on high pressure. When the time has elapsed, release pressure naturally.

Remove the lid and add all other. Stir while adjusting the seasonings. Serve and enjoy

Per Serving

308 Calories 11g Fat

Zucchini Patties

Prep time: 15 minutes | **Cook time:** 5 minutes | **Serves:**2

Ingredients:

2 medium zucchinis, shredded
1 teaspoon salt, divided
2 eggs
2 tablespoons chickpea flour
1 tablespoon chopped fresh mint
1 scallion, chopped
2 tablespoons extra-virgin olive oil

Directions:

Put the shredded zucchini in a fine-mesh strainer and season with ½ teaspoon of salt. Set aside.

Beat together the eggs, chickpea flour, mint, scallion, and remaining ½ teaspoon of salt in a medium bowl.

Squeeze the zucchini to drain as much liquid as possible. Add the zucchini to the egg mixture and stir until well incorporated. Heat the olive oil in a large skillet over medium-high heat.

Drop the zucchini mixture by spoonfuls into the skillet. Gently flatten the zucchini with the back of a spatula.

Cook for 2 to 3 minutes or until golden brown. Flip and cook for an additional 2 minutes.

Remove from the heat and serve on a plate.

Per Serving

calories: 264 | fat: 20.0g | protein: 9.8g | carbs: 16.1g

Creamy Sweet Potatoes and Collards

Prep time: 20 minutes | **Cook time:** 35 minutes | **Serves:**2

Ingredients:

1 tablespoon avocado oil
3 garlic cloves, chopped
1 yellow onion, diced
½ teaspoon crushed red pepper flakes
1 large sweet potato, peeled and diced
2 bunches collard greens (about 2 pounds/907 g), stemmed, leaves chopped int
1-inch squares
1 (14.5-ounce / 411-g) can diced tomatoes with juice
1 (15-ounce / 425-g) can red kidney beans or chickpeas, drained and rinsed
1½ cups water
½ cup unsweetened coconut milk
Salt and black pepper, to taste

Directions:

In a large, deep skillet over medium heat, melt the avocado oil. Add the garlic, onion, and red pepper flakes and cook for 3 minutes. Stir in the sweet potato and collards.

Add the tomatoes with their juice, beans, water, and coconut milk and mix well. Bring the mixture just to a boil.

Reduce the heat to medium-low, cover, and simmer for about 30 minutes, or until softened.

Season to taste with salt and pepper and serve.

Per Serving calories: 445 fat: 9.6g protein: 18.1g carbs: 73.1g

Zucchini Crisp

Prep time: 10 minutes | **Cook time:** 20 minutes | **Serves:**2

Ingredients:

4 zucchinis, sliced into ½-inch rounds
½ cup unsweetened almond milk
1 teaspoon fresh lemon juice
1 teaspoon arrowroot powder
½ teaspoon salt, divided
½ cup whole wheat bread crumbs
¼ cup nutritional yeast
¼ cup hemp seeds
½ teaspoon garlic powder
¼ teaspoon crushed red pepper
¼ teaspoon black pepper

Directions:

Preheat the oven to 375°F (190°C). Line two baking sheets with parchment paper and set aside.

Put the zucchini in a medium bowl with the almond milk, lemon juice, arrowroot powder, and ¼ teaspoon of salt. Stir to mix well.

In a large bowl with a lid, thoroughly combine the bread crumbs, nutritional yeast, hemp seeds, garlic powder, crushed red pepper and black pepper. Add the zucchini in batches and shake until the slices are evenly coated.

Arrange the zucchini on the prepared baking sheets in a single layer.

Bake in the preheated oven for about 20 minutes, or until the zucchini slices are golden brown. Season with the remaining ¼ teaspoon of salt before serving.

Per Serving

calories: 255 | fat: 11.3g | protein: 8.6g | carbs: 31.9g

Roasted Vegetables and Zucchini Pasta (Italian)

Preparation Time: 10 minutes **Cooking Time:** 7 minutes **Servings:** 2

Ingredients:

¼ cup raw pine nuts
1 tablespoon extra-virgin olive oil
2 garlic cloves, minced
4 cups leftover vegetables
4 medium zucchinis, cut into long strips resembling noodles

Directions:

Heat oil in a large skillet over medium heat and sauté the garlic for 2 minutes.

Add the leftover vegetables and place the zucchini noodles on top. Let it cook for five minutes. Garnish with pine nuts.

Per Serving

Calories: 288; Carbs: 23.6g; Protein: 8.2g; Fat: 19.2g

Paprika Cauliflower Steaks with Walnut Sauce

Prep time: 5 minutes | **Cook time:** 30 minutes | **Serves:** 2

Ingredients:

Walnut Sauce:
½ cup raw walnut halves
2 tablespoons virgin olive oil, divided
1 clove garlic, chopped
1 small yellow onion, chopped
½ cup unsweetened almond milk

Salt and pepper, to taste
2 tablespoons fresh lemon juice
Paprika Cauliflower:
1 medium head cauliflower
1 teaspoon sweet paprika
1 teaspoon minced fresh thyme leaves (about 2 sprigs)

Directions:

Preheat the oven to 350ºF (180ºC).

Make the walnut sauce: Toast the walnuts in a large, ovenproof skillet over medium heat until fragrant and slightly darkened, about 5 minutes. Transfer the walnuts to a blender. Heat 1 tablespoon of olive oil in the skillet. Add the garlic and onion and sauté for about 2 minutes, or until slightly softened. Transfer the garlic and onion into the blender, along with the almond milk, lemon juice, salt, and pepper. Blend the ingredients until smooth and creamy. Keep the sauce warm while you prepare the cauliflower.

Make the paprika cauliflower: Cut two 1-inch-thick "steaks" from the center of the cauliflower. Lightly moisten the steaks with water and season both sides with paprika, thyme, salt, and pepper. Heat the remaining 1 tablespoon of olive oil in the skillet over medium-high heat. Add the cauliflower steaks and sear for about 3 minutes until evenly browned. Flip the cauliflower steaks and transfer the skillet to the oven. Roast in the preheated oven for about 20 minutes until crisp-tender. Serve the cauliflower steaks warm with the walnut sauce on the side.

Per Serving calories: 367 | fat: 27.9g | protein: 7.0g | carbs: 22.7g

Potato and Kale Bowls

Prep time: 10 minutes | **Cook time:** 10 minutes | **Serves:** 4

Ingredients:

1 tablespoon olive oil
1 small onion, peeled and diced
1 stalk celery, diced
2 cloves garlic, minced
4 medium potatoes, peeled and diced
2 bunches kale, washed, deveined, and chopped

1½ cups vegetable broth
2 teaspoons salt
½ teaspoon ground black pepper
¼ teaspoon caraway seeds
1 tablespoon apple cider vinegar
4 tablespoons sour cream

Directions:

Press the Sauté button on Instant Pot. Heat oil. Add onion and celery and stir-fry for 3 to 5 minutes until onions are translucent. Add garlic and cook for an additional minute. Add potatoes in an even layer. Add chopped kale in an even layer. Add broth. Lock lid.

Press the Manual button and adjust time to 5 minutes. Let the pressure release naturally for 10 minutes. Quick release any additional pressure until float valve drops and then unlock lid; then drain broth. Stir in salt, pepper, caraway seeds, and vinegar; slightly mash the potatoes in the Instant Pot. Garnish each serving with 1 tablespoon sour cream.

Per Serving
calories: 259 | fat: 5.5g | protein: 7.9g | carbs: 47.6g

Eggplant and Millet Pilaf

Prep time: 5 minutes | **Cook time:** 17 minutes | **Serves:** 4

Ingredients:

1 tablespoon olive oil
¼ cup peeled and diced onion
1 cup peeled and diced eggplant
1 small Roma tomato, seeded and diced
1 cup millet

2 cups vegetable broth
1 teaspoon sea salt
¼ teaspoon ground black pepper
⅛ teaspoon saffron
⅛ teaspoon cayenne pepper
1 tablespoon chopped fresh chives

Directions:

Press Sauté button on Instant Pot. Add the olive oil. Add onion and cook for 3 to 5 minutes until translucent. Toss in eggplant and stir-fry for 2 more minutes. Add diced tomato.

Add millet to Instant Pot in an even layer. Gently pour in broth. Lock lid. Press the Rice button (the Instant Pot will determine the time, about 10 minutes pressurized cooking time). When timer beeps, let pressure release naturally for 5 minutes. Quick release any additional pressure until float valve drops and then unlock lid.

Transfer pot ingredients to a serving bowl. Season with salt, pepper, saffron, and cayenne pepper. Garnish with chives.

Per Serving
calories: 238 | fat: 5.6g | protein: 6.0g | carbs: 40.8g

Sautéed Cabbage (Spanish)

Preparation Time: 10 minutes
Cooking Time: 12 to 14 minutes **Serving:** 4 to 6

Ingredients:

1 small head green cabbage (about 1¼ pounds / 567 g), cored and sliced thin
3/4 teaspoon salt, divided
¼ cup chopped fresh parsley

2 tablespoons extra-virgin olive oil, divided 1 onion, halved and sliced thin
¼ teaspoon black pepper
1½ teaspoons lemon juice

Directions:

Place the cabbage in a large bowl with cold water. Let sit for 3 minutes. Drain well.

Heat 1 tablespoon of the oil in a skillet over medium-high heat until shimmering. Add the onion and ¼ teaspoon of the salt and cook for 5 to 7 minutes, or until softened and lightly browned. Transfer to a bowl.

Heat the remaining 1 tablespoon of the oil in now-empty skillet over medium-high heat until shimmering. Add the cabbage and sprinkle with the remaining ½ teaspoon of the salt and black pepper. Cover and cook for about 3 minutes, without stirring, or until cabbage is wilted and lightly browned on bottom.

Stir and continue to cook for about 4 minutes, uncovered, or until the cabbage is crisp-tender and lightly browned in places, stirring once halfway through cooking. Off heat, stir in the cooked onion, parsley and lemon juice.

Transfer to a plate and serve.

Per Serving

calories: 117 fat: 7g protein: 3g carbs: 13g

Quick Spinach Focaccia (Italian)

Preparation Time: 10 minutes **Cooking Time:** 25 minutes
Servings: 12

Ingredients:

10 eggs
¼ tsp garlic powder
½ tsp dried basil

2 cups spinach, chopped
¼ tsp onion powder
1 ½ cups parmesan cheese, grated Salt

Directions:

Preheat the oven to 400 F. Grease muffin tin and set aside.

In a large bowl, whisk eggs with basil, garlic powder, onion powder, and salt.

Add cheese and spinach and stir well.

Pour egg mixture into the prepared muffin tin and bake 15 minutes.

Serve and enjoy.

Per Serving

110 Calories 7g Fat 9g Protein

Ratatouille (Italian)

Preparation Time: 15 minutes **Cooking Time:** 40 minutes
Serving: 6

Ingredients:

2 russet potatoes, cubed
1 eggplant, cubed
1 zucchini, cubed
1 red bell pepper, chopped
1 teaspoon dried parsley
1 teaspoon dried oregano
½ teaspoon black pepper
1/3 cup olive oil
1 (8-ounce / 227-g) can tomato paste

½ cup Roma tomatoes, cubed
1 red onion, chopped
1 teaspoon dried mint
½ teaspoon salt
2 garlic cloves, minced
¼ teaspoon red pepper flakes
¼ cup vegetable broth
¼ cup water

Directions:

Preheat the air fryer to 320ºF (160ºC).

In a large bowl, combine the potatoes, tomatoes, eggplant, zucchini, onion, bell pepper, garlic, mint, parsley, oregano, salt, black pepper, and red pepper flakes.

In a small bowl, mix together the olive oil, tomato paste, broth, and water. Pour the oil-and-tomato-paste mixture over the vegetables and toss until everything is coated.

Pour the coated vegetables into the air fryer basket in an even layer and roast for 20 minutes. After 20 minutes, stir well and spread out again. Roast for an additional 10 minutes, then repeat the process and cook for another 10 minutes.

Per Serving

calories: 280 fat: 13g protein: 6g carbs: 40g

Tortellini in Red Pepper Sauce (Italian)

Prep time: 15 minutes Cook time: 10 minutes **Servings:** 4

Ingredients:

1 (16-ounce) container fresh cheese tortellini (usually green and white pasta)
¼ cup tahini

1 (16-ounce) jar roasted red peppers, drained
1 teaspoon garlic powder
1 tablespoon red pepper oil (optional)

Directions:

Bring a large pot of water to a boil and cook the tortellini according to package directions.

In a blender, combine the red peppers with the garlic powder and process until smooth. Once blended, add the tahini until the sauce is thickened. If the sauce gets too thick, add up to 1 tablespoon red pepper oil (if using).

Once tortellini are cooked, drain and leave pasta in colander. Add the sauce to the bottom of the empty pot and heat for 2 minutes. Then, add the tortellini back into the pot and cook for 2 more minutes. Serve and enjoy!

Per Serving

Calories: 530; Carbs: 95.4g; Protein: 8.0g; Fat: 18.5g

Celeriac Mix with Cauliflower (Italian)

Preparation Time: 10 minutes **Cooking Time:** 12 minutes
Servings: 6

Ingredients:

1 head cauliflower 1 small celery root
1 tablespoon. chopped rosemary
¼ cup butter
1 tablespoon. chopped thyme
1 cup cream cheese

Directions:

Skin the celery root and cut it into small pieces.

Cut the cauliflower into similar sized pieces and combine.

Toast the herbs in the butter in a large pan, until they become fragrant.

Add the cauliflower and celery root and stir to combine.

Season and cook at medium-high until moisture in the vegetables releases itself, then cover and cook on low for 10-12 minutes.

Once the vegetables are soft, remove them from the heat and place them in the blender.

Make it smooth, then put the cream cheese and puree again.

Season and serve.

Per Serving
225 Calories 20g Fat 5g Protein

Delicious Feta with Fresh Spinach (Greek)

Preparation Time: 10 minutes **Cooking Time:** 0 minutes
Servings: 6

Ingredients:

6 cups fresh baby spinach, chopped
1 (16-ounce) package orzo pasta, cooked according to package directions, rinsed, drained, and cooled
1/4 cup extra-virgin olive oil
Freshly ground black pepper
¼ cup scallions, white and green parts, chopped
3/4 cup crumbled feta cheese 1/4 cup halved Kalamata olives
1/2 cup red wine vinegar
1½ teaspoons freshly squeezed lemon juice Sea salt

Directions:

In a large bowl, combine the spinach, scallions, and cooled orzo.

Sprinkle with the feta and olives.

In a small bowl, whisk the vinegar, olive oil, and lemon juice. Season with sea salt and pepper.

Add the dressing to the salad and gently toss to combine. Refrigerate until serving.

Per Serving
255 Calories 8g Protein 8g Fat

Cheddar Fondue with Tomato Sauce (Italian)

Preparation Time: 10 minutes **Cooking Time:** 30 minutes
Servings: 4

Ingredients:

1 garlic clove, halved
2/3 cup dry white wine
6 tablespoons. Butter, cubed
1-½ teaspoons. Dried basil
Dash cayenne pepper
Cubed French bread and cooked shrimp
6 medium tomatoes, seeded and diced
2 cups shredded cheddar cheese
1 tablespoon. All-purpose flour

Directions:

Rub the bottom and sides of a fondue pot with a garlic clove.

Set aside and discard the garlic.

3. Combine wine, butter, basil, cayenne, and tomatoes in a large saucepan.

On a medium-low heat, bring the mixture to a simmer, then decrease the heat to low.

Mix cheese with flour.

Add to tomato mixture gradually while stirring after each addition until cheese is melted.

Pour into the preparation fondue pot and keep warm.

Enjoy with shrimp and bread cubes.

Per Serving
118 Calories 10g Fat 4g Protein

Easy Roasted Radishes (Greek)

Preparation Time: 5 minutes **Cooking Time:** 18 minutes
Serving: 4

Ingredients:

1-pound (454 g) radishes, ends trimmed
½ teaspoon sea salt if needed
2 tbsp olive oil

Directions:

Preheat the air fryer to 360°F (182°C).

In a large bowl, combine the radishes with olive oil and sea salt.

Pour the radishes into the air fryer and cook for 10 minutes. Stir or turn the radishes over and cook for 8 minutes more, then serve.

Per Serving
calories: 78 | fat: 9g | protein: 1g | carbs: 4g

Mediterranean Baked Chickpeas (Spanish)

Preparation Time: 15 minutes **Cooking Time:** 15 minutes
Servings: 6

Ingredients:

1 tablespoon extra-virgin olive oil

2 teaspoons smoked paprika

4 cups halved cherry tomatoes

1 cup crumbled feta

½ cup plain, unsweetened, full-fat Greek yogurt, for serving

½ medium onion, chopped

3 garlic cloves, chopped

¼ teaspoon ground cumin

2 (15-ounce) cans chickpeas, drained and rinsed

Directions:

Preheat the oven to 425°F.

In an oven-safe sauté pan or skillet, heat the oil over medium heat and sauté the onion and garlic. Cook for about 5 minutes, until softened and fragrant. Stir in the paprika and cumin and cook for 2 minutes. Stir in the tomatoes and chickpeas. Bring to a simmer for 5 to 10 minutes before placing in the oven.

Roast in oven for 25 to 30 minutes, until bubbling and thickened. To serve, top with Greek yogurt and feta.

Per Serving

Calories: 330; Carbs: 75.4g; Protein: 9.0g; Fat: 18.5g

Falafel Bites (Italian)

Preparation Time: 10 minutes **Cooking Time:** 15 minutes
Servings: 4

Ingredients:

1 2/3 cups falafel mix

1¼ cups water

1 tablespoon Pickled Onions (optional)

Turnips (optional)

Extra-virgin olive oil spray

1 tablespoon Pickled

2 tablespoons Tzatziki Sauce (optional)

Directions:

In a large bowl, carefully stir the falafel mix into the water. Mix well. Let stand 15 minutes to absorb the water. Form mixes into 1-inch balls and arrange on a baking sheet.

Preheat the broiler to high.

Take the balls and flatten slightly with your thumb (so they won't roll around on the baking sheet). Spray with olive oil, and then broil for 2 to 3 minutes on each side, until crispy and brown.

To fry the falafel, fill a pot with ½ inch of cooking oil and heat over medium-high heat to 375°F. Fry the balls for about 3 minutes, until brown and crisp. Drain on paper towels and serve with pickled onions, pickled turnips, and tzatziki sauce (if using).

Per Serving

Calories: 530; Carbs: 95.4g; Protein: 8.0g; Fat: 18.5g

Vegetable Hummus Wraps (Greek)

Prep time: 15 minutes **Cooking Time:** 10 minutes
Serving: 6

Ingredients:

1 large eggplant

½ cup extra-virgin olive oil

1 teaspoon salt

1 large onion

6 lavash wraps or large pita bread

1 cup hummus

Directions:

Preheat a grill, large grill pan, or lightly oiled large skillet on medium heat.

Slice the eggplant and onion into circles. Brush the vegetables with olive oil and sprinkle with salt.

Cook the vegetables on both sides, about 3 to 4 minutes each side.

To make the wrap, lay the lavash or pita flat. Spread about 2 tablespoons of hummus on the wrap.

Evenly divide the vegetables among the wraps, layering them along one side of the wrap. Gently fold over the side of the wrap with the vegetables, tucking them in and making a tight wrap.

Lay the wrap seam side-down and cut in half or thirds.

You can also wrap each sandwich with plastic wrap to help it hold its shape and eat it later.

Per Serving

calories: 362 | fat: 26g | protein: 15g | carbs: 28g

Summer Veggies in Instant Pot (Spanish)

Prep time: 10 minutes **Cooking Time:** 7 mins **Servings:** 6

Ingredients:

2 cups okra, sliced

1 cup mushroom, sliced

1 ½ cups onion, sliced

2 tablespoons basil, chopped 1 tablespoon thyme, chopped

1 cup grape tomatoes

2 cups bell pepper, sliced

2 ½ cups zucchini, sliced

½ cups balsamic vinegar

½ cups olive oil Salt and pepper

Directions:

Place all in the Instant Pot.

Stir the contents and close the lid.

Close the lid and press the Manual button.

Adjust the cooking time to 7 minutes.

Do quick pressure release.

Once cooled, evenly divide into serving size, keep in your preferred container, and refrigerate until ready to eat.

Per Serving

Calories: 233; Carbs: 7g; Protein: 3g; Fat: 18g

Beet and Watercress Salad (Greek)

Preparation Time: 15 minutes **Cooking Time:** 8 minutes
Serving: 4

Ingredients:

1 pounds (907 g) beets, scrubbed, trimmed and cut into ¾-inch pieces
1 teaspoon caraway seeds
1 tablespoon white wine vinegar, divided
¼ cup coarsely chopped fresh dill
1 tablespoon extra-virgin olive oil, divided, plus more for drizzling
¼ cup hazelnuts, toasted, skinned and chopped
½ cup water
1 cup plain Greek yogurt
1 small garlic clove, minced
½ teaspoon table salt, plus more for seasoning
1 teaspoon grated orange zest
5 ounces (142 g) watercress, torn into bite-size pieces
Black pepper, to taste
2 tablespoons orange juice
Coarse sea salt, to taste

Directions:

Combine the beets, water, caraway seeds and table salt in the Instant Pot. Set the lid in place. Select the Manual mode and set the cooking time for 8 minutes on High Pressure. When the timer goes off, do a quick pressure release.

Carefully open the lid. Using a slotted spoon, transfer the beets to a plate. Set aside to cool slightly.

In a small bowl, combine the yogurt, garlic and 3 tablespoons of the beet cooking liquid. In a large bowl, toss the watercress with 2 teaspoons of the oil and 1 teaspoon of the vinegar. Season with table salt and pepper.

Spread the yogurt mixture over a serving dish. Arrange the watercress on top of the yogurt mixture, leaving 1-inch border of the yogurt mixture.

Add the beets to now-empty large bowl and toss with the orange zest and juice, the remaining 2 teaspoons of the vinegar and the remaining 1 teaspoon of the oil. Season with table salt and pepper.

Arrange the beets on top of the watercress mixture. Drizzle with the olive oil and sprinkle with the dill, hazelnuts and sea salt.

Serve immediately.

Per Serving

calories: 240 | fat: 15g | protein: 9g | carbs: 19g

Zucchini Garlic Fries (Italian)

Preparation Time: 15 minutes **Cooking Time:** 20 minutes
Servings: 6

Ingredients:

¼ teaspoon garlic powder
2 large egg whites, beaten
Salt and pepper to taste
½ cup almond flour
3 medium zucchinis, sliced into fry sticks

Directions:

Preheat oven to 400oF.

Mix all in a bowl until the zucchini fries are well coated.

Place fries on cookie sheet and spread evenly.

Put in oven and cook for 20 minutes.

Halfway through cooking time, stir fries.

Per Serving

Calories: 11; Carbs: 1.1g; Protein: 1.5g; Fat: 0.1g

Mediterranean Lentil Sloppy Joes (Italian)

Preparation Time: 5 minutes **Cooking Time:** 15 minutes
Servings: 4

Ingredients:

1 tablespoon extra-virgin olive oil
1 cup chopped bell pepper, any color (about 1 medium bell pepper) 2 garlic cloves, minced (about 1 teaspoon)
1 (14.5-ounce) can low-sodium or no-salt-added diced tomatoes, undrained
¼ teaspoon kosher or sea salt
1½ cups chopped seedless cucumber (1 medium cucumber)
1 cup chopped onion (about ½ medium onion)
1 (15-ounce) can lentils, drained and rinsed
1 cup chopped romaine lettuce
1 teaspoon ground cumin
4 whole-wheat pita breads, split open
1 teaspoon dried thyme

Directions:

In a medium saucepan over medium-high heat, heat the oil. Add the onion and bell pepper and cook for 4 minutes, stirring frequently. Add the garlic and cook for 1 minute, stirring frequently. Add the lentils, tomatoes (with their liquid), cumin, thyme, and salt. Turn the heat to medium and cook, stirring occasionally, for 10 minutes, or until most of the liquid has evaporated.

Stuff the lentil mixture inside each pita. Lay the cucumbers and lettuce on top of the lentil mixture and serve.

Per Serving

Calories: 334 Total Fat: 5g Saturated Fat: 1g Cholesterol: 0mg
Total Carbohydrates: 58g Protein: 16g

Stir Fried Bok Choy (Spanish)

Preparation Time: 5 minutes **Cooking Time:** 13 minutes
Servings: 4

Ingredients:

3 tablespoons coconut oil

4 cloves of garlic, minced

1 onion, chopped

2 tablespoons sesame oil

Salt and pepper to taste

2 heads bok choy, rinsed and chopped

2 teaspoons coconut aminos

2 tablespoons sesame seeds, toasted

Directions:

Heat the oil in a pot for 2 minutes.

Sauté the garlic and onions until fragrant, around 3 minutes.

Stir in the bok choy, coconut aminos, salt and pepper.

Cover pan and cook for 5 minutes.

Stir and continue cooking for another 3 minutes.

Drizzle with sesame oil and sesame seeds on top before serving.

Per Serving

Calories: 358; Carbs: 5.2g; Protein: 21.5g; Fat: 28.4g

Nutritious Vegan Cabbage (Spanish)

Preparation Time: 35 minutes **Cooking Time:** 15 minutes
Servings: 6

Ingredients:

3 cups green cabbage

1 can tomatoes

carrots

2 tbsp. vinegar

onion Cups vegetable broth

3 stalks celery

sage

Directions:

Mix 1 tbsp. of lemon juice. 2 garlic cloves and the rest of in the instant pot and. Lid and set time for fifteen minutes on high pressure.

Release pressure naturally then remove the lid. Remove the soup from the instant pot.

Serve and enjoy.

Per Serving

67 Calories 0.4g Fat

Crispy Artichokes (Spanish)

Preparation Time: 10 minutes **Cooking Time:** 15 minutes
Serving: 2

Ingredients:

1 large sweet potato (about 8 ounces / 227 g)

1 cup chopped onion

1 garlic clove

½ cup crumbled

1 tablespoon balsamic vinegar

Gorgonzola cheese

1 large egg

2 tablespoons extra-virgin olive oil, divided

1 cup old-fashioned rolled oats

¼ teaspoon kosher salt

1 tablespoon dried oregano

Directions:

Using a fork, pierce the sweet potato all over and microwave on high for 4 to 5 minutes, until softened in the center. Cool slightly before slicing in half.

Meanwhile, in a large skillet over medium-high heat, heat 1 tablespoon of the olive oil. Add the onion and sauté for 5 minutes.

Spoon the sweet potato flesh out of the skin and put the flesh in a food processor. Add the cooked onion, egg, garlic, oats, oregano, vinegar and salt. Pulse until smooth. Add the cheese and pulse four times to barely combine.

Form the mixture into four burgers. Place the burgers on a plate, and press to flatten each to about ¾-inch thick.

Wipe out the skillet with a paper towel. Heat the remaining 1 tablespoon of the oil over medium-high heat for about 2 minutes. Add the burgers to the hot oil, then reduce the heat to medium. Cook the burgers for 5 minutes per side.

Transfer the burgers to a plate and serve.

Per Serving

calories: 290 | fat: 12g | protein: 12g | carbs: 43g

Rosemary Roasted Red Potatoes (Greek)

Preparation Time: 5 minutes **Cooking Time:** 20 minutes
Serving: 6

Ingredients:

1 pound (454 g) red
potatoes, quartered
½ teaspoon kosher salt
4 rosemary sprigs

¼ cup olive oil
1 garlic clove, minced
¼ teaspoon black pepper

Directions:

Preheat the air fryer to 360°F (182°C).

In a large bowl, toss the potatoes with the olive oil, salt,
pepper, and garlic until well coated.

Pour the potatoes into the air fryer basket and top with the
sprigs of rosemary.

Roast for 10 minutes, then stir or toss the potatoes and
roast for 10 minutes more.

Remove the rosemary sprigs and serve the potatoes.
Season with additional salt and pepper, if needed.

Per Serving

calories: 133 | fat: 9g | protein: 1g | carbs: 12g

Savoy Cabbage with Coconut Cream Sauce (Spanish)

Prep time: 5 minutes **Cooking Time:** 20 mins **Servings:** 4

Ingredients:

1 tablespoons olive oil
1 onion, chopped
1 head savoy cabbage,
chopped finely
Salt and pepper to taste
2 cups bone broth

2 cloves of garlic, minced
1 bay leaf
1 cup coconut milk, freshly
squeezed
2 tablespoons chopped
parsley

Directions:

Heat oil in a pot for 2 minutes.

Stir in the onions, bay leaf, and garlic until fragrant, around
3 minutes.

Add the rest of the , except for the parsley and mix well.

Cover pot, bring to a boil, and let it simmer for 5 minutes
or until cabbage is tender to taste.

Stir in parsley and serve.

Per Serving

Calories: 195; Carbs: 12.3g; Protein: 2.7g; Fat: 19.7g

Delicious Tomato Broth (Spanish)

Preparation Time: 10 minutes **Cooking Time:** 15 minutes
Servings: 2

Ingredients:

14 oz can fire-roasted
tomatoes
½ cup heavy cream
1 cup cheddar cheese,
grated
1 ½ cups vegetable stock

½ tsp dried basil
½ tsp dried oregano Pepper
½ cup parmesan cheese,
grated
Salt
¼ cup zucchini, grated

Directions:

Add tomatoes, stock, zucchini, oregano, basil, pepper, and
salt into the instant pot and stir well.

Seal pot and cook on high pressure for 5 minutes.

Release pressure using quick release. Remove lid.

Set pot on sauté mode. Add heavy cream, parmesan
cheese, and cheddar cheese and stir well and cook until
cheese is melted.

Serve and enjoy.

Per Serving

460 Calories 35g Fat 24g Protein

Chapter 7
Poultry and Meats

Herbed-Mustard-Coated Pork Tenderloin

Prep time: 10 minutes | **Cook time:** 15 minutes | **Serves:**4

Ingredients:

3 tablespoons fresh rosemary leaves

¼ cup Dijon mustard

½ cup fresh parsley leaves

6 garlic cloves

½ teaspoon sea salt

¼ teaspoon freshly ground black pepper

1 tablespoon extra-virgin olive oil

1 (1½-pound / 680-g) pork tenderloin

Directions:

Preheat the oven to 400ºF (205ºC).

Put all the ingredients, except for the pork tenderloin, in a food processor. Pulse until it has a thick consistency.

Put the pork tenderloin on a baking sheet, then rub with the mixture to coat well.

Put the sheet in the preheated oven and bake for 15 minutes or until the internal temperature of the pork reaches at least 165ºF (74ºC). Flip the tenderloin halfway through the cooking time.

Transfer the cooked pork tenderloin to a large plate and allow to cool for 5 minutes before serving.

Per Serving

calories: 363 | fat: 18.1g | protein: 2.2g | carbs: 4.9g

Grilled Pork Chops

Prep time: 20 minutes | **Cook time:** 10 minutes | **Serves:**4

Ingredients:

¼ cup extra-virgin olive oil

2 tablespoons fresh thyme leaves

1 teaspoon smoked paprika

1 teaspoon salt

4 pork loin chops, ½-inch-thick

Directions:

In a small bowl, mix together the olive oil, thyme, paprika, and salt. Put the pork chops in a plastic zip-top bag or a bowl and coat them with the spice mix. Let them marinate for 15 minutes.

Preheat the grill to high heat. Cook the pork chops for 4 minutes on each side until cooked through. Serve warm.

Per Serving

calories: 282 | fat: 23.0g | protein: 21.0g | carbs: 1.0g

Macadamia Pork

Prep time: 10 minutes | **Cook time:** 10 minutes | **Serves:**4

Ingredients:

1 (1-pound / 454-g) pork tenderloin, cut into ½-inch slices and pounded thin

1 teaspoon sea salt, divided

1 tablespoon extra-virgin olive oil

¼ teaspoon freshly ground black pepper, divided

½ cup macadamia nuts

1 cup unsweetened coconut milk

Directions:

Preheat the oven to 400ºF (205ºC).

On a clean work surface, rub the pork with ½ teaspoon of the salt and ⅛ teaspoon of the ground black pepper. Set aside. Ground the macadamia nuts in a food processor, then combine with remaining salt and black pepper in a bowl. Stir to mix well and set aside.

Combine the coconut milk and olive oil in a separate bowl. Stir to mix well.

Dredge the pork chops into the bowl of coconut milk mixture, then dunk into the bowl of macadamia nut mixture to coat well. Shake the excess off.

Put the well-coated pork chops on a baking sheet, then bake for 10 minutes or until the internal temperature of the pork reaches at least 165ºF (74ºC). Transfer the pork chops to a serving plate and serve immediately.

Per Serving

calories: 436 | fat: 32.8g | protein: 33.1g | carbs: 5.9g

Lemon Beef (Spanish)

Preparation Time: 10 minutes **Cooking Time:** 6 hours **Servings:** 4

Ingredients:

1 lb. beef chuck roast

1 teaspoon chili powder

1/2 teaspoon salt

1 garlic clove, crushed

2 cups lemon-lime soda

1 fresh lime juice

Directions:

Place beef chuck roast into the slow cooker. Season roast with garlic, chili powder, and salt. Pour lemon-lime soda over the roast.

Cover slow cooker with lid and cook on low for 6 hours. Shred the meat using fork.

Add lime juice over shredded roast and serve.

Per Serving

Calories 355 Fat 16.8 g Carbohydrates 14 g Sugar 11.3 g Protein 35.5 g Cholesterol 120 mg

Grilled Chicken and Zucchini Kebabs

Prep time: 10 minutes | **Cook time:** 20 minutes | **Serves:**4

Ingredients:

¼ cup extra-virgin olive oil
2 tablespoons balsamic vinegar
1 teaspoon dried oregano, crushed between your fingers
1 pound (454 g) boneless, skinless chicken breasts, cut into 1½-inch pieces
2 medium zucchinis, cut into 1-inch pieces
½ cup Kalamata olives, pitted and halved
2 tablespoons olive brine
¼ cup torn fresh basil leaves
Nonstick cooking spray

Special Equipment:

14 to 15 (12-inch) wooden skewers, soaked for at least 30 minutes

Directions:

Spray the grill grates with nonstick cooking spray. Preheat the grill to medium-high heat.

In a small bowl, whisk together the olive oil, vinegar, and oregano. Divide the marinade between two large plastic zip-top bags.

Add the chicken to one bag and the zucchini to another. Seal and massage the marinade into both the chicken and zucchini.

Thread the chicken onto 6 wooden skewers. Thread the zucchini onto 8 or 9 wooden skewers. Cook the kebabs in batches on the grill for 5 minutes, flip, and grill for 5 minutes more, or until any chicken juices run clear.

Remove the chicken and zucchini from the skewers to a large serving bowl. Toss with the olives, olive brine, and basil and serve.

Per Serving

calories: 283 | fat: 15.0g | protein: 11.0g | carbs: 26.0g

Slow Cooker Mediterranean Beef Stew (Greek)

Prep time: 10 mins **Cooking Time:** 10 hours **Servings:** 10

Ingredients:

Beef meat (for stew) 3 pounds Beef broth 2 cups 10 cloves Chopped onion Salt ½ tbsp.
2 tablespoons Tomato sauce 15 ounces Balsamic vinegar ½ cup
Pepper ½ tbsp
Baby mushrooms
16 ounces Garlic, minced
1 large Diced tomatoes in a can
14½ ounces Jar capers, drained 2 ounces Drained black olives
6 ounces Dried rosemary

Directions:

Put all the except the for garnishing in a 6-quart slow cooker and combine.

Cover the cooker and slow cook for 10 hours. Add pepper and salt as required. Garnish with parmesan and chopped parsley while serving.

Per Serving

Calories: 273 Carbohydrate: 16g Protein: 33g Sugars: 6g

Almond-Crusted Chicken Tenders with Honey

Prep time: 10 minutes | **Cook time:** 20 minutes | **Serves:**4

Ingredients:

1 tablespoon honey
1 tablespoon whole-grain or Dijon mustard
¼ teaspoon freshly ground black pepper
¼ teaspoon kosher or sea salt
1 pound (454 g) boneless, skinless chicken breast tenders or tenderloins
1 cup almonds, roughly chopped
Nonstick cooking spray

Directions:

Preheat the oven to 425°F (220°C). Line a large, rimmed baking sheet with parchment paper. Place a wire cooling rack on the parchment-lined baking sheet, and spray the rack well with nonstick cooking spray.

In a large bowl, combine the honey, mustard, pepper, and salt. Add the chicken and toss gently to coat. Set aside.

Dump the almonds onto a large sheet of parchment paper and spread them out. Press the coated chicken tenders into the nuts until evenly coated on all sides. Place the chicken on the prepared wire rack.

Bake in the preheated oven for 15 to 20 minutes, or until the internal temperature of the chicken measures 165°F (74°C) on a meat thermometer and any juices run clear.

Cool for 5 minutes before serving.

Per Serving

calories: 222 | fat: 7.0g | protein: 11.0g | carbs: 29.0g

Greek-Style Lamb Burgers

Prep time: 10 minutes | **Cook time:** 10 minutes | **Serves:**4

Ingredients:

1 pound (454 g) ground lamb
½ teaspoon salt
½ teaspoon freshly ground black pepper
4 tablespoons crumbled feta cheese
Buns, toppings, and tzatziki, for serving (optional)

Directions:

Preheat the grill to high heat. In a large bowl, using your hands, combine the lamb with the salt and pepper.

Divide the meat into 4 portions. Divide each portion in half to make a top and a bottom. Flatten each half into a 3-inch circle. Make a dent in the center of one of the halves and place 1 tablespoon of the feta cheese in the center. Place the second half of the patty on top of the feta cheese and press down to close the 2 halves together, making it resemble a round burger. Grill each side for 3 minutes, for medium-well. Serve on a bun with your favorite toppings and tzatziki sauce, if desired.

Per Serving

calories: 345 | fat: 29.0g | protein: 20.0g | carbs: 1.0g

Parsley-Dijon Chicken and Potatoes

Prep time: 5 minutes | **Cook time:** 22 minutes | **Serves:** 6

Ingredients:

1 tablespoon extra-virgin olive oil

1½ pounds (680 g) boneless, skinless chicken thighs, cut into 1-inch cubes, patted dry

1½ pounds (680 g) Yukon Gold potatoes, unpeeled, cut into ½-inch cubes

2 garlic cloves, minced

¼ cup dry white wine

1 cup low-sodium or no-salt-added chicken broth

1 tablespoon Dijon mustard

¼ teaspoon freshly ground black pepper

¼ teaspoon kosher or sea salt

1 cup chopped fresh flat-leaf (Italian) parsley, including stems

1 tablespoon freshly squeezed lemon juice

Directions:

In a large skillet over medium-high heat, heat the oil. Add the chicken and cook for 5 minutes, stirring only after the chicken has browned on one side. Remove the chicken and reserve on a plate.

Add the potatoes to the skillet and cook for 5 minutes, stirring only after the potatoes have become golden and crispy on one side. Push the potatoes to the side of the skillet, add the garlic, and cook, stirring constantly, for 1 minute. Add the wine and cook for 1 minute, until nearly evaporated. Add the chicken broth, mustard, salt, pepper, and reserved chicken. Turn the heat to high and bring to a boil. Once boiling, cover, reduce the heat to medium-low, and cook for 10 to 12 minutes, until the potatoes are tender and the internal temperature of the chicken measures 165°F (74°C) on a meat thermometer and any juices run clear. During the last minute of cooking, stir in the parsley. Remove from the heat, stir in the lemon juice, and serve.

Per Serving

calories: 324 | fat: 9.0g | protein: 16.0g | carbs: 45.0g

Herb Pork Roast (Spanish)

Preparation Time: 10 minutes **Cooking Time:** 14 hours **Servings:** 10

Ingredients:

4 lbs. pork roast boneless or bone-in

1 tablespoon dry herb mix

4 garlic cloves cut into slivers

1 tablespoon salt

Directions:

Using a sharp knife make small cuts all over meat then insert garlic slivers into the cuts.

In a small bowl, mix together Italian herb mix and salt and rub all over pork roast. Place pork roast in the crock pot. Cover and cook on low for 14 hours. Remove meat from crock pot and shred using a fork. Serve and enjoy.

Per Serving

Calories 327 Fat 8 g Carbohydrates 0.5 g Sugar 0 g Protein 59 g Cholesterol 166 mg

Potato Lamb and Olive Stew

Prep time: 20 minutes | **Cook time:** 3 hours 42 minutes | **Serves:** 10

Ingredients:

4 tablespoons almond flour

¾ cup low-sodium chicken stock

1¼ pounds (567 g) small potatoes, halved

3 cloves garlic, minced

4 large shallots, cut into ½-inch wedges

3 sprigs fresh rosemary

1 tablespoon lemon zest

Coarse sea salt and black pepper, to taste

3½ pounds (1.6 kg) lamb shanks, fat trimmed and cut crosswise into 1½- inch pieces

2 tablespoons extra-virgin olive oil

½ cup dry white wine

1 cup pitted green olives, halved

2 tablespoons lemon juice

Directions:

Combine 1 tablespoon of almond flour with chicken stock in a bowl. Stir to mix well. Put the flour mixture, potatoes, garlic, shallots, rosemary, and lemon zest in the slow cooker. Sprinkle with salt and black pepper. Stir to mix well. Set aside.

Combine the remaining almond flour with salt and black pepper in a large bowl, then dunk the lamb shanks in the flour and toss to coat.

Heat the olive oil in a nonstick skillet over medium-high heat until shimmering.

Add the well-coated lamb and cook for 10 minutes or until golden brown. Flip the lamb pieces halfway through the cooking time. Transfer the cooked lamb to the slow cooker.

Pour the wine in the same skillet, then cook for 2 minutes or until it reduces in half. Pour the wine in the slow cooker.

Put the slow cooker lid on and cook on high for 3 hours and 30 minutes or until the lamb is very tender.

In the last 20 minutes of the cooking, open the lid and fold in the olive halves to cook.

Pour the stew on a large plate, let them sit for 5 minutes, then skim any fat remains over the face of the liquid.

Drizzle with lemon juice and sprinkle with salt and pepper. Serve warm.

Per Serving

calories: 309 | fat: 10.3g | protein: 36.9g | carbs: 16.1g

Slow Cook Lamb Shanks with Cannellini Beans Stew

Prep time: 20 minutes | **Cook time:** 10 hours 15 minutes | Serves:12

Ingredients:

1 (19-ounce / 539-g) can cannellini beans, rinsed and drained
1 large yellow onion, chopped
2 medium-sized carrots, diced
1 large stalk celery, chopped
2 cloves garlic, thinly sliced

4 (1½-pound / 680-g) lamb shanks, fat trimmed
2 teaspoons tarragon
½ teaspoon sea salt
¼ teaspoon ground black pepper
1 (28-ounce / 794-g) can diced tomatoes, with the juice

Directions:

Combine the beans, onion, carrots, celery, and garlic in the slow cooker. Stir to mix well.

Add the lamb shanks and sprinkle with tarragon, salt, and ground black pepper.

Pour in the tomatoes with juice, then cover the lid and cook on high for an hour.

Reduce the heat to low and cook for 9 hours or until the lamb is super tender.

Transfer the lamb on a plate, then pour the bean mixture in a colander over a separate bowl to reserve the liquid.

Let the liquid sit for 5 minutes until set, then skim the fat from the surface of the liquid. Pour the bean mixture back to the liquid.

Remove the bones from the lamb heat and discard the bones. Put the lamb meat and bean mixture back to the slow cooker. Cover and cook to reheat for 15 minutes or until heated through.

Pour them on a large serving plate and serve immediately.

Per Serving

calories: 317 | fat: 9.7g | protein: 52.1g | carbs: 7.0g

Beef, Tomato, and Lentils Stew

Prep time: 10 minutes | **Cook time:** 10 minutes | Serves:4

Ingredients:

1 tablespoon extra-virgin olive oil
1 pound (454 g) extra-lean ground beef
1 onion, chopped
1 (14-ounce / 397-g) can chopped tomatoes with garlic and basil, drained

1 (14-ounce / 397-g) can lentils, drained
½ teaspoon sea salt
⅛ teaspoon freshly ground black pepper

Directions:

Heat the olive oil in a pot over medium-high heat until shimmering.

Add the beef and onion to the pot and sauté for 5 minutes or until the beef is lightly browned.

Add the remaining ingredients. Bring to a boil. Reduce the heat to medium and cook for 4 more minutes or until the lentils are tender. Keep stirring during the cooking.

Pour them in a large serving bowl and serve immediately.

Per Serving

calories: 460 | fat: 14.8g | protein: 44.2g | carbs: 36.9g

Beef Kebabs with Onion and Pepper

Prep time: 15 minutes | **Cook time:** 10 minutes | Serves:6

Ingredients:

2 pounds (907 g) beef fillet
1½ teaspoons salt
1 teaspoon freshly ground black pepper
½ teaspoon ground nutmeg

½ teaspoon ground allspice
⅓ cup extra-virgin olive oil
1 large onion, cut into 8 quarters
1 large red bell pepper, cut into 1-inch cubes

Directions:

Preheat the grill to high heat.

Cut the beef into 1-inch cubes and put them in a large bowl.

In a small bowl, mix together the salt, black pepper, allspice, and nutmeg.

Pour the olive oil over the beef and toss to coat. Evenly sprinkle the seasoning over the beef and toss to coat all pieces.

Skewer the beef, alternating every 1 or 2 pieces with a piece of onion or bell pepper.

To cook, place the skewers on the preheated grill, and flip every 2 to 3 minutes until all sides have cooked to desired doneness, 6 minutes for medium-rare, 8 minutes for well done. Serve hot.

Per Serving

calories: 485 | fat: 36.0g | protein: 35.0g | carbs: 4.0g

Chicken Bruschetta Burgers

Prep time: 10 minutes | **Cook time:** 16 minutes | **Serves:** 2

Ingredients:

1 tablespoon olive oil
2 garlic cloves, minced
3 tablespoons finely minced onion
1 teaspoon dried basil
3 tablespoons minced sun-dried tomatoes packed in olive oil
8 ounces (227 g) ground chicken breast
¼ teaspoon salt
3 pieces small Mozzarella balls, minced

Directions:

Heat the olive oil in a nonstick skillet over medium-high heat. Add the garlic and onion and sauté for 5 minutes until tender. Stir in the basil. Remove from the skillet to a medium bowl. Add the tomatoes, ground chicken, and salt and stir until incorporated. Mix in the Mozzarella balls.

Divide the chicken mixture in half and form into two burgers, each about ¾-inch thick.

Heat the same skillet over medium-high heat and add the burgers. Cook each side for 5 to 6 minutes, or until they reach an internal temperature of 165°F (74°C).

Serve warm.

Per Serving

calories: 300 | fat: 17.0g | protein: 32.2g | carbs: 6.0g

Quick Chicken Salad Wraps

Prep time: 15 minutes | **Cook time:** 0 minutes | **Serves:** 2

Ingredients:

Tzatziki Sauce:
½ cup plain Greek yogurt
1 tablespoon freshly squeezed lemon juice
Pinch garlic powder
1 teaspoon dried dill
Salt and freshly ground black pepper, to taste
1 scallion, chopped
¼ cup pitted black olives

Salad Wraps:
2 (8-inch) whole-grain pita bread
1 cup shredded chicken meat
2 cups mixed greens
2 roasted red bell peppers, thinly sliced
½ English cucumber, peeled if desired and thinly sliced

Directions:

Make the tzatziki sauce: In a bowl, whisk together the yogurt, lemon juice, garlic powder, dill, salt, and pepper until creamy and smooth.

Make the salad wraps: Place the pita bread on a clean work surface and spoon ¼ cup of the tzatziki sauce onto each piece of pita bread, spreading it all over. Top with the shredded chicken, mixed greens, red pepper slices, cucumber slices, black olives, finished by chopped scallion.

Roll the salad wraps and enjoy.

Per Serving

calories: 428 | fat: 10.6g | protein: 31.1g | carbs: 50.9g

Chicken Cacciatore

Prep time: 15 minutes | **Cook time:** 1 hour and 30 minutes
Serves: 2

Ingredients:

1½ pounds (680 g) bone-in chicken thighs, skin removed and patted dry
Salt, to taste
2 tablespoons olive oil
½ large onion, thinly sliced
4 ounces (113 g) baby bella mushrooms, sliced
1 red sweet pepper, cut into 1-inch pieces
1 (15-ounce / 425-g) can crushed fire-roasted tomatoes
1 fresh rosemary sprig
½ cup dry red wine
1 teaspoon Italian herb seasoning
½ teaspoon garlic powder
3 tablespoons flour

Directions:

Season the chicken thighs with a generous pinch of salt.

Heat the olive oil in a Dutch oven over medium-high heat. Add the chicken and brown for 5 minutes per side.

Add the onion, mushrooms, and sweet pepper to the Dutch oven and sauté for another 5 minutes.

Add the tomatoes, rosemary, wine, Italian seasoning, garlic powder, and salt, stirring well.

Bring the mixture to a boil, then reduce the heat to low. Allow to simmer slowly for at least 1 hour, stirring occasionally, or until the chicken is tender and easily pulls away from the bone.

Measure out 1 cup of the sauce from the pot and put it into a bowl. Add the flour and whisk well to make a slurry.

Increase the heat to medium-high and slowly whisk the slurry into the pot. Stir until it comes to a boil and cook until the sauce is thickened.

Remove the chicken from the bones and shred it, and add it back to the sauce before serving, if desired.

Per Serving

calories: 520 | fat: 23.1g | protein: 31.8g | carbs: 37.0g

Chicken Gyros with Tzatziki Sauce

Prep time: 15 minutes | **Cook time:** 10 minutes | **Serves:** 2

Ingredients:

2 tablespoons freshly squeezed lemon juice

2 tablespoons olive oil, divided, plus more for oiling the grill

1 teaspoon minced fresh oregano

½ teaspoon garlic powder

Salt, to taste

8 ounces (227 g) chicken tenders

1 small eggplant, cut into 1-inch strips lengthwise

1 small zucchini, cut into ½-inch strips lengthwise

½ red pepper, seeded and cut in half lengthwise

½ English cucumber, peeled and minced

¾ cup plain Greek yogurt

1 tablespoon minced fresh dill

2 (8-inch) pita breads

Directions:

Combine the lemon juice, 1 tablespoon of olive oil, oregano, garlic powder, and salt in a medium bowl. Add the chicken and let marinate for 30 minutes.

Place the eggplant, zucchini, and red pepper in a large mixing bowl and sprinkle with salt and the remaining 1 tablespoon of olive oil. Toss well to coat. Let the vegetables rest while the chicken is marinating.

Make the tzatziki sauce: Combine the cucumber, yogurt, salt, and dill in a medium bowl. Stir well to incorporate and set aside in the refrigerator.

When ready, preheat the grill to medium-high heat and oil the grill grates.

Drain any liquid from the vegetables and put them on the grill.

Remove the chicken tenders from the marinade and put them on the grill.

Grill the chicken and vegetables for 3 minutes per side, or until the chicken is no longer pink inside.

Remove the chicken and vegetables from the grill and set aside. On the grill, heat the pitas for about 30 seconds, flipping them frequently.

Divide the chicken tenders and vegetables between the pitas and top each with ¼ cup of the prepared sauce. Roll the pitas up like a cone and serve.

Per Serving

calories: 586 | fat: 21.9g | protein: 39.0g | carbs: 62.0g

Crispy Pesto Chicken

Prep time: 15 minutes | **Cook time:** 50 minutes | **Serves:** 2

Ingredients:

12 ounces (340 g) small red potatoes (3 or 4 potatoes), scrubbed and diced into 1-inch pieces

1 tablespoon olive oil

½ teaspoon garlic powder

¼ teaspoon salt

1 (8-ounce / 227-g) boneless, skinless chicken breast

3 tablespoons prepared pesto

Directions:

Preheat the oven to 425°F (220°C). Line a baking sheet with parchment paper.

Combine the potatoes, olive oil, garlic powder, and salt in a medium bowl. Toss well to coat.

Arrange the potatoes on the parchment paper and roast for 10 minutes. Flip the potatoes and roast for an additional 10 minutes.

Meanwhile, put the chicken in the same bowl and toss with the pesto, coating the chicken evenly.

Check the potatoes to make sure they are golden brown on the top and bottom. Toss them again and add the chicken breast to the pan.

Turn the heat down to 350°F (180°C) and roast the chicken and potatoes for 30 minutes. Check to make sure the chicken reaches an internal temperature of 165°F (74°C) and the potatoes are fork-tender.

Let cool for 5 minutes before serving.

Per Serving

calories: 378 | fat: 16.0g | protein: 29.8g | carbs: 30.1g

Lemon Lamb Leg (Greek)

Preparation Time: 10 minutes **Cooking Time:** 8 hours
Servings: 12

Ingredients:

4 lbs. lamb leg, boneless and slice of fat 1 tablespoon rosemary, crushed

1/4 cup water

1/4 cup lemon juice

1 teaspoon black pepper

1/4 teaspoon salt

Directions:

Place lamb into the crock pot.

Add remaining into the crock pot over the lamb.

Cover and cook on low for 8 hours.

Remove lamb from crock pot and sliced.

Serve and enjoy.

Per Serving

Calories 275 Fat 10.2 g Carbohydrates

Beef Stew with Beans and Zucchini

Prep time: 20 minutes | **Cook time:** 6 to 8 hours | **Serves:**2

Ingredients:

1 (15-ounce / 425-g) can diced or crushed tomatoes with basil
1 teaspoon beef base
2 tablespoons olive oil, divided
8 ounces (227 g) baby bella (cremini) mushrooms, quartered
2 garlic cloves, minced
½ large onion, diced
1 pound (454 g) cubed beef stew meat
3 tablespoons flour
¼ teaspoon salt
Pinch freshly ground black pepper
¾ cup dry red wine
¼ cup minced brined olives
1 fresh rosemary sprig
1 (15-ounce / 425-g) can white cannellini beans, drained and rinsed
1 medium zucchini, cut in half lengthwise and then cut into 1-inch pieces.

Directions:

Place the tomatoes into a slow cooker and set it to low heat. Add the beef base and stir to incorporate.

Heat 1 tablespoon of olive oil in a large sauté pan over medium heat. Add the mushrooms and onion and sauté for 10 minutes, stirring occasionally, or until they're golden. Add the garlic and cook for 30 seconds more. Transfer the vegetables to the slow cooker.

In a plastic food storage bag, combine the stew meat with the flour, salt, and pepper. Seal the bag and shake well to combine. Heat the remaining 1 tablespoon of olive oil in the sauté pan over high heat.

Add the floured meat and sear to get a crust on the outside edges. Deglaze the pan by adding about half of the red wine and scraping up any browned bits on the bottom. Stir so the wine thickens a bit and transfer to the slow cooker along with any remaining wine.

Stir the stew to incorporate the ingredients. Stir in the olives and rosemary, cover, and cook for 6 to 8 hours on Low. About 30 minutes before the stew is finished, add the beans and zucchini to let them warm through. Serve warm.

Per Serving

calories: 389 | fat: 15.1g | protein: 30.8g | carbs: 25.0g

Greek Beef Kebabs

Prep time: 15 minutes | **Cook time:** 20 minutes | **Serves:**2

Ingredients:

6 ounces (170 g) beef sirloin tip, trimmed of fat and cut into 2-inch pieces
3 cups of any mixture of vegetables: mushrooms, summer squash, zucchini, onions, red peppers, cherry tomatoes
½ cup olive oil
¼ cup freshly squeezed lemon juice
2 tablespoons balsamic vinegar
2 teaspoons dried oregano
1 teaspoon garlic powder
1 teaspoon salt
1 teaspoon minced fresh rosemary
Cooking spray

Directions:

Put the beef in a plastic freezer bag.

Slice the vegetables into similar-size pieces and put them in a second freezer bag.

Make the marinade: Mix the olive oil, lemon juice, balsamic vinegar, oregano, garlic powder, salt, and rosemary in a measuring cup. Whisk well to combine. Pour half of the marinade over the beef, and the other half over the vegetables.

Put the beef and vegetables in the refrigerator to marinate for 4 hours.

When ready, preheat the grill to medium-high heat and spray the grill grates with cooking spray.

Thread the meat onto skewers and the vegetables onto separate skewers.

Grill the meat for 3 minutes per side. They should only take 10 to 12 minutes to cook, depending on the thickness of the meat.

Grill the vegetables for about 3 minutes per side, or until they have grill marks and are softened. Serve hot.

Per Serving calories: 284 | fat: 18.2g | protein: 21.0g | carbs: 9.0g

Gyro Burgers with Tahini Sauce

Prep time: 15 minutes | **Cook time:** 10 minutes | **Serves:** 4

Ingredients:

2 tablespoons extra-virgin olive oil
1 tablespoon dried oregano
1¼ teaspoons garlic powder, divided
1 teaspoon ground cumin
½ teaspoon freshly ground black pepper
¼ teaspoon kosher or sea salt
1 pound (454 g) beef flank steak, top round steak, or lamb leg steak, center cut, about 1 inch thick
1 medium green bell pepper, halved and seeded
2 tablespoons tahini or peanut butter
1 tablespoon hot water (optional)
½ cup plain Greek yogurt
1 tablespoon freshly squeezed lemon juice
1 cup thinly sliced red onion
4 (6-inch) whole-wheat pita breads, warmed
Nonstick cooking spray

Directions:

Set an oven rack about 4 inches below the broiler element. Preheat the oven broiler to high. Line a large, rimmed baking sheet with aluminum foil. Place a wire cooling rack on the foil, and spray the rack with nonstick cooking spray. Set aside.

In a small bowl, whisk together the olive oil, oregano, 1 teaspoon of garlic powder, cumin, pepper, and salt. Rub the oil mixture on all sides of the steak, reserving 1 teaspoon of the mixture. Place the steak on the prepared rack. Rub the remaining oil mixture on the bell pepper, and place on the rack, cut-side down. Press the pepper with the heel of your hand to flatten.

Broil for 5 minutes. Flip the steak and the pepper pieces, and broil for 2 to 5 minutes more, until the pepper is charred and the internal temperature of the meat measures 145°F (63°C) on a meat thermometer. Put the pepper and steak on a cutting board to rest for 5 minutes.

Meanwhile, in a small bowl, whisk the tahini until smooth (adding 1 tablespoon of hot water if your tahini is sticky). Add the remaining ¼ teaspoon of garlic powder and the yogurt and lemon juice, and whisk thoroughly.

Slice the steak crosswise into ¼-inch-thick strips. Slice the bell pepper into strips. Divide the steak, bell pepper, and onion among the warm pita breads. Drizzle with tahini sauce and serve.

Per Serving

calories: 348 | fat: 15.0g | protein: 33.0g | carbs: 20.0g

Grilled Lemon Chicken

Prep time: 10 minutes | **Cook time:** 12 to 14 minutes
Serves: 2

Ingredients:

1 (4-ounce / 113-g) boneless, skinless chicken breasts
Marinade:
4 tablespoons freshly squeezed lemon juice
2 tablespoons olive oil, plus more for greasing the grill grates
1 teaspoon dried basil
1 teaspoon paprika
½ teaspoon dried thyme
¼ teaspoon salt
¼ teaspoon garlic powder

Directions:

Make the marinade: Whisk together the lemon juice, olive oil, basil, paprika, thyme, salt, and garlic powder in a large bowl until well combined.

Add the chicken breasts to the bowl and let marinate for at least 30 minutes.

When ready to cook, preheat the grill to medium-high heat. Lightly grease the grill grates with the olive oil. Discard the marinade and arrange the chicken breasts on the grill grates.

Grill for 12 to 14 minutes, flipping the chicken halfway through, or until a meat thermometer inserted in the center of the chicken reaches 165°F (74°C).

Let the chicken cool for 5 minutes and serve warm.

Per Serving

calories: 251 | fat: 15.5g | protein: 27.3g | carbs: 1.9g

Spiced Roast Chicken

Prep time: 10 minutes | **Cook time:** 35 minutes | **Serves:** 6

Ingredients:

1 teaspoon garlic powder
1 teaspoon ground paprika
½ teaspoon ground cumin
½ teaspoon ground coriander
½ teaspoon salt
¼ teaspoon ground cayenne pepper
6 chicken legs
1 teaspoon extra-virgin olive oil

Directions:

Preheat the oven to 400°F (205°C).

Combine the garlic powder, paprika, cumin, coriander, salt, and cayenne pepper in a small bowl.

On a clean work surface, rub the spices all over the chicken legs until completely coated.

Heat the olive oil in an ovenproof skillet over medium heat.

Add the chicken thighs and sear each side for 8 to 10 minutes, or until the skin is crispy and browned. Transfer the skillet to the preheated oven and continue cooking for 10 to 15 minutes, or until the juices run clear and it registers an internal temperature of 165°F (74°C). Remove from the heat and serve on plates.

Per Serving

calories: 275 | fat: 15.6g | protein: 30.3g | carbs: 0.9g

Roasted Chicken Thighs With Basmati Rice

Prep time: 15 minutes | **Cook time:** 50 to 55 minutes
Serves: 2

Ingredients:

Chicken:
½ teaspoon cumin
½ teaspoon cinnamon
½ teaspoon paprika
¼ teaspoon ginger powder
¼ teaspoon garlic powder
¼ teaspoon coriander
¼ teaspoon salt
⅛ teaspoon cayenne pepper
¼ teaspoon salt

10 ounces (284 g) boneless, skinless chicken thighs (about 4 pieces)
Rice:
1 tablespoon olive oil
½ small onion, minced
½ cup basmati rice
2 pinches saffron
1 cup low-sodium chicken stock

Directions:
Make the Chicken

Preheat the oven to 350ºF (180ºC). Combine the cumin, cinnamon, paprika, ginger powder, garlic powder, coriander, salt, and cayenne pepper in a small bowl. Using your hands to rub the spice mixture all over the chicken thighs.

Transfer the chicken thighs to a baking dish. Roast in the preheated oven for 35 to 40 minutes, or until the internal temperature reaches 165ºF (74ºC) on a meat thermometer.

Meanwhile, heat the olive oil in a skillet over medium-high heat. Sauté the onion for 5 minutes until fragrant, stirring occasionally.

Stir in the basmati rice, saffron, chicken stock, and salt. Reduce the heat to low, cover, and bring to a simmer for 15 minutes, until light and fluffy.

Remove the chicken from the oven to a plate and serve with the rice.

Per Serving
calories: 400 | fat: 9.6g | protein: 37.2g | carbs: 40.7g

Roasted Pork Meat (Spanish)

Preparation Time: 5 minutes **Cooking Time:** 55 minutes
Servings: 6

Ingredients:

3 pounds of roast pork
Salt and pepper
1 sliced onion

1 tablespoon vegetable oil
2 cups of water

Directions:

Pour vegetable oil into the pot. Brown the pork on both sides in medium pressure over medium heat and then remove from the pot.

Pour the water into the pot. Put the pork on the rack of the pot. Season with salt, pepper and sliced onions.

Close and secure the lid. Place the pressure regulator on the vent tube and cook 55 minutes once the pressure regulator begins to rock slowly. Let the pressure decrease on its own.

Per Serving
Calories: 483, Carbohydrates: 0g, Fat: 27g, Protein: 53g, Cholesterol: 171mg,

Yogurt Chicken Breasts

Prep time: 10 minutes | **Cook time:** 10 minutes | **Serves:** 4

Ingredients:

1 pound (454 g) boneless, skinless chicken breasts, cut into 2-inch strips
1 tablespoon extra-virgin olive oil
Yogurt Sauce:
½ cup plain Greek yogurt
2 tablespoons water

Pinch saffron (3 or 4 threads)
3 garlic cloves, minced
½ onion, chopped
2 tablespoons chopped fresh cilantro
Juice of ½ lemon
½ teaspoon salt

Directions:

Make the yogurt sauce: Place the yogurt, water, saffron, garlic, onion, cilantro, lemon juice, and salt in a blender, and pulse until completely mixed.

Transfer the yogurt sauce to a large bowl, along with the chicken strips. Toss to coat well.

Cover with plastic wrap and marinate in the refrigerator for at least 1 hour, or up to overnight. When ready to cook, heat the olive oil in a large skillet over medium heat.

Add the chicken strips to the skillet, discarding any excess marinade. Cook each side for 5 minutes, or until cooked through.

Let the chicken cool for 5 minutes before serving.

Per Serving
calories: 154 | fat: 4.8g | protein: 26.3g | carbs: 2.9g

Coconut Chicken Tenders

Prep time: 10 minutes | **Cook time:** 15 to 20 minutes | **Serves:** 6

Ingredients:

4 chicken breasts, each cut lengthwise into 3 strips
½ teaspoon salt
¼ teaspoon freshly ground black pepper

½ cup coconut flour
2 eggs
2 tablespoons unsweetened plain almond milk
1 cup unsweetened coconut flakes

Directions:

Preheat the oven to 400ºF (205ºC). Line a baking sheet with parchment paper. On a clean work surface, season the chicken with salt and pepper.

In a small bowl, add the coconut flour. In a separate bowl, whisk the eggs with almond milk until smooth. Place the coconut flakes on a plate.

One at a time, roll the chicken strips in the coconut flour, then dredge them in the egg mixture, shaking off any excess, and finally in the coconut flakes to coat.

Arrange the coated chicken pieces on the baking sheet. Bake in the preheated oven for 15 to 20 minutes, flipping the chicken halfway through, or until the chicken is golden brown and cooked through. Remove from the oven and serve on plates.

Per Serving
calories: 215 | fat: 12.6g | protein: 20.2g | carbs: 8.9g

Sautéed Ground Turkey with Brown Rice

Prep time: 20 minutes | **Cook time:** 45 minutes | **Serves:** 2

Ingredients:

1 tablespoon olive oil
½ medium onion, minced
2 garlic cloves, minced
8 ounces (227 g) ground turkey breast
½ cup chopped roasted red peppers, (about 2 jarred peppers)
¼ cup sun-dried tomatoes, minced
1¼ cups low-sodium chicken stock
½ cup brown rice
1 teaspoon dried oregano
Salt, to taste
2 cups lightly packed baby spinach

Directions:

In a skillet, heat the olive oil over medium heat. Sauté the onion for 5 minutes, stirring occasionally.

Stir in the garlic and sauté for 30 seconds more until fragrant.

Add the turkey breast and cook for about 7 minutes, breaking apart with a wooden spoon, until the turkey is no longer pink.

Stir in the roasted red peppers, tomatoes, chicken stock, brown rice, and oregano and bring to a boil.

When the mixture starts to boil, cover, and reduce the heat to medium- low. Bring to a simmer until the rice is tender, stirring occasionally, about 30 minutes. Sprinkle with the salt.

Add the baby spinach and keep stirring until wilted. Remove from the heat and serve warm.

Per Serving

calories: 445 | fat: 16.8g | protein: 30.2g | carbs: 48.9g

Baked Teriyaki Turkey Meatballs

Prep time: 20 minutes | **Cook time:** 20 minutes | **Serves:** 6

Ingredients:

1 pound (454 g) lean ground turkey
1 egg, whisked
¼ cup finely chopped scallions, both white and green parts
2 garlic cloves, minced
2 tablespoons reduced-sodium tamari or gluten-free soy sauce
1 teaspoon grated fresh ginger
1 tablespoon honey
2 teaspoons mirin
1 teaspoon olive oil

Directions:

Preheat the oven to 400ºF (205ºC). Line a baking sheet with parchment paper and set aside.

Mix together the ground turkey, whisked egg, scallions, garlic, tamari, ginger, honey, mirin, and olive oil in a large bowl, and stir until well blended.

Using a tablespoon to scoop out rounded heaps of the turkey mixture, and then roll them into balls with your hands. Transfer the balls to the prepared baking sheet.

Bake in the preheated oven for 20 minutes, flipping the balls with a spatula halfway through, or until the meatballs are browned and cooked through.Serve warm.

Per Serving calories: 158 fat: 8.6g protein: 16.2g carbs: 4.0g

Ground Beef, Tomato, and Kidney Bean Chili

Prep time: 10 minutes | **Cook time:** 15 minutes | **Serves:** 4

Ingredients:

1 tablespoon extra-virgin olive oil
1 pound (454 g) extra-lean ground beef
1 onion, chopped
2 (14-ounce / 397-g) cans kidney beans
2 (28-ounce / 794-g) cans chopped tomatoes, juice reserved
Chili Spice:
1 teaspoon garlic powder
1 tablespoon chili powder
½ teaspoon sea salt

Directions:

Heat the olive oil in a pot over medium-high heat until shimmering.

Add the beef and onion to the pot and sauté for 5 minutes or until the beef is lightly browned and the onion is translucent.

Add the remaining ingredients. Bring to a boil. Reduce the heat to medium and cook for 10 more minutes. Keep stirring during the cooking.

Pour them in a large serving bowl and serve immediately.

Per Serving

calories: 891 | fat: 20.1g | protein: 116.3g | carbs: 62.9g

Ground Beef, Tomato, and Kidney Bean Chili

Prep time: 10 minutes | **Cook time:** 15 minutes | **Serves:** 4

Ingredients:

1 tbsp extra-virgin olive oil
1 pound (454 g) extra-lean ground beef
1 onion, chopped
2 (14-ounce / 397-g) cans kidney beans
2 (28-ounce / 794-g) cans chopped tomatoes, juice reserved
Chili Spice:
1 teaspoon garlic powder
1 tablespoon chili powder
½ teaspoon sea salt

Directions:

Heat the olive oil in a pot over medium-high heat until shimmering.

Add the beef and onion to the pot and sauté for 5 minutes or until the beef is lightly browned and the onion is translucent.

Add the remaining. Bring to a boil. Reduce the heat to medium and cook for 10 more minutes. Keep stirring during the cooking.

Pour them in a large serving bowl and serve immediately.

Per Serving

calories: 891 | fat: 20.1g | protein: 116.3g | carbs: 62.9g

Lamb Tagine with Couscous and Almonds

Prep time: 15 minutes | **Cook time:** 7 hours 7 minutes | **Serves:** 6

Ingredients:

2 tablespoons almond flour
Juice and zest of 1 navel orange
2 tablespoons extra-virgin olive oil
2 pounds (907 g) boneless lamb leg, fat trimmed and cut into 1½-inch cubes
½ cup low-sodium chicken stock
2 large white onions, chopped
1 teaspoon pumpkin pie spice
¼ teaspoon crushed saffron threads
1 teaspoon ground cumin
¼ teaspoon ground red pepper flakes
½ teaspoon sea salt
2 tablespoons raw honey
1 cup pitted dates
3 cups cooked couscous, for serving
2 tablespoons toasted slivered almonds, for serving

Directions:

Combine the almond flour with orange juice in a large bowl. Stir until smooth, then mix in the orange zest. Set aside.

Heat the olive oil in a nonstick skillet over medium-high heat until shimmering.

Add the lamb cubes and sauté for 7 minutes or until lightly browned.

Pour in the flour mixture and chicken stock, then add the onions, pumpkin pie spice, saffron, cumin, ground red pepper flakes, and salt. Stir to mix well.

Pour them in the slow cooker. Cover and cook on low for 6 hours or until the internal temperature of the lamb reaches at least 145ºF (63ºC).

When the cooking is complete, mix in the honey and dates, then cook for another an hour.

Put the couscous in a tagine bowl or a large bowl, then top with lamb mixture. Scatter with slivered almonds and serve immediately.

Per Serving

calories: 447 | fat: 10.2g | protein: 36.3g | carbs: 53.5g

Chermoula Roasted Pork Tenderloin

Prep time: 15 minutes | **Cook time:** 20 minutes | **Serves:** 2

Ingredients:

½ cup fresh cilantro
½ cup fresh parsley
6 small garlic cloves
3 tablespoons olive oil, divided
3 tablespoons freshly squeezed lemon juice
2 teaspoons cumin
1 teaspoon smoked paprika
½ teaspoon salt, divided
Pinch freshly ground black pepper
1 (8-ounce / 227-g) pork tenderloin

Directions:

Preheat the oven to 425ºF (220ºC).

In a food processor, combine the cilantro, parsley, garlic, 2 tablespoons of olive oil, lemon juice, cumin, paprika, and ¼ teaspoon of salt. Pulse 15 to 20 times, or until the mixture is fairly smooth. Scrape the sides down as needed to incorporate all the ingredients. Transfer the sauce to a small bowl and set aside.

Season the pork tenderloin on all sides with the remaining ¼ teaspoon of salt and a generous pinch of black pepper. Heat the remaining 1 tablespoon of olive oil in a sauté pan. Sear the pork for 3 minutes, turning often, until golden brown on all sides.

Transfer the pork to a baking dish and roast in the preheated oven for 15 minutes, or until the internal temperature registers 145ºF (63ºC). Cool for 5 minutes before serving.

Per Serving

calories: 169 | fat: 13.1g | protein: 11.0g | carbs: 2.9g

Lamb Kofta (Spiced Meatballs)

Prep time: 15 minutes | **Cook time:** 30 minutes | **Serves:** 2

Ingredients:

¼ cup walnuts
1 garlic clove
½ small onion
1 roasted piquillo pepper
2 tablespoons fresh mint
2 tablespoons fresh parsley
¼ teaspoon cumin
¼ teaspoon allspice
¼ teaspoon salt
Pinch cayenne pepper
8 ounces (227 g) lean ground lamb

Directions:

Preheat the oven to 350ºF (180ºC). Line a baking sheet with aluminum foil.

In a food processor, combine the walnuts, garlic, onion, roasted pepper, mint, parsley, cumin, allspice, salt, and cayenne pepper. Pulse about 10 times to combine everything.

Transfer the spice mixture to a large bowl and add the ground lamb. With your hands or a spatula, mix the spices into the lamb.

Roll the lamb into 1½-inch balls (about the size of golf balls). Arrange the meatballs on the prepared baking sheet and bake for 30 minutes, or until cooked to an internal temperature of 165ºF (74ºC). Serve warm.

Per Serving

calories: 409 | fat: 22.9g | protein: 22.0g | carbs: 7.1g

Beef, Artichoke & Mushroom Stew (Italian)

Preparation Time: 20 minutes
Cooking Time: 2 hours and 15 minutes **Servings:** 6

Ingredients:

For Beef Marinade: 1 onion, chopped

1 garlic clove, crushed

2 tablespoons fresh thyme, hopped

½ cup dry red wine 2 tablespoons tomato puree

2 tablespoons olive oil

1 teaspoon cayenne pepper

Pinch of salt and ground black pepper

1½ pounds beef stew meat, cut into large chunks For

2 tablespoons all-purpose flour ½ cup water

½ cup dry red wine 12 ounces jar artichoke hearts, drained and cut into small chunks

4 ounces button mushrooms, sliced

Salt and ground black pepper, as required

Stew: 2 tablespoons olive oil

Directions:

For marinade: in a large bowl, add all the except the beef and mix well.

Add the beef and coat with the marinade generously.

Refrigerate to marinate overnight.

Remove the beef from bowl, reserving the marinade.

In a large pan, heat the oil and sear the beef in 2 batches for about 5 minutes or until browned.

With a slotted spoon, transfer the beef into a bowl.

In the same pan, add the reserved marinade, flour, water and wine and stir to combine.

Stir in the cooked beef and bring to a boil.

Reduce the heat to low and simmer, covered for about 2 hours, stirring occasionally.

Stir in the artichoke hearts and mushrooms and simmer for about 30 minutes.

Stir in the salt and black pepper and bring to a boil over high heat.

Remove from the eat ad serve hot.

Per Serving

Calories 367 Total Fat 16.6 g Saturated Fat 4 g Cholesterol 101mg Total Carbs 9.6 g Sugar 2.2 g Potassium 624 mg Protein 36.7 g

Beef & Tapioca Stew (Greek)

Preparation Time: 20 minutes
Cooking Time: 1 hour and 45 minutes **Servings:** 8

Ingredients:

1 tablespoon olive oil

2 pounds boneless beef chuck roast, cut into ¾-inch cubes

2 tbsp ground cinnamon

2 cups beef broth

1 (14½-ounce) can diced tomatoes with juice

¼ cup quick-cooking tapioca

3 cups sweet potato, peeled and cubed

¼ teaspoon garlic powder

Ground black pepper, as required

2 medium onions, cut into thin wedges

¼ cup red wine vinegar

1 tablespoon honey

2 cups prunes, pitted

Directions:

In a Dutch oven, heat 1 tablespoon of oil over medium-high heat and sear the beef cubes in 2 batches for bout 4-5 minutes or until browned.

Drain off the grease from the pan.

Stir in the tomatoes, tapioca, honey, cinnamon, garlic powder, black pepper, vinegar and broth and bring to a boil.

Reduce the heat to low and simmer, covered for about 1 hour, stirring occasionally.

Stir in the onions and sweet potato and simmer, covered for about 20-30 minutes. Stir in the prunes and cook for about 3-5 minutes. Serve hot.

Per Serving

Calories 675 Total Fat34. 1 g Saturated Fat 13 g Cholesterol 117 mg Total Carbs 59.6 g Sugar 26 mg Potassium 1150 mg Protein 34.1 g

Basil Cheese Pork Roast (Italian)

Preparation Time: 10 minutes **Cooking Time:** 6 hours
Servings: 8

Ingredients:

1 lbs. lean pork roast, boneless

1 teaspoon garlic powder

½ cup cheddar cheese, grated

1 tablespoon parsley

1 teaspoon dried oregano

1 teaspoon dried basil

30 oz can tomato, diced

Pepper

Salt

Directions:

Add the meat into the crock pot.

Mix together tomatoes, oregano, basil, garlic powder, parsley, cheese, pepper, and salt and pour over meat.

Cover and cook on low for 6 hours.

Serve and enjoy.

Per Serving

Calories 260 Fat 9 g Carbohydrates 5.5 g Sugar 3.5 g Protein 35 g Cholesterol 97 mg

Pork Ribs with Barbecue Sauce (Spanish)

Preparation Time: 5 minutes **Cooking Time:** 15 minutes
Servings: 6

Ingredients:

3 pounds of pork ribs in portions
½ cup of water
¼ cup chopped onion
1 teaspoon salt
1 cup of ketchup
1 cup of water
½ cup vinegar
¼ cup sugar
1 teaspoon chili powder
1 teaspoon celery seeds

Directions:

Put the ribs and water in the pot. Close and secure the lid. Place the pressure regulator on the vent tube and cook 5 minutes once the pressure regulator begins to rock slowly. Cool the pot quickly. Drain the liquid.

Mix the remaining and pour them over the ribs in the pot. Stir to cover the ribs.

Close and secure the lid. Place the pressure regulator on the vent tube and cook 10 minutes once the pressure regulator begins to rock slowly.

Let the pressure decrease on its own. Remove the ribs. Boil the sauce, without the lid, until the desired consistency is achieved.

Per Serving

Calories: 427, Carbohydrates: 0g, Fat: 27g, Protein: 47g, Sugar: 0g, Cholesterol: 107mg

Easy Pork Kabobs (Greek)

Preparation Time: 10 minutes
Cooking Time: 4 hours 20 minutes **Servings:** 6

Ingredients:

1 lbs. pork tenderloin, cut into 1-inch cubes
½ cup olive oil
2 garlic cloves, chopped
½ cup red wine vinegar
1 onion, chopped
Pepper Salt
2 tablespoon fresh parsley, chopped

Directions:

In a large zip-lock bag, mix together red wine vinegar, parsley, garlic, onion, and oil.

Add meat to bag and marinate in the refrigerator for overnight.

Remove marinated pork from refrigerator and thread onto soaked wooden skewers. Season with pepper and salt.

Preheat the grill over high heat.

Grill pork for 3-4 minutes on each side. Serve and enjoy.

Per Serving

Calories 375 Fat 22 g Carbohydrates 2.5 g Sugar 1 g Protein 40 g Cholesterol 110 mg

Apricot Pork Meat (Spanish)

Preparation Time: 5 minutes **Cooking Time:** 60 minutes
Servings: 8

Ingredients:

3 pounds boneless rolled pork
½ cup teriyaki sauce
¼ cup cider vinegar
1 large onion sliced
1 teaspoon dried mustard
¼ teaspoon black pepper
½ cup ketchup
1 teaspoon of paprika
1/3 Cup of canned apricots
¼ cup dark brown sugar, packaged
2 cups of water

Directions:

Put the creed meat in a large plastic bag or glass dish. Combine ketchup, teriyaki sauce, canned food, vinegar, brown sugar, paprika, mustard and pepper. Mix together and pour over pork. Refrigerate overnight.

Remove the pork from the marinade and keep the marinade. Brown pork on both sides in the pressure cooker over medium heat. Remove pork from the pot.

Place the pressure regulator on the vent tube and cook 60 minutes once the pressure regulator begins to rock slowly. Let the pressure decrease on its own. Put in a saucepan the marinade that it kept and boil until it thickens, stirring occasionally.

Remove the meat and onions from the pressure cooker. Add onions to the thickened marinade and serve with sliced pork. Onions can be stepped on before adding to the sauce and served with rice, if desired.

Per Serving

Calories: 332, Carbohydrates: 0g, Fat: 13g, Protein: 47g, Sugar: 0g, Cholesterol: 77mg

Feta Lamb Patties (Greek)

Preparation Time: 10 minutes **Cooking Time:** 12 minutes
Servings: 4

Ingredients:

1 lb. ground lamb
1/4 cup mint leaves, chopped
1/4 cup roasted red pepper, chopped
1/4 cup onion, chopped
1/2 teaspoon garlic powder
1/2 cup feta cheese, crumbled
Pepper Salt

Directions:

Add all into the bowl and mix until well combined. Spray pan with cooking spray and heat over medium-high heat. Make small patties from meat mixture and place on hot pan and cook for 6-7 minutes on each side. Serve and enjoy.

Per Serving

Calories 270 Fat 12 g Carbohydrates 2.9 g Sugar 1.7 g Protein 34.9 g Cholesterol 119 mg

Tomato Pork Chops (Spanish)

Prep time: 10 minutes **Cooking Time:** 6 hours **Servings:** 4

Ingredients:

4 pork chops, bone-in	½ small onion, chopped
1 tablespoon garlic, minced	6 oz can tomato paste
¼ teaspoon red pepper flakes	1 tablespoon dried Italian seasoning oz can tomato, diced
1 teaspoon Worcestershire sauce	2 teaspoon olive oil
¼ teaspoon pepper	
1 teaspoon kosher salt	

Directions:

Heat oil in a pan over medium-high heat.

Season pork chops with pepper and salt.

Sear pork chops in pan until brown from both the sides.

Transfer pork chops into the crock pot.

Add remaining over pork chops.

Cover and cook on low for 6 hours. Serve and enjoy.

Per Serving

Calories 325 Fat 23.4 g Carbohydrates 10 g Sugar 6 g Protein 20 g Cholesterol 70 mg

Greek Pork Chops (Greek)

Prep time: 10 minutes **Cooking Time:** 6 mins **Servings:** 8

Ingredients:

8 pork chops, boneless	2 tablespoon Worcestershire
4 teaspoon dried oregano	1 teaspoon ground mustard
Salt	2 teaspoon garlic powder
3 tablespoon fresh lemon juice	2 teaspoon onion powder
sauce ¼ cup olive oil	Pepper

Directions:

Whisk together oil, garlic powder, onion powder, oregano, Worcestershire sauce, lemon juice, mustard, pepper, and salt.

Place pork chops in a baking dish then pour marinade over pork chops and coat well. Place in refrigerator overnight.

Preheat the grill.

Place pork chops on hot grill and cook for 3-4 mins on each side.

Serve and enjoy.

Per Serving

Calories 324 Fat 26.5 g Carbohydrates 2.5 g Sugar 1.3 g Protein 18 g Cholesterol 69 mg

Pork Cacciatore (Italian)

Prep time: 10 minutes **Cooking Time:** 6 hours **Servings:** 6

Ingredients:

1 ½ lbs. pork chops	1 teaspoon dried oregano
3 tablespoon tomato paste	2 cups mushrooms, sliced
14 oz can tomato, diced	1 small onion, diced
1 garlic clove, minced	¼ teaspoon pepper
2 tablespoon olive oil	1 cup beef broth
½ teaspoon salt	

Directions:

Heat oil in a pan over medium-high heat.

Add pork chops in pan and cook until brown on both the sides.

Transfer pork chops into the crock pot.

Pour remaining over the pork chops.

Cover and cook on low for 6 hours. Serve and enjoy.

Per Serving

Calories 440 Fat 33 g Carbohydrates 6 g Sugar 3 g Protein 28 g Cholesterol 97 mg

Pork with Tomato & Olives (Greek)

Preparation Time: 10 minutes **Cooking Time:** 30 minutes **Servings:** 6

Ingredients:

6 pork chops, boneless and cut into thick slices	1/2 cup olives, pitted and sliced
1/8 teaspoon ground cinnamon	8 oz can tomato, crushed
1/4 cup beef broth	1 large onion, sliced
1 tablespoon olive oil	2 garlic cloves, chopped

Directions:

Heat olive oil in a pan over medium-high heat.

Place pork chops in a pan and cook until lightly brown and set aside.

Cook garlic and onion in the same pan over medium heat, until onion is softened.

Add broth and bring to boil over high heat.

Return pork to pan and stir in crushed tomatoes and remaining .

Cover and simmer for 20 minutes.

Serve and enjoy.

Per Serving

Calories 321 Fat 23 g Carbohydrates 7 g Sugar 1 g Protein 19 g Cholesterol 70 mg

Tender Lamb Chops (Greek)

Preparation Time: 10 minutes **Cooking Time:** 6 hours
Servings: 8

Ingredients:

8 lamb chops
1 teaspoon dried oregano
1 onion, sliced
½ teaspoon dried thyme
2 garlic cloves, minced
Pepper and salt

Directions:

Add sliced onion into the slow cooker.

Combine together thyme, oregano, pepper, and salt. Rub over lamb chops.

Place lamb chops in slow cooker and top with garlic.

Pour ¼ cup water around the lamb chops.

Cover and cook on low for 6 hours.

Serve and enjoy.

Per Serving

Calories 40 Fat 1.9 g Carbohydrates 2.3 g Sugar 0.6 g Protein 3.4 g Cholesterol 0 mg

Sun-dried Tomato Chuck Roast (Italian)

Preparation Time: 10 minutes **Cooking Time:** 10 hours
Servings: 6

Ingredients:

1 lbs. beef chuck roast
25 garlic cloves, peeled
½ cup beef broth
¼ cup olives, sliced
¼ cup sun-dried tomatoes, chopped
1 teaspoon dried Italian seasoning, crushed
2 tablespoon balsamic vinegar

Directions:

Place meat into the crock pot.

Pour remaining over meat.

Cover and cook on low for 10 hours.

Shred the meat using fork.

Serve and enjoy.

Per Serving

Calories 582 Fat 43 g Carbohydrates 5 g Sugar 0.5 g Protein 40g Cholesterol 156 mg 0.4 g Sugar 0.1 g Protein 42 g Cholesterol 132 mg

Herb Ground Beef (Spanish)

Preparation Time: 10 minutes **Cooking Time:** 15 minutes
Servings: 4

1 lb. ground beef
½ teaspoon dried basil
1 teaspoon garlic, minced
1 teaspoon pepper
¼ teaspoon nutmeg
½ teaspoon dried parsley
½ teaspoon dried oregano
1 tablespoon olive oil
½ teaspoon dried thyme
½ teaspoon dried rosemary
1 teaspoon salt

Directions:

Heat oil in a pan over medium heat.

Add ground meat to the pan and fry until cooked.

Add remaining and stir well.

Serve and enjoy.

Per Serving

Calories 215 Fat 7.2 g Carbohydrates 1 g Sugar 0.2 g Protein 34 g Cholesterol 101 mg

Easy Beef Kofta (Spanish)

Preparation Time: 10 minutes **Cooking Time:** 10 minutes
Servings: 8

Ingredients:

1 lbs. ground beef
1 onion, minced
1 cup fresh parsley, chopped
1 teaspoon salt
4 garlic cloves, minced
2 teaspoon cumin
¼ teaspoon pepper

Directions:

Add all into the mixing bowl and mix until combined.

Roll meat mixture into the kabab shapes and cook in a hot pan for 4-6 minutes on each side or until cooked.

Serve and enjoy.

Per Serving

Calories 223 Fat 7.3 g Carbohydrates 2.5 g Sugar 0.7 g Protein 35 g Cholesterol 101 mg

Smoky Pork & Cabbage (Italian)

Preparation Time: 10 minutes **Cooking Time:** 8 hours
Servings: 6

Ingredients:

3 lbs. pork roast

1/3 cup liquid smoke

1 cup water

1/2 cabbage head, chopped

1 tablespoon kosher salt

Directions:

Rub pork with kosher salt and place into the crock pot.

Pour liquid smoke over the pork. Add water.

Cover and cook on low for 7 hours.

Remove pork from crock pot and add cabbage in the bottom of crock pot.

Place pork on top of the cabbage.

Cover again and cook for 1 hour more.

Shred pork with a fork and serve.

Per Serving

Calories 484 Fat 21.5 g Carbohydrates 4 g Sugar 1.9 g Protein 66 g Cholesterol 195 mg

Jalapeno Lamb Patties (Spanish)

Prep time: 10 minutes **Cooking Time:** 8 mins **Servings:** 4

Ingredients:

1 lb. ground lamb

5 basil leaves, minced

1 tablespoon garlic, minced

¼ cup fresh parsley, chopped

¼ teaspoon pepper

1 jalapeno pepper, minced

10 mint leaves, minced

1 teaspoon dried oregano

1 cup feta cheese, crumbled

½ teaspoon kosher salt

Directions:

Add all into the mixing bowl and mix until well combined.

Preheat the grill to 450 F.

Spray grill with cooking spray.

Make four equal shape patties from meat mixture and place on hot grill and cook for 3 minutes. Turn patties to another side and cook for 4 minutes. Serve and enjoy.

Per Serving

Calories 317 Fat 16 g Carbohydrates 3 g Sugar 1.7 g Protein 37.5 g Cholesterol 135 mg

Basil Parmesan Pork Roast (Spanish)

Prep time: 10 minutes **Cooking Time:** 6 hours **Servings:** 8

Ingredients:

2 lbs. lean pork roast, boneless

½ cup parmesan cheese, grated

1 teaspoon dried oregano

1 tablespoon parsley

1 tbsp garlic powder Pepper

28 oz can tomato, diced Salt

1 teaspoon dried basil

Directions:

Add the meat into the crock pot.

Mix together tomatoes, oregano, basil, garlic powder, parsley, cheese, pepper, and salt and pour over meat.

Cover and cook on low for 6 hours. Serve and enjoy.

Per Serving

Calories 294 Fat 11.6 g Carbohydrates 5 g Sugar 3 g Protein 38 g Cholesterol 105 mg

Seasoned Pork Chops (Spanish)

Preparation Time: 10 minutes **Cooking Time:** 4 hours
Servings: 4

Ingredients:

4 pork chops

1 tablespoon poultry seasoning

1/4 cup olive oil

2 garlic cloves, minced

Pepper and salt

1 cup chicken broth

Directions:

In a bowl, whisk together olive oil, poultry seasoning, garlic, broth, pepper, and salt.

Pour olive oil mixture into the slow cooker then place pork chops to the crock pot.

Cover and cook on high for 4 hours.

Serve and enjoy.

Per Serving

Calories 386 Fat 32.9 g Carbohydrates 3 g Sugar 1 g Protein 20 g Cholesterol 70 mg

Chapter 8
Fish and Seafood

Cioppino (Seafood Tomato Stew)

Prep time: 10 minutes | **Cook time:** 20 minutes | **Serves:** 2

Ingredients:

2 tablespoons olive oil
½ small onion, diced
½ green pepper, diced
2 teaspoons dried basil
2 teaspoons dried oregano
½ cup dry white wine
1 (14.5-ounce / 411-g) can diced tomatoes with basil
1 (8-ounce / 227-g) can no-salt-added tomato sauce

1 (6.5-ounce / 184-g) can minced clams with their juice
8 ounces (227 g) peeled, deveined raw shrimp
4 ounces (113 g) any white fish (a thick piece works best)
3 tablespoons fresh parsley
Salt and freshly ground black pepper, to taste

Directions:

In a Dutch oven, heat the olive oil over medium heat.

Saut é the onion and green pepper for 5 minutes, or until tender. Stir in the basil, oregano, wine, diced tomatoes, and tomato sauce and bring to a boil.

Once boiling, reduce the heat to low and bring to a simmer for 5 minutes.

Add the clams, shrimp, and fish and cook for about 10 minutes, or until the shrimp are pink and cooked through.

Scatter with the parsley and add the salt and black pepper to taste. Remove from the heat and serve warm.

Per Serving
calories: 221 | fat: 7.7g | protein: 23.1g | carbs: 10.9g

Fried Cod Fillets

Prep time: 5 minutes | **Cook time:** 10 minutes | **Serves:** 4

Ingredients:

½ cup all-purpose flour
1 teaspoon garlic powder
1 teaspoon salt

4 (4- to 5-ounce / 113- to 142-g) cod fillets
1 tablespoon extra-virgin olive oil

Directions:

Mix together the flour, garlic powder, and salt in a shallow dish. Dredge each piece of fish in the seasoned flour until they are evenly coated.

Heat the olive oil in a medium skillet over medium-high heat. Once hot, add the cod fillets and fry for 6 to 8 minutes, flipping the fish halfway through, or until the fish is opaque and flakes easily.

Remove from the heat and serve on plates.

Per Serving calories: 333 fat: 18.8g protein: 21.2g carbs: 20.0g

Lemon Grilled Shrimp

Prep time: 20 minutes | **Cook time:** 4 to 6 minutes | **Serves:** 4

Ingredients:

2 tablespoons garlic, minced
3 tablespoons fresh Italian parsley, finely chopped
¼ cup extra-virgin olive oil
½ cup lemon juice

1 teaspoon salt
2 pounds (907 g) jumbo shrimp (21 to 25), peeled and deveined
Special Equipment:
4 wooden skewers, soaked in water for at least 30 minutes

Directions:

Whisk together the garlic, parsley, olive oil, lemon juice, and salt in a large bowl.

Add the shrimp to the bowl and toss well, making sure the shrimp are coated in the marinade. Set aside to sit for 15 minutes.

When ready, skewer the shrimps by piercing through the center. You can place about 5 to 6 shrimps on each skewer. Preheat the grill to high heat.

Grill the shrimp for 4 to 6 minutes, flipping the shrimp halfway through, or until the shrimp are pink on the outside and opaque in the center. Serve hot.

Per Serving
calories: 401 | fat: 17.8g | protein: 56.9g | carbs: 3.9g

Dill Baked Sea Bass

Prep time: 10 minutes | **Cook time:** 10 to 15 minutes | **Serves:** 6

Ingredients:

¼ cup olive oil
2 pounds (907 g) sea bass
Sea salt and freshly ground pepper, to taste

1 garlic clove, minced
¼ cup dry white wine
3 teaspoons fresh dill
2 teaspoons fresh thyme

Directions:

Preheat the oven to 425ºF (220ºC).

Brush the bottom of a roasting pan with the olive oil. Place the fish in the pan and brush the fish with oil.

Season the fish with sea salt and freshly ground pepper. Combine the remaining ingredients and pour over the fish.

Bake in the preheated oven for 10 to 15 minutes, depending on the size of the fish. Serve hot.

Per Serving
calories: 224 | fat: 12.1g | protein: 28.1g | carbs: 0.9g

Baked Lemon Salmon

Prep time: 5 minutes | **Cook time:** 20 minutes | **Serves:**4

Ingredients:

¼ teaspoon dried thyme
Zest and juice of ½ lemon
¼ teaspoon salt
Nonstick cooking spray

½ teaspoon freshly ground black pepper
1 pound (454 g) salmon fillet

Directions:

Preheat the oven to 425ºF (220ºC). Coat a baking sheet with nonstick cooking spray.

Mix together the thyme, lemon zest and juice, salt, and pepper in a small bowl and stir to incorporate.

Arrange the salmon, skin-side down, on the coated baking sheet. Spoon the thyme mixture over the salmon and spread it all over.

Bake in the preheated oven for about 15 to 20 minutes, or until the fish flakes apart easily. Serve warm.

Per Serving calories: 162 | fat: 7.0g | protein: 23.1g | carbs:

Garlic Shrimp with Mushrooms

Prep time: 10 minutes | **Cook time:** 15 minutes | **Serves:**4

Ingredients:

1 pound (454 g) fresh shrimp, peeled, deveined, and patted dry
1 teaspoon salt
1 cup extra-virgin olive oil
8 large garlic cloves, thinly sliced

4 ounces (113 g) sliced mushrooms (shiitake, baby bella, or button)
½ teaspoon red pepper flakes
¼ cup chopped fresh flat-leaf Italian parsley

Directions:

In a bowl, season the shrimp with salt. Set aside.

Heat the olive oil in a large skillet over medium-low heat.

Add the garlic and cook for 3 to 4 minutes until fragrant, stirring occasionally.

Sauté the mushrooms for 5 minutes, or until they start to exude their juices. Stir in the shrimp and sprinkle with red pepper flakes and sauté for 3 to 4 minutes more, or until the shrimp start to turn pink.

Remove the skillet from the heat and add the parsley. Stir to combine and serve warm.

Per Serving

calories: 619 | fat: 55.5g | protein: 24.1g | carbs: 3.7g

Lemony Shrimp with Orzo Salad

Prep time: 10 minutes | **Cook time:** 22 minutes | **Serves:**4

Ingredients:

1 cup orzo
1 hothouse cucumber, deseeded and chopped
½ cup finely diced red onion
2 tablespoons extra-virgin olive oil
2 pounds (907 g) shrimp, peeled and deveined

3 lemons, juiced
Salt and freshly ground black pepper, to taste
¾ cup crumbled feta cheese
2 tablespoons dried dill
1 cup chopped fresh flat-leaf parsley

Directions:

Bring a large pot of water to a boil. Add the orzo and cook covered for 15 to 18 minutes, or until the orzo is tender. Transfer to a colander to drain and set aside to cool.

Mix the cucumber and red onion in a bowl. Set aside.

Heat the olive oil in a medium skillet over medium heat until it shimmers.

Reduce the heat, add the shrimp, and cook each side for 2 minutes until cooked through.

Add the cooked shrimp to the bowl of cucumber and red onion. Mix in the cooked orzo and lemon juice and toss to combine. Sprinkle with salt and pepper. Scatter the top with the feta cheese and dill. Garnish with the parsley and serve immediately.

Per Serving

calories: 565 | fat: 17.8g | protein: 63.3g | carbs: 43.9g

Spicy Grilled Shrimp with Lemon Wedges

Prep time: 15 minutes | **Cook time:** 6 minutes | **Serves:**6

Ingredients:

1 large clove garlic, crushed
1 teaspoon coarse salt
1 teaspoon paprika
½ teaspoon cayenne pepper
2 teaspoons lemon juice

2 tablespoons plus
1 teaspoon olive oil, divided
2 pounds (907 g) large shrimp, peeled and deveined
8 wedges lemon, for garnish

Directions:

Preheat the grill to medium heat.

Stir together the garlic, salt, paprika, cayenne pepper, lemon juice, and 2 tablespoons of olive oil in a small bowl until a paste forms. Add the shrimp and toss until well coated.

Grease the grill grates lightly with remaining 1 teaspoon of olive oil. Grill the shrimp for 4 to 6 minutes, flipping the shrimp halfway through, or until the shrimp is totally pink and opaque. Garnish the shrimp with lemon wedges and serve hot.

Per Serving

calories: 163 | fat: 5.8g | protein: 25.2g | carbs: 2.8g

Avocado Shrimp Ceviche

Prep time: 15 minutes | **Cook time:** 0 minutes | **Serves:**4

Ingredients:

1 pound (454 g) fresh shrimp, peeled, deveined, and cut in half lengthwise
1 small red or yellow bell pepper, cut into ½-inch chunks
½ small red onion, cut into thin slivers
½ English cucumber, peeled and cut into ½-inch chunks
¼ cup chopped fresh cilantro
⅓ cup freshly squeezed lime juice
2 tablespoons freshly squeezed clementine juice
2 tablespoons freshly squeezed lemon juice
1 teaspoon salt
½ teaspoon freshly ground black pepper
2 ripe avocados, peeled, pitted, and cut into ½-inch chunks
½ cup extra-virgin olive oil

Directions:

Place the shrimp, bell pepper, red onion, cucumber, and cilantro in a large bowl and toss to combine.

In a separate bowl, stir together the olive oil, lime, clementine, and lemon juice, salt, and black pepper until smooth. Pour the mixture into the bowl of shrimp and vegetable mixture and toss until they are completely coated.

Cover the bowl with plastic wrap and transfer to the refrigerator to marinate for at least 2 hours, or up to 8 hours.

When ready, stir in the avocado chunks and toss to incorporate. Serve immediately.

Per Serving

calories: 496 | fat: 39.5g | protein: 25.3g | carbs: 13.8g

Baked Salmon with Basil and Tomato

Prep time: 10 minutes | **Cook time:** 20 minutes | **Serves:**2

Ingredients:

2 (6-ounce / 170-g) boneless salmon fillets
1 tablespoon dried basil
1 tomato, thinly sliced
1 tablespoon olive oil
2 tablespoons grated Parmesan cheese
Nonstick cooking spray

Directions:

Preheat the oven to 375ºF (190ºC). Line a baking sheet with a piece of aluminum foil and mist with nonstick cooking spray.

Arrange the salmon fillets onto the aluminum foil and scatter with basil. Place the tomato slices on top and drizzle with olive oil. Top with the grated Parmesan cheese.

Bake for about 20 minutes, or until the flesh is opaque and it flakes apart easily.

Remove from the oven and serve on a plate.

Per Serving

calories: 403 | fat: 26.5g | protein: 36.3g | carbs: 3.8g

Cod with Parsley Pistou

Prep time: 15 minutes | **Cook time:** 10 minutes | **Serves:**4

Ingredients:

1 cup packed roughly chopped fresh flat-leaf Italian parsley
Zest and juice of 1 lemon
1 to 2 small garlic cloves, minced
1 teaspoon salt
½ teaspoon freshly ground black pepper
1 cup extra-virgin olive oil, divided
1 pound (454 g) cod fillets, cut into 4 equal-sized pieces

Directions:

Make the pistou: Place the parsley, lemon zest and juice, garlic, salt, and pepper in a food processor until finely chopped. With the food processor running, slowly drizzle in ¾ cup of olive oil until a thick sauce forms. Set aside.

Heat the remaining ¼ cup of olive oil in a large skillet over medium-high heat.

Add the cod fillets, cover, and cook each side for 4 to 5 minutes, until browned and cooked through.

Remove the cod fillets from the heat to a plate and top each with generous spoonfuls of the prepared pistou. Serve immediately.

Per Serving

calories: 580 | fat: 54.6g | protein: 21.1g | carbs: 2.8g

Mediterranean Braised Cod with Vegetables

Prep time: 10 minutes | **Cook time:** 18 minutes | **Serves:**2

Ingredients:

1 tablespoon olive oil
½ medium onion, minced
2 garlic cloves, minced
1 teaspoon oregano
1 (15-ounce / 425-g) can artichoke hearts in water, drained and halved
1 (15-ounce / 425-g) can diced tomatoes with basil
¼ cup pitted Greek olives, drained
10 ounces (284 g) wild cod
Salt and freshly ground black pepper, to taste

Directions:

In a skillet, heat the olive oil over medium-high heat.

Sauté the onion for about 5 minutes, stirring occasionally, or until tender. Stir in the garlic and oregano and cook for 30 seconds more until fragrant.

Add the artichoke hearts, tomatoes, and olives and stir to combine. Top with the cod. Cover and cook for 10 minutes, or until the fish flakes easily with a fork and juices run clean. Sprinkle with the salt and pepper. Serve warm.

Per Serving

calories: 332 | fat: 10.5g | protein: 29.2g | carbs: 30.7g

Lemon-Parsley Swordfish

Prep time: 10 minutes | **Cook time:** 17 to 20 minutes | **Serves:** 4

Ingredients:

1 cup fresh Italian parsley	2 cloves garlic
¼ cup lemon juice	½ teaspoon salt
¼ cup extra-virgin olive oil	4 swordfish steaks
¼ cup fresh thyme	Olive oil spray

Directions:

Preheat the oven to 450°F (235°C). Grease a large baking dish generously with olive oil spray.

Place the parsley, lemon juice, olive oil, thyme, garlic, and salt in a food processor and pulse until smoothly blended.

Arrange the swordfish steaks in the greased baking dish and spoon the parsley mixture over the top.

Bake in the preheated oven for 17 to 20 minutes until flaky.

Divide the fish among four plates and serve hot.

Per Serving

calories: 396 | fat: 21.7g | protein: 44.2g | carbs: 2.9g

Baked Salmon with Tarragon Mustard Sauce

Prep time: 5 minutes | **Cook time:** 12 minutes | **Serves:** 4

Ingredients:

1¼ pounds (567 g) salmon fillet (skin on or removed), cut into 4 equal pieces	2 tablespoons chopped fresh tarragon
¼ cup Dijon mustard	½ teaspoon salt
¼ cup avocado oil mayonnaise	¼ teaspoon freshly ground black pepper
Zest and juice of ½ lemon	4 tablespoons extra-virgin olive oil, for serving

Directions:

Preheat the oven to 425°F (220°C). Line a baking sheet with parchment paper. Arrange the salmon pieces on the prepared baking sheet, skin-side down.

Stir together the mustard, avocado oil mayonnaise, lemon zest and juice, tarragon, salt, and pepper in a small bowl. Spoon the mustard mixture over the salmon.

Bake for 10 to 12 minutes, or until the top is golden and salmon is opaque in the center.

Divide the salmon among four plates and drizzle each top with 1 tablespoon of olive oil before serving.

Per Serving

calories: 386 | fat: 27.7g | protein: 29.3g | carbs: 3.8g

Glazed Broiled Salmon

Prep time: 5 minutes | **Cook time:** 5 to 10 minutes | **Serves:** 4

Ingredients:

4 (4-ounce / 113-g) salmon fillets	1 teaspoon coconut aminos
	1 teaspoon rice vinegar
2 tablespoons raw honey	3 tablespoons miso paste

Directions:

Preheat the broiler to High. Line a baking dish with aluminum foil and add the salmon fillets.

Whisk together the miso paste, honey, coconut aminos, and vinegar in a small bowl. Pour the glaze over the fillets and spread it evenly with a brush.

Broil for about 5 minutes, or until the salmon is browned on top and opaque. Brush any remaining glaze over the salmon and broil for an additional 5 minutes if needed. The cooking time depends on the thickness of the salmon.

Let the salmon cool for 5 minutes before serving.

Per Serving

calories: 263 | fat: 8.9g | protein: 30.2g | carbs: 12.8g

Honey-Mustard Roasted Salmon

Prep time: 5 minutes | **Cook time:** 15 to 20 minutes | **Serves:** 4

Ingredients:

2 tablespoons whole-grain mustard	¼ teaspoon freshly ground black pepper
2 garlic cloves, minced	1 pound (454 g) salmon fillet
1 tablespoon honey	
¼ teaspoon salt	Nonstick cooking spray

Directions:

Preheat the oven to 425°F (220°C). Coat a baking sheet with nonstick cooking spray.

Stir together the mustard, garlic, honey, salt, and pepper in a small bowl.

Arrange the salmon fillet, skin-side down, on the coated baking sheet. Spread the mustard mixture evenly over the salmon fillet.

Roast in the preheated oven for 15 to 20 minutes, or until it flakes apart easily and reaches an internal temperature of 145°F (63°C). Serve hot.

Per Serving

calories: 185 | fat: 7.0g | protein: 23.2g | carbs: 5.8g

Baked Fish with Pistachio Crust

Prep time: 10 minutes | **Cook time:** 15 to 20 minutes | Serves:4

Ingredients:

½ cup extra-virgin olive oil, divided

1 pound (454 g) flaky white fish (such as cod, haddock, or halibut), skin removed

½ cup shelled finely chopped pistachios

½ cup ground flaxseed

Zest and juice of 1 lemon, divided

1 teaspoon ground cumin

1 teaspoon ground allspice

½ teaspoon salt

¼ teaspoon freshly ground black pepper

Directions:

Preheat the oven to 400ºF (205ºC).

Line a baking sheet with parchment paper or aluminum foil and drizzle 2 tablespoons of olive oil over the sheet, spreading to evenly coat the bottom.

Cut the fish into 4 equal pieces and place on the prepared baking sheet. In a small bowl, combine the pistachios, flaxseed, lemon zest, cumin, allspice, salt, and pepper. Drizzle in ¼ cup of olive oil and stir well.

Divide the nut mixture evenly on top of the fish pieces. Drizzle the lemon juice and remaining 2 tablespoons of olive oil over the fish and bake until cooked through, 15 to 20 minutes, depending on the thickness of the fish.

Cool for 5 minutes before serving.

Per Serving

calories: 509 | fat: 41.0g | protein: 26.0g | carbs: 9.0g

Haddock with Cucumber Sauce

Prep time: 10 minutes | **Cook time:** 10 minutes | **Serves:**4

Ingredients:

¼ cup plain Greek yogurt

½ scallion, white and green parts, finely chopped

½ English cucumber, grated, liquid squeezed out

2 teaspoons chopped fresh mint

1 teaspoon honey

Sea salt and freshly ground black pepper, to taste

4 (5-ounce / 142-g) haddock fillets, patted dry

Nonstick cooking spray

Directions:

In a small bowl, stir together the yogurt, cucumber, scallion, mint, honey, and a pinch of salt. Set aside.

Season the fillets lightly with salt and pepper.

Place a large skillet over medium-high heat and spray lightly with cooking spray.

Cook the haddock, turning once, until it is just cooked through, about 5 minutes per side.

Remove the fish from the heat and transfer to plates.

Serve topped with the cucumber sauce.

Per Serving

calories: 164 | fat: 2.0g | protein: 27.0g | carbs: 4.0g

Sole Piccata with Capers

Prep time: 10 minutes | **Cook time:** 17 minutes | **Serves:**4

Ingredients:

1 teaspoon extra-virgin olive oil

4 (5-ounce / 142-g) sole fillets, patted dry

3 tablespoons almond butter

2 teaspoons minced garlic

2 tablespoons all-purpose flour

2 cups low-sodium chicken broth

Juice and zest of ½ lemon

2 tablespoons capers

Directions:

Place a large skillet over medium-high heat and add the olive oil.

Sear the sole fillets until the fish flakes easily when tested with a fork, about 4 minutes on each side. Transfer the fish to a plate and set aside.

Return the skillet to the stove and add the butter.

Sauté the garlic until translucent, about 3 minutes.

Whisk in the flour to make a thick paste and cook, stirring constantly, until the mixture is golden brown, about 2 minutes.

Whisk in the chicken broth, lemon juice and zest.

Cook for about 4 minutes until the sauce is thickened.

Stir in the capers and serve the sauce over the fish.

Per Serving

calories: 271 | fat:13.0g | protein: 30.0g | carbs: 7.0g

Crispy Herb Crusted Halibut

Prep time: 10 minutes | **Cook time:** 20 minutes | **Serves:**4

Ingredients:

4 (5-ounce / 142-g) halibut fillets, patted dry

Extra-virgin olive oil, for brushing

½ cup coarsely ground unsalted pistachios

Pinch freshly ground black pepper

1 tablespoon chopped fresh parsley

1 teaspoon chopped fresh basil

1 teaspoon chopped fresh thyme

Pinch sea salt

Directions:

Preheat the oven to 350ºF (180ºC). Line a baking sheet with parchment paper.

Place the fillets on the baking sheet and brush them generously with olive oil.

In a small bowl, stir together the pistachios, parsley, basil, thyme, salt, and pepper.

Spoon the nut mixture evenly on the fish, spreading it out so the tops of the fillets are covered.

Bake in the preheated oven until it flakes when pressed with a fork, about 20 minutes. Serve immediately.

Per Serving

calories: 262 fat: 11.0g protein: 32.0g carbs: 4.0g

Breaded Shrimp

Prep time: 10 minutes | **Cook time:** 4 to 6 minutes | Serves:4

Ingredients:

2 large eggs
1 tablespoon water
2 cups seasoned Italian bread crumbs
1 teaspoon salt

1 cup flour
1 pound (454 g) large shrimp (21 to 25), peeled and deveined
Extra-virgin olive oil, as needed

Directions:

In a small bowl, beat the eggs with the water, then transfer to a shallow dish. Add the bread crumbs and salt to a separate shallow dish, then mix well.

Place the flour into a third shallow dish.

Coat the shrimp in the flour, then the beaten egg, and finally the bread crumbs. Place on a plate and repeat with all of the shrimp. Heat a skillet over high heat. Pour in enough olive oil to coat the bottom of the skillet. Cook the shrimp in the hot skillet for 2 to 3 minutes on each side. Remove and drain on a paper towel. Serve warm.

Per Serving

calories: 714 | fat: 34.0g | protein: 37.0g | carbs: 63.0g

Pesto Shrimp over Zoodles

Prep time: 15 minutes | **Cook time:** 10 minutes | Serves:4

Ingredients:

1 pound (454 g) fresh shrimp, peeled and deveined
Salt and freshly ground black pepper, to taste
2 tablespoons extra-virgin olive oil
½ small onion, slivered

8 ounces (227 g) store-bought jarred pesto
¾ cup crumbled goat or feta cheese, plus additional for serving
2 large zucchini, spiralized, for serving
¼ cup chopped flat-leaf Italian parsley, for garnish

Directions:

In a bowl, season the shrimp with salt and pepper. Set aside.

In a large skillet, heat the olive oil over medium-high heat. Sauté the onion until just golden, 5 to 6 minutes.

Reduce the heat to low and add the pesto and cheese, whisking to combine and melt the cheese. Bring to a low simmer and add the shrimp. Reduce the heat back to low and cover. Cook until the shrimp is cooked through and pink, about 3 to 4 minutes.

Serve the shrimp warm over zoodles, garnishing with chopped parsley and additional crumbled cheese.

Per Serving

calories: 491 | fat: 35.0g | protein: 29.0g | carbs: 15.0g

Salt and Pepper Calamari and Scallops

Prep time: 5 minutes | **Cook time:** 10 minutes | **Serves:**4

Ingredients:

8 ounces (227 g) calamari steaks, cut into ½-inch-thick rings
8 ounces (227 g) sea scallops
1½ teaspoons salt, divided

1 teaspoon garlic powder
1 teaspoon freshly ground black pepper
⅓ cup extra-virgin olive oil
2 tablespoons almond butter

Directions:

Place the calamari and scallops on several layers of paper towels and pat dry. Sprinkle with 1 teaspoon of salt and allow to sit for 15 minutes at room temperature.

Pat dry with additional paper towels. Sprinkle with pepper and garlic powder.

In a deep medium skillet, heat the olive oil and butter over medium-high heat. When the oil is hot but not smoking, add the scallops and calamari in a single layer to the skillet and sprinkle with the remaining ½ teaspoon of salt. Cook for 2 to 4 minutes on each side, depending on the size of the scallops, until just golden but still slightly opaque in center.

Using a slotted spoon, remove from the skillet and transfer to a serving platter. Allow the cooking oil to cool slightly and drizzle over the seafood before serving.

Per Serving

calories: 309 | fat: 25.0g | protein: 18.0g | carbs: 3.0g

Grilled Lemon Pesto Salmon

Prep time: 5 minutes | **Cook time:** 6 to 10 minutes | Serves:2

Ingredients:

10 ounces (283 g) salmon fillet (1 large piece or 2 smaller ones)
Salt and freshly ground black pepper, to taste

2 tablespoons prepared pesto sauce
1 large fresh lemon, sliced
Cooking spray

Directions:

reheat the grill to medium-high heat. Spray the grill grates with cooking spray. Season the salmon with salt and black pepper. Spread the pesto sauce on top.

Make a bed of fresh lemon slices about the same size as the salmon fillet on the hot grill, and place the salmon on top of the lemon slices. Put additional lemon slices on top of the salmon. Grill the salmon for 6 to 10 minutes, or until the fish is opaque and flakes apart easily. Serve hot.

Per Serving

calories: 316 | fat: 21.1g | protein: 29.0g | carbs: 1.0g

Baked Cod with Vegetables

Prep time: 15 minutes | **Cook time:** 25 minutes | **Serves:** 2

Ingredients:

1 pound (454 g) thick cod fillet, cut into 4 even portions

¼ teaspoon onion powder (optional)

¼ teaspoon paprika

3 tablespoons extra-virgin olive oil

4 medium scallions

½ cup fresh chopped basil, divided

3 tablespoons minced garlic (optional)

2 teaspoons freshly ground black pepper

¼ teaspoon dry marjoram (optional)

6 sun-dried tomato slices

½ cup dry white wine

½ cup crumbled feta cheese

1 (15-ounce / 425-g) can oil-packed artichoke hearts, drained

1 lemon, sliced

1 cup pitted kalamata olives

1 teaspoon capers (optional)

4 small red potatoes, quartered

2 teaspoons salt

Directions:

Preheat the oven to 375ºF (190ºC).

Season the fish with paprika and onion powder (if desired).

Heat an ovenproof skillet over medium heat and sear the top side of the cod for about 1 minute until golden. Set aside.

Heat the olive oil in the same skillet over medium heat. Add the scallions, ¼ cup of basil, garlic (if desired), salt, pepper, marjoram (if desired), tomato slices, and white wine and stir to combine. Bring to a boil and remove from heat.

Evenly spread the sauce on the bottom of skillet. Place the cod on top of the tomato basil sauce and scatter with feta cheese. Place the artichokes in the skillet and top with the lemon slices.

Scatter with the olives, capers (if desired), and the remaining ¼ cup of basil. Remove from the heat and transfer to the preheated oven. Bake for 15 to 20 minutes, or until it flakes easily with a fork.

Meanwhile, place the quartered potatoes on a baking sheet or wrapped in aluminum foil. Bake in the oven for 15 minutes until fork-tender.

Cool for 5 minutes before serving.

Per Serving

calories: 1168 | fat: 60.0g | protein: 63.8g | carbs: 94.0g

Slow Cooker Salmon in Foil

Prep time: 5 minutes | **Cook time:** 2 hours | **Serves:** 2

Ingredients:

2 (6-ounce / 170-g) salmon fillets

1 tablespoon olive oil

2 cloves garlic, minced

½ tablespoon lime juice

1 teaspoon finely chopped fresh parsley

¼ teaspoon black pepper

Directions:

Spread a length of foil onto a work surface and place the salmon fillets in the middle. Mix together the olive oil, garlic, lime juice, parsley, and black pepper in a small bowl. Brush the mixture over the fillets. Fold the foil over and crimp the sides to make a packet.

Place the packet into the slow cooker, cover, and cook on High for 2 hours, or until the fish flakes easily with a fork.

Serve hot.

Per Serving calories: 446 | fat: 20.7g | protein: 65.4g | carbs: 1.5g

Dill Chutney Salmon

Prep time: 5 minutes | **Cook time:** 3 minutes | **Serves:** 2

Ingredients:

Chutney:

¼ cup fresh dill

¼ cup extra virgin olive oil

Juice from ½ lemon

Sea salt, to taste

Fish:

2 cups water

2 salmon fillets

Juice from ½ lemon

¼ teaspoon paprika

Salt and freshly ground pepper to taste

Directions:

Pulse all the chutney ingredients in a food processor until creamy. Set aside. Add the water and steamer basket to the Instant Pot. Place salmon fillets, skin-side down, on the steamer basket. Drizzle the lemon juice over salmon and sprinkle with the paprika. Secure the lid. Select the Manual mode and set the cooking time for 3 minutes at High Pressure.

Once cooking is complete, do a quick pressure release. Carefully open the lid. Season the fillets with pepper and salt to taste. Serve topped with the dill chutney.

Per Serving calories: 636 | fat: 41.1g | protein: 65.3g | carbs: 1.9g

Garlic-Butter Parmesan Salmon and Asparagus

Prep time: 10 minutes | **Cook time:** 15 minutes | **Serves:** 2

Ingredients:

2 (6-ounce / 170-g) salmon fillets, skin on and patted dry
Pink Himalayan salt
Freshly ground black pepper, to taste

1 pound (454 g) fresh asparagus, ends snapped off
3 tablespoons almond butter
2 garlic cloves, minced
¼ cup grated Parmesan cheese

Directions:

Preheat the oven to 400ºF (205ºC). Line a baking sheet with aluminum foil. Season both sides of the salmon fillets with salt and pepper. Put the salmon in the middle of the baking sheet and arrange the asparagus around the salmon.

Heat the almond butter in a small saucepan over medium heat. Add the minced garlic and cook for about 3 minutes, or until the garlic just begins to brown. Drizzle the garlic-butter sauce over the salmon and asparagus and scatter the Parmesan cheese on top. Bake in the preheated oven for about 12 minutes, or until the salmon is cooked through and the asparagus is crisp-tender.

You can switch the oven to broil at the end of cooking time for about 3 minutes to get a nice char on the asparagus.

Let cool for 5 minutes before serving.

Per Serving

calories: 435 | fat: 26.1g | protein: 42.3g | carbs: 10.0g

Steamed Trout with Lemon Herb Crust

Prep time: 10 minutes | **Cook time:** 15 minutes | **Serves:** 2

Ingredients:

3 tablespoons olive oil
3 garlic cloves, chopped
2 tablespoons fresh lemon juice
1 tablespoon chopped fresh mint
1 tablespoon chopped fresh parsley

¼ teaspoon dried ground thyme
1 teaspoon sea salt
1 pound (454 g) fresh trout (2 pieces)
2 cups fish stock

Directions:

Stir together the olive oil, garlic, lemon juice, mint, parsley, thyme, and salt in a small bowl. Brush the marinade onto the fish. Insert a trivet in the Instant Pot. Pour in the fish stock and place the fish on the trivet.

Secure the lid. Select the Steam mode and set the cooking time for 15 minutes at High Pressure. Once cooking is complete, do a quick pressure release. Carefully open the lid. Serve warm.

Per Serving

calories: 477 | fat: 29.6g | protein: 51.7g | carbs: 3.6g

Lemon Rosemary Roasted Branzino

Prep time: 15 minutes | **Cook time:** 30 minutes | **Serves:** 2

Ingredients:

4 tablespoons extra-virgin olive oil, divided
2 (8-ounce / 227-g) branzino fillets, preferably at least 1 inch thick
1 garlic clove, minced
1 bunch scallions (white part only), thinly sliced
10 to 12 small cherry tomatoes, halved

1 large carrot, cut into ¼-inch rounds
½ cup dry white wine
2 tablespoons paprika
2 teaspoons kosher salt
½ tablespoon ground chili pepper
2 rosemary sprigs or 1 tablespoon dried rosemary
1 small lemon, thinly sliced
½ cup sliced pitted kalamata olives

Directions:

Heat a large ovenproof skillet over high heat until hot, about 2 minutes. Add 1 tablespoon of olive oil and heat for 10 to 15 seconds until it shimmers.

Add the branzino fillets, skin-side up, and sear for 2 minutes. Flip the fillets and cook for an additional 2 minutes. Set aside. Swirl 2 tablespoons of olive oil around the skillet to coat evenly.

Add the garlic, scallions, tomatoes, and carrot, and sauté for 5 minutes, or until softened.

Add the wine, stirring until all ingredients are well combined. Carefully place the fish over the sauce.

Preheat the oven to 450ºF (235ºC).

Brush the fillets with the remaining 1 tablespoon of olive oil and season with paprika, salt, and chili pepper. Top each fillet with a rosemary sprig and lemon slices. Scatter the olives over fish and around the skillet.

Roast for about 10 minutes until the lemon slices are browned. Serve hot.

Per Serving calories: 724 | fat: 43.0g | protein: 57.7g | carbs: 25.0g

Hazelnut Crusted Sea Bass

Prep time: 10 minutes | **Cook time:** 15 minutes | **Serves:** 2

Ingredients:

2 tablespoons almond butter

2 sea bass fillets

⅓ cup roasted hazelnuts

A pinch of cayenne pepper

Directions:

Preheat the oven to 425°F (220°C). Line a baking dish with waxed paper. Brush the almond butter over the fillets.

Pulse the hazelnuts and cayenne in a food processor.

Coat the sea bass with the hazelnut mixture, then transfer to the baking dish. Bake in the preheated oven for about 15 minutes. Cool for 5 minutes before serving.

Per Serving

calories: 468 | fat: 30.8g | protein: 40.0g | carbs: 8.8g

Roasted Trout Stuffed with Veggies

Prep time: 10 minutes | **Cook time:** 25 minutes | **Serves:** 2

Ingredients:

2 (8-ounce / 227-g) whole trout fillets, dressed (cleaned but with bones and skin intact)

1 tablespoon extra-virgin olive oil

¼ teaspoon salt

⅛ teaspoon freshly ground black pepper

1 small onion, thinly sliced

½ red bell pepper, seeded and thinly sliced

1 poblano pepper, seeded and thinly sliced

2 or 3 shiitake mushrooms, sliced

1 lemon, sliced

Nonstick cooking spray

Directions:

Preheat the oven to 425°F (220°C). Spray a baking sheet with nonstick cooking spray. Rub both trout fillets, inside and out, with the olive oil. Season with salt and pepper. Mix together the onion, bell pepper, poblano pepper, and mushrooms in a large bowl. Stuff half of this mixture into the cavity of each fillet. Top the mixture with 2 or 3 lemon slices inside each fillet.

Place the fish on the prepared baking sheet side by side. Roast in the preheated oven for 25 minutes, or until the fish is cooked through and the vegetables are tender.

Remove from the oven and serve on a plate.

Per Serving

calories: 453 | fat: 22.1g | protein: 49.0g | carbs: 13.8g

Lemony Trout with Caramelized Shallots

Prep time: 10 minutes | **Cook time:** 20 minutes | **Serves:** 2

Ingredients:

Shallots:

1 teaspoon almond butter

2 shallots, thinly sliced Dash salt

Trout:

1 tablespoon plus

1 teaspoon almond butter, divided

2 (4-ounce / 113-g) trout fillets

3 tablespoons capers

¼ cup freshly squeezed lemon juice

¼ teaspoon salt

Dash freshly ground black pepper

1 lemon, thinly sliced

Directions:

In a large skillet over medium heat, cook the butter, shallots, and salt for 20 minutes, stirring every 5 minutes, or until the shallots are wilted and caramelized. Make the Trout Meanwhile, in another large skillet over medium heat, heat 1 teaspoon of almond butter.

Add the trout fillets and cook each side for 3 minutes, or until flaky. Transfer to a plate and set aside.

In the skillet used for the trout, stir in the capers, lemon juice, salt, and pepper, then bring to a simmer. Whisk in the remaining 1 tablespoon of almond butter. Spoon the sauce over the fish. Garnish the fish with the lemon slices and caramelized shallots before serving.

Per Serving

calories: 344 | fat: 18.4g | protein: 21.1g | carbs: 14.7g

Tomato Tuna Melts

Prep time: 5 minutes | **Cook time:** 3 to 4 minutes | **Serves:** 2

Ingredients:

1 (5-ounce / 142-g) can chunk light tuna packed in water, drained

2 tablespoons plain Greek yogurt

2 tablespoons finely chopped celery

1 tablespoon finely chopped red onion

2 teaspoons freshly squeezed lemon juice

Pinch cayenne pepper

1 large tomato, cut into ¾-inch-thick rounds

½ cup shredded Cheddar cheese

Directions:

Preheat the broiler to High. Stir together the tuna, yogurt, celery, red onion, lemon juice, and cayenne pepper in a medium bowl. Place the tomato rounds on a baking sheet. Top each with some tuna salad and Cheddar cheese.

Broil for 3 to 4 minutes until the cheese is melted and bubbly. Cool for 5 minutes before serving.

Per Serving

calories: 244 | fat: 10.0g | protein: 30.1g | carbs: 6.9g

Mackerel and Green Bean Salad

Prep time: 10 minutes | **Cook time:** 10 minutes | **Serves:** 2

Ingredients:

2 cups green beans
1 tablespoon avocado oil
2 mackerel fillets
4 cups mixed salad greens
2 hard-boiled eggs, sliced

1 avocado, sliced
2 tablespoons lemon juice
2 tablespoons olive oil
1 teaspoon Dijon mustard
Salt and black pepper, to taste

Directions:

Cook the green beans in a medium saucepan of boiling water for about 3 minutes until crisp-tender. Drain and set aside.

Melt the avocado oil in a pan over medium heat. Add the mackerel fillets and cook each side for 4 minutes.

Divide the greens between two salad bowls. Top with the mackerel, sliced egg, and avocado slices.

In another bowl, whisk together the lemon juice, olive oil, mustard, salt, and pepper, and drizzle over the salad. Add the cooked green beans and toss to combine, then serve.

Per Serving

calories: 737 | fat: 57.3g | protein: 34.2g | carbs: 22.1g

Shrimp and Pea Paella

Prep time: 20 minutes | **Cook time:** 60 minutes | **Serves:** 2

Ingredients:

2 tablespoons olive oil
1 garlic clove, minced
½ large onion, minced
1 cup diced tomato
½ cup short-grain rice
½ teaspoon sweet paprika
½ cup dry white wine

1¼ cups low-sodium chicken stock
8 ounces (227 g) large raw shrimp
1 cup frozen peas
¼ cup jarred roasted red peppers, cut into strips
Salt, to taste

Directions:

Heat the olive oil in a large skillet over medium-high heat.

Add the garlic and onion and sauté for 3 minutes, or until the onion is softened. Add the tomato, rice, and paprika and stir for 3 minutes to toast the rice.

Add the wine and chicken stock and stir to combine. Bring the mixture to a boil.

Cover and reduce the heat to medium-low, and simmer for 45 minutes, or until the rice is just about tender and most of the liquid has been absorbed.

Add the shrimp, peas, and roasted red peppers. Cover and cook for an additional 5 minutes. Season with salt to taste and serve.

Per Serving

calories: 646 | fat: 27.1g | protein: 42.0g | carbs: 59.7g

Garlic Shrimp with Arugula Pesto

Prep time: 20 minutes | **Cook time:** 5 minutes | **Serves:** 2

Ingredients:

3 cups lightly packed arugula
½ cup lightly packed basil leaves
¼ cup walnuts
3 tablespoons olive oil
3 medium garlic cloves
2 tablespoons grated Parmesan cheese
1 tablespoon freshly squeezed lemon juice

Salt and freshly ground black pepper, to taste
1 (10-ounce / 283-g) package zucchini noodles
8 ounces (227 g) cooked, shelled shrimp
2 Roma tomatoes, diced

Directions:

Process the arugula, basil, walnuts, olive oil, garlic, Parmesan cheese, and lemon juice in a food processor until smooth, scraping down the sides as needed. Season with salt and pepper to taste.

Heat a skillet over medium heat. Add the pesto, zucchini noodles, and cooked shrimp. Toss to combine the sauce over the noodles and shrimp, and cook until heated through. Taste and season with more salt and pepper as needed. Serve topped with the diced tomatoes.

Per Serving calories: 435 | fat: 30.2g | protein: 33.0g | carbs: 15.1g

Steamed Bass

Prep time: 10 minutes | **Cook time:** 8 minutes | **Serves:** 4

Ingredients:

1½ cups water
1 lemon, sliced
4 sea bass fillets
4 sprigs thyme
1 white onion, cut into thin rings

2 turnips, chopped
2 pinches salt
1 pinch ground black pepper
2 teaspoons olive oil

Directions:

Add water and set a rack into the pot.

Line a parchment paper to the bottom of the steamer basket. Place lemon slices in a single layer on the rack.

Arrange fillets on the top of the lemons, cover with onion and thyme sprigs. Top with turnip slices.

Drizzle pepper, salt, and olive oil over the mixture. Put steamer basket onto the rack. Seal lid and cook on Low pressure for 8 minutes. Release the pressure quickly.

Serve over the delicate onion rings and thinly turnips.

Per Serving

calories: 177 | fat: 4.9g | protein: 24.7g | carbs: 7.8g

Baked Oysters with Vegetables

Prep time: 30 minutes | **Cook time:** 15 to 17 minutes | **Serves:**2

Ingredients:

2 cups coarse salt, for holding the oysters
1 dozen fresh oysters, scrubbed
1 tablespoon almond butter
¼ cup finely chopped scallions, both white and green parts
½ cup finely chopped artichoke hearts

¼ cup finely chopped red bell pepper
1 garlic clove, minced
1 tablespoon finely chopped fresh parsley
Zest and juice of ½ lemon
Pinch salt
Freshly ground black pepper, to taste

Directions:

Pour the salt into a baking dish and spread to evenly fill the bottom of the dish.

Prepare a clean work surface to shuck the oysters. Using a shucking knife, insert the blade at the joint of the shell, where it hinges open and shut. Firmly apply pressure to pop the blade in, and work the knife around the shell to open. Discard the empty half of the shell. Using the knife, gently loosen the oyster, and remove any shell particles. Set the oysters in their shells on the salt, being careful not to spill the juices. Preheat the oven to 425°F (220°C).

Heat the almond butter in a large skillet over medium heat. Add the scallions, artichoke hearts, and bell pepper, and cook for 5 to 7 minutes. Add the garlic and cook for 1 minute more. Remove from the heat and stir in the parsley, lemon zest and juice, and season to taste with salt and pepper. Divide the vegetable mixture evenly among the oysters. Bake in the preheated oven for 10 to 12 minutes, or until the vegetables are lightly browned. Serve warm.

Per Serving

calories: 135 | fat: 7.2g | protein: 6.0g | carbs: 10.7g

Instant Pot Poached Salmon

Prep time: 10 minutes | **Cook time:** 3 minutes | **Serves:**4

Ingredients:

1 lemon, sliced ¼ inch thick
4 (6-ounce / 170-g) skinless salmon fillets, 1½ inches thick

½ teaspoon salt
¼ teaspoon pepper
½ cup water

Directions:

Layer the lemon slices in the bottom of the Instant Pot.

Season the salmon with salt and pepper, then arrange the salmon (skin- side down) on top of the lemon slices. Pour in the water. Secure the lid. Select the Manual mode and set the cooking time for 3 minutes at High Pressure.

Once cooking is complete, do a quick pressure release. Carefully open the lid. Serve warm.

Per Serving calories: 350 | fat: 23.0g | protein: 35.0g | carbs: 0g

Steamed Cod

Prep time: 15 minutes | **Cook time:** 7 minutes | **Serves:**4

Ingredients:

1 pound (454 g) cherry tomatoes, halved
1 bunch fresh thyme sprigs
4 fillets cod
1 teaspoon olive oil
1 clove garlic, pressed
3 pinches salt

2 cups water
1 cup white rice
1 cup Kalamata olives
2 tablespoons pickled capers
1 tablespoon olive oil
1 pinch ground black pepper

Directions:

Line a parchment paper on the basket of your instant pot. Place about half the tomatoes in a single layer on the paper. Sprinkle with thyme, reserving some for garnish.

Arrange cod fillets on top. Sprinkle with a little bit of olive oil. Spread the garlic, pepper, salt, and remaining tomatoes over the fish. In the pot, mix rice and water.

Lay a trivet over the rice and water. Lower steamer basket onto the trivet. Seal the lid, and cook for 7 minutes on Low Pressure. Release the pressure quickly.

Remove the steamer basket and trivet from the pot. Use a fork to fluff rice. Plate the fish fillets and apply a garnish of olives, reserved thyme, pepper, remaining olive oil, and capers. Serve with rice.

Per Serving

calories: 352 | fat: 9.1g | protein: 22.2g | carbs: 44.7g

Rosemary Cod with Cherry Tomato

Prep time: 20 minutes | **Cook time:** 5 minutes | **Serves:**6

Ingredients:

1½ pounds (680 g) cherry tomatoes, halved
2½ tablespoons fresh rosemary, chopped
6 (4-ounce / 113-g) cod fillets

3 garlic cloves, minced
2 tablespoons olive oil
Salt and freshly ground black pepper, to taste

Directions:

Add the olive oil, half of the tomatoes and rosemary to the insert of the Instant Pot. Place the cod fillets over these tomatoes. Then add more tomatoes to the pot.

Add the garlic to the pot. Then secure the lid.

Select the Manual function with High Pressure for 5 minutes. After the beep, use the quick release to discharge all the steam. Serve cod fillets with tomatoes and sprinkle a pinch of salt and pepper on top.

Per Serving

calories: 143 | fat: 5.2g | protein: 18.8g | carbs: 5.0g

Catfish and Shrimp Jambalaya

Prep time: 20 minutes | **Cook time:** 4 hours 45 minutes | Serves:

Ingredients:

4 ounces (113 g) catfish (cut into 1-inch cubes)
4 ounces (113 g) shrimp (peeled and deveined)
1 tablespoon olive oil
2 bacon slices, chopped
1¼ cups vegetable broth
¾ cup sliced celery stalk
¼ teaspoon minced garlic
½ cup chopped onion
1 cup canned diced tomatoes
1 cup uncooked long-grain white rice
½ tablespoon Cajun seasoning
¼ teaspoon dried thyme
¼ teaspoon cayenne pepper
½ teaspoon dried oregano
Salt and freshly ground black pepper, to taste

Directions:

Select the Sauté function on your Instant Pot and add the oil into it.

Put the onion, garlic, celery, and bacon to the pot and cook for 10 minutes.

Add all the remaining ingredients to the pot except seafood. Stir well, then secure the cooker lid. Select the Slow Cook function on a medium mode. Keep the pressure release handle on venting position. Cook for 4 hours.

Once done, remove the lid and add the seafood to the gravy.

Secure the lid again, keep the pressure handle in the venting position.

Cook for another 45 minutes then serve.

Per Serving
calories: 437 | fat: 13.1g | protein: 21.3g | carbs: 56.7g

Balsamic-Honey Glazed Salmon

Prep time: 2 minutes | **Cook time:** 8 minutes | **Serves:**4

Ingredients:

½ cup balsamic vinegar
1 tablespoon honey
4 (8-ounce / 227-g) salmon fillets
Sea salt and freshly ground pepper, to taste
1 tablespoon olive oil

Directions:

Heat a skillet over medium-high heat. Combine the vinegar and honey in a small bowl.

Season the salmon fillets with the sea salt and freshly ground pepper; brush with the honey-balsamic glaze.

Add olive oil to the skillet, and sear the salmon fillets, cooking for 3 to 4 minutes on each side until lightly browned and medium rare in the center.

Let sit for 5 minutes before serving.

Per Serving
calories: 454 | fat: 17.3g | protein: 65.3g | carbs: 9.7g

Salmon and Potato Casserole

Prep time: 20 minutes | **Cook time:** 8 hours | **Serves:**4

Ingredients:

½ tablespoon olive oil
8 ounces (227 g) cream of mushroom soup
¼ cup water
3 medium potatoes (peeled and sliced)
3 tablespoons flour
1 (1-pound / 454-g) can salmon (drained and flaked)
½ cup chopped scallion
¼ teaspoon ground nutmeg
Salt and freshly ground black pepper, to taste

Directions:

Pour mushroom soup and water in a separate bowl and mix them well.

Add the olive oil to the Instant Pot and grease it lightly.

Place half of the potatoes in the pot and sprinkle salt, pepper, and half of the flour over it.

Now add a layer of half of the salmon over potatoes, then a layer of half of the scallions.

Repeat these layers and pour mushroom soup mix on top.

Top it with nutmeg evenly.

Secure the lid and set its pressure release handle to the venting position.

Select the Slow Cook function with Medium heat on your Instant Pot.

Let it cook for 8 hours then serve.

Per Serving
calories: 388 | fat: 11.6g | protein: 34.6g | carbs: 37.2g

Lemony Salmon

Prep time: 10 minutes | **Cook time:** 3 minutes | **Serves:**3

Ingredients:

1 cup water
3 lemon slices
1 (5-ounce / 142-g) salmon fillet
1 teaspoon fresh lemon juice
Salt and ground black pepper, to taste
Fresh cilantro to garnish

Directions:

Add the water to the Instant pot and place a trivet inside.

In a shallow bowl, place the salmon fillet. Sprinkle salt and pepper over it.

Squeeze some lemon juice on top then place a lemon slice over the salmon fillet.

Cover the lid and lock it. Set its pressure release handle to Sealing position.

Use Steam function on your cooker for 3 minutes to cook.

After the beep, do a Quick release and release the pressure.

Remove the lid, then serve with the lemon slice and fresh cilantro on top.

Per Serving
calories: 161 | fat: 5.0g | protein: 26.6g | carbs: 0.7g

Salmon and Tomato Curry

Prep time: 10 minutes | **Cook time:** 12 minutes | **Serves:**8

Ingredients:

3 pounds (1.4 kg) salmon fillets (cut into pieces)
2 tablespoons olive oil
2 Serrano peppers, chopped
1 teaspoon ground turmeric
4 tablespoons curry powder
4 teaspoons ground cumin
4 curry leaves
2 tablespoons fresh lemon juice
2½ cups tomatoes, chopped
4 teaspoons ground coriander
2 small yellow onions, chopped
2 teaspoons red chili powder
4 garlic cloves, minced
4 cups unsweetened coconut milk
Fresh cilantro leaves to garnish

Directions:

Put the oil and curry leaves to the insert of the Instant Pot. Select the Sauté function to cook for 30 secs.

Add the garlic and onions to the pot, cook for 5 minutes.

Stir in all the spices and cook for another 1 minute. Put the fish, Serrano pepper, coconut milk, and tomatoes while cooking.

Cover and lock the lid. Seal the pressure release valve.

Select the Manual function at Low Pressure for 5 minutes.

After the beep, do a Natural release to release all the steam. Remove the lid and squeeze in lemon juice. Garnish with fresh cilantro leaves and serve.

Per Serving

calories: 551 | fat: 40.6g | protein: 38.9g | carbs: 10.6g

Spicy Cumin Salmon

Prep time: 10 minutes | **Cook time:** 2 minutes | **Serves:**8

Ingredients:

2 cups water
2 garlic cloves, minced
2 teaspoons powdered stevia
8 lemon slices
2 tablespoons red chili powder
2 teaspoons ground cumin
Salt and freshly grated black pepper, to taste
2 pounds (907 g) salmon fillet, cut into 8 pieces

Directions:

Pour two cups of water in the insert of the Instant Pot. Set the trivet in it.

In a separate bowl, add all the ingredients except the lemon slices and mix them well.

Pour this mixture over the salmon fillets and rub it all over it. Place the salmon slices over the trivet in a single layer.

Top each fillet with a lemon slice. Secure the lid and select Steam function for 2 minutes. After the beep, do a Quick release and then remove the lid. Serve immediately.

Per Serving

calories: 151 | fat: 4.7g | protein: 23.3g | carbs: 3.1g

Rosemary Salmon with Feta Cheese

Prep time: 5 minutes | **Cook time:** 3 minutes | **Serves:**6

Ingredients:

1½ pounds (680 g) salmon fillets
1½ cups water
¼ cup olive oil
1½ garlic cloves, minced
1½ tablespoons feta cheese, crumbled
½ teaspoon dried oregano
3 tablespoons fresh lemon juice
Salt and freshly ground black pepper, to taste
3 fresh rosemary sprigs
3 lemon slices

Directions:

Take a large bowl and add the garlic, feta cheese, salt, pepper, lemon juice, and oregano. Whisk well all the ingredients.

Add the water to the Instant pot then place the steamer trivet in it.

Arrange the salmon fillets over the trivet in a single layer.

Pour the cheese mixture over these fillets.

Place a lemon slice and a rosemary sprig over each fillet.

Secure the lid.

Select the Steam function on your cooker and set 3 minutes cooking time.

After it is done, carefully do a Quick release. Remove the lid.

Serve hot.

Per Serving

calories: 229 | fat: 14.0g | protein: 23.4g | carbs: 1.3g

Mahi-Mahi Meal

Prep time: 15 minutes | **Cook time:** 7 minutes | **Serves:**4

Ingredients:

1½ cups water
4 (4-ounce / 113-g) mahi-mahi fillets
Salt and freshly ground black pepper, to taste
4 garlic cloves, minced
4 tablespoons fresh lime juice
4 tablespoons erythritol
2 teaspoons red pepper flakes, crushed

Directions:

Sprinkle some salt and pepper over Mahi-Mahi fillets for seasoning. In a separate bowl add all the remaining ingredients and mix well.

Add the water to the Instant pot and place the trivet in it.

Arrange the seasoned fillets over the trivet in a single layer.

Pour the prepared sauce on top of each fillet.

Cover and secure the lid.

Set the Steam function on your cooker for 5 minutes.

Once it beeps, do a quick release then remove the lid.

Serve the steaming hot Mahi-Mahi and enjoy.

Per Serving calories: 228 | fat: 1.4g | protein: 38.0g | carbs: 14.2g

Mussels with Onions

Prep time: 10 minutes | **Cook time:** 7 minutes | **Serves:**8

Ingredients:

2 tablespoons olive oil
2 medium yellow onions, chopped
1 teaspoon dried rosemary, crushed
2 garlic cloves, minced
2 cups chicken broth
4 pounds (1.8 kg) mussels, cleaned and debearded
¼ cup fresh lemon juice
Salt and ground black pepper as needed

Directions:

Put the oil to the Instant Pot and select the Sauté function for cooking. Add the onions and cook for 5 minutes with occasional stirring.

Add the rosemary and garlic to the pot. Stir and cook for 1 minute. Pour the chicken broth and lemon juice into the cooker, sprinkle some salt and black pepper over it.

Place the trivet inside the cooker and arrange the mussels over it. Select the Manual function at Low Pressure for 1 minute. Secure the lid and let the mussels cook.

After the beep, do a Quick release then remove the lid.

Serve the mussels with its steaming hot soup in a bowl.

Per Serving

calories: 249 | fat: 8.8g | protein: 28.5g | carbs: 11.9g

Cod Curry

Prep time: 5 minutes | **Cook time:** 12 minutes | **Serves:**8

Ingredients:

3 pounds (1.4 kg) cod fillets, cut into bite-sized pieces
2 tablespoons olive oil
4 curry leaves
4 medium onions, chopped
2 tablespoons fresh ginger, grated finely
4 garlic cloves, minced
4 tablespoons curry powder
2 Serrano peppers, seeded and chopped
4 teaspoons ground cumin
4 teaspoons ground coriander
2 teaspoons red chili powder
1 teaspoon ground turmeric
4 cups unsweetened coconut milk
2½ cups tomatoes, chopped
2 tablespoons fresh lemon juice

Directions:

Add the oil to the Instant Pot and select Sauté function for cooking. Add the curry leaves and cook for 30 seconds. Stir the onion, garlic, and ginger into the pot and cook 5 minutes. Add all the spices to the mixture and cook for another 1½ minutes. Hit Cancel then add the coconut milk, Serrano pepper, tomatoes, and fish to the pot.

Secure the lid and select the Manual settings with Low Pressure and 5 minutes cooking time. After the beep, do a Quick release and remove the lid. Drizzle lemon juice over the curry then stir. Serve immediately.

Per Serving

calories: 424 | fat: 29.1g | protein: 30.2g | carbs: 14.4g

Shrimps with Northern Beans

Prep time: 10 minutes | **Cook time:** 25 minutes | **Serves:**3

Ingredients:

1½ tablespoons olive oil
1 medium onion, chopped
½ small green bell pepper, seeded and chopped
½ celery stalk, chopped
1 garlic clove, minced
1 tablespoon fresh parsley, chopped
½ teaspoon red pepper
½ teaspoon cayenne pepper
½ pound (227 g) great northern beans, rinsed, soaked, and drained
1 cup chicken broth
1 bay leaf
½ pound (227 g) medium shrimp, peeled and deveined

Directions:

Select the Sauté function on your Instant pot, then add the oil, onion, celery, bell pepper and cook for 5 minutes.

Now add the parsley, garlic, spices, and bay leaf to the pot and cook for another 2 minutes. Pour in the chicken broth then add the beans to it. Secure the cooker lid.

Select the Manual function for 15 minutes with medium pressure. After the beep, do a Natural release for 10 minutes and remove the lid. Add the shrimp to the beans and cook them together on the Manual function for 2 minutes at High Pressure. Do a Quick release, keep it aside for 10 minutes, then remove the lid. Serve hot.

Per Serving

calories: 405 | fat: 9.1g | protein: 29.1g | carbs: 53.1g

Shrimp and Potato Curry

Prep time: 5 minutes | **Cook time:** 9 minutes | **Serves:**8

Ingredients:

2 tablespoons olive oil
1½ medium onions, chopped
1½ teaspoons ground cumin
2 teaspoons red chili powder
2 teaspoons ground turmeric
6 medium tomatoes, chopped
2 pounds (907 g) medium shrimp, peeled and deveined
1½ tablespoons fresh lemon juice
Salt, to taste
½ cup fresh cilantro, chopped

Directions:

Select the Sauté function on your Instant Pot. Add the oil and onions then cook for 2 minutes.

Add the tomatoes, potatoes, cilantro, lemon juice and all the spices into the pot and secure the lid.

Select the Manual function at medium pressure for 5 minutes. Do a natural release then remove the lid. Stir shrimp into the pot. Secure the lid again then set the Manual function with High Pressure for 2 minutes.

After the beep, use Natural release and let it stand for 10 minutes. Remove the lid and serve hot.

Per Serving

calories: 197 | fat: 5.0g | protein: 18.1g | carbs: 20.3g

Sardines and Plum Tomato Curry

Prep time: 10 minutes | **Cook time:** 8 hours 2 minutes | Serves:4

Ingredients:

1 tablespoon olive oil
1 pound (454 g) fresh sardines, cubed
2 plum tomatoes, chopped finely
½ large onion, sliced
1 garlic clove, minced
½ cup tomato purée
Salt and ground black pepper, to taste

Directions:

Select the Sauté function on your Instant pot then add the oil and sardines to it. Let it sauté for 2 minutes then add all the remaining ingredients.

Cover the lid and select Slow Cook function for 8 hours.

Remove the lid and stir the cooked curry. Serve warm.

Per Serving

calories: 292 | fat: 16.5g | protein: 28.9g | carbs: 6.0g

Salmon and Mushroom Hash with Pesto

Prep time: 15 minutes | **Cook time:** 20 minutes | Serves:6

Ingredients:

Pesto:
¼ cup extra-virgin olive oil
1 bunch fresh basil
Juice and zest of 1 lemon
⅓ cup water
¼ teaspoon salt, plus additional as needed

Hash:
2 tablespoons extra-virgin olive oil
6 cups mixed mushrooms (brown, white, shiitake, cremini, portobello, etc.), sliced
1 pound (454 g) wild salmon, cubed

Directions:

Make the pesto: Pulse the olive oil, basil, juice and zest, water, and salt in a blender or food processor until smoothly blended. Set aside.

Heat the olive oil in a large skillet over medium heat.

Stir-fry the mushrooms for 6 to 8 minutes, or until they begin to exude their juices.

Add the salmon and cook each side for 5 to 6 minutes until cooked through.

Fold in the prepared pesto and stir well. Taste and add additional salt as needed. Serve warm.

Per Serving

calories: 264 | fat: 14.7g | protein: 7.0g | carbs: 30.9g

Spiced Citrus Sole

Prep time: 10 minutes | **Cook time:** 10 minutes | **Serves:**4

Ingredients:

1 teaspoon garlic powder
1 teaspoon chili powder
½ teaspoon lemon zest
½ teaspoon lime zest
¼ teaspoon smoked paprika
2 teaspoons freshly squeezed lime juice
¼ teaspoon freshly ground black pepper Pinch sea salt
4 (6-ounce / 170-g) sole fillets, patted dry
1 tablespoon extra-virgin olive oil

Directions:

Preheat the oven to 450°F (235°C). Line a baking sheet with aluminum foil and set aside.

Mix together the garlic powder, chili powder, lemon zest, lime zest, paprika, pepper, and salt in a small bowl until well combined.

Arrange the sole fillets on the prepared baking sheet and rub the spice mixture all over the fillets until well coated. Drizzle the olive oil and lime juice over the fillets.

Bake in the preheated oven for about 8 minutes until flaky.

Remove from the heat to a plate and serve.

Per Serving

calories: 183 | fat: 5.0g | protein: 32.1g | carbs: 0g

Asian-Inspired Tuna Lettuce Wraps

Prep time: 10 minutes | **Cook time:** 0 minutes | **Serves:**2

Ingredients:

⅓ cup almond butter
1 tablespoon freshly squeezed lemon juice
1 teaspoon low-sodium soy sauce
1 teaspoon curry powder
½ teaspoon sriracha, or to taste
½ cup canned water chestnuts, drained and chopped
2 (2.6-ounce / 74-g) package tuna packed in water, drained
2 large butter lettuce leaves

Directions:

Stir together the almond butter, lemon juice, soy sauce, curry powder, sriracha in a medium bowl until well mixed. Add the water chestnuts and tuna and stir until well incorporated.

Place 2 butter lettuce leaves on a flat work surface, spoon half of the tuna mixture onto each leaf and roll up into a wrap. Serve immediately.

Per Serving

calories: 270 | fat: 13.9g | protein: 19.1g | carbs: 18.5g

Crispy Tilapia with Mango Salsa

Prep time: 5 minutes | **Cook time:** 10 minutes | **Serves:** 2

Ingredients:

Salsa:
1 cup chopped mango
2 tablespoons chopped fresh cilantro
2 tablespoons chopped red onion
2 tablespoons freshly squeezed lime juice
½ jalapeño pepper, seeded and minced
Pinch salt
Tilapia:
1 tablespoon paprika
1 teaspoon onion powder
½ teaspoon dried thyme
½ teaspoon freshly ground black pepper
¼ teaspoon cayenne pepper
½ teaspoon garlic powder
¼ teaspoon salt
½ pound (227 g) boneless tilapia fillets
2 teaspoons extra-virgin olive oil
1 lime, cut into wedges, for serving

Directions:

Make the salsa: Place the mango, cilantro, onion, lime juice, jalapeño, and salt in a medium bowl and toss to combine. Set aside.

Make the tilapia: Stir together the paprika, onion powder, thyme, black pepper, cayenne pepper, garlic powder, and salt in a small bowl until well mixed. Rub both sides of fillets generously with the mixture.

Heat the olive oil in a large skillet over medium heat.

Add the fish fillets and cook each side for 3 to 5 minutes until golden brown and cooked through.

Divide the fillets among two plates and spoon half of the prepared salsa onto each fillet. Serve the fish alongside the lime wedges.

Per Serving
calories: 239 | fat: 7.8g | protein: 25.0g | carbs: 21.9g

Peppercorn-Seared Tuna Steaks

Prep time: 5 minutes | **Cook time:** 10 minutes | **Serves:** 2

Ingredients:

2 (5-ounce / 142-g) ahi tuna steaks
1 teaspoon kosher salt
¼ teaspoon cayenne pepper
2 tablespoons olive oil
1 teaspoon whole peppercorns

Directions:

On a plate, Season the tuna steaks on both sides with salt and cayenne pepper.

In a skillet, heat the olive oil over medium-high heat until it shimmers.

Add the peppercorns and cook for about 5 minutes, or until they soften and pop.

Carefully put the tuna steaks in the skillet and sear for 1 to 2 minutes per side, depending on the thickness of the tuna steaks, or until the fish is cooked to the desired level of doneness. Cool for 5 minutes before serving.

Per Serving
calories: 260 | fat: 14.3g | protein: 33.4g | carbs: 0.2g

Mediterranean Grilled Sea Bass

Prep time: 20 minutes | **Cook time:** 20 minutes | **Serves:** 6

Ingredients:

¼ teaspoon onion powder
¼ teaspoon garlic powder
¼ teaspoon paprika
Lemon pepper and sea salt to taste
2 pounds (907 g) sea bass
3 tablespoons extra-virgin olive oil, divided
2 large cloves garlic, chopped
1 tablespoon chopped Italian flat leaf parsley

Directions:

Preheat the grill to high heat.

Place the onion powder, garlic powder, paprika, lemon pepper, and sea salt in a large bowl and stir to combine.

Dredge the fish in the spice mixture, turning until well coated.

Heat 2 tablespoon of olive oil in a small skillet. Add the garlic and parsley and cook for 1 to 2 minutes, stirring occasionally. Remove the skillet from the heat and set aside. Brush the grill grates lightly with remaining 1 tablespoon olive oil.

Grill the fish for about 7 minutes. Flip the fish and drizzle with the garlic mixture and cook for an additional 7 minutes, or until the fish flakes when pressed lightly with a fork. Serve hot.

Per Serving
calories: 200 | fat: 10.3g | protein: 26.9g | carbs: 0.6g

Alfredo Tuscan Shrimp with Penne

Prep time: 5 minutes | **Cook time:** 5 minutes | **Serves:** 3

Ingredients:

1 pound (454 g) shrimp
1 jar alfredo sauce
1½ cups fresh spinach
3 cups water
1 cup sun-dried tomatoes
1 box penne pasta
1½ teaspoons Tuscan seasoning

Directions:

Add the water and pasta to a pot over a medium heat, boil until it cooks completely. Then strain the pasta and keep it aside. Select the Sauté function on your Instant Pot and add the tomatoes, shrimp, Tuscan seasoning, and alfredo sauce into it.

Stir and cook until shrimp turn pink in color.

Now add the spinach leaves to the pot and cook for 5 minutes.

Add the pasta to the pot and stir well.

Serve hot.

Per Serving
calories: 1361 | fat: 70.1g | protein: 55.9g | carbs: 134.4g

Braised Branzino with Wine Sauce

Prep time: 15 minutes | **Cook time:** 15 mins | **Serves:** 2 to 3

Ingredients:

Sauce:
¾ cup dry white wine
2 tablespoons white wine vinegar
2 tablespoons cornstarch
1 tablespoon honey
Fish:
1 large branzino, butterflied and patted dry
2 tablespoons onion powder
2 tablespoons paprika
½ tablespoon salt
6 tablespoons extra-virgin olive oil, divided
4 garlic cloves, thinly sliced
4 scallions, both green and white parts, thinly sliced
1 large tomato, cut into ¼-inch cubes
4 kalamata olives, pitted and chopped

Directions:

Make the sauce: Mix together the white wine, vinegar, cornstarch, and honey in a bowl and keep stirring until the honey has dissolved. Set aside.

Make the fish: Place the fish on a clean work surface, skin-side down. Sprinkle the onion powder, paprika, and salt to season. Drizzle 2 tablespoons of olive oil all over the fish.

Heat 2 tablespoons of olive oil in a large skillet over high heat until it shimmers.

Add the fish, skin-side up, to the skillet and brown for about 2 minutes. Carefully flip the fish and cook for another 3 minutes. Remove from the heat to a plate and set aside.

Add the remaining 2 tablespoons olive oil to the skillet and swirl to coat. Stir in the garlic cloves, scallions, tomato, and kalamata olives and sauté for 5 minutes. Pour in the prepared sauce and stir to combine.

Return the fish (skin-side down) to the skillet, flipping to coat in the sauce. Reduce the heat to medium-low, and cook for an additional 5 minutes until cooked through.

Using a slotted spoon, transfer the fish to a plate and serve warm.

Per Serving
calories: 1059 | fat: 71.9g | protein: 46.2g | carbs: 55.8g

Canned Sardine Donburi (Rice Bowl)

Prep time: 10 minutes | **Cook time:** 40 to 50 minutes | **Serves:** 4 to 6

Ingredients:

4 cups water
2 cups brown rice, rinsed well
½ teaspoon salt
3 (4-ounce / 113-g) cans
3 scallions, sliced thin
1-inch piece fresh ginger, grated
4 tablespoons sesame oil

Directions:

Place the water, brown rice, and salt to a large saucepan and stir to combine. Allow the mixture to boil over high heat.

Once boiling, reduce the heat to low, and cook covered for 45 to 50 minutes, or until the rice is tender.

Meanwhile, roughly mash the sardines with a fork in a medium bowl.

When the rice is done, stir in the mashed sardines, scallions, and ginger.

Divide the mixture into four bowls. Top each bowl with a drizzle of sesame oil. Serve warm.

Per Serving
calories: 603 | fat: 23.6g | protein: 25.2g | carbs: 73.8g

Baked Halibut Steaks with Vegetables

Prep time: 15 minutes | **Cook time:** 20 minutes | **Serves:** 4

Ingredients:

2 teaspoon olive oil, divided
1 clove garlic, peeled and minced
½ cup minced onion
1 cup diced zucchini
2 cups diced fresh tomatoes
⅓ cup crumbled feta cheese
2 tablespoons chopped fresh basil
¼ teaspoon salt
¼ teaspoon ground black pepper
4 (6-ounce / 170-g) halibut steaks

Directions:

Preheat oven to 450ºF (235ºC). Coat a shallow baking dish lightly with 1 teaspoon of olive oil.

In a medium saucepan, heat the remaining 1 teaspoon of olive oil.

Add the garlic, onion, and zucchini and mix well. Cook for 5 minutes, stirring occasionally, or until the zucchini is softened.

Remove the saucepan from the heat and stir in the tomatoes, basil, salt, and pepper.

Place the halibut steaks in the coated baking dish in a single layer. Spread the zucchini mixture evenly over the steaks. Scatter the top with feta cheese.

Bake in the preheated oven for about 15 minutes, or until the fish flakes when pressed lightly with a fork. Serve hot.

Per Serving
calories: 258 | fat: 7.6g | protein: 38.6g | carbs: 6.5g

Spicy Haddock Stew

Prep time: 15 minutes | **Cook time:** 35 minutes | **Serves:**6

Ingredients:

¼ cup coconut oil
1 tablespoon minced garlic
1 onion, chopped
2 celery stalks, chopped
½ fennel bulb, thinly sliced
1 carrot, diced
1 sweet potato, diced
1 (15-ounce / 425-g) can low-sodium diced tomatoes
1 cup coconut milk
1 cup low-sodium chicken broth
¼ teaspoon red pepper flakes
12 ounces (340 g) haddock, cut into 1-inch chunks
2 tablespoons chopped fresh cilantro, for garnish

Directions:

In a large saucepan, heat the coconut oil over medium-high heat. Add the garlic, onion, and celery and sauté for about 4 minutes, stirring occasionally, or until they are tender.

Stir in the fennel bulb, carrot, and sweet potato and sauté for 4 minutes more. Add the diced tomatoes, coconut milk, chicken broth, and red pepper flakes and stir to incorporate, then bring the mixture to a boil. Once it starts to boil, reduce the heat to low, and bring to a simmer for about 15 minutes, or until the vegetables are fork-tender.

Add the haddock chunks and continue simmering for about 10 minutes, or until the fish is cooked through.

Sprinkle the cilantro on top for garnish before serving.

Per Serving

calories: 276 | fat: 20.9g | protein: 14.2g | carbs: 6.8g

Orange Flavored Scallops

Prep time: 10 minutes | **Cook time:** 10 minutes | **Serves:**4

Ingredients:

2 pounds (907 g) sea scallops, patted dry
Sea salt and freshly ground black pepper, to taste
2 tablespoons extra-virgin olive oil
1 tablespoon minced garlic
¼ cup freshly squeezed orange juice
1 teaspoon orange zest
2 teaspoons chopped fresh thyme, for garnish

Directions:

In a bowl, lightly season the scallops with salt and pepper. Set aside.

Heat the olive oil in a large skillet over medium-high heat until it shimmers. Add the garlic and sauté for about 3 minutes, or until fragrant.

Stir in the seasoned scallops and sear each side for about 4 minutes, or until the scallops are browned.

Remove the scallops from the heat to a plate and set aside.

Add the orange juice and zest to the skillet, scraping up brown bits from bottom of skillet.

Drizzle the sauce over the scallops and garnish with the thyme before serving.

Per Serving

calories: 266 | fat: 7.6g | protein: 38.1g | carbs: 7.9g

Garlic Skillet Salmon

Prep time: 5 minutes | **Cook time:** 14 to 16 minutes | **Serves:**4

Ingredients:

1 tablespoon extra-virgin olive oil
2 garlic cloves, minced
1 teaspoon smoked paprika
1½ cups grape or cherry tomatoes, quartered
1 (12-ounce / 340-g) jar roasted red peppers, drained and chopped
1 tablespoon water
¼ teaspoon freshly ground black pepper
¼ teaspoon kosher or sea salt
1 pound (454 g) salmon fillets, skin removed and cut into 8 pieces
1 tablespoon freshly squeezed lemon juice

Directions:

In a large skillet over medium heat, heat the oil. Add the garlic and smoked paprika and cook for 1 minute, stirring often. Add the tomatoes, roasted peppers, water, black pepper, and salt. Turn up the heat to medium-high, bring to a simmer, and cook for 3 minutes, stirring occasionally and smashing the tomatoes with a wooden spoon toward the end of the cooking time.

Add the salmon to the skillet, and spoon some of the sauce over the top. Cover and cook for 10 to 12 minutes, or until the salmon is cooked through and just starts to flake.

Remove the skillet from the heat, and drizzle lemon juice over the top of the fish. Stir the sauce, then break up the salmon into chunks with a fork. Serve hot.

Per Serving

calories: 255 | fat: 11.7g | protein: 24.2g | carbs: 5.9g

Salmon Baked in Foil

Prep time: 5 minutes | **Cook time:** 25 minutes | **Serves:**4

Ingredients:

2 cups cherry tomatoes
3 tablespoons extra-virgin olive oil
3 tablespoons lemon juice
3 tablespoons almond butter
1 teaspoon oregano
½ teaspoon salt
4 (5-ounce / 142-g) salmon fillets

Directions:

Preheat the oven to 400ºF (205ºC). Cut the tomatoes in half and put them in a bowl. Add the olive oil, lemon juice, butter, oregano, and salt to the tomatoes and gently toss to combine.

Cut 4 pieces of foil, about 12-by-12 inches each. Place the salmon fillets in the middle of each piece of foil.

Divide the tomato mixture evenly over the 4 pieces of salmon. Bring the ends of the foil together and seal to form a closed pocket. Place the 4 pockets on a baking sheet. Bake in the preheated oven for 25 minutes. Remove from the oven and serve on a plate.

Per Serving

calories: 410 | fat: 32.0g | protein: 30.0g | carbs: 4.0g

Seared Salmon with Lemon Cream Sauce

Prep time: 10 minutes | **Cook time:** 20 minutes | **Serves:** 4

Ingredients:

4 (5-ounce / 142-g) salmon fillets
Sea salt and freshly ground black pepper, to taste
1 tablespoon extra-virgin olive oil
½ cup low-sodium vegetable broth

Juice and zest of 1 lemon
1 teaspoon chopped fresh thyme
½ cup fat-free sour cream
1 teaspoon honey
1 tablespoon chopped fresh chives

Directions:

Preheat the oven to 400°F (205°C).

Season the salmon lightly on both sides with salt and pepper. Place a large ovenproof skillet over medium-high heat and add the olive oil.

Sear the salmon fillets on both sides until golden, about 3 minutes per side. Transfer the salmon to a baking dish and bake in the preheated oven until just cooked through, about 10 minutes.

Meanwhile, whisk together the vegetable broth, lemon juice and zest, and thyme in a small saucepan over medium-high heat until the liquid reduces by about one-quarter, about 5 minutes.

Whisk in the sour cream and honey.

Stir in the chives and serve the sauce over the salmon.

Per Serving

calories: 310 | fat: 18.0g | protein: 29.0g | carbs: 6.0g

Fennel Poached Cod with Tomatoes

Prep time: 10 minutes | **Cook time:** 20 minutes | **Serves:** 4

Ingredients:

1 tablespoon olive oil
1 cup thinly sliced fennel
½ cup thinly sliced onion
1 tablespoon minced garlic
1 (15-ounce / 425-g) can diced tomatoes

2 cups chicken broth
½ cup white wine
Juice and zest of 1 orange
1 pinch red pepper flakes
1 bay leaf
1 pound (454 g) cod

Directions:

Heat the olive oil in a large skillet. Add the onion and fennel and cook for 6 minutes, stirring occasionally, or until translucent. Add the garlic and cook for 1 minute more. Add the tomatoes, chicken broth, wine, orange juice and zest, red pepper flakes, and bay leaf, and simmer for 5 minutes to meld the flavors.

Carefully add the cod in a single layer, cover, and simmer for 6 to 7 minutes. Transfer fish to a serving dish, ladle the remaining sauce over the fish, and serve.

Per Serving

calories: 336 | fat: 12.5g | protein: 45.1g | carbs:11.0g

Tuna and Zucchini Patties

Prep time: 10 minutes | **Cook time:** 12 minutes | **Serves:** 4

Ingredients:

3 slices whole-wheat sandwich bread, toasted
2 (5-ounce / 142-g) cans tuna in olive oil, drained
1 cup shredded zucchini
1 large egg, lightly beaten
¼ cup diced red bell pepper
1 tablespoon dried oregano

1 teaspoon lemon zest
¼ teaspoon freshly ground black pepper
¼ teaspoon kosher or sea salt
1 tablespoon extra-virgin olive oil
Salad greens or 4 whole-wheat rolls, for serving (optional)

Directions:

Crumble the toast into bread crumbs with your fingers (or use a knife to cut into ¼-inch cubes) until you have 1 cup of loosely packed crumbs. Pour the crumbs into a large bowl. Add the tuna, zucchini, beaten egg, bell pepper, oregano, lemon zest, black pepper, and salt. Mix well with a fork. With your hands, form the mixture into four (½-cup-size) patties. Place them on a plate, and press each patty flat to about ¾-inch thick.

In a large skillet over medium-high heat, heat the oil until it's very hot, about 2 minutes.

Add the patties to the hot oil, then reduce the heat down to medium. Cook the patties for 5 minutes, flip with a spatula, and cook for an additional 5 minutes. Serve the patties on salad greens or whole-wheat rolls, if desired.

Per Serving

calories: 757 | fat: 72.0g | protein: 5.0g | carbs: 26.0g

Scallop Teriyaki

Prep time: 5 minutes | **Cook time:** 5 minutes | **Serves:** 6

Ingredients:

2 pounds (907 g) jumbo sea scallops
2 tablespoons olive oil
6 tablespoons pure maple syrup

1 cup coconut aminos
1 teaspoon ground ginger
1 teaspoon garlic powder
1 teaspoon sea salt

Directions:

Add the olive oil to the Instant pot and heat it on the Sauté settings of your pot. Add the scallops to the pot and cook for a minute from each side.

Stir in all the remaining ingredients in the pot and mix them well. Secure the lid and select the Steam function to cook for 3 minutes. After the beep, do a Quick release then remove the lid. Serve hot.

Per Serving

calories: 228 | fat: 5.3g | protein: 23.4g | carbs: 21.4g

Mediterranean Cod Stew

Prep time: 10 minutes | **Cook time:** 20 minutes | **Serves:**6

Ingredients:

2 tablespoons extra-virgin olive oil
2 cups chopped onion
2 garlic cloves, minced
¾ teaspoon smoked paprika
1 (14.5-ounce / 411-g) can diced tomatoes, undrained
1 (12-ounce / 340-g) jar roasted red peppers, drained and chopped
1 cup sliced olives, green or black
⅓ cup dry red wine
¼ teaspoon kosher or sea salt
¼ teaspoon freshly ground black pepper
1½ pounds (680 g) cod fillets, cut into 1-inch pieces
3 cups sliced mushrooms

Directions:

In a large stockpot over medium heat, heat the oil. Add the onion and cook for 4 minutes, stirring occasionally. Add the garlic and smoked paprika and cook for 1 minute, stirring often. Mix in the tomatoes with their juices, roasted peppers, olives, wine, pepper, and salt, and turn the heat to medium-high. Bring the mixture to a boil. Add the cod fillets and mushrooms, and reduce the heat to medium.

Cover and cook for about 10 minutes, stirring a few times, until the cod is gcooked through and flakes easily, and serve.

Per Serving

calories: 167 | fat: 5.0g | protein: 19.0g | carbs: 11.0g

Coconut Tangy Cod Curry

Prep time: 5 minutes | **Cook time:** 3 minutes | **Serves:**6

Ingredients:

1 (28-ounce / 794-g) can coconut milk
Juice of 2 lemons
2 tablespoons red curry paste
2 teaspoons fish sauce
2 teaspoons honey
4 teaspoons Sriracha
4 cloves garlic, minced
2 teaspoons ground turmeric
2 teaspoons ground ginger
1 teaspoon sea salt
1 teaspoon white pepper
2 pounds (907 g) codfish, cut into 1-inch cubes
½ cup chopped fresh cilantro, for garnish
4 lime wedges, for garnish

Directions:

Add all the ingredients, except the cod cubes and garnish, to a large bowl and whisk them well. Arrange the cod cube at the base of the Instant Pot and pour the coconut milk mixture over it. Secure the lid and hit the Manual key, select High Pressure with 3 minutes cooking time.

After the beep, do a Quick release then remove the lid.

Garnish with fresh cilantro and lemon wedges then serve.

Per Serving

calories: 396 | fat: 29.1g | protein: 26.6g | carbs: 11.4g

Teriyaki Salmon

Prep time: 10 minutes | **Cook time:** 8 minutes | **Serves:**4

Ingredients:

4 (8-ounce / 227-g) thick salmon fillets.
1 cup soy sauce
2 cups water
½ cup mirin
2 tablespoons sesame oil
4 teaspoons sesame seeds
2 cloves garlic, minced
2 tablespoons freshly grated ginger
4 tablespoons brown sugar
1 tablespoon corn starch
4 green onions, minced

Directions:

Add the soy sauce, sesame oil, sesame seeds, mirin, ginger, water, garlic, green onions, and brown sugar to a small bowl. Mix them well. In a shallow dish place the salmon fillets and pour half of the prepared mixture over the fillets. Let it marinate for 30 minutes in a refrigerator.

Pour 1 cup of water into the insert of your Instant pot and place trivet inside it. Arrange the marinated salmon fillets over the trivet and secure the lid.

Select the Manual settings with High Pressure and 8 minutes cooking time. Meanwhile, take a skillet and add the remaining marinade mixture in it.

Let it cook for 2 minutes, then add the corn starch mixed with water. Stir well and cook for 1 minute.

Check the pressure cooker, do a Quick release if it is done.

Transfer the fillets to a serving platter and pour the sesame mixture over it. Garnish with chopped green chilies then serve hot.

Per Serving

calories: 622 | fat: 28.6g | protein: 51.3g | carbs: 29.6g

Mahi-Mahi and Tomato Bowls

Prep time: 5 minutes | **Cook time:** 14 minutes | **Serves:**3

Ingredients:

3 (4-ounce / 113-g) mahi-mahi fillets
1½ tablespoons olive oil
½ yellow onion, sliced
½ teaspoon dried oregano
1 tablespoon fresh lemon juice
Salt and freshly ground black pepper, to taste
1 (14-ounce / 397-g) can sugar-free diced tomatoes

Directions:

Add the olive oil to the Instant Pot. Select the Sauté function on it. Add all the ingredient to the pot except the fillets. Cook them for 10 minutes. Press the Cancel key, then add the mahi-mahi fillets to the sauce.

Cover the fillets with sauce by using a spoon.

Secure the lid and set the Manual function at High Pressure for 4 minutes. After the beep, do a Quick release then remove the lid. Serve the fillets with their sauce, poured on top.

Per Serving
calories: 265 | fat: 8.6g | protein: 39.1g | carbs: 7.0g

Shrimps with Broccoli

Prep time: 5 minutes | **Cook time:** 10 minutes | **Serves:** 2

Ingredients:

2 teaspoons vegetable oil
2 tablespoons corn starch
1 cup broccoli florets
¼ cup chicken broth
8 ounces (227 g) large shrimp, peeled and deveined
¼ cup soy sauce
¼ cup water
¼ cup sliced carrots
3 tablespoons rice vinegar
2 teaspoons sesame oil
1 tablespoon chili garlic sauce
Coriander leaves to garnish
Boiled rice or noodles, for serving

Directions:

Add 1 tablespoon of corn starch and shrimp to a bowl. Mix them well then set it aside.

In a small bowl, mix the remaining corn starch, chicken broth, carrots, chili garlic sauce, rice vinegar and soy sauce together. Keep the mixture aside.

Select the Sauté function on your Instant pot, add the sesame oil and broccoli florets to the pot and sauté for 5 minutes. Add the water to the broccoli, cover the lid and cook for 5 minutes. Stir in shrimp and vegetable oil to the broccoli, sauté it for 5 minutes. Garnish with coriander leaves on top. Serve with rice or noodles.

Per Serving

calories: 300 | fat: 16.5g | protein: 19.6g | carbs: 17.1g

Salmon with Lemon & Dill (Spanish)

Prep time: 15 minutes **Cooking Time:** 2 hours **Servings:** 4

Ingredients:

Cooking spray
1 tablespoon fresh dill, chopped
Salt and pepper to taste
1 teaspoon olive oil
1 clove garlic, minced
1 lemon, sliced
2 lb. salmon

Directions:

Spray your slow cooker with oil.

Brush both sides of salmon with olive oil.

Season the salmon with salt, pepper, dill and garlic

Add to the slow cooker.

Put the lemon slices on top.

Cover the pot and cook on high for 2 hours.

Per Serving

Calories 313 Fat 15.2g Carbohydrate 0.7g Protein 44.2g Sugars 0g

Shrimp and Tomato Creole

Prep time: 20 minutes | **Cook time:** 7 hours 10 minutes | **Serves:** 4

Ingredients:

1 pound (454 g) shrimp (peeled and deveined)
1 tablespoon olive oil
1 (28-ounce / 794-g) can crush whole tomatoes
1 cup celery stalk (sliced)
¾ cup chopped white onion
½ cup green bell pepper (chopped)
1 (8-ounce / 227-g) can tomato sauce
½ teaspoon minced garlic
¼ teaspoon ground black pepper
1 tablespoon Worcestershire sauce
4 drops hot pepper sauce
Salt, to taste
White rice for serving

Directions:

Put the oil to the Instant Pot along with all the ingredients except the shrimp. Secure the cooker lid and keep the pressure handle valve turned to the venting position.

Select the Slow Cook function on your cooker and set it on medium heat. Let the mixture cook for 6 hours.

Remove the lid afterwards and add the shrimp to the pot.

Stir and let the shrimp cook for another 1 hour on Slow Cook function. Keep the lid covered with pressure release handle in the venting position. To serve, pour the juicy shrimp creole over steaming white rice.

Per Serving

calories: 231 | fat: 4.8g | protein: 27.6g | carbs: 23.8g

Tuna with Shirataki Noodles

Prep time: 5 minutes | **Cook time:** 4 minutes | **Serves:** 2

Ingredients:

½ can tuna, drained
8 ounces (227 g) Shirataki noodles
½ cup frozen peas
1 (14-ounce / 397-g) can cream mushroom soup
2 ounces (57 g) shredded Cheddar cheese
1½ cups water

Directions:

Add the water with noodles to the base of your Instant Pot.

Place the tuna and peas over it. Then pour the mushroom soup on top.

Secure the lid and cook with the Manual function at High Pressure for 4 minutes.

After the beep, do a Quick release then remove the lid.

Stir in shredded cheese to the tuna mix.

Serve warm.

Per Serving

calories: 362 | fat: 11.1g | protein: 19.5g | carbs: 46.5g

Shrimp and Spaghetti Squash Bowls

Prep time: 5 minutes | **Cook time:** 25 minutes | **Serves:** 4

Ingredients:

½ cup dry white wine
¼ teaspoon crushed red pepper flakes
1 large shallot, finely chopped
1 pound (454 g) jumbo shrimp, peeled and deveined

1 (28-ounce / 794-g) can crushed tomatoes
2 cloves garlic, minced
2½ pounds (1.1 kg) spaghetti squash
1 teaspoon olive oil
Salt and pepper, to taste
Parsley leaves (garnish)

Directions:

At first, sprinkle some salt and pepper over the shrimp and keep them in a refrigerator until further use.

Hit the Sauté function on your Instant Pot, then add the olive oil and red pepper flakes into it. Sauté for 1 minute.

Add the shallot and cook for 3 minutes. Then add the garlic, cook for 1 minute.

Add the dry wine, tomatoes, and whole spaghetti squash in the pot. Select Manual settings with medium pressure for 20 minutes. After the beep, do a Natural release. Remove the lid and the spaghetti squash.

Cut squash in half, remove its seed and stab with a fork to form spaghetti strands out of it. Keep them aside.

Select the Sauté function on your instant pot again, stir in shrimp. Mix well the shrimp with sauce. To serve, top the spaghetti squash with shrimp and sauce. Garnish it with parsley.

Per Serving

calories: 222 | fat: 4.4g | protein: 19.3g | carbs: 30.1g

Asparagus Smoked Salmon (Spanish)

Preparation Time: 15 minutes **Cooking Time:** 5 hours **Servings:** 6

Ingredients:

1 tablespoon extra-virgin olive oil
2 teaspoons chopped fresh dill, plus additional for garnish
¼ teaspoon freshly ground black pepper
6 ounces smoked salmon, flaked
½ teaspoon kosher salt

1 cup heavy (whipping) cream
6 large eggs
12 ounces asparagus, trimmed and sliced
11/2 cups shredded Havarti or Monterey Jack cheese

Directions:

Brush butter into a cooker

Whisk in the heavy cream with eggs, dill, salt, and pepper.

Stir in the cheese and asparagus.

Gently fold in the salmon and then pour the mixture into the prepared insert. Cover and cook on low or 3 hours on high. Serve warm, garnished with additional fresh dill.

Per Serving

Calories 388 Fat 19 Carbs 1.0 Protein 21

Grits with Shrimp

Prep time: 5 minutes | **Cook time:** 15 minutes | **Serves:** 8

Ingredients:

1 tablespoon oil
2 cups quick grits
12 ounces (340 g) Parmesan cheese, shredded
2 cups heavy cream

24 ounces (680 g) tail-on shrimp
2 tablespoons Old Bay seasoning
A pinch of ground black pepper
4 cups water

Directions:

Add a tablespoon of oil to the Instant Pot. Select the Sauté function for cooking.

Add the shrimp to the oil and drizzle old bay seasoning over it.

Cook the shrimp for 3-4 minutes while stirring then set them aside.

Now add the water, cream, and quick grits to the pot. Select the Manual function for 3 minutes at High Pressure.

After the beep, do a Quick release then remove the lid.

Add the shredded cheese to the grits then stir well.

Take a serving bowl, first pour in the creamy grits mixture then top it with shrimp.

Sprinkle black pepper on top then serve hot.

Per Serving

calories: 528 | fat: 38.6g | protein: 30.7g | carbs: 15.2g

Grilled Salmon (Spanish)

Prep time: 15 minutes **Cooking Time:** 16 mins **Servings:** 6

Ingredients:

1 1/2 pounds salmon fillet
Pepper to taste
1/3 cup of brown sugar
1/3 cup of water

Garlic powder to taste
1/3 cup soy sauce
1/4 cup vegetable oil

Directions:

Season the salmon fillets with lemon pepper, salt, and garlic powder.

Mix the soy sauce, brown sugar, water, and vegetable oil in a small bowl until the sugar is dissolved. Place the fish in a big resealable plastic bag with the soy sauce mixture, seal, and let marinate for at least 2 hours.

Preheat the grill on medium heat.

Lightly oil the grill. Place the salmon on the preheated grill and discard the marinade. Cook salmon 6 to 8 minutes per side or until the fish flakes easily with a fork.

Per Serving

318 calories 20.1 grams of fat 13.2 g carbohydrates 20.5 g of protein 56 mg cholesterol

Fish Tacos (Italian)

Preparation Time: 40 minutes **Cooking Time:** 15 minutes
Servings: 8

Ingredients:

1 cup flour
1 teaspoon baking powder
1/2 teaspoon of salt
1 cup of beer
1/2 cup of mayonnaise
1 lime, juice
1/2 teaspoon ground cumin
1/2 teaspoon dried dill
1 teaspoon ground cayenne pepper
1/2 medium cabbage, finely shredded
2 tablespoons corn flour
1 egg
1 liter of oil for frying
1/2 cup of yogurt
1 jalapeño pepper, minced
1 cup Finely chopped capers
1/2 teaspoon dried oregano
1 pound of cod fillets, 2-3 ounces each
8 corn tortillas

Directions:

Prepare beer dough: combine flour, corn flour, baking powder and salt in a large bowl. Mix the egg and the beer and stir in the flour mixture quickly.

To make a white sauce: combine yogurt and mayonnaise in a medium bowl. Gradually add fresh lime juice until it is slightly fluid — season with jalapeño, capers, oregano, cumin, dill, and cayenne pepper.

Heat the oil in a frying pan.

Lightly sprinkle the fish with flour. Dip it in the beer batter and fry until crispy and golden brown. Drain on kitchen paper. Heat the tortillas. Place the fried fish in a tortilla and garnish with grated cabbage and white sauce.

Per Serving
409 calories 18.8 g of fat 43 grams of carbohydrates 17.3 g of protein 54 mg cholesterol.

Leftover Salmon Salad Power Bowls (Greek)

Preparation Time: 10 minutes **Cooking Time:** 10 minutes
Servings: 1

Ingredients:

½ cup raspberries
1 tablespoon balsamic glaze
2 sprigs of thyme, chopped
2 tablespoon olive oil
Salmon Salt and pepper to taste
½ cup zucchini, sliced
4 cups seasonal greens
1 lemon, juice squeezed
4 ounces leftover grilled

Directions:

Heat oil in a skillet over medium flame and sauté the zucchini. Season with salt and pepper to taste.

In a mixing bowl, mix all together.

Toss to combine everything.

Sprinkle with nut cheese.

Per Serving
Calories: 450.3; Fat: 35.5 g; Protein: 23.4g; Carbs: 9.3 g

Grilled Tilapia with Mango Salsa (Spanish)

Preparation Time: 45 minutes **Cooking Time:** 10 minutes
Servings: 2

Ingredients:

1/3 cup extra virgin olive oil
1 tablespoon lemon juice
1 teaspoon dried basil
1/2 teaspoon salt
2 tilapia fillets (1 oz. each)
1/2 red pepper, diced
2 tablespoons chopped red onion
2 tablespoons lime juice
Salt and pepper to taste
1 tablespoon lemon juice
1 tablespoon chopped fresh parsley
1 clove of garlic, minced
1 teaspoon ground black pepper
1 large ripe mango, peeled, pitted and diced
1 tablespoon chopped fresh coriander
1 jalapeño pepper, seeded and minced

Directions:

Mix extra virgin olive oil, 1 tablespoon lemon juice, parsley, garlic, basil, 1 teaspoon pepper, and 1/2 teaspoon salt in a bowl, then pour into a resealable plastic bag. Add the tilapia fillets, cover with the marinade, remove excess air, and close the bag. Marinate in the fridge for 1 hour.

Prepare the mango salsa by combining the mango, red pepper, red onion, coriander, and jalapeño pepper in a bowl. Add the lime juice and 1 tablespoon lemon juice and mix well. Season with salt and pepper and keep until serving.

Preheat a grill over medium heat and lightly oil. Remove the tilapia from the marinade and remove the excess. Discard the rest of the marinade. Grill the fillets until the fish is no longer translucent in the middle and flake easily with the fork for 3 to 4 minutes on each side, depending on the thickness of the fillets. Serve the tilapia topped with mango salsa.

Per Serving
634 calories 40.2 grams of fat 33.4 g carbohydrates 36.3 g of protein 62 mg cholesterol

One-Pot Seafood Chowder (Greek)

Prep time: 10 minutes **Cooking Time:** 10 mins **Servings:** 3

Ingredients:

3 cans coconut milk
1 can corn, drained
3 cans clams, chopped
2 cans shrimps, canned
4 large potatoes, diced
1 tablespoon garlic, minced
Salt and pepper to taste
1 package fresh shrimps, shelled and deveined
2 carrots, peeled and chopped
2 celery stalks, chopped

Directions:

Place all in a pot and give a good stir to mix everything. Close the lid and turn on the heat to medium.

Bring to a boil and allow to simmer for 10 minutes. Place in individual containers. Put a label and store in the fridge. Allow to warm at room temperature before heating in the microwave oven.

Per Serving Calories: 532; Carbs: 92.5g; Protein: 25.3g

Herbed Salmon Loaf with Sauce (Italian)

Preparation Time: 5 minutes **Cooking Time:** 5 hours
Servings: 4

Ingredients:

For the Salmon Meatloaf:
1cup fresh bread crumbs
1/3 cup whole milk
1 egg
1/4 cup scallions, chopped
1 teaspoon ground coriander
1/2 teaspoon fenugreek
1/4 teaspoon white pepper
1/2 cup cucumber, chopped
Salt, to taste

1 can (7 1/2 ounce) salmon, drained
1 tablespoon fresh lemon juice 1 teaspoon dried rosemary
1 teaspoon mustard seed
1/2 teaspoon salt
1/2 teaspoon dill weed
1/2 cup reduced-fat plain yogurt

Directions:

Line your crock pot with a foil.

Mix all for the salmon meatloaf until everything is well incorporated; form into loaf and place in the crock pot.

Cover with a suitable lid and cook on low heat setting 5 hours.

Combine all of the for the sauce; whisk to combine.

Serve your meatloaf with prepared sauce.

Per Serving

Calories: 145 Fat: 11 g Carbs: 2 g Protein: 11 g

Scallops in Wine 'n Olive Oil (Greek)

Preparation Time: 10 minutes **Cooking Time:** 8 minutes
Servings: 4

Ingredients:

¼ teaspoon salt
1 ½ lbs. large sea scallops
2 tablespoon olive oil
Black pepper – optional

½ cup dry white wine
1 ½ teaspoon chopped fresh tarragon

Directions:

On medium high fire, place a large nonstick fry pan and heat oil.

Add scallops and fry for 3 minutes per side or until edges are lightly browned. Transfer to a serving plate.

On same pan, add salt, tarragon and wine while scraping pan to loosen browned bits.

Turn off fire.

Pour sauce over scallops and serve.

Per Serving

Calories: 205.2; Fat: 8 g; Protein: 28.6 g; Carbohydrates: 4.7 g

Warm Caper Tapenade on Cod (Greek)

Preparation Time: 10 minutes **Cooking Time:** 30 minutes
Servings: 4

Ingredients:

¼ cup chopped cured olives
1 cup halved cherry tomatoes
1 ½ teaspoon chopped fresh oregano
1 teaspoon balsamic vinegar
1 tablespoon capers, rinsed and chopped

¼ teaspoon freshly ground pepper
1 tablespoon minced shallot
1 lb. cod fillet
3 teaspoon extra virgin olive oil, divided

Directions:

Grease baking sheet with cooking spray and preheat oven to 450 F.

Place cod on prepared baking sheet. Rub with 2 teaspoon oil and season with pepper.

Roast in oven for 15 to 20 minutes or until cod is flaky.

While waiting for cod to cook, on medium fire, place a small fry pan and heat 1 teaspoon oil.

Sauté shallots for a minute.

Add tomatoes and cook for two minutes or until soft.

Add capers and olives. Sauté for another minute.

Add vinegar and oregano. Turn off fire and stir to mix well.

Evenly divide cod into 4 serving and place on a plate.

1 To serve, top cod with Caper-Olive-Tomato Tapenade and enjoy.

Per Serving

Calories: 107; Fat: 2.9g; Protein: 17.6g; Carbs: 2.0g

Tomato Basil Cauliflower Rice (Spanish)

Preparation Time: 5 minutes **Cooking Time:** 10 minutes
Servings: 4

Ingredients:

Salt and pepper to taste
Dried parsley for garnish
½ teaspoon garlic, minced
½ teaspoon marjoram
1 large head of cauliflower
1 teaspoon oil

¼ cup tomato paste
1 teaspoon dried oregano
½ teaspoon onion powder
1 ½ teaspoon dried basil

Directions:

Cut the cauliflower into florets and place in the food processor.

Pulse until it has a coarse consistency similar with rice. Set aside.

In a skillet, heat the oil and sauté the garlic and onion for three minutes. Add the rest of the . Cook for 8 minutes.

Per Serving

Calories: 106; Carbs: 15.1g; Protein: 3.3g; Fat: 5.0g

Berries and Grilled Calamari (Spanish)

Preparation Time: 10 minutes **Cooking Time:** 5 minutes **Servings:** 4

Ingredients:

¼ cup dried cranberries
¼ cup olive oil
½ lemon, juiced
1 ½ pounds calamari tube, cleaned
1 granny smith apple, sliced thinly
Sea salt to taste
Freshly grated pepper to taste
¼ cup extra virgin olive oil
¼ cup sliced almonds
¾ cup blueberries
2 tablespoons apple cider vinegar
6 cups fresh spinach
1 tablespoon fresh lemon juice

Directions:

In a small bowl, make the vinaigrette by mixing well the tablespoon of lemon juice, apple cider vinegar, and extra virgin olive oil. Season with pepper and salt to taste. Set aside.

Turn on the grill to medium fire and let the grates heat up for a minute or two.

In a large bowl, add olive oil and the calamari tube. Season calamari generously with pepper and salt.

Place seasoned and oiled calamari onto heated grate and grill until cooked or opaque. This is around two minutes per side.

As you wait for the calamari to cook, you can combine almonds, cranberries, blueberries, spinach, and the thinly sliced apple in a large salad bowl. Toss to mix.

Remove cooked calamari from grill and transfer on a chopping board. Cut into ¼-inch thick rings and throw into the salad bowl.

Drizzle with vinaigrette and toss well to coat salad.

Serve and enjoy!

Per Serving
Calories: 567; Fat: 24.5g; Protein: 54.8g; Carbs: 30.6g

Dill Relish on White Sea Bass (Greek)

Prep time: 10 mins **Cooking Time:** 12 minutes **Servings:** 4

Ingredients:

1 ½ tablespoon chopped white onion
1 teaspoon Dijon mustard
1 ½ teaspoon chopped fresh dill
1 lemon, quartered
1 teaspoon lemon juice
1 teaspoon pickled baby capers, drained
4 pieces of 4-oz white sea bass fillets

Directions:

Preheat oven to 375oF.

Mix lemon juice, mustard, dill, capers and onions in a small bowl.

Prepare four aluminum foil squares and place 1 fillet per foil.

Squeeze a lemon wedge per fish.

Evenly divide into 4 the dill spread and drizzle over fillet.

Close the foil over the fish securely and pop in the oven.

Bake for 10 to 12 minutes or until fish is cooked through.

Remove from foil and transfer to a serving platter, serve and enjoy.

Per Serving
Calories: 115; Protein: 7g; Fat: 1g; Carbs: 12g

Sweet Potatoes Oven Fried (Spanish)

Preparation Time: 10 minutes **Cooking Time:** 30 minutes **Servings:** 7

Ingredients:

1 small garlic clove, minced
1 teaspoon grated orange rind
¼ teaspoon pepper
1 tablespoon fresh parsley, chopped finely
1 tablespoon olive oil
¼ teaspoon salt
4 medium sweet potatoes, peeled and sliced to ¼-inch thickness

Directions:

In a large bowl mix well pepper, salt, olive oil and sweet potatoes.

In a greased baking sheet, in a single layer arrange sweet potatoes.

Pop in a preheated 400oF oven and bake for 15 minutes, turnover potato slices and return to oven. Bake for another 15 minutes or until tender.

Meanwhile, mix well in a small bowl garlic, orange rind and parsley, sprinkle over cooked potato slices and serve.

You can store baked sweet potatoes in a lidded container and just microwave whenever you want to eat it. Do consume within 3 days.

Per Serving
Calories: 176; Carbs: 36.6g; Protein: 2.5g; Fat: 2.5g

Tasty Avocado Sauce over Zoodles (Italian)

Preparation Time: 10 minutes **Cooking Time:** 10 minutes
Servings: 2

Ingredients:

1 zucchini peeled and spiralized into noodles
1/3 cup water
1 avocado peeled and pitted
12 sliced cherry tomatoes
Pepper and salt to taste
2 tablespoon lemon juice
4 tablespoon pine nuts
1 1/4 cup basil

Directions:

Make the sauce in a blender by adding pine nuts, lemon juice, avocado, water, and basil. Pulse until smooth and creamy. Season with pepper and salt to taste. Mix well.

Place zoodles in salad bowl. Pour over avocado sauce and toss well to coat.

Add cherry tomatoes, serve, and enjoy.

Per Serving
Calories: 313; Protein: 6.8g; Carbs: 18.7g; Fat: 26.8g

Vegan Sesame Tofu and Eggplants (Greek)

Preparation Time: 10 minutes **Cooking Time:** 20 minutes
Servings: 4

Ingredients:

5 tablespoons olive oil
2 teaspoons Swerve sweetener
2 whole eggplants, sliced
Salt and pepper to taste
1 cup fresh cilantro, chopped
1-pound firm tofu, sliced
¼ cup soy sauce
3 tablespoons rice vinegar
¼ cup sesame seeds
4 tablespoons toasted sesame oil

Directions:

Heat the oil in a pan for 2 minutes.

Pan fry the tofu for 3 minutes on each side.

Stir in the rice vinegar, sweetener, eggplants, and soy sauce. Season with salt and pepper to taste.

Cover and cook for 5 minutes on medium fire. Stir and continue cooking for another 5 minutes.

Toss in the sesame oil, sesame seeds, and cilantro.

Serve and enjoy.

Per Serving
Calories: 616; Carbs: 27.4g; Protein: 23.9g; Fat: 49.2g

Simple Cod Piccata (Italian)

Preparation Time: 10 minutes **Cooking Time:** 15 minutes
Servings: 3

Ingredients:

¼ cup capers, drained
¾ cup chicken stock
1/3 cup almond flour
2 tablespoon fresh parsley, chopped
2 tablespoon grapeseed oil
½ teaspoon salt
1-pound cod fillets, patted dry
3 tablespoon extra-virgin oil
3 tablespoon lemon juice

Directions:

In a bowl, combine the almond flour and salt.

Dredge the fish in the almond flour to coat. Set aside.

Heat a little bit of olive oil to coat a large skillet. Heat the skillet over medium high heat. Add grapeseed oil. Cook the cod for 3 minutes on each side to brown. Remove from the plate and place on a paper towel- lined plate.

In a saucepan, mix together the chicken stock, capers and lemon juice. Simmer to reduce the sauce to half. Add the remaining grapeseed oil.

Drizzle the fried cod with the sauce and sprinkle with parsley.

Per Serving
Calories: 277.1; Fat: 28.3 g; Protein: 1.9 g; Carbs: 3.7 g

Yummy Salmon Panzanella (Italian)

Preparation Time: 10 minutes **Cooking Time:** 10 minutes
Servings: 4

Ingredients:

¼ cup thinly sliced fresh basil
¼ teaspoon freshly ground pepper, divided
1 lb. center cut salmon, skinned and cut into 4 equal portions
1 medium cucumber, peeled, seeded, and cut into 1-inch slices
2 thick slices day old whole grain bread, sliced into 1-inch cubes
¼ cup thinly sliced red onion
½ teaspoon salt
3 tablespoon virgin olive oil
2 large tomatoes, cut into 1-inch pieces
1 tablespoon capers, rinsed and chopped
8 Kalamata olives, pitted and chopped
3 tablespoon red wine vinegar

Directions:

Grease grill grate and preheat grill to high.

In a large bowl, whisk 1/8 teaspoon pepper, capers, vinegar, and olives. Add oil and whisk well.

Stir in basil, onion, cucumber, tomatoes, and bread.

Season both sides of salmon with remaining pepper and salt.Grill on high for 4 minutes per side. Into 4 plates, evenly divide salad, top with grilled salmon, and serve.

Per Serving
Calories: 383; Fat: 20.6g; Protein: 34.8g; Carbs: 13.6g

Vegetarian Coconut Curry (Spanish)

Preparation Time: 10 minutes **Cooking Time:** 30 minutes
Servings: 4

Ingredients:

4 tablespoons coconut oil	2 cups fresh spinach leaves
1 medium onion, chopped	2 teaspoons fish sauce
1 teaspoon minced ginger	1 teaspoon minced garlic
1 cup broccoli florets	Salt and pepper to taste
1 tablespoon garam masala	½ cup coconut milk

Directions:

Heat oil in a pot.

Sauté the onion and garlic until fragrant, around 3 minutes.

Stir in the rest of the , except for spinach leaves.

Season with salt and pepper to taste.

Cover and cook on medium fire for 5 minutes.

Stir and add spinach leaves. Cover and cook for another 2 minutes.

Turn off fire and let it sit for two more minutes before serving.

Per Serving
Calories: 210; Carbs: 6.5g; Protein: 2.1g; Fat: 20.9g

Healthy Poached Trout (Greek)

Preparation Time: 10 minutes
Cooking Time: 10 minutes **Servings:** 2

Ingredients:

1 8-oz boneless, skin on trout fillet	2 leeks, halved
6-8 slices lemon	2 cups chicken broth or water
	salt and pepper to taste

Directions:

On medium fire, place a large nonstick skillet and arrange leeks and lemons on pan in a layer. Cover with soup stock or water and bring to a simmer.

Meanwhile, season trout on both sides with pepper and salt. Place trout on simmering pan of water. Cover and cook until trout are flaky, around 8 minutes.

In a serving platter, spoon leek and lemons on bottom of plate, top with trout and spoon sauce into plate. Serve and enjoy.

Per Servings
Calories: 360.2; Protein: 13.8g; Fat: 7.5g; Carbs: 51.5g

Salmon with Potatoes (Spanish)

Prep time: 10 minutes **Cooking Time:** 15 mins **Servings** 4

Ingredients:

1 1/2 lbs. Salmon fillets, boneless and cubed	1 cup fish stock
2 tbsp. parsley, chopped	2 tbsp. olive oil
1 tsp. garlic, minced	1 lb. baby potatoes, halved
Salt	Pepper

Directions:

Add oil into the inner pot of instant pot and set the pot on sauté mode.

Add garlic and sauté for 2 minutes.

Add remaining and stir well.

Cover the pot with lid and cook on high for 13 minutes.

Once done, release pressure using quick release. Remove lid.

Serve and enjoy.

Per Serving
Calories 362 Fat 18.1 g Carbohydrates 14.5 g Sugar 0 g Protein 37.3 g Cholesterol 76 mg

Fish Stew (Greek)

Prep time: 15 minutes
Cooking Time: 1 hour and 24 minutes **Servings:** 2

Ingredients:

1 lb. white fish	1 tablespoon lime juice
2 cloves garlic, sliced	1 jalapeno pepper, sliced
1 red pepper, sliced	1 teaspoon paprika
2 cups chicken broth	2 cups tomatoes, chopped
1 onion, sliced	Salt and pepper to taste
	2oz. coconut milk

Directions:

Marinate the fish in lime juice for 10 minutes.

Pour the olive oil into a pan over medium heat.

Add the onion, garlic and peppers.

Cook for 4 minutes.

Add the rest of the except the coconut milk.

Cover the pot.

Cook on low for 1 hour.

Stir in the coconut milk and simmer for 10 minutes

Per Serving
Calories 323 Fat 28.6g Carbohydrate 1.1g Protein 9.3g Sugars 6.2g

Minty-Cucumber Yogurt Topped Grilled Fish(Greek)

Prep time: 10 minutes **Cooking Time:** 2 mins **Servings:** 4

Ingredients:

¼ cup 2% plain Greek yogurt	¼ teaspoon + 1/8 teaspoon salt
¼ teaspoon black pepper fresh mint leaves	½ green onion, finely chopped
½ teaspoon dried oregano	1 tablespoon finely chopped
3 tablespoons finely chopped English cucumber	Cooking oil as needed
4 5-oz cod fillets	

Directions:

Brush grill grate with oil and preheat grill to high.

Season cod fillets on both sides with pepper, ¼ teaspoon salt and oregano.

Grill cod for 3 minutes per side or until cooked to desired doneness.

Mix thoroughly 1/8 teaspoon salt, onion, mint, cucumber and yogurt in a small bowl. Serve cod with a dollop of the dressing. This dish can be paired with salad greens or brown rice.

Per Serving
Calories: 253.5; Protein: 25.5g; Fat: 1g; Carbs: 5g

Soy-Ginger Braised Squid (Spanish)

Prep time: 5 minutes **Cooking Time:** 8 hours **Servings:** 6

Ingredients:

18-ounce wild-caught squid, cut into rings	2 bay leaves
1 tablespoon grated ginger	2 scallions, chopped
½ cup swerve sweetener	1 bulb. of garlic, peeled & minced
¼ cup oyster sauce	¼ cup soy sauce
¼ cup white wine	¼ cup avocado oil

Directions:

Plug in a 6-quart slow cooker, add all the and stir until mixed.

Shut with lid and cook for 8 hours at low heat setting or until cooked through.

Serve straightaway.

Per Serving
Calories: 154 Fat: 13 g Protein: 15 g Carbs: 3.4 g Sugar: 1.9 g

Sea Bass in Coconut Cream Sauce (Spanish)

Prep time: 5 minutes **Cooking Time:** 1 hour **Servings:** 3

Ingredients:

18-ounce wild-caught sea bass	4 stalks of bock Choy
2 stalks of scallions, sliced	5 jalapeno peppers
1 tablespoon grated ginger	1 tablespoon fish sauce, unsweetened
1 1/2 teaspoon salt	2 cups coconut cream

Directions:

Stir together all the except for bok choy and fish in a bowl and add this mixture in a 6-quarts slow cooker.

Plug in the slow cooker, then add fish, top with bok choy and shut with lid.

Cook sea bass for 1 hour and 30 minutes or until cooked.

Serve straightaway.

Per Serving
Calories: 315 Fat: 17 g Protein: 15 g Carbs: 2.4 g Sugar: 3.2 g

Chapter 9
Fruits and Desserts

Rice Pudding with Roasted Orange

Prep time: 10 minutes | **Cook time:** 19 to 20 minutes | **Serves:**6

Ingredients:

2 medium oranges
2 teaspoons extra-virgin olive oil
⅛ teaspoon kosher salt
2 large eggs
2 cups unsweetened almond milk
1 cup orange juice
1 cup uncooked instant brown rice
¼ cup honey
½ teaspoon ground cinnamon
1 teaspoon vanilla extract
Cooking spray

Directions:

Preheat the oven to 450ºF (235ºC). Spritz a large, rimmed baking sheet with cooking spray. Set aside.

Slice the unpeeled oranges into ¼-inch rounds. Brush with the oil and sprinkle with salt. Place the slices on the baking sheet and roast for 4 minutes. Flip the slices and roast for 4 more minutes, or until they begin to brown. Remove from the oven and set aside.

Crack the eggs into a medium bowl. In a medium saucepan, whisk together the milk, orange juice, rice, honey and cinnamon. Bring to a boil over medium-high heat, stirring constantly. Reduce the heat to medium- low and simmer for 10 minutes, stirring occasionally.

Using a measuring cup, scoop out ½ cup of the hot rice mixture and whisk it into the eggs. While constantly stirring the mixture in the pan, slowly pour the egg mixture back into the saucepan.

Cook on low heat for 1 to 2 minutes, or until thickened, stirring constantly. Remove from the heat and stir in the vanilla. Let the pudding stand for a few minutes for the rice to soften. The rice will be cooked but slightly chewy. For softer rice, let stand for another half hour. Top with the roasted oranges. Serve warm or at room temperature.

Per Serving

calories: 204 | fat: 6.0g | protein: 5.0g | carbs: 34.0g

Cherry Walnut Brownies

Prep time: 10 minutes | **Cook time:** 20 minutes | **Serves:**9

Ingredients:

2 large eggs
½ cup 2% plain Greek yogurt
½ cup sugar ⅓ cup honey
¼ cup extra-virgin olive oil
1 teaspoon vanilla extract
½ cup whole-wheat pastry flour
⅓ cup unsweetened dark chocolate cocoa powder
¼ teaspoon baking powder
¼ teaspoon salt
⅓ cup chopped walnuts
9 fresh cherries, stemmed and pitted
Cooking spray

Directions:

Preheat the oven to 375ºF (190ºC) and set the rack in the middle of the oven. Spritz a square baking pan with cooking spray. In a large bowl, whisk together the eggs, yogurt, sugar, honey, oil and vanilla.

In a medium bowl, stir together the flour, cocoa powder, baking powder and salt. Add the flour mixture to the egg mixture and whisk until all the dry ingredients are incorporated. Fold in the walnuts.

Pour the batter into the prepared pan. Push the cherries into the batter, three to a row in three rows, so one will be at the center of each brownie once you cut them into squares. Bake the brownies for 20 minutes, or until just set. Remove from the oven and place on a rack to cool for 5 minutes. Cut into nine squares and serve.

Per Serving

calories: 154 | fat: 6.0g | protein: 3.0g | carbs: 24.0g

Watermelon and Blueberry Salad

Prep time: 5 minutes | **Cook time:** 0 minutes **Serves:**6 to 8

Ingredients:

1 medium watermelon
1 cup fresh blueberries
⅓ cup honey
2 tablespoons lemon juice
2 tablespoons finely chopped fresh mint leaves

Directions:

Cut the watermelon into 1-inch cubes. Put them in a bowl.

Evenly distribute the blueberries over the watermelon.

In a separate bowl, whisk together the honey, lemon juice and mint. Drizzle the mint dressing over the watermelon and blueberries. Serve cold.

Per Serving

calories: 238 | fat: 1.0g | protein: 4.0g | carbs: 61.0g

Crispy Sesame Cookies

Prep time: 5 minutes | **Cook time:** 8 to 10 minutes | **Serves:** 14 to 16

Ingredients:

1 cup hulled sesame seeds
1 cup sugar

8 tablespoons almond butter
2 large eggs
1¼ cups flour

Directions:

Preheat the oven to 350ºF (180ºC).

Toast the sesame seeds on a baking sheet for 3 minutes. Set aside and let cool. Using a mixer, whisk together the sugar and butter. Add the eggs one at a time until well blended. Add the flour and toasted sesame seeds and mix until well blended. Drop spoonfuls of cookie dough onto a baking sheet and form them into round balls, about 1-inch in diameter, similar to a walnut.

Put in the oven and bake for 5 to 7 minutes, or until golden brown. Let the cookies cool for 5 minutes before serving.

Per Serving

calories: 218 | fat: 12.0g | protein: 4.0g | carbs: 25.0g

Mint Banana Chocolate Sorbet

Prep time: 4 hours 5 minutes | **Cook time:** 0 minutes | **Serves:** 1

Ingredients:

1 frozen banana
1 tablespoon almond butter
2 tablespoons minced fresh mint

2 to 3 tablespoons dark chocolate chips (60% cocoa or higher)
2 to 3 tablespoons goji (optional)

Directions:

Put the banana, butter, and mint in a food processor. Pulse to purée until creamy and smooth.

Add the chocolate and goji, then pulse for several more times to combine well. Pour the mixture in a bowl or a ramekin, then freeze for at least 4 hours before serving chilled.

Per Serving

calories: 213 | fat: 9.8g | protein: 3.1g | carbs: 2.9g

Pecan and Carrot Cake

Prep time: 15 minutes | **Cook time:** 45 minutes | **Serves:** 12

Ingredients:

½ cup coconut oil, at room temperature, plus more for greasing the baking dish
2 teaspoons pure vanilla extract
¼ cup pure maple syrup 6 eggs
½ cup coconut flour
1 teaspoon baking powder

1 teaspoon baking soda
½ teaspoon ground nutmeg
1 teaspoon ground cinnamon
⅛ teaspoon sea salt
½ cup chopped pecans
3 cups finely grated carrots

Directions:

Preheat the oven to 350ºF (180ºC). Grease a 13-by-9-inch baking dish with coconut oil.

Combine the vanilla extract, maple syrup, and ½ cup of coconut oil in a large bowl. Stir to mix well.

Break the eggs in the bowl and whisk to combine well. Set aside. Combine the coconut flour, baking powder, baking soda, nutmeg, cinnamon, and salt in a separate bowl. Stir to mix well. Make a well in the center of the flour mixture, then pour the egg mixture into the well. Stir to combine well. Add the pecans and carrots to the bowl and toss to mix well. Pour the mixture in the single layer on the baking dish. Bake in the preheated oven for 45 minutes or until puffed and the cake spring back when lightly press with your fingers. Remove the cake from the oven. Allow to cool for at least 15 minutes, then serve.

Per Serving

calories: 255 | fat: 21.2g | protein: 5.1g | carbs: 12.8g

Raspberry Yogurt Basted Cantaloupe

Prep time: 15 minutes | **Cook time:** 0 minutes | **Serves:** 6

Ingredients:

2 cups fresh raspberries, mashed
1 cup plain coconut yogurt
½ teaspoon vanilla extract

1 cantaloupe, peeled and sliced
½ cup toasted coconut flakes

Directions:

Combine the mashed raspberries with yogurt and vanilla extract in a small bowl. Stir to mix well.

Place the cantaloupe slices on a platter, then top with raspberry mixture and spread with toasted coconut.

Serve immediately.

Per Serving

calories: 75 | fat: 4.1g | protein: 1.2g | carbs: 10.9g

Apple Compote

Prep time: 15 minutes | **Cook time:** 10 minutes | **Serves:**4

Ingredients:

6 apples, peeled, cored, and chopped
¼ cup raw honey

1 teaspoon ground cinnamon
¼ cup apple juice
Sea salt, to taste

Directions:

Put all the ingredients in a stockpot. Stir to mix well, then cook over medium-high heat for 10 minutes or until the apples are glazed by honey and lightly saucy. Stir constantly. Serve immediately.

Per Serving calories: 246 | fat: 0.9g | protein: 1.2g | carbs: 66.3g

Peanut Butter and Chocolate Balls

Prep time: 45 minutes | **Cook time:** 0 mins | **Serves:**15 balls

Ingredients:

¾ cup creamy peanut butter
¼ cup unsweetened cocoa powder
2 tablespoons softened almond butter

½ teaspoon vanilla extract
1¾ cups maple syrup

Directions:

Line a baking sheet with parchment paper.

Combine all the ingredients in a bowl. Stir to mix well.

Divide the mixture into 15 parts and shape each part into a 1-inch ball. Arrange the balls on the baking sheet and refrigerate for at least 30 minutes, then serve chilled.

Per Serving (1 ball)

calories: 146 | fat: 8.1g | protein: 4.2g | carbs: 16.9g

Spiced Sweet Pecans

Prep time: 4 minutes | **Cook time:** 17 minutes | **Serves:**4

Ingredients:

1 cup pecan halves
3 tablespoons almond butter
1 teaspoon ground cinnamon

½ teaspoon ground nutmeg
¼ cup raw honey
¼ teaspoon sea salt

Directions:

Preheat the oven to 350ºF (180ºC). Line a baking sheet with parchment paper. Combine all the ingredients in a bowl. Stir to mix well, then spread the mixture in the single layer on the baking sheet with a spatula. Bake in the preheated oven for 16 minutes or until the pecan halves are well browned.

Serve immediately.

Per Serving calories: 324 | protein: 3.2g | carbs: 13.9g

Greek Yogurt Affogato with Pistachios

Prep time: 5 minutes | **Cook time:** 0 minutes | **Serves:**4

Ingredients:

24 ounces (680 g) vanilla Greek yogurt
2 teaspoons sugar
4 shots hot espresso

4 tablespoons chopped unsalted pistachios
4 tablespoons dark chocolate chips

Directions:

Spoon the yogurt into four bowls or tall glasses.

Mix ½ teaspoon of sugar into each of the espresso shots.

Pour one shot of the hot espresso over each bowl of yogurt.

Top each bowl with 1 tablespoon of the pistachios and 1 tablespoon of the chocolate chips and serve.

Per Serving

calories: 190 | fat: 6.0g | protein: 20.0g | carbs: 14.0g

Grilled Peaches with Whipped Ricotta

Prep time: 5 minutes | **Cook time:** 14 to 22 minutes | **Serves:**4

Ingredients:

4 peaches, halved and pitted
2 teaspoons extra-virgin olive oil
¾ cup whole-milk Ricotta cheese

1 tablespoon honey
¼ teaspoon freshly grated nutmeg
4 sprigs mint
Cooking spray

Directions:

Spritz a grill pan with cooking spray. Heat the grill pan to medium heat.

Place a large, empty bowl in the refrigerator to chill.

Brush the peaches all over with the oil. Place half of the peaches, cut-side down, on the grill pan and cook for 3 to 5 minutes, or until grill marks appear.

Using tongs, turn the peaches over. Cover the grill pan with aluminum foil and cook for 4 to 6 minutes, or until the peaches are easily pierced with a sharp knife. Set aside to cool. Repeat with the remaining peaches.

Remove the bowl from the refrigerator and add the Ricotta. Using an electric beater, beat the Ricotta on high for 2 minutes. Add the honey and nutmeg and beat for 1 more minute. Divide the cooled peaches among 4 serving bowls. Top with the Ricotta mixture and a sprig of mint and serve.

Per Serving

calories: 176 | fat: 8.0g | protein: 8.0g | carbs: 20.0g

Honey Baked Cinnamon Apples

Prep time: 5 minutes | **Cook time:** 20 minutes | **Serves:** 2

Ingredients:

1 teaspoon extra-virgin olive oil

4 firm apples, peeled, cored, and sliced

½ teaspoon salt

1½ teaspoons ground cinnamon, divided

2 tablespoons unsweetened almond milk

2 tablespoons honey

Directions:

Preheat the oven to 375ºF (190ºC). Coat a small casserole dish with the olive oil.

Toss the apple slices with the salt and ½ teaspoon of the cinnamon in a medium bowl. Spread the apples in the prepared casserole dish and bake in the preheated oven for 20 minutes. Meanwhile, in a small saucepan, heat the milk, honey, and remaining 1 teaspoon of cinnamon over medium heat, stirring frequently. When it reaches a simmer, remove the pan from the heat and cover to keep warm. Divide the apple slices between 2 plates and pour the sauce over the apples. Serve warm.

Per Serving

calories: 310 | fat: 3.4g | protein: 1.7g | carbs: 68.5g

Strawberries with Balsamic Vinegar

Prep time: 5 minutes | **Cook time:** 0 minutes | **Serves:** 2

Ingredients:

2 cups strawberries, hulled and sliced

2 tablespoons sugar

2 tablespoons balsamic vinegar

Directions:

Place the sliced strawberries in a bowl, sprinkle with the sugar, and drizzle lightly with the balsamic vinegar.

Toss to combine well and allow to sit for about 10 minutes before serving.

Per Serving calories: 92 | fat: 0.4g | protein: 1.0g | carbs: 21.7g

Frozen Mango Raspberry Delight

Prep time: 5 minutes | **Cook time:** 0 minutes | **Serves:** 2

Ingredients:

3 cups frozen raspberries

1 mango, peeled and pitted

1 peach, peeled and pitted

1 teaspoon honey

Directions:

Place all the ingredients into a blender and purée, adding some water as needed.

Put in the freezer for 10 minutes to firm up if desired. Serve chilled or at room temperature.

Per Serving

calories: 276 | fat: 2.1g | protein: 4.5g | carbs: 60.3g

Grilled Stone Fruit with Honey

Prep time: 8 minutes | **Cook time:** 6 minutes | **Serves:** 2

Ingredients:

3 apricots, halved and pitted

2 plums, halved and pitted

2 peaches, halved and pitted

½ cup low-fat ricotta cheese

2 tablespoons honey

Cooking spray

Directions:

Preheat the grill to medium heat. Spray the grill grates with cooking spray.

Arrange the fruit, cut side down, on the grill, and cook for 2 to 3 minutes per side, or until lightly charred and softened.

Serve warm with a sprinkle of cheese and a drizzle of honey.

Per Serving

calories: 298 | fat: 7.8g | protein: 11.9g | carbs: 45.2g

Mascarpone Baked Pears

Prep time: 10 minutes | **Cook time:** 20 minutes | **Serves:** 2

Ingredients:

2 ripe pears, peeled

1 tablespoon plus 2 teaspoons honey, divided

1 teaspoon vanilla, divided

¼ teaspoon ground coriander

¼ teaspoon ginger

¼ cup minced walnuts

¼ cup mascarpone cheese

Pinch salt

Cooking spray

Directions:

Preheat the oven to 350ºF (180ºC). Spray a small baking dish with cooking spray.

Slice the pears in half lengthwise. Using a spoon, scoop out the core from each piece. Put the pears, cut side up, in the baking dish.

Whisk together 1 tablespoon of honey, ½ teaspoon of vanilla, ginger, and coriander in a small bowl. Pour this mixture evenly over the pear halves.

Scatter the walnuts over the pear halves.

Bake in the preheated oven for 20 minutes, or until the pears are golden and you're able to pierce them easily with a knife.

Meanwhile, combine the mascarpone cheese with the remaining 2 teaspoons of honey, ½ teaspoon of vanilla, and a pinch of salt. Stir to combine well.

Divide the mascarpone among the warm pear halves and serve.

Per Serving

calories: 308 | fat: 16.0g | protein: 4.1g | carbs: 42.7g

Mixed Berry Crisp

Prep time: 15 minutes | **Cook time:** 30 minutes | **Serves:**2

Ingredients:

1½ cups frozen mixed berries, thawed

1 tablespoon coconut sugar

1 tablespoon almond butter

¼ cup oats

¼ cup pecans

Directions:

Preheat the oven to 350ºF (180ºC). Divide the mixed berries between 2 ramekins Place the coconut sugar, almond butter, oats, and pecans in a food processor, and pulse a few times, until the mixture resembles damp sand.

Divide the crumble topping over the mixed berries.

Put the ramekins on a sheet pan and bake for 30 minutes, or until the top is golden and the berries are bubbling.

Serve warm.

Per Serving

calories: 268 | fat: 17.0g | protein: 4.1g | carbs: 26.8g

Orange Mug Cakes

Prep time: 10 minutes | **Cook time:** 3 minutes | **Serves:**2

Ingredients:

6 tablespoons flour

2 tablespoons sugar

1 teaspoon orange zest

½ teaspoon baking powder

Pinch salt

1 egg

2 tablespoons olive oil

2 tablespoons unsweetened almond milk

2 tablespoons freshly squeezed orange juice

½ teaspoon orange extract

½ teaspoon vanilla extract

Directions:

Combine the flour, sugar, orange zest, baking powder, and salt in a small bowl. In another bowl, whisk together the egg, olive oil, milk, orange juice, orange extract, and vanilla extract. Add the dry ingredients to the wet ingredients and stir to incorporate. The batter will be thick.

Divide the mixture into two small mugs. Microwave each mug separately. The small ones should take about 60 seconds, and one large mug should take about 90 seconds, but microwaves can vary. Cool for 5 minutes before serving.

Per Serving calories: 303 | fat: 16.9g | protein: 6.0g | carbs: 32.5g

Fruit and Nut Chocolate Bark

Prep time: 15 minutes | **Cook time:** 2 minutes | **Serves:**2

Ingredients:

2 tablespoons chopped nuts

3 ounces (85 g) dark chocolate chips

¼ cup chopped dried fruit (blueberries, apricots, figs, prunes, or any combination of those)

Directions:

Line a sheet pan with parchment paper and set aside.

Add the nuts to a skillet over medium-high heat and toast for 60 seconds, or just fragrant. Set aside to cool.

Put the chocolate chips in a microwave-safe glass bowl and microwave on High for 1 minute.

Stir the chocolate and allow any unmelted chips to warm and melt. If desired, heat for an additional 20 to 30 seconds. Transfer the chocolate to the prepared sheet pan. Scatter the dried fruit and toasted nuts over the chocolate evenly and gently pat in so they stick.

Place the sheet pan in the refrigerator for at least 1 hour to let the chocolate harden. When ready, break into pieces and serve.

Per Serving calories: 285 | fat: 16.1g | protein: 4.0g | carbs: 38.7g

Crunchy Almond Cookies

Prep time: 5 minutes | **Cook time:** 5 to 7 minutes | **Serves:**4

Ingredients:to 6

½ cup sugar

8 tablespoons almond butter

1 large egg

1½ cups all-purpose flour

1 cup ground almonds

Directions:

Preheat the oven to 375ºF (190ºC). Line a baking sheet with parchment paper.

Using a mixer, whisk together the sugar and butter. Add the egg and mix until combined. Alternately add the flour and ground almonds, ½ cup at a time, while the mixer is on slow.

Drop 1 tablespoon of the dough on the prepared baking sheet, keeping the cookies at least 2 inches apart.

Put the baking sheet in the oven and bake for about 5 to 7 minutes, or until the cookies start to turn brown around the edges.

Let cool for 5 minutes before serving.

Per Serving

calories: 604 | fat: 36.0g | protein: 11.0g | carbs: 63.0g

Walnut and Date Balls

Prep time: 5 minutes | **Cook time:** 8 to 10 minutes | **Serves:** 6 to 8

Ingredients:

1 cup walnuts

1 cup unsweetened shredded coconut

14 medjool dates, pitted

8 tablespoons almond butter

Directions:

Preheat the oven to 350ºF (180ºC).

Put the walnuts on a baking sheet and toast in the oven for 5 minutes.

Put the shredded coconut on a clean baking sheet. Toast for about 3 to 5 minutes, or until it turns golden brown. Once done, remove it from the oven and put it in a shallow bowl.

In a food processor, process the toasted walnuts until they have a medium chop. Transfer the chopped walnuts into a medium bowl.

Add the dates and butter to the food processor and blend until the dates become a thick paste. Pour the chopped walnuts into the food processor with the dates and pulse just until the mixture is combined, about 5 to 7 pulses.

Remove the mixture from the food processor and scrape it into a large bowl.

To make the balls, spoon 1 to 2 tablespoons of the date mixture into the palm of your hand and roll around between your hands until you form a ball. Put the ball on a clean, lined baking sheet. Repeat until all the mixture is formed into balls.

Roll each ball in the toasted coconut until the outside of the ball is coated. Put the ball back on the baking sheet and repeat.

Put all the balls into the refrigerator for 20 minutes before serving. Store any leftovers in the refrigerator in an airtight container.

Per Serving

calories: 489 | fat: 35.0g | protein: 5.0g | carbs: 48.0g

Apple and Berries Ambrosia

Prep time: 15 minutes | **Cook time:** 0 minutes | **Serves:** 4

Ingredients:

2 cups unsweetened coconut milk, chilled

2 tablespoons raw honey

1 apple, peeled, cored, and chopped

2 cups fresh raspberries

2 cups fresh blueberries

Directions:

Spoon the chilled milk in a large bowl, then mix in the honey. Stir to mix well.

Then mix in the remaining ingredients. Stir to coat the fruits well and serve immediately.

Per Serving calories: 386 fat: 21.1g protein: 4.2g carbs: 45.9g

Banana, Cranberry, and Oat Bars

Prep time: 15 mins | **Cook time:** 40 mins | Makes 16 bars

Ingredients:

2 tablespoon extra-virgin olive oil

2 medium ripe bananas, mashed

½ cup almond butter

½ cup maple syrup

⅓ cup dried cranberries

1½ cups old-fashioned rolled oats

¼ cup oat flour

¼ cup ground flaxseed

¼ teaspoon ground cloves

½ cup shredded coconut

½ teaspoon ground cinnamon

1 teaspoon vanilla extract

Directions:

Preheat the oven to 400ºF (205ºC). Line a 8-inch square pan with parchment paper, then grease with olive oil.

Combine the mashed bananas, almond butter, and maple syrup in a bowl. Stir to mix well.

Mix in the remaining ingredients and stir to mix well until thick and sticky.

Spread the mixture evenly on the square pan with a spatula, then bake in the preheated oven for 40 minutes or until a toothpick inserted in the center comes out clean.

Remove them from the oven and slice into 16 bars to serve.

Per Serving

calories: 145 | fat: 7.2g | protein: 3.1g | carbs: 18.9g

Chocolate and Avocado Mousse

Prep time: 40 minutes | **Cook time:** 5 mins | **Serves:** 4 to 6

Ingredients:

8 ounces (227 g) dark chocolate (60% cocoa or higher), chopped

¼ cup unsweetened coconut milk

2 ripe avocados, deseeded

¼ cup raw honey

Sea salt, to taste

2 tablespoons coconut oil

Directions:

Put the chocolate in a saucepan. Pour in the coconut milk and add the coconut oil.

Cook for 3 minutes or until the chocolate and coconut oil melt. Stir constantly.

Put the avocado in a food processor, then drizzle with honey and melted chocolate. Pulse to combine until smooth.

Pour the mixture in a serving bowl, then sprinkle with salt. Refrigerate to chill for 30 minutes and serve.

Per Serving

calories: 654 | fat: 46.8g | protein: 7.2g | carbs: 55.9g

Berry and Rhubarb Cobbler

Prep time: 15 minutes | **Cook time:** 35 minutes | **Serves:**8

Ingredients:

Cobbler:
1 cup fresh raspberries
2 cups fresh blueberries
1 cup sliced (½-inch) rhubarb pieces
1 tablespoon arrowroot powder
¼ cup unsweetened apple juice
¼ cup raw honey

Topping:
1 cup almond flour
1 tablespoon arrowroot powder
½ cup shredded coconut
¼ cup raw honey
½ cup coconut oil
2 tablespoons melted coconut oil

Directions:

Make the Cobbler

Preheat the oven to 350ºF (180ºC). Grease a baking dish with melted coconut oil.

Combine the ingredients for the cobbler in a large bowl. Stir to mix well.

Spread the mixture in the single layer on the baking dish. Set aside.

Make the Topping

Combine the almond flour, arrowroot powder, and coconut in a bowl. Stir to mix well.

Fold in the honey and coconut oil. Stir with a fork until the mixture crumbled.

Spread the topping over the cobbler, then bake in the preheated oven for 35 minutes or until frothy and golden brown.

Serve immediately.

Per Serving

calories: 305 | fat: 22.1g | protein: 3.2g | carbs: 29.8g

Chocolate, Almond, and Cherry Clusters

Prep time: 15 mins | **Cook time:** 3 mins | Makes 10 clusters

Ingredients:

1 cup dark chocolate (60% cocoa or higher), chopped
1 tablespoon coconut oil
½ cup dried cherries
1 cup roasted salted almonds

Directions:

Line a baking sheet with parchment paper.

Melt the chocolate and coconut oil in a saucepan for 3 minutes. Stir constantly.

Turn off the heat and mix in the cherries and almonds.

Drop the mixture on the baking sheet with a spoon. Place the sheet in the refrigerator and chill for at least 1 hour or until firm.

Serve chilled.

Per Serving

calories: 197 | fat: 13.2g | protein: 4.1g | carbs: 17.8g

Citrus Cranberry and Quinoa Energy Bites

Prep time: 25 minutes | **Cook time:** 0 mins | Makes 12 bites

Ingredients:

2 tablespoons almond butter
2 tablespoons maple syrup
¾ cup cooked quinoa
1 tablespoon dried cranberries
1 tablespoon chia seeds
¼ cup ground almonds
¼ cup sesame seeds, toasted
Zest of 1 orange
½ teaspoon vanilla extract

Directions:

Line a baking sheet with parchment paper.

Combine the butter and maple syrup in a bowl. Stir to mix well.

Fold in the remaining ingredients and stir until the mixture holds together and smooth.

Divide the mixture into 12 equal parts, then shape each part into a ball.

Arrange the balls on the baking sheet, then refrigerate for at least 15 minutes.

Serve chilled.

Per Serving (1 bite)

calories: 110 | fat: 10.8g | protein: 3.1g | carbs: 4.9g

Coconut Blueberries with Brown Rice

Prep time: 55 minutes | **Cook time:** 10 minutes | **Serves:**4

Ingredients:

1 cup fresh blueberries
2 cups unsweetened coconut milk
1 teaspoon ground ginger
¼ cup maple syrup
Sea salt, to taste
2 cups cooked brown rice

Directions:

Put all the ingredients, except for the brown rice, in a pot. Stir to combine well.

Cook over medium-high heat for 7 minutes or until the blueberries are tender.

Pour in the brown rice and cook for 3 more minute or until the rice is soft. Stir constantly.

Serve immediately.

Per Serving

calories: 470 | fat: 24.8g | protein: 6.2g | carbs: 60.1g

Blueberry and Oat Crisp

Prep time: 15 minutes | **Cook time:** 20 minutes | **Serves:**4

Ingredients:

2 tablespoons coconut oil, melted, plus more for greasing

4 cups fresh blueberries

Juice of ½ lemon

2 teaspoons lemon zest

¼ cup maple syrup

1 cup gluten-free rolled oats

½ cup chopped pecans

½ teaspoon ground cinnamon

Sea salt, to taste

Directions:

Preheat the oven to 350°F (180°C). Grease a baking sheet with coconut oil.

Combine the blueberries, lemon juice and zest, and maple syrup in a bowl. Stir to mix well, then spread the mixture on the baking sheet.

Combine the remaining ingredients in a small bowl. Stir to mix well. Pour the mixture over the blueberries mixture.

Bake in the preheated oven for 20 minutes or until the oats are golden brown.

Serve immediately with spoons.

Per Serving

calories: 496 | fat: 32.9g | protein: 5.1g | carbs: 50.8g

Glazed Pears with Hazelnuts

Prep time: 10 minutes | **Cook time:** 20 minutes | **Serves:**4

Ingredients:

4 pears, peeled, cored, and quartered lengthwise

1 cup apple juice

1 tablespoon grated fresh ginger

½ cup pure maple syrup

¼ cup chopped hazelnuts

Directions:

Put the pears in a pot, then pour in the apple juice. Bring to a boil over medium-high heat, then reduce the heat to medium-low. Stir constantly.

Cover and simmer for an additional 15 minutes or until the pears are tender.

Meanwhile, combine the ginger and maple syrup in a saucepan. Bring to a boil over medium-high heat. Stir frequently. Turn off the heat and transfer the syrup to a small bowl and let sit until ready to use.

Transfer the pears in a large serving bowl with a slotted spoon, then top the pears with syrup.

Spread the hazelnuts over the pears and serve immediately.

Per Serving

calories: 287 | fat: 3.1g | protein: 2.2g | carbs: 66.9g

Lemony Blackberry Granita

Prep time: 10 minutes | **Cook time:** 0 minutes | **Serves:**4

Ingredients:

1 pound (454 g) fresh blackberries

1 teaspoon chopped fresh thyme

½ cup raw honey

½ cup water

¼ cup freshly squeezed lemon juice

Directions:

Put all the ingredients in a food processor, then pulse to purée.

Pour the mixture through a sieve into a baking dish. Discard the seeds remain in the sieve.

Put the baking dish in the freezer for 2 hours. Remove the dish from the refrigerator and stir to break any frozen parts.

Return the dish back to the freezer for an hour, then stir to break any frozen parts again.

Return the dish to the freezer for 4 hours until the granita is completely frozen.

Remove it from the freezer and mash to serve.

Per Serving

calories: 183 | fat: 1.1g | protein: 2.2g | carbs: 45.9g

Lemony Tea and Chia Pudding

Prep time: 30 minutes | **Cook time:** 0 minutes
Serves:3 to 4

Ingredients:

2 teaspoons matcha green tea powder (optional)

2 tablespoons ground chia seeds

1 to 2 dates

2 cups unsweetened coconut milk

Zest and juice of 1 lime

Directions:

Put all the ingredients in a food processor and pulse until creamy and smooth.

Pour the mixture in a bowl, then wrap in plastic. Store in the refrigerator for at least 20 minutes, then serve chilled.

Per Serving

calories: 225 | fat: 20.1g | protein: 3.2g | carbs: 5.9g:

Sweet Spiced Pumpkin Pudding

Prep time: 2 hours 10 minutes | **Cook time:** 0 minutes | **Serves:** 6

Ingredients:

1 cup pure pumpkin purée
2 cups unsweetened coconut milk
1 teaspoon ground cinnamon
¼ teaspoon ground nutmeg
½ teaspoon ground ginger
Pinch cloves
¼ cup pure maple syrup
2 tablespoons chopped pecans, for garnish

Directions:

Combine all the ingredients, except for the chopped pecans, in a large bowl. Stir to mix well.

Wrap the bowl in plastic and refrigerate for at least 2 hours.

Remove the bowl from the refrigerator and discard the plastic. Spread the pudding with pecans and serve chilled.

Per Serving

calories: 249 | fat: 21.1g | protein: 2.8g | carbs: 17.2g

Cozy Superfood Hot Chocolate

Prep time: 5 minutes | **Cook time:** 8 minutes | **Serves:** 2

Ingredients:

2 cups unsweetened almond milk
1 tablespoon avocado oil
1 tablespoon collagen protein powder
2 teaspoons coconut sugar
2 tablespoons cocoa powder
1 teaspoon ground cinnamon
1 teaspoon ground ginger
1 teaspoon vanilla extract
½ teaspoon ground turmeric
Dash salt
Dash cayenne pepper (optional)

Directions:

In a small saucepan over medium heat, warm the almond milk and avocado oil for about 7 minutes, stirring frequently.

Fold in the protein powder, which will only properly dissolve in a heated liquid.

Stir in the coconut sugar and cocoa powder until melted and dissolved.

Carefully transfer the warm liquid into a blender, along with the cinnamon, ginger, vanilla, turmeric, salt, and cayenne pepper (if desired). Blend for 15 seconds until frothy.

Serve immediately.

Per Serving

calories: 217 | fat: 11.0g | protein: 11.2g | carbs: 14.8g

Mango and Coconut Frozen Pie

Prep time: 1 hour 10 minutes | **Cook time:** 0 minutes | **Serves:** 8

Ingredients:

Crust:
1 cup cashews
½ cup rolled oats
1 cup soft pitted dates
1 cup unsweetened coconut milk

Filling:
2 large mangoes, peeled and chopped
½ cup unsweetened shredded coconut
½ cup water

Directions:

Combine the ingredients for the crust in a food processor. Pulse to combine well.

Pour the mixture in an 8-inch springform pan, then press to coat the bottom. Set aside.

Combine the ingredients for the filling in the food processor, then pulse to purée until smooth.

Pour the filling over the crust, then use a spatula to spread the filling evenly. Put the pan in the freeze for 30 minutes.

Remove the pan from the freezer and allow to sit for 15 minutes under room temperature before serving.

Per Serving (1 slice)

calories: 426 | fat: 28.2g | protein: 8.1g | carbs: 14.9g

Mini Nuts and Fruits Crumble

Prep time: 15 minutes | **Cook time:** 15 minutes | **Serves:** 6

Ingredients:

Topping:
¼ cup coarsely chopped hazelnuts
1 cup coarsely chopped walnuts
1 teaspoon ground cinnamon
Sea salt, to taste
1 tablespoon melted coconut oil

Filling:
6 fresh figs, quartered
2 nectarines, pitted and sliced
1 cup fresh blueberries
2 teaspoons lemon zest
½ cup raw honey
1 teaspoon vanilla extract

Directions:
Make the Topping:
1. Combine the ingredients for the topping in a bowl. Stir to mix well. Set aside until ready to use.

Make the Filling:

Preheat the oven to 375°F (190°C).

Combine the ingredients for the fillings in a bowl. Stir to mix well.

Divide the filling in six ramekins, then divide and top with nut topping.

Bake in the preheated oven for 15 minutes or until the topping is lightly browned and the filling is frothy.

Serve immediately.

Per Serving

calories: 336 | fat: 18.8g | protein: 6.3g | carbs: 41.9g

Chapter 10
Sauces, Dips, and Dressings

Creamy Cucumber Dip

Prep time: 10 minutes | **Cook time:** 0 minutes | **Serves:** 6

Ingredients:

1 medium cucumber, peeled and grated

¼ teaspoon salt

1 cup plain Greek yogurt

2 garlic cloves, minced

1 tablespoon extra-virgin olive oil

1 tablespoon freshly squeezed lemon juice

¼ teaspoon freshly ground black pepper

Directions:

Place the grated cucumber in a colander set over a bowl and season with salt. Allow the cucumber to stand for 10 minutes. Using your hands, squeeze out as much liquid from the cucumber as possible. Transfer the grated cucumber to a medium bowl.

Add the yogurt, garlic, olive oil, lemon juice, and pepper to the bowl and stir until well blended.

Cover the bowl with plastic wrap and refrigerate for at least 2 hours to blend the flavors.

Serve chilled.

Per Serving (¼ cup)

calories: 47 | fat: 2.8g | protein: 4.2g | carbs: 2.7g

Italian Dressing

Prep time: 5 minutes | **Cook time:** 0 minutes | **Serves:** 12

Ingredients:

½ cup extra-virgin olive oil

¼ cup red wine vinegar

1 teaspoon dried Italian seasoning

1 teaspoon Dijon mustard

¼ teaspoon salt

¼ teaspoon freshly ground black pepper

1 garlic clove, minced

Directions:

Place all the ingredients in a mason jar and cover. Shake vigorously for 1 minute until completely mixed.

Store in the refrigerator for up to 1 week.

Per Serving (1 tablespoon)

calories: 80 | fat: 8.6g | protein: 0g | carbs: 0g

Ranch-Style Cauliflower Dressing

Prep time: 10 minutes | **Cook time:** 0 minutes | **Serves:** 8

Ingredients:

2 cups frozen cauliflower, thawed

½ cup unsweetened plain almond milk

2 tablespoons apple cider vinegar

2 tablespoons extra-virgin olive oil

1 garlic clove, peeled

2 teaspoons finely chopped fresh parsley

2 teaspoons finely chopped scallions (both white and green parts)

1 teaspoon finely chopped fresh dill

½ teaspoon onion powder

½ teaspoon Dijon mustard

½ teaspoon salt

¼ teaspoon freshly ground black pepper

Directions:

Place all the ingredients in a blender and pulse until creamy and smooth.

Serve immediately, or transfer to an airtight container to refrigerate for up to 3 days.

Per Serving (2 tablespoons)

calories: 41 | fat: 3.6g | protein: 1.0g | carbs: 1.9g

Asian-Inspired Vinaigrette

Prep time: 5 minutes | **Cook time:** 0 minutes | **Serves:** 2

Ingredients:

¼ cup extra-virgin olive oil

3 tablespoons apple cider vinegar

1 garlic clove, minced

1 tablespoon peeled and grated fresh ginger

1 tablespoon chopped fresh cilantro

1 tablespoon freshly squeezed lime juice

½ teaspoon sriracha

Directions:

Add all the ingredients in a small bowl and stir to mix well.

Serve immediately, or store covered in the refrigerator and shake before using.

Per Serving

calories: 251 | fat: 26.8g | protein: 0g | carbs: 1.8g

Not Old Bay Seasoning

Prep time: 10 minutes | **Cook time:** 0 minutes
Makes about ½ cup

Ingredients:

3 tablespoons sweet paprika
1 tablespoon mustard seeds
2 tablespoons celery seeds
2 teaspoons freshly ground
black pepper
1½ teaspoons cayenne
pepper

1 teaspoon red pepper
flakes
½ teaspoon ground ginger
½ teaspoon ground nutmeg
½ teaspoon ground
cinnamon
¼ teaspoon ground cloves

Directions:

Mix together all the ingredients in an airtight container until well combined.

You can store it in a cool, dry, and dark place for up to 3 months.

Per Serving (1 tablespoon)

calories: 26 | fat: 1.9g | protein: 1.1g | carbs: 3.6g

Tzatziki

Prep time: 15 minutes | **Cook time:** 0 mins | **Serves:** 4 to 6

Ingredients:

½ English cucumber, finely
chopped
1 teaspoon salt, divided
1 cup plain Greek yogurt
8 tablespoons olive oil,
divided

1 garlic clove, finely minced
1 to 2 tablespoons chopped
fresh dill
1 teaspoon red wine vinegar
½ teaspoon freshly ground
black pepper

Directions:

In a food processor, pulse the cucumber until puréed. Place the cucumber on several layers of paper towels lining the bottom of a colander and sprinkle with ½ teaspoon of salt. Allow to drain for 10 to 15 minutes. Using your hands, squeeze out any remaining liquid.

In a medium bowl, whisk together the cucumber, yogurt, 6 tablespoons of olive oil, garlic, dill, vinegar, remaining ½ teaspoon of salt, and pepper until very smooth.

Drizzle with the remaining 2 tablespoons of olive oil. Serve immediately or refrigerate until ready to serve.

Per Serving calories: 286 | fat: 29.0g | protein: 3.0g

Harissa Sauce

Prep time: 10 minutes | **Cook time:** 20 minutes
Makes 3 to 4 cups

Ingredients:

1 large red bell pepper,
deseeded, cored, and cut
into chunks
1 yellow onion, cut into
thick rings
4 garlic cloves, peeled
1 cup vegetable broth

2 tablespoons tomato paste
1 tablespoon tamari
1 teaspoon ground cumin
1 tablespoon Hungarian
paprika

Directions:

Preheat the oven to 450°F (235°C). Line a baking sheet with parchment paper.

Place the bell pepper on the prepared baking sheet, flesh-side up, and space out the onion and garlic around the pepper.

Roast in the preheated oven for 20 minutes. Transfer to a blender.

Add the vegetable broth, tomato paste, tamari, cumin, and paprika. Purée until smooth. Served chilled or warm.

Per Serving (¼ cup)

calories: 15 | fat: 1.0g | protein: 1.0g | carbs: 3.0g

Pineapple Salsa

Prep time: 10 minutes | **Cook time:** 0 mins | **Serves:** 6 to 8

Ingredients:

1 pound (454 g) fresh or
thawed frozen pineapple,
finely diced, juices reserved
1 white or red onion, finely
diced

1 bunch cilantro or mint,
leaves only, chopped
1 jalapeño, minced
(optional)
Salt, to taste

Directions:

Stir together the pineapple with its juice, onion, cilantro, and jalapeño (if desired) in a medium bowl. Season with salt to taste and serve.

The salsa can be refrigerated in an airtight container for up to 2 days.

Per Serving

calories: 55 | fat: 0.1g | protein: 0.9g | carbs: 12.7g

Garlic Lemon-Tahini Dressing

Prep time: 5 minutes | **Cook time:** 0 mins | **Serves:** 8 to 10

Ingredients:

½ cup tahini
¼ cup extra-virgin olive oil
¼ cup freshly squeezed lemon juice

1 garlic clove, finely minced
2 teaspoons salt

Directions:

In a glass mason jar with a lid, combine the tahini, olive oil, lemon juice, garlic, and salt. Cover and shake well until combined and creamy.

Store in the refrigerator for up to 2 weeks.

Per Serving

calories: 121 | fat: 12.0g | protein: 2.0g | carbs: 3.0g

Creamy Grapefruit and Tarragon Dressing

Prep time: 5 minutes | **Cook time:** 0 mins | **Serves:** 4 to 6

Ingredients:

½ cup avocado oil mayonnaise
2 tablespoons Dijon mustard
1 teaspoon dried tarragon or 1 tablespoon chopped fresh tarragon

½ teaspoon salt
Zest and juice of ½ grapefruit
¼ teaspoon freshly ground black pepper
1 to 2 tablespoons water (optional)

Directions:

In a large mason jar with a lid, combine the mayonnaise, Dijon, tarragon, grapefruit zest and juice, salt, and pepper and whisk well with a fork until smooth and creamy. If a thinner dressing is preferred, thin out with water.

Serve immediately or refrigerate until ready to serve.

Per Serving

calories: 86 | fat: 7.0g | protein: 1.0g | carbs: 6.0g

Vinaigrette

Prep time: 5 minutes | **Cook time:** 0 minutes | Makes 1 cup

Ingredients:

½ cup extra-virgin olive oil
¼ cup red wine vinegar
1 tablespoon Dijon mustard
1 teaspoon dried rosemary

½ teaspoon salt
½ teaspoon freshly ground black pepper

Directions:

In a cup or a mansion jar with a lid, combine the olive oil, vinegar, mustard, rosemary, salt, and pepper and shake until well combined.

Serve chilled or at room temperature.

Per Serving

calories: 124 | fat: 14.0g | protein: 0g | carbs: 1.0g

Ginger Teriyaki Sauce

Prep time: 5 minutes | **Cook time:** 0 minutes | **Serves:** 2

Ingredients:

¼ cup pineapple juice
¼ cup low-sodium soy sauce
2 tablespoons packed coconut sugar

1 tablespoon grated fresh ginger
1 tablespoon arrowroot powder or cornstarch
1 teaspoon garlic powder

Directions:

Whisk the pineapple juice, soy sauce, coconut sugar, ginger, arrowroot powder, and garlic powder together in a small bowl.

Store in an airtight container in the fridge for up to 5 days.

Per Serving

calories: 37 | fat: 0.1g | protein: 1.1g | carbs: 12.0g

Aioli

Prep time: 5 minutes | **Cook time:** 0 mins | Makes ½ cup

Ingredients:

½ cup plain Greek yogurt
2 teaspoons Dijon mustard

½ teaspoon hot sauce
¼ teaspoon raw honey
Pinch salt

Directions:

In a small bowl, whisk together the yogurt, mustard, hot sauce, honey, and salt.

Serve immediately or refrigerate in an airtight container for up to 3 days.

Per Serving

calories: 47 | fat: 2.5g | protein: 2.1g | carbs: 3.5g

Parsley Vinaigrette

Prep time: 5 minutes | **Cook time:** 0 minutes | Makes about ½ cup

Ingredients:

½ cup lightly packed fresh parsley, finely chopped
⅓ cup extra-virgin olive oil

3 tablespoons red wine vinegar
1 garlic clove, minced
¼ teaspoon salt, plus additional as needed

Directions:

Place all the ingredients in a mason jar and cover. Shake vigorously for 1 minute until completely mixed.

Taste and add additional salt as needed.

Serve immediately or serve chilled.

Per Serving (1 tablespoon)

calories: 92 | fat: 10.9g | protein: 0g | carbs: 0g

Hot Pepper Sauce

Prep time: 10 minutes | **Cook time:** 20 mins | Makes 4 cups

Ingredients:

1 red hot fresh chiles, deseeded
2 dried chiles
2 garlic cloves, peeled
½ small yellow onion, roughly chopped
2 cups water
2 cups white vinegar

Directions:

Place all the ingredients except the vinegar in a medium saucepan over medium heat. Allow to simmer for 20 minutes until softened. Transfer the mixture to a food processor or blender. Stir in the vinegar and pulse until very smooth. Serve immediately or transfer to a sealed container and refrigerate for up to 3 months.

Per Serving (2 tablespoons)

calories: 20 | fat: 1.2g | protein: 0.6g | carbs: 4.4g

Lemon-Tahini Sauce

Prep time: 10 minutes | **Cook time:** 0 mins | Makes 1 cup

Ingredients:

½ cup tahini
1 garlic clove, minced
Juice and zest of 1 lemon
½ teaspoon salt, plus more as needed
½ cup warm water, plus more as needed

Directions:

Combine the tahini and garlic in a small bowl. Add the lemon juice and zest and salt to the bowl and stir to mix well. Fold in the warm water and whisk until well combined and creamy. Feel free to add more warm water if you like a thinner consistency. Taste and add more salt as needed. Store the sauce in a sealed container in the refrigerator for up to 5 days.

Per Serving (¼ cup)

calories: 179 | fat: 15.5g | protein: 5.1g | carbs: 6.8g

Peanut Sauce with Honey

Prep time: 5 minutes | **Cook time:** 0 minutes | **Serves:** 4

Ingredients:

¼ cup peanut butter
1 tablespoon peeled and grated fresh ginger
1 tablespoon honey
1 tablespoon low-sodium soy sauce
1 garlic clove, minced
Juice of 1 lime
Pinch red pepper flakes

Directions:

Whisk together all the ingredients in a small bowl until well incorporated. Transfer to an airtight container and refrigerate for up to 5 days.

Per Serving

calories: 117 | fat: 7.6g | protein: 4.1g | carbs: 8.8g

Peri-Peri Sauce

Prep time: 10 minutes | **Cook time:** 5 minutes | **Serves:** 4

Ingredients:

1 tomato, chopped
1 red onion, chopped
1 red bell pepper, deseeded and chopped
1 red chile, deseeded and chopped
4 garlic cloves, minced
2 tablespoons extra-virgin olive oil
Juice of 1 lemon
1 tablespoon dried oregano
1 tablespoon smoked paprika
1 teaspoon sea salt

Directions:

Process all the ingredients in a food processor or a blender until smooth. Transfer the mixture to a small saucepan over medium-high heat and bring to a boil, stirring often.

Reduce the heat to medium and allow to simmer for 5 minutes until heated through. You can store the sauce in an airtight container in the refrigerator for up to 5 days.

Per Serving

calories: 98 | fat: 6.5g | protein: 1.0g | carbs: 7.8g

Cilantro-Tomato Salsa

Prep time: 10 minutes | **Cook time:** 0 minutes | **Serves:** 6

Ingredients:

2 or 3 medium, ripe tomatoes, diced
1 serrano pepper, seeded and minced
½ red onion, minced
¼ cup minced fresh cilantro
Juice of 1 lime
¼ teaspoon salt, plus more as needed

Directions:

Place the tomatoes, serrano pepper, onion, cilantro, lime juice, and salt in a small bowl and mix well. Taste and add additional salt, if needed. Store in an airtight container in the refrigerator for up to 3 days.

Per Serving (¼ cup)

calories: 17 | fat: 0g | protein: 1.0g | carbs: 3.9g

Cheesy Pea Pesto

Prep time: 5 minutes | **Cook time:** 0 minutes | **Serves:** 4

Ingredients:

½ cup fresh green peas
½ cup grated Parmesan cheese
¼ cup extra-virgin olive oil
¼ cup pine nuts
¼ cup fresh basil leaves
2 garlic cloves, minced
¼ teaspoon sea salt

Directions:

Add all the ingredients to a food processor or blender and pulse until the nuts are chopped finely. Transfer to an airtight container and refrigerate for up to 2 days. You can also store it in ice cube trays in the freezer for up to 6 months.

Per Serving

calories: 247 | fat: 22.8g | protein: 7.1g | carbs: 4.8g

Guacamole

Prep time: 10 minutes | **Cook time:** 0 minutes | **Serves:**6

Ingredients:

2 large avocados
¼ white onion, finely diced
1 small, firm tomato, finely diced
¼ cup finely chopped fresh cilantro

2 tablespoons freshly squeezed lime juice
¼ teaspoon salt
Freshly ground black pepper, to taste

Directions:

Slice the avocados in half and remove the pits. Using a large spoon to scoop out the flesh and add to a medium bowl.

Mash the avocado flesh with the back of a fork, or until a uniform consistency is achieved. Add the onion, tomato, cilantro, lime juice, salt, and pepper to the bowl and stir to combine.

Serve immediately, or transfer to an airtight container and refrigerate until chilled.

Per Serving (¼ cup)

calories: 81 | fat: 6.8g | protein: 1.1g | carbs: 5.7g

Lentil-Tahini Dip

Prep time: 10 minutes | **Cook time:** 15 mins | **Makes 3 cups**

Ingredients:

1 cup dried green or brown lentils, rinsed
2½ cups water, divided

⅓ cup tahini
1 garlic clove
½ teaspoon salt, plus more as needed

Directions:

Add the lentils and 2 cups of water to a medium saucepan and bring to a boil over high heat.

Once it starts to boil, reduce the heat to low, and then cook for 14 minutes, stirring occasionally, or the lentils become tender but still hold their shape. You can drain any excess liquid.

Transfer the lentils to a food processor, along with the remaining water, tahini, garlic, and salt and process until smooth and creamy.

Taste and adjust the seasoning if needed. Serve immediately.

Per Serving (¼ cup)

calories: 100 | fat: 3.9g | protein: 5.1g | carbs: 10.7g

Lemon-Dill Cashew Dip

Prep time: 10 minutes | **Cook time:** 0 mins | **Makes 1 cup**

Ingredients:

¾ cup cashews, soaked in water for at least 4 hours and drained well
¼ cup water

Juice and zest of 1 lemon
2 tablespoons chopped fresh dill
¼ teaspoon salt, plus more as needed

Directions:

Put the cashews, water, lemon juice and zest in a blender and blend until smooth.

Add the dill and salt to the blender and blend again.

Taste and adjust the seasoning, if needed.

Transfer to an airtight container and refrigerate for at least 1 hour to blend the flavors.

Serve chilled.

Per Serving (1 tablespoon)

calories: 37 | fat: 2.9g | protein: 1.1g | carbs: 1.9g

Homemade Blackened Seasoning

Prep time: 10 minutes | **Cook time:** 0 minutes | **Makes about ½ cup**

Ingredients:

2 tablespoons smoked paprika
2 tablespoons garlic powder
2 tablespoons onion powder
1 tablespoon sweet paprika

1 teaspoon dried dill
1 teaspoon freshly ground black pepper
½ teaspoon ground mustard
¼ teaspoon celery seeds

Directions:

Add all the ingredients to a small bowl and mix well.

Serve immediately, or transfer to an airtight container and store in a cool, dry and dark place for up to 3 months.

Per Serving (1 tablespoon)

calories: 22 | fat: 0.9g | protein: 1.0g | carbs: 4.7g

Basil Pesto

Prep time: 5 minutes | **Cook time:** 0 minutes | Makes 1 cup

Ingredients:

2 cups packed fresh basil leaves

3 garlic cloves, peeled

½ cup freshly grated Parmesan cheese

½ cup extra-virgin olive oil

⅓ cup pine nuts

Kosher salt and freshly ground black pepper, to taste

Directions:

Place all the ingredients, except for the salt and pepper, in a food processor. Pulse a few times until smoothly pur é ed. Season with salt and pepper to taste.

Store in an airtight container in the fridge for up to 2 weeks.

Per Serving

calories: 100 | fat: 10.2g | protein: 2.2g | carbs: 1.2g

Orange-Garlic Dressing

Prep time: 5 minutes | **Cook time:** 0 minutes | **Serves:**2

Ingredients:

¼ cup extra-virgin olive oil

1 orange, zested

2 tablespoons freshly squeezed orange juice

¾ teaspoon za'atar seasoning

1 teaspoon garlic powder

½ teaspoon salt

¼ teaspoon Dijon mustard

Freshly ground black pepper, to taste

Directions:

Whisk together all ingredients in a bowl until well combined. Serve immediately or refrigerate until ready to serve.

Per Serving

calories: 287 | fat: 26.7g | protein: 1.2g | carbs: 12.0g

Creamy Cider Yogurt Dressing

Prep time: 5 minutes | **Cook time:** 0 minutes | **Serves:**2

Ingredients:

1 cup plain, unsweetened, full-fat Greek yogurt

½ cup extra-virgin olive oil

½ lemon, juiced

1 tablespoon chopped fresh oregano

1 tablespoon apple cider vinegar

½ teaspoon dried parsley

½ teaspoon kosher salt

¼ teaspoon garlic powder

¼ teaspoon freshly ground black pepper

Directions:

In a large bowl, whisk all ingredients to combine.

Serve chilled or at room temperature.

Per Serving

calories: 407 | fat: 40.7g | protein: 8.3g | carbs: 3.8g

Basic French Vinaigrette

Prep time: 5 minutes | **Cook time:** 0 minutes | **Serves:**2

Ingredients:

3 tablespoons apple cider vinegar

2 tablespoons minced shallot (or 1 tablespoon minced red onion)

1 tablespoon balsamic vinegar

½ teaspoon dried thyme

1 teaspoon Dijon mustard

¼ cup olive oil

Salt and black pepper, to taste

Directions:

Stir together the apple cider vinegar, shallot, and balsamic vinegar in a medium jar with a tight-fitting lid. Allow to sit for 5 minutes.

Stir in the mustard and thyme. Whisk in the olive oil in a slow, steady stream and season to taste with salt and pepper.

Store in an airtight container in the fridge for up to 5 days.

Per Serving

calories: 256 | fat: 27.1g | protein: 0.3g | carbs: 3.4g

Chapter 11
DINNER

Salad Skewers (Greek)

Preparation Time: 10 minutes **Cooking Time:** 0 minutes
Servings: 1

Ingredients:

1 wooden skewers, soaked in water for 30 minutes before use
1 yellow pepper, cut into eight squares.
For the dressing:
1 tbsp. extra-virgin olive oil.
Juice of ½ lemon.
3.5-oz. (about 10cm) cucumber, cut into four slices and halved. oz. feta, cut into 8 cubes.
A right amount of salt and freshly ground black pepper

8 cherry tomatoes.
. 8 large black olives.
. Few leaves oregano,chppd
½ red onion, chopped in half and separated into eight pieces.
1 tsp. balsamic vinegar.
Few leaves basil, finely chopped (or ½ tsp dried mixed herbs to replace basil and oregano).
½ clove garlic, peeled and crushed

Directions:

Thread each skewer in the order with salad olive, tomato, yellow pepper, red onion, cucumber, feta, basil, olive, yellow pepper, red ointment, cucumber, feta. Put all the ingredients of the dressing in a small bowl and blend well together. Pour over the spoils.

Per Serving

Calories: 315 g. Fat: 30 g. Protein: 56 g. Carbs: 45 g.
Cholesterol: 230 mg. Sugar: 0 g.

Creamy Strawberry & Cherry Smoothie (Greek)

Prep time: 10 minutes **Cooking Time:** 15 mins **Servings:** 1

Ingredients:

1 ½ oz. strawberries.
1 tbsp. plain full-fat yogurt..

oz. frozen pitted cherries.
oz. unsweetened soya milk

Directions:

Place the ingredients into a blender then process until smooth. Serve and enjoy.

Per Serving

Calories: 132 g. Fat: 30 g. Protein: 56 g. Carbs: 45 g.
Cholesterol: 230 mg. Sugar: 0 g.

Italian Style Ground Beef (Italian)

Preparation Time: 10 minutes **Cooking Time:** 20 minutes
Servings: 4

Ingredients:

2 lbs. ground beef
Salt
3 tbsp olive oil
1/2 tsp dried sage
2 tsp thyme

eggs, lightly beaten
1/4 tsp dried basil
1 1/2 tsp dried parsley
1 tsp oregano
1 tsp rosemary Pepper

Directions:

Pour 1 1/2 cups of water into the instant pot then place the trivet in the pool.

Spray loaf pan with cooking spray.Add all ingredients into the mixing bowl and mix until well combined.

Transfer meat mixture into the prepared loaf pan and place loaf pan on top of the trivet in the pot.

Seal pot with lid and cook on high for 35 minutes. Once done, allow to release pressure naturally for 10 minutes then release remaining using quick release. Remove lid. Serve and enjoy.

Per Serving

Calories 365 Fat 18 Sugar 0.1 g Protein 47.8 g

Turkey With Cauliflower Couscous (Italian)

Preparation Time: 20 minutes **Cooking Time:** 50 minutes
Servings: 1

Ingredients:

3 oz. turkey.
1 tsp. fresh ginger.
1 pepper Bird's Eye.
1 clove of garlic.
oz. dried tomatoes.
0.3-oz. parsley.
¼ fresh lemon juice.

1- oz. cauliflower.
3 tbsps. extra virgin olive oil.
2 tsps. turmeric.
Dried sage to taste.
1 tbsp. capers.
2 oz. red onion.

Directions:

Blend the raw cauliflower tops and cook them in a tsp. of extra virgin olive oil, garlic, red onion, chili pepper, ginger, and a tsp. of turmeric.

Leave to flavor on the fire for a minute, then add the chopped sun-dried tomatoes and 5 g of parsley. Season the turkey slice with a tsp. of extra virgin olive oil, the dried sage, and cook it in another tsp. of extra virgin olive oil. Once ready, season with a tbsp. of capers, ¼ of lemon juice, 5 g of parsley, a tbsp. of water and add the cauliflower.

Per Serving

Calories: 120 g. Fat: 10 g. Protein: 56 g. Carbs: 45 g.
Cholesterol: 230 mg. Sugar: 0 g.

Spicy Chicken Shawarma (Greek)

Preparation Time: 15 minutes **Cooking Time:** 6 minutes
Servings: 4

Ingredients:

1 lb. chicken breast	4 (6-inch) halved pitas
½ cup plum tomato, chopped	½ cup cucumber, chopped
¼ cup red onion, chopped	5 tbsps. plain low-fat
2 tbsps. lemon juice, divided	Greek-style yogurt, divided
2 tbsps. parsley, finely	1 tbsp. Tahini
chopped	2 tbsps. extra-virgin olive oil
½ tsp. salt	½ tsp. crushed red pepper
¼ tsp. ground cumin	¼ tsp. ground ginger
1/8 tsp. ground coriander	

Directions:

Combine the parsley, salt, red pepper, ginger, cumin, coriander, 1 tbsp. yogurt, 1 tbsp. juice, and 2 cloves of garlic. Add the chicken, stir to coat. Preheat the oil in a nonstick pan over medium-high heat. Add the chicken mixture to the pan and cook for 6 minutes.

In the meantime, combine the remaining 1 tbsp. lemon juice, the remaining ¼ cup of yogurt, the remaining 1 clove of garlic, and the tahini, mixing well. Put 1 ½ tsp. the tahini mixture inside each half of the pita, divide the chicken between the pita halves. Fill each half of the pita with 1 tbsp. cucumber, 1 tbsp. tomato, and 1 ½ tsp. onion.

Per Serving
Calories: 440 Protein: 37 g. Fat: 19 g.

Parmesan Honey Pork Loin Roast (Italian)

Preparation Time: 10 minutes **Cooking Time:** 5 hours
Servings: 8

Ingredients:

3 lbs. pork loin	2/3 cup grated parmesan
1 tbsp. oregano	cheese
½ cup honey	3 tbsps. soy sauce
1 tbsp. basil	2 tbsps. garlic, chopped
½ tsp. salt	2 tbsps. cornstarch
¼ cup chicken broth	Olive oil or nonstick
2 tbsps. olive oil	cooking spray

Directions:

Spray your slow cooker with olive oil or nonstick cooking spray.

Place the pork loin in the slow cooker.In a small mixing bowl, combine the cheese, honey, soy sauce, oregano, basil, garlic, olive oil, and salt. Stir with a fork to mix well, then pour over the pork loin.Cook on low for 5–6 hours.

Remove the pork loin and put it on a serving platter.

Pour the juices from the slow cooker into a small saucepan. Create a slurry by mixing the cornstarch into the chicken broth and whisking until smooth. Bring the contents of the saucepan to a boil, then whisk in the slurry and let simmer until thickened. Pour over the pork loin and serve.

Per Serving
Calories: 449 Fat: 15 g. Protein: 55 g.

Fried Whole Tilapia (Spanish)

Preparation Time: 10 minutes **Cooking Time:** 25 minutes
Servings: 2

Ingredients:

10-oz. tilapia.	5 garlic cloves, mince.
4 large onions, chopped.	1 tsp. cumin powder.
2 tbsps. red chili powder.	2 tbsps. oil.
1 tsp. coriander powder.	Black pepper to taste.
Salt to taste.	2 tbsps. soy sauce.
2 tbsps. fish sauce.	1 tsp. turmeric powder

Directions:

Take the tilapia fish and clean it well without taking off the skin. You need to fry it whole, so you have to be careful about cleaning the gut inside.

Cut few slits on the skin so the seasoning gets inside well.

Marinate the fish with fish sauce, soy sauce, red chili powder, cumin powder, turmeric powder, coriander powder, salt, and pepper.

Coat half of the onions in the same mixture too.

Let them marinate for 1 hour.

In a skillet heat the oil. Fry the fish for 8 minutes on each side.

Transfer the fish to a serving plate.

Fry the marinated onions until they become crispy.

Add the remaining raw onions on top and serve hot.

Per Serving
Calories: 368 g. Fats: 30.1 g. Carbs: 9.2 g. Proteins: 16.6 g.

Artichoke Petals Bites (Spanish)

Preparation Time: 10 minutes **Cooking Time:** 10 minutes
Servings: 8

Ingredients:

8 oz. artichoke petals,	½ cup almond flour.
boiled, drained, without salt.	4 oz. Parmesan, grated
	2 tbsps. almond butter,
	melted.

Directions:

In the mixing bowl, mix up together almond flour and grated Parmesan.

Preheat the oven to 355° F.

Dip the artichoke petals in the almond butter and then coat in the almond flour mixture.

Place them in the tray.

Transfer the tray to the preheated oven and cook the petals for 10 minutes.

Chill the cooked petal bites a little before serving.

Per Serving
Calories: 140 g. Fat: 6.4 g Carbs: 14.6 g. Protein: 10 g.

Mediterranean Pearl Couscous (Italian)

Preparation Time: 4 minutes **Cooking Time:** 10 minutes
Servings: 6

Ingredients:

For the Lemon Dill Vinaigrette: 1 large lemon, juice of Couscous Extra virgin olive oil
1 tsp garlic powder
Salt and pepper
2 cups Pearl Couscous, Israeli
1/2 English cucumber
14 oz. can good quality artichoke hearts
1/2 cup Kalamata olives

1/3 cup Extra virgin olive oil
1 tsp dill weed
1/3 cup finely chopped red onions
For the Israeli Couscous:
2 cups grape tomatoes, halved
15 oz. can chickpeas
15–20 fresh basil leaves
3 oz. fresh baby mozzarella or feta cheese

Directions:

Make the lemon-dill vinaigrette, scourge lemon juice, olive oil, dill weed, garlic powder, salt and pepper then keep aside

In a medium-sized heavy pot, heat two tbsp. of olive oil

Sauté the couscous in the olive oil briefly until golden brown, then add cups of boiling water (or follow the instructed on the package), and cook according to package.

Once done, drain in a colander, set aside in a bowl and allow to cool

In a large mixing bowl, combine the extra virgin olive oil, grape tomatoes, red onions, cucumber, chickpeas, artichoke hearts, and Kalamata olives

Then add in the couscous and the basil, mix together gently

Now, give the lemon-dill vinaigrette a quick whisk and add to the couscous salad, mix to combine

Taste and adjust salt, if needed

Distribute among the containers, store for 2-3 days

To Serve: Add in the mozzarella cheese, garnish with more fresh basil and enjoy!

Per Serving

Calories: 393 Fat: 13g Protein: 13g

Mediterranean Tuna Noodle Casserole (Italian)

Preparation Time: 15 minutes **Cooking Time:** 40 minutes
Servings: 5

Ingredients:

10 oz. dried egg noodles
Pepper to taste
1 lb. small red potatoes, sliced ¼-inch thick
¾ cup drained capers
4 sliced scallions
½ cup black olives, sliced
4 tbsps. unsalted butter
6 oz. drained olive oil-packed tuna

9 oz. halved frozen artichoke hearts
¾ cup Parmesan cheese, finely grated
½ cup flat-leaf parsley, finely chopped
¼ cup flour
2 tsps. Kosher salt, divided
2 tbsps. olive oil
2 cup milk

Directions:

Place a grill in the middle of the oven and heat to 400°F. Lightly coat a 2-quart baking tray with oil. Set aside.

Bring a large pan of salt and water to a boil. Add the noodles and cook for 2 minutes less than recommended in the package directions. Strain noodles. Season immediately with olive oil so that they don't pile up. Set aside.

Fill the pan with water again and bring to a boil. Add the potato slices and cook for 4 minutes. Drain well, then bring them back to the pan.

Heat the butter in a small saucepan over medium heat, while the noodles and potatoes are cooking. When it melts and expands, add the flour and cook for 5 minutes mixing constantly, until the sauce thickens slightly for 5 minutes. Add 1 tsp. salt and pepper to taste.

Add the egg noodles to the potato pan, then pour the sauce over it. Add and mix the remaining 1 tsp. salt, capers, olive oil, tuna, artichoke hearts, shallots, parsley, and ½ cup of Parmesan cheese. Taste and season with more salt as needed.

Transfer to the baking tray and distribute it in a uniform layer. Season with the remaining ¼ cup of Parmesan and bake, uncovered, for 25 min.

Per Serving

Calories: 457 Protein: 37 g. Fat: 21 g.

Olive Feta Beef (Greek)

Preparation Time: 10 minutes **Cooking Time:** 6 hours
Servings: 8

Ingredients:

1 lbs. beef stew meat, cut into half-inch pieces	30 oz. can tomato, diced
½ cup feta cheese, crumbled.	½ tsp. salt.
	¼ tsp. pepper.
	1 cup olives, pitted, and cut in half.

Directions:

Add all ingredients into the crockpot and stir well.

Cover and cook on high for 6 hours.

Season with pepper and salt.Stir well and serve.

Per Serving
Calories: 370 g. Fat: 12 g. Carbs: 10 g. Protein: 50 g.

African Chicken Curry (Greek)

Prep time: 10 minutes **Cooking Time:** 30 mins **Servings:** 4

Ingredients:

1 lb. whole chicken.	½ onion.
½ cup coconut milk.	½ bay leaf.
1 ½ tsps. olive oil.	½ cup peeled tomatoes.
1 clove garlic	1 tsp. curry powder.
½ lemon, juiced..	1 tsp. salt.

Directions:

Keep the skin of the chicken.

Cut your chicken into 8 pieces. It looks good when you keep the size not too small or not too big.

Discard the skin of the onion and garlic and mince the garlic and dice the onion.

Cut the tomato wedges.

Now in a pot add the olive oil and heat over medium heat.

Add the garlic and fry until it becomes brown.

Add the diced onion and caramelize it.

Add the bay leaf, and chicken pieces.

Fry the chicken pieces until they are golden.

Add the curry powder, coconut milk, and salt.

Cover and cook for 10 minutes on high heat.

Lower the heat to medium-low and add the lemon juice.

Add the tomato wedges and coconut milk.

Cook for another 10 minutes.

Serve hot with rice or tortilla.

Per Serving
Calories: 354 g. Fats: 10 g. Proteins: 18 g. Carbs: 17 g.

Prawn Arrabbiata (Greek)

Preparation Time: 10 minutes **Cooking Time:** 40 minutes
Servings: 1

Ingredients:

Raw or cooked prawns (Ideally king prawns). oz. buckwheat pasta.	1 tbsp. extra-virgin olive oil. For the arrabbiata sauce:
Red onion, finely chopped.	1 tsp. dried mixed herbs.
1.2-oz. celery, finely chopped.	1 garlic clove, finely chopped
1 Bird's eye chili, finely chopped.	1 tbsp. chopped parsley.
14-oz. tinned chopped tomatoes	1 tsp. extra-virgin olive oil.
	2 tbsps. white wine (optional).

Directions:

Firstly, fry the onion, garlic, celery, and chili over medium-low heat and dry herbs in the oil for 1–2 minutes. Switch the flame to medium, then add the wine and cook for 1 minute. Add the tomatoes and leave the sauce to cook for 20–30 minutes over medium-low heat until it has a nice rich consistency. If you feel the sauce becomes too thick, add some water.

While the sauce is cooking, boil a pan of water, and cook the pasta as directed by the packet. Drain, toss with the olive oil when cooked to your liking, and keep in the pan until needed.

Add the raw prawns to the sauce and cook for another 3–4 minutes until they have turned pink and opaque, then attach the parsley and serve. If you use cooked prawns add the parsley, bring the sauce to a boil and eat.

Add the cooked pasta to the sauce, blend well, and serve gently.

Per Serving
Calories: 185 g. Fat: 30 g. Protein: 56 g. Carbs: 45 g. Cholesterol: 230 mg. Sugar: 0 g.

Lime Chicken with Black Beans (Spanish)

Preparation Time: 15 minutes **Cooking Time:** 30 minutes
Servings: 8

Ingredients:

8 chicken thighs (boneless and skinless)	1 cup black beans
1 cup canned tomatoes	3 tablespoons lime juice
	4 teaspoons garlic powder

Directions:

Marinate the chicken in a mixture of lime juice and garlic powder.

Add the chicken to the Instant Pot. Pour the tomatoes on top of the chicken. Seal the pot. Set it to manual. Cook at high pressure for 10 minutes. Release the pressure naturally. Stir in the black beans. Press sauté to simmer until black beans are cooked.

Per Serving
Calories 370; Total Fat 11.2g; Saturated Fat 3.1g; Cholesterol 130mg

Coated Cauliflower Head (Spanish)

Preparation Time: 10 minutes **Cooking Time:** 40 minutes **Servings:** 6

Ingredients:

2-lb. cauliflower head.	1 tbsp. butter softened.
3 tbsps. olive oil.	1 tsp. salt.
1 egg, whisked.	1 tsp. dried cilantro.
1 tsp. Tahini paste.	1 tsp. dried oregano.
1 tsp. ground coriander.	

Directions:

Trim cauliflower head if needed.

Preheat oven to 350° F.

In the mixing bowl, mix up together olive oil, softened butter, ground coriander, salt, whisked egg, dried cilantro, dried oregano, and tahini paste.

Then brush the cauliflower head with this mixture generously and transfer it to the tray.

Bake the cauliflower head for 40 minutes.

Brush it with the remaining oil mixture every 10 minutes.

Per Serving
Calories: 131 g. Fat: 10.3 g. Carbs: 8.4 g. Protein: 4.1 g.

Chicken Sausage and Peppers (Spanish)

Preparation Time: 10 minutes **Cooking Time:** 20 minutes **Servings:** 6

Ingredients:

1 tbsps. extra-virgin olive oil	1 red bell pepper
6 Italian chicken sausage links	pepper Pinch red pepper flakes
1 green bell pepper	3 garlic cloves, minced
½ cup dry white wine	½ tsp. sea salt
¼ tsp. freshly ground black	1 onion

Directions:

Heat the olive oil in a skillet at medium-high heat.

Add the sausages and cook for 5–7 minutes, turning occasionally, until browned, and they reach an internal temperature of 165°F. With tongs, remove the sausage from the pan and set it aside on a platter, tented with aluminum foil to keep warm.

Put the skillet back to heat and add the onion, red bell pepper, and green bell pepper. Cook them for 5–7 minutes.

Cook the garlic for 30 seconds, stirring constantly.

Stir in the wine, sea salt, pepper, and red pepper flakes. Scrape and fold in any browned bits from the bottom. Simmer for 4 minutes more. Spoon the peppers over the sausages and serve.

Per Serving
Calories: 173 Protein: 22 g. Fat: 5 g.

Chicken Merlot with Mushrooms (Spanish)

Prep time: 10 minutes **Cooking Time:** 40 mins **Servings:** 2

Ingredients:

6 boneless, skinless chicken breasts, cubed.	1 large red onion, chopped.
¾ cup chicken broth.	2 cloves garlic, minced.
¼ cup Merlot.	1 (6 oz.) can tomato paste.
2 tbsps. basil, chopped finely.	3 tbsps. chia seeds.
	Salt and pepper to taste
1 (10 oz.) package buckwheat ramen noodles, cooked.	3 cups mushrooms, sliced..
	2 tbsps. Parmesan, shaved.
	2 tsps. sugar

Directions:

Rinse chicken; set aside.

Add mushrooms, onion, and garlic to the crockpot and mix.

Place chicken cubes on top of the vegetables and do not mix.

In a large bowl, combine broth, tomato paste, wine, chia seeds, basil, sugar, salt, and pepper. Pour over the chicken.

Cover and cook on low for 7–8 hours or on high for 3 ½–4 hours.

To serve, spoon chicken, mushroom mixture, and sauce over hot cooked buckwheat ramen noodles. Top with shaved Parmesan.

Per Serving
Calories: 213 g. Fat: 10 g. Protein: 56 g. Carbs: 45 g. Cholesterol: 230 mg. Sugar: 0 g.

Garlic Herb Grilled Chicken Breast (Greek)

Prep time: 7 minutes **Cooking Time:** 20 mins **Servings:** 4

Ingredients:

1 ¼ lb. chicken breasts, skinless and boneless.	1 tbsp. garlic & herb seasoning blend.
2 tsps. olive oil.	Salt andPepper.

Directions:

Pat dries the chicken breasts, coat it with olive oil, and season it with salt and pepper on both sides.

Season the chicken with garlic and herb seasoning or any other seasoning of your choice.

Turn the grill on and oil the grate.

Place the chicken on the hot grate and let it grill till the sides turn white.

Flip them over and let them cook again.

When the internal temperature is about 160° F, it is most likely cooked.

Set aside for 15 minutes. Chop into pieces.

Per Serving
Calories: 187 g. Fats: 6 g. Protein: 32 g. Carbs: 5 g.

Stuffed Beef Loin in Sticky Sauce (Italian)

Preparation Time: 15 minutes **Cooking Time:** 6 minutes
Servings: 4

Ingredients:

1 tbsp. Erythritol.
½ tsp. tomato sauce.
½ cup of water.
3 oz. celery root, grated.
3 oz. bacon, sliced.
¾ tsps. garlic, diced.

1 tbsp. lemon juice.
¼ tsp. dried rosemary.
9 oz. beef loin.
1 tbsp. walnuts, chopped.
2 tsps. butter.
1 tbsp. olive oil.
1 tsp. salt.

Directions:

Cut the beef loin into the layer and spread it with the dried rosemary, butter, and salt.

Then place over the beef loin: grated celery root, sliced bacon, walnuts, and diced garlic.

Roll the beef loin and brush it with olive oil. Secure the meat with the help of the toothpicks.

Place it in the tray and add a ½ cup of water.

Cook the meat in the preheated to 365° F oven for 40 minutes.

Meanwhile, make the sticky sauce: mix up together Erythritol, lemon juice, 4 tbsps. of water, and butter.

Preheat the mixture until it starts to boil. Then add tomato sauce and whisk it well.

Bring the sauce to boil and remove from the heat.

When the beef loin is cooked, remove it from the oven and brush it with the cooked sticky sauce very generously.

Slice the beef roll and sprinkle with the remaining sauce.

Per Serving

Calories: 248 g. Fat: 17.5 g. Carbs: 2.2 g. Protein:20.7 g.

Excellent Beef Meal (Spanish)

Prep time: 15 minutes **Cooking Time:** 7 hours 4 minutes
Servings: 6

Ingredients:

1 tbsp. vegetable oil
2 lb. beef stew meat
1 can artichoke hearts
1 onion
1 container beef broth
1 can tomato sauce
1 tsp. dried basil
1/2 tsp. ground cumin

4 garlic cloves
1 can diced tomatoes with juice 1/2 C.
1 bay leaf, crumbled
Kalamata olives, pitted
1 tsp. dried oregano
1 tsp. dried parsley

Directions:

In a skillet, heat the oil over medium-high heat and cook the beef for about 2 minutes per side.

Transfer the beef into a slow cooker and top with artichoke hearts, followed by the onion and garlic.

Place the remaining ingredients on top. Set the slow cooker on "Low" and cook, covered for about 7 hours.

Per Serving

Calories: 410; Carbohydrates: 0.9g; Protein: 53.1g;

Osso Bucco (Spanish)

Preparation Time: 30 minutes **Cooking Time:** 8 hours
Servings: 2–4

Ingredients:

beef shanks or veal shanks
1 tsp. sea salt
2 medium onions, diced
2 medium carrots, diced
1 (14 oz.) can diced tomatoes 2 tsps.
1–2 tbsps. olive oil

½ tsp. ground black pepper
3 tbsps. whole wheat flour
4 garlic cloves, minced
2 celery stalks, diced
½ cup beef or vegetable dried thyme leaves stock

Directions:

Season the shanks on both sides, then dip in the flour to coat.

Heat a large skillet over high heat. Add the olive oil. When the oil is hot, add the shanks and brown evenly on both sides. When browned, transfer to the slow cooker.

Pour the stock into the skillet and let simmer for 3–5 minutes while stirring to deglaze the pan.

Add the rest of the ingredients to the slow cooker and pour the stock from the skillet over the top.

Click slow cooker to low and cook for 8 hours.

Serve the Osso Bucco over quinoa, brown rice, or even cauliflower rice.

Per Serving

Calories: 589 Fat: 21.3 g. Protein: 74.7g.

Lamb Shanks with Red Wine (Greek)

Preparation Time: 20 minutes **Cooking Time:** 5 hours
Servings: 4

Ingredients:

1 tbsps. olive oil
2 tbsps. flour
2 garlic cloves, crushed
2/3 cup red wine

4 lamb shanks, trimmed
1 onion, chopped
3 cups tomato sauce

Directions:

Heat a skillet over high heat. Add the olive oil.

Season the lamb shanks, then roll in the flour. Shake off excess flour and place the shanks in the skillet to brown on all sides.

Spray the slow cooker with olive oil and place the browned shanks in the slow cooker.

Add the crushed garlic to the red wine. Mix with the tomato sauce and then, pour the mixture over the lamb shanks and cook on low for 5–6 hours.

Per Serving

Calories: 354 Fat: 12 g. Protein: 42 g.

Spanish Meatballs (Spanish)

Preparation Time: 20 minutes **Cooking Time:** 5 hours
Servings: 6

Ingredients:

1 lb. ground turkey 1 lb. ground pork	1 (20 oz.) can tomatoes, diced
2 eggs	2 tbsps. olive oil
¾ cup sweet onion, minced, divided	¼ cup plus
1 tbsp. breadcrumbs	3 tbsps fresh parsley, chopped.
1 ½ tsp. paprika (sweet or hot)	1 ½ tsp. cumin

Directions:

Spray the slow cooker with olive oil.

In a mixing bowl, mix the ground meat, eggs, about half of the onions, the breadcrumbs, and the spices.

Wash your hands and mix until everything is well combined. Shape into meatballs.

Mix 2 tbsps. of olive oil over medium heat. When the skillet and oil are hot, add the meatballs and brown on all sides. When they are done, transfer them to the slow cooker.

Add the rest of the onions and the tomatoes to the skillet and allow them to cook for a few minutes, scraping the brown bits from the meatballs up to add flavor.

Pour the tomatoes over the meatballs in the slow cooker and cook on low for 5 hours.

Per Serving
Calories: 372 Fat: 21.7 g. Protein: 28.5g.

Flavorful Beef Bourguignon (Spanish)

Preparation Time: 10 minutes **Cooking Time:** 20 minutes
Servings: 4

Ingredients:

1 1/2 lbs. beef chuck roast, cut into chunks	2 tbsp fresh thyme
2/3 cup beef stock	1 bay leaf
1 tsp garlic, minced	2 tbsp tomato paste
2/3 cup dry red wine	8 oz mushrooms, sliced
1 onion, sliced	4 carrots, cut into chunks
Pepper Salt	1 tbsp olive oil

Directions:

Add oil into the instant pot and set the pot on sauté mode.

Add meat and sauté until brown. Add onion and sauté until softened.

Add remaining ingredient and stir well.

Seal pot with lid and cook on high for 12 minutes.

Once done, allow to release pressure naturally. Remove lid. Stir well and serve.

Per Serving
Calories 744 Fat 51.3 g Carbohydrates 14.5 g Sugar 6.5 g

Deliciously Simple Beef (Spanish)

Preparation Time: 10 minutes **Cooking Time:** 10 hours
Servings: 4

Ingredients:

1 large onion, sliced thinly	1 tsp. dried oregano
1/4 C. extra-virgin olive oil	1 tbsp. garlic, minced
Salt and freshly ground black pepper, to taste	2 lb. beef chuck roast, cut into bite-sized pieces
2 tbsp. fresh lemon juice	

Directions:

In a slow cooker, place all the ingredients except for beef cubes and stir to combine.

Add the beef cubes and stir to combine.

Set the slow cooker on "Low" and cook, covered for about 8-10 hours.

Serve hot.

Per Serving
Calories: 553; Carbohydrates: 4.6g; Protein: 62.8g; Fat: 30.3g; Sugar: 18g;

Tuna and Kale (Greek)

Preparation Time: 5 minutes **Cooking Time:** 20 minutes
Servings: 4

Ingredients:

1-lb. tuna fillets, boneless, skinless, and cubed.	1 cup kale, torn.
2 tbsps. olive oil.	½ cup cherry tomatoes, cubed.
	1 yellow onion, chopped

Directions:

Heat up a pan with the oil over medium heat, add the onion and sauté for 5 minutes.

Add the tuna and the other ingredients, toss, cook everything for 15 minutes more, divide between plates and serve.

Per Serving
Calories: 251 g. Fat: 4 g. Protein: 56 g. Carbs: 45 g. Cholesterol: 230 mg. Sugar: 0 g.

Country Chicken Breasts (Spanish)

Preparation Time: 10 minutes **Cooking Time:** 45 minutes
Servings: 2

Ingredients:

2 medium green apples, diced.
1 small red onion, finely diced.
2 tbsps. dried currants.
1 tbsp. curry powder.
¼ tsp. chili pepper flakes.
1/3 cup slivered almonds
6 skinless, boneless chicken breasts, halved.
1 cup long-grain white rice.

1 small green bell pepper, chopped.
3 cloves garlic, minced.
Salt and pepper to taste.
1 tsp. ground ginger.
1 tsp. turmeric.
1 can (14 ½ oz.) diced tomatoes.
½ cup chicken broth.
Chopped parsley.
1-lb. large raw shrimp, shelled and deveined.

Directions:

Rinse chicken, pat dry, and set aside.

In a large crockpot, combine apples, onion, bell pepper, garlic, currants, curry powder, turmeric, ginger, and chili pepper flakes. Stir in tomatoes.

Arrange chicken, overlapping pieces slightly, on top of tomato mixture.

Pour in broth and do not mix or stir. Cover and cook for 6–7 hours on low. Preheat oven to 200° F.

Carefully transfer chicken to an oven-safe plate, cover lightly, and keep warm in the oven.

Stir rice into the remaining liquid. Increase cooker heat setting to high; cover and cook, stirring once or twice, until rice is almost tender to bite, 30–35 minutes. Stir in shrimp, cover, and cook until shrimp are opaque in center, about 10 more minutes.

Meanwhile, toast almonds in a small pan over medium heat until golden brown, 5–8 minutes, stirring occasionally. Set aside.

To serve, season the rice mixture to taste with salt and pepper. Mound in a warm serving dish and arrange chicken on top. Sprinkle with parsley and almonds.

Per Serving

Calories: 155 g. Fat: 5 g. Protein: 56 g. Carbs: 45 g.
Cholesterol: 230 mg. Sugar: 0 g.

Greek Lamb Chop (Greek)

Preparation Time: 10 minutes **Cooking Time:** 8 minutes
Servings: 8

Ingredients:

8 trimmed lamb loin chops
2 tbsps. lemon juice
½ tsp. salt

1 tbsp. dried oregano
1 tbsp. garlic, minced
¼ tsp. black pepper
Cooking spray

Directions:

Preheat the broiler.

Combine oregano, garlic, lemon juice, salt, and pepper and rub on both sides of the lamb. Place the lamb on a broiler pan coated with cooking spray and cook for 4 minutes on each side.

Per Serving

Calories: 457 Protein: 49 g. Fat: 20 g.

Beef Cabbage Stew (Spanish)

Preparation Time: 30 minutes **Cooking Time:** 2 hours
Servings: 8

Ingredients:

1 lbs. beef stew meat.
1 cube beef bouillon.
8-oz. plum tomatoes, chopped.
1 cup hot chicken broth.
4 onions, chopped.

¼ cup chopped celery.
2 bay leaves.
Salt and pepper to taste.
1 cabbage.
8-oz. tomato sauce.
1 tsp. Greek seasoning

Directions:

Cut off the stem of the cabbage. Separate the leaves carefully. Wash well and rinse off. Set aside for now.

Fry the beef in a large pan over medium-low heat for about 8–10 minutes or until you get a brown color.

3. Into the pan, pour in of the chicken broth.

Add the beef bouillon, and mix well.

Add the black pepper, salt and mix again.

Add the lid and cook on medium-low heat for about 1 hour.

Take off the heat and transfer the mix into a bowl.

Spread the cabbage leaves on a flat surface.

Fill the middle using the beef mixture. Use a generous portion of filling, it will give your stew a better taste.

Wrap the cabbage leaves tightly. Use a kitchen thread to tie it. Finish it with the remaining leaves and filling.

In a pot heat the oil over fry the onion for 1 minute.

Add the remaining chicken broth. Add in the celery and tomato sauce and cook for another 10 minutes.

Add the Greek seasonings, and mix well. Bring to boil and then carefully add the wrapped cabbage. Cover and cook for another 10 minutes. Serve hot.

Per Serving

Calories: 372 g. Fats: 22.7 g. Carbs: 9 g. Protein: 31.8 g.

Steamed Trout with Lemon Herb Crust (Spanish)

Preparation Time: 10 minutes **Cooking Time:** 15 minutes
Servings: 2

Ingredients:

3 tbsps. olive oil	3 garlic cloves, chopped
1 tbsp. fresh mint, chopped	1 tbsp. fresh parsley, chopped
2 tbsps. fresh lemon juice	
¼ tsp. dried ground thyme	1 lb. (454 g.) fresh trout (2 pieces) 2 cups fish stock
1 tsp. sea salt	

Directions:

Blend the olive oil, garlic, lemon juice, mint, parsley, thyme, and salt. Brush the marinade onto the fish.

Insert a trivet in the electric pressure cooker. Fill in the fish stock and place the fish on the trivet.

Secure the lid. Select the STEAM mode and set the cooking time for 15 minutes at high pressure.

Once cooking is complete, do a quick pressure release. Carefully open the lid. Serve warm.

Per Serving
Calories: 477 Fat: 30 g. Protein: 52 g.

Lamb with String Beans (Spanish)

Preparation Time: 10 minutes **Cooking Time:** 1 hour
Servings: 6

Ingredients:

¼ cup extra-virgin olive oil	1 tsp. sea salt
6 lamb chops	2 tbsps. tomato paste
½ tsp. black pepper	1 lb. green beans
1 ½ cups hot water	1 onion
2 tomatoes	

Directions:

In a skillet at medium-high heat, pour 2 tbsps. of olive oil.

Season the lamb chops with ½ tsp. sea salt and 1/8 tsp. pepper. Cook the lamb in the hot oil for 4 minutes. Transfer the meat to a platter and set it aside.

Put back to the heat then put the 2 tbsps. of olive oil. Heat until it shimmers.

Blend the tomato paste and the hot water. Mix to the hot skillet along with the green beans, onion, tomatoes, and the remaining ½ tsp. sea salt and ¼ tsp. pepper. Bring to a simmer.

Return the lamb chops to the pan. Bring to boil and reduce the heat to medium-low. Simmer for 45 minutes until the beans are soft, adding additional water as needed to adjust the thickness of the sauce.

Per Serving
Calories: 439 Protein: 50 g. Fat: 22 g.

Chicken Piccata (Italian)

Preparation Time: 10 minutes **Cooking Time:** 10 minutes
Servings: 6

Ingredients:

½ cup whole-wheat flour	½ tsp. sea salt
1/8 tsp. freshly ground black pepper	3 tbsps. extra-virgin olive oil
1 ½ lb. boneless	1 cup unsalted chicken broth
½ cup dry white wine	1 lemon zest
¼ cup capers, drained and rinsed	¼ cup fresh parsley leaves, chopped
1 lemon juice	

Directions:

In a shallow dish, whisk the flour, sea salt, and pepper. Dredge the chicken in the flour and tap off any excess.

Heat the olive oil in a pan over medium-high heat.

Add the chicken and cook for 4 minutes. Remove the chicken from the pan and set aside, tented with aluminum foil to keep warm.

Return to the heat and mix the broth, wine, lemon juice, and lemon zest, and capers. Simmer for 3–4 minutes, stirring. Remove the skillet from the heat and return the chicken to the pan. Turn to coat. Stir in the parsley and serve.

Per Serving
Calories: 153 Protein: 8 g. Fat: 9 g.

Chicken and Tzatziki Pitas (Greek)

Preparation Time: 10 minutes **Cooking Time:** 0 minutes
Servings: 8

Ingredients:

2 pita breads	10 oz chicken fillet, grilled
8 teaspoons tzatziki sauce	1 cup lettuce, chopped

Directions:

Cut every pita bread on the halves to get 8 pita pockets.

Then fill every pita pocket with chopped lettuce and sprinkle greens with tzatziki sauce.

Chop chicken fillet and add it in the pita pockets too.

Per Serving
calories 106, fat 3.8, carbs 6.1, protein 11

One-Pan Tuscan Chicken (Italian)

Preparation Time: 10 minutes **Cooking Time:** 25 minutes
Servings: 6

Ingredients:

¼ cup extra-virgin olive oil, divided
1 red bell pepper
3 garlic cloves
1 (14 oz.) can white beans
½ tsp. sea salt
1/8 tsp. red pepper flakes
¼ cup fresh basil leaves, chopped
1 onion
1 lb. boneless chicken
½ cup dry white wine
2 (14 oz.) can tomatoes
1 tbsp Italian seasoning
1/8 tsp. freshly ground black pepper

Directions:

In a huge skillet over medium-high heat, preheat 2 tbsps. of olive oil. Add the chicken and cook for 6 minutes, stirring. Take out the chicken and set it aside on a platter, tented with aluminum foil to keep warm.

Return the skillet to heat and heat the remaining 2 tbsps. of olive oil. Add the onion and red bell pepper. Cook for 5 minutes.

Cook the garlic for 30 seconds. Stir in the wine. Cook for 1 minute, stirring.

Add the crushed and chopped tomatoes, white beans, Italian seasoning, sea salt, pepper, and red pepper flakes. Bring to a simmer and reduce the heat to medium. Cook for 5 minutes, stirring occasionally.

Take the chicken and any juices that have collected back to the skillet. Cook for 1–2 minutes. Pull out from the heat and stir in the basil before serving.

Per Serving
Calories: 271 Protein: 14 g. Fat: 0.1 g.

Mediterranean Rice and Sausage (Italian)

Preparation Time: 15 minutes **Cooking Time:** 8 hours
Servings: 6

Ingredients:

1 ½ lb. Italian sausage, crumbled
2 cups long-grain rice, uncooked
½ cup water
2 tbsps. steak sauce
1 medium onion, chopped
1 (14 oz.) can diced tomatoes with juice
1 medium green pepper, diced Olive oil

Directions:

Spray your slow cooker with olive oil or nonstick cooking spray.

Add the sausage, onion, and steak sauce to the slow cooker. Cook on low for 8–10 hours.

After 8 hours, add the rice, tomatoes, water, and green pepper. Stir to combine thoroughly. Cook for 20–25 minutes.

Per Serving
Calories: 650 Fat: 36 g. Protein: 22 g.

Chicken Kapama (Spanish)

Preparation Time: 10 minutes **Cooking Time:** 90 minutes
Servings: 4

Ingredients:

1 (32 oz.) can tomatoes, chopped
3 tbsps. extra-virgin olive oil
½ tsp. dried oregano
½ tsp. sea salt
4 boneless, skinless chicken breast halves
¼ cup dry white wine
2 tbsps. tomato paste
¼ tsp. red pepper flakes
1 cinnamon stick
1/8 tsp. black pepper
2 whole cloves

Directions:

In a pot over medium-high heat, mix the tomatoes, wine, tomato paste, olive oil, red pepper flakes, allspice, oregano, cloves, cinnamon stick, sea salt, and pepper. Bring to a simmer, stirring occasionally. Adjust the heat to medium-low and simmer for 30 minutes, stirring occasionally. Remove and discard the whole cloves and cinnamon stick from the sauce and let the sauce cool.

Preheat the oven to 350°F.

Place the chicken in a 9-by-13-inch baking dish. Drizzle sauce over the chicken and cover the pan with aluminum foil. Bake for 45 minutes.

Per Serving
Calories: 220 Protein: 8 g. Fat: 14 g.

Spinach and Feta-Stuffed Chicken Breasts (Greek)

Preparation Time: 10 minutes **Cooking Time:** 45 minutes
Servings: 4

Ingredients:

2 tbsps. extra-virgin olive oil
1 lb. fresh baby spinach
½ tsp. sea salt
4 chicken breast halves
½ cup Feta cheese, crumbled
3 garlic cloves, minced
1 lemon zest
1/8 tsp. freshly ground black pepper

Directions:

Preheat the oven to 350°F.

Preheat the oil and skillet over medium-high heat.

Cook the spinach for 3–4 minutes. Cook the garlic, lemon zest, sea salt, and pepper. Cool slightly and mix in the cheese.

Spread the spinach and cheese mixture in an even layer over the chicken pieces and roll the breast around the filling. Hold closed with toothpicks or butcher's twine.

Place the breasts in a 9-by-13-inch baking dish and bake for 30–40 minutes. Take away from the oven and let rest for 5 minutes before slicing and serving.

Per Serving
Calories: 263 Protein: 17 g. Fat: 20 g.

Roasted Trout Stuffed with Veggies (Greek)

Preparation Time: 10 minutes **Cooking Time:** 25 minutes
Servings: 2

Ingredients:

1 (8 oz.) whole trout fillets	¼ tsp. salt
1 tbsp. extra-virgin olive oil	1 poblano pepper
1/8 tsp. black pepper	1 small onion, thinly sliced
½ red bell pepper	2–3 shiitake mushrooms,
Cooking spray	sliced 1 lemon, sliced

Directions:

Set the oven to 425ºF (220°C). Coat the baking sheet with nonstick cooking spray.

Rub both trout fillets, inside and out, with olive oil. Season with salt and pepper.

Mix the onion, bell pepper, poblano pepper, and mushrooms in a large bowl. Stuff half of this mix into the cavity of each fillet. Top the mixture with 2–3 lemon slices inside each fillet.

Place the fish on the prepared baking sheet side by side. Roast in the preheated oven for 25 minutes.

Pull out from the oven and serve on a plate.

Per Serving

Calories: 453 Fat: 22 g. Protein: 49 g.

Chicken Gyros with Tzatziki (Italian)

Preparation Time: 10 minutes **Cooking Time:** 80 minutes
Servings: 6

Ingredients:

1 lb. ground chicken breast	2 tbsps. dried rosemary
1 onion	1 tbsp. dried marjoram
½ tsp. sea salt	¼ tsp. freshly ground black
6 garlic cloves, minced	pepper Tzatziki Sauce

Directions:

Preheat the oven to 350°F.

In a stand mixer, blend the chicken, onion, rosemary, marjoram, garlic, sea salt, and pepper.

Press the mixture into a loaf pan. Bake for 1 hour. Pull out from the oven and set it aside for 20 minutes before slicing.

Slice the gyro and spoon the tzatziki sauce over the top.

Per Serving

Calories: 289 Protein: 50 g. Fat: 1 g.

Veal Pot Roast (Spanish)

Preparation Time: 20 minutes **Cooking Time:** 5 hours
Servings: 6–8

Ingredients:

1 tbsps. olive oil	2 lbs. boneless veal roast
Salt and pepper	4 medium carrots, peeled
2 parsnips, peeled and halved	2 white turnips, peeled and quartered
2 sprigs of fresh thyme	1 orange, scrubbed and zested
10 garlic cloves, peeled	1 cup chicken or veal stock

Directions:

Heat a large skillet over medium-high heat.

Coat veal roast all over with olive oil, then season with salt and pepper.

When the skillet is hot, add the veal roast and sear on all sides.

Once the veal roast is cooked on all sides, transfer it to the slow cooker.

Toss the carrots, parsnips, turnips, and garlic into the skillet. Stir and cook for 5 minutes—not all the way through, just to get some of the brown bits from the veal and give them a bit of color.

Transfer the vegetables to the slow cooker, placing them all around the meat.

Top the veal roast with the thyme and the zest from the orange. Slice orange in half and squeeze the juice over the top of the meat.

Add the chicken stock, then cook the veal roast on LOW for 5 hours.

Per Serving

Calories: 426 Fat: 12.8 g. Protein: 48.8 g.

Slow Cooker Salmon in Foil (Italian)

Preparation Time: 5 minutes **Cooking Time:** 2 hours
Servings: 2

Ingredients:

1 (6 oz./170 g.) salmon fillets	2 garlic cloves, minced
½ tbsp. lime juice	1 tbsp. olive oil
¼ tsp. black pepper	1 tsp. fresh parsley, finely chopped

Directions:

Spread a length of foil onto a work surface and place the salmon fillets in the middle.

Blend the olive oil, garlic, lime juice, parsley, and black pepper. Brush the mixture over the fillets. Fold the foil over and crimp the sides to make a packet.

Place the packet into the slow cooker, cover, and cook on HIGH for 2 hours. Serve hot.

Per Serving

Calories: 446 Fat: 21 g. Protein: 65 g.

Chicken with Kale and Chili Salsa (Italian)

Preparation Time: 5 minutes **Cooking Time:** 45 minutes
Servings: 1

Ingredients:

3 oz. buckwheat.

1 tbsp. extra-virgin olive oil.

3 oz. kale, chopped. oz. red onion, sliced.

1 tomato.

1 bird's eye chili, chopped.

1 tsp. chopped fresh ginger.

Juice of ½ lemon, divided.

4 oz. skinless, boneless chicken breast.

1 handful parsley.

2 tsps. ground turmeric.

Directions:

Start with the salsa: Remove the eye out of the tomato and finely chop it, making sure to keep as much of the liquid as you can. Mix it with chili, parsley, and lemon juice. You could add everything to a blender for different results.

Heat your oven to 220° F. Marinate the chicken with a little oil, 1 tsp. of turmeric, and lemon juice. Let it rest for 5–10 mins.

Heat a pan over medium heat until it is hot then add marinated chicken and allow it to cook for a minute on both sides (until it is pale gold). Transfer the chicken to the oven if the pan is not ovenproof, place it in a baking tray and bake for 8–10 minutes or until it is cooked through. Take the chicken out of the oven, cover with foil, and let it rest for 5 minutes before you serve.

Meanwhile, in a steamer, steam the kale for about 5 minutes.

In a little oil, fry the ginger and red onions until they are soft but not colored, and then add in the cooked kale and fry it for a minute.

Cook the buckwheat in accordance with the packet directions with the remaining turmeric. Serve alongside the vegetables, salsa, and chicken.

Per Serving

Calories: 134.8 g. Fat: 30 g. Protein: 56 g. Carbs: 45 g. Cholesterol: 230 mg. Sugar: 0 g.

Dijon and Herb Pork Tenderloin (Spanish)

Preparation Time: 10 minutes **Cooking Time:** 30 minutes
Servings: 6

Ingredients:

½ cup fresh Italian parsley leaves 3 tbsps. fresh rosemary leaves

1 tbsp. extra-virgin olive oil

¼ tsp. freshly ground black pepper

1 tbsps. fresh thyme leaves

3 tbsps. Dijon mustard

1 (1 ½ lb.) pork tenderloin

½ tsp. sea salt

4 garlic cloves, minced

Directions:

Preheat the oven to 400°F.

In a blender, pulse the parsley, rosemary, thyme, mustard, olive oil, garlic, sea salt, and pepper. Spread the mixture evenly over the pork and place it on a rimmed baking sheet.

Bake for 20 minutes. Remove from the oven and set it aside for 10 minutes before slicing and serving.

Per Serving

Calories: 393 Protein: 74 g. Fat: 12 g.

Appendix 1 Measurement Conversion Chart

VOLUME EQUIVALENTS(DRY)

US STANDARD	METRIC (APPROXIMATE)
1/8 teaspoon	0.5 mL
1/4 teaspoon	1 mL
1/2 teaspoon	2 mL
3/4 teaspoon	4 mL
1 teaspoon	5 mL
1 tablespoon	15 mL
1/4 cup	59 mL
1/2 cup	118 mL
3/4 cup	177 mL
1 cup	235 mL
2 cups	475 mL
3 cups	700 mL
4 cups	1 L

VOLUME EQUIVALENTS(LIQUID)

US STANDARD	US STANDARD (OUNCES)	METRIC (APPROXIMATE)
2 tablespoons	1 fl.oz.	30 mL
1/4 cup	2 fl.oz.	60 mL
1/2 cup	4 fl.oz.	120 mL
1 cup	8 fl.oz.	240 mL
1 1/2 cup	12 fl.oz.	355 mL
2 cups or 1 pint	16 fl.oz.	475 mL
4 cups or 1 quart	32 fl.oz.	1 L
1 gallon	128 fl.oz.	4 L

TEMPERATURES EQUIVALENTS

FAHRENHEIT(F)	CELSIUS(C) (APPROXIMATE)
225 °F	107 °C
250 °F	120 °C
275 °F	135 °C
300 °F	150 °C
325 °F	160 °C
350 °F	180 °C
375 °F	190 °C
400 °F	205 °C
425 °F	220 °C
450 °F	235 °C
475 °F	245 °C
500 °F	260 °C

WEIGHT EQUIVALENTS

US STANDARD	METRIC (APPROXIMATE)
1 ounce	28 g
2 ounces	57 g
5 ounces	142 g
10 ounces	284 g
15 ounces	425 g
16 ounces (1 pound)	455 g
1.5 pounds	680 g
2 pounds	907 g

Appendix 2   Dirty Dozen and Clean Fifteen

The Environmental Working Group (EWG) is a nonprofit, nonpartisan organization dedicated to protecting human health and the environment Its mission is to empower people to live healthier lives in a healthier environment. This organization publishes an annual list of the twelve kinds of produce, in sequence, that have the highest amount of pesticide residue-the Dirty Dozen-as well as a list of the fifteen kinds ofproduce that have the least amount of pesticide residue-the Clean Fifteen.

THE DIRTY DOZEN	THE CLEAN FIFTEEN
• The 2016 Dirty Dozen includes the following produce. These are considered among the year's most important produce to buy organic:	• The least critical to buy organically are the Clean Fifteen list. The following are on the 2016 list:

Dirty Dozen:

Strawberries	Spinach
Apples	Tomatoes
Nectarines	Bell peppers
Peaches	Cherry tomatoes
Celery	Cucumbers
Grapes	Kale/collard greens
Cherries	Hot peppers

Clean Fifteen:

Avocados	Papayas
Corn	Kiw
Pineapples	Eggplant
Cabbage	Honeydew
Sweet peas	Grapefruit
Onions	Cantaloupe
Asparagus	Cauliflower
Mangos	

• The Dirty Dozen list contains two additional itemskale/collard greens and hot peppers-because they tend to contain trace levels of highly hazardous pesticides.

• Some of the sweet corn sold in the United States are made from genetically engineered (GE) seedstock. Buy organic varieties of these crops to avoid GE produce.

Appendix 3   Index

Leave a Review

As an independent author with a small marketing budget, reviews are my livelihood on this platform. If you enjoyed this book, I'd appreciate it if you could leave your honest feedback.

I read EVERY single review because I love the feedback from MY readers!

Thank you for staying with me.

96919349R00111